Women's Untold Stories

Women's Untold Stories

Breaking Silence, Talking Back, Voicing Complexity

edited by

MARY ROMERO AND ABIGAIL J. STEWART

ROUTLEDGE
New York London

Published in 1999 by
Routledge
29 West 35th Street
New York, NY 10001

Published in Great Britain by
Routledge
11 New Fetter Lane
London EC4P 4EE

Copyright ©1999 by Routledge

Printed in the United States of America on acid-free paper.

Library of Congress Cataloging-in-Publication Data

    Women's untold stories: breaking silence, talking back, voicing complexity / by Mary
       Romero and Abigail J. Stewart, eds.
        p. cm.
    Includes bibliographical references.
    ISBN 0-415-92206-2 (hardcover). — ISBN 0-415-92207-0 (pbk.)
       1. Women—United States—Social conditions.   2. Minority women—United States—
Social conditions.   3. Women employees—United States.   4. Feminism—United States.
I. Romero, Mary. II. Stewart, Abigail J.
HQ1421.W677 1999
305.42'0973—dc21   98-420007
                                                            CIP

Contents

Acknowledgments   *vii*

Introduction   Mary Romero and Abigail J. Stewart   *ix*

Breaking Silence

1   Rosario Ceballo
"The Only Black Woman Walking the Face of the Earth
Who Cannot Have a Baby": Two Women's Stories   *3*

2   Karin A. Martin and Lisa Kane Low
"Kind of Neanderthal" or "Perfectly Normal": Giving Birth at Home   *20*

3   Lora Bex Lempert
"An Unbelievable Kind of Thing": A Mother's Response
to the Disclosure of Incest   *37*

4   Janet E. Malley
Life on the Home Front: Housewives' Experiences of World War II   *53*

5   Donna K. Nagata
Expanding the Internment Narrative: Multiple Layers
of Japanese American Women's Experiences   *71*

6   Aída Hurtado
Cross-border Existence: One Woman's Migration Story   *83*

Talking Back

7   PJ McGann
Skirting the Gender Normal Divide: A Tomboy Life Story   *105*

8   Sandra Schwartz Tangri and Joan Mechelle Browne
Climbing out of the Pit: From the Black Middle Class
to Homeless and (Almost) Back Again   *125*

9 | MARY ROMERO
One of the Family, or Just the Mexican Maid's Daughter?:
Belonging, Identity, and Social Mobility   142

10 | MARIXSA ALICEA AND JENNIFER FRIEDMAN
Millie's Story: Motherhood, Heroin, and Methadone   159

11 | AMY SCHULZ, FAYE KNOKI, AND URSULA KNOKI-WILSON
"How Would You Write about That?": Identity, Language, and
Knowledge in the Narratives of Two Navajo Women   174

Voicing Complexity

12 | ABIGAIL J. STEWART
"I've Got to Try to Make a Difference":
A White Woman in the Civil Rights Movement   195

13 | JOAN M. OSTROVE
A Continuing Commitment to Social Change:
Portraits of Activism throughout Adulthood   212

14 | THAOMEE XIONG AND BEVERLY DANIEL TATUM
"In My Heart I Will Always Be Hmong":
One Hmong American Woman's Pioneering Journey toward Activism   227

15 | ANNA NEUMANN
Inventing a Labor of Love: Scholarship as a Woman's Work   243

16 | MARÍA A. GUTIÉRREZ SOLDATENKO
Berta's Story: Journey from Sweatshop to Showroom   256

Contributors   271

Index   277

Acknowledgments

WE ARE GRATEFUL TO MANY PEOPLE who provided support at various stages in development of this project. Most importantly we are grateful to the chapter authors, who participated in our demanding collective process of generating, reviewing, and commenting on chapters, as well as creating a shared vision for the book. They have been true collaborators. We are also grateful to the other participants in the Center for Feminist Conversation conferences whose projects turned out not to fit within the framework of this volume. We learned from them both in their discussions of their work and in their feedback about the work represented in this book.

The first two meetings in Amherst, Massachusetts, were graciously hosted by Faye Crosby, who not only provided for our creature comforts but also created an environment in which warmth and trust were always at hand. She innovated a fund-raising technique from grateful participants and friends of the center that provided an enormous subsidy for our last meeting. Finally, she secured the help of SunWok Eoh, Ginny Farmer, Suzanne Klonis, Marilyn V. Patton, and Kimberly van Cleve, who added immeasurably to our enjoyment and stimulation. We are also grateful to Bonnie Strickland for sharing her home and lake to refresh our bodies and souls after long work days.

Our third meeting in Ann Arbor, Michigan, was equally well supported by the ministrations of Brigit Macomber, Patricia Smith, Katherine E. Brown, Jane Hassinger and Erica Stovall. In addition, Faye Crosby found the time and energy to join in our collective deliberations, adding her humor, energy, and insight to the group's.

We appreciate the enthusiasm and encouragement received from our editor at Routledge, Heidi Freund, and external reviewer of our proposal, Jean O'Barr. As we moved into the book phase, many others provided us with help: Shea Settimi and Liana Fredley from Routledge offered information and support at crucial points, as did Patricia Smith and Elizabeth Searl from the Institute for Research on Women and Gender at the University of Michigan. Mary Fran Draisker, College of Public Programs Publications Office at Arizona State University, contributed valuable expertise in preparing the final manuscript. Joanne Leonard offered her powerful artistic vision of women's participation in narrative possibilities for the cover of the book (contained in a detail from her work, *Map of a ground-note echoing*); we are grateful for her talent and her collaboration. Finally, Eric Margolis and David Winter offered humor, patience, help, support, and criticism in the proportions we needed.

Introduction

MARY ROMERO AND ABIGAIL J. STEWART

E MET AT LOGAN AIRPORT IN BOSTON and drove across Massachusetts to the Center for Feminist Conversation, where we had agreed to co-lead a workshop on gender, ethnicity, and life narratives. The car was filled with energy generated by high hopes for meeting interesting new toilers in the feminist/narrative vineyard and reconnecting with familiar ones; fears of conflict over paradigms or—worse—boredom; and anxiety about the complexities of "facilitating" and feminist process. We were happy for the rare chance to spend time together talking about the work we both have cared about. We've come simultaneously overprepared (laden with bibliographies and references) and totally unprepared for the days ahead. Through a frustratingly ambiguous process of recruitment and self-selection, a group of women academics was assembling to spend three days together in conversation. We had agreed to aim for no product—fostering the process of interdisciplinary exchange, mutual stimulation, and support was the only goal. We had all sent each other brief descriptions of our research projects, along with some sense of what we hoped to get help with at the workshop.

We turned out to be a wonderfully motley group. We came from different disciplines and different kinds of teaching and nonteaching environments. We had different personal and professional experiences with gender, sexuality, ethnicity, and life narratives and were at very different life and career stages. Our motleyness was reassuring: it meant there would be room for our many differences within our lack of similarity. In addition to the researchers, a group of women students from Smith College, who worked at the center conferences, found time to join various sessions. These students were as diverse as our group and added another dimension to our conference experience. We all relaxed into laughter and conversation and dove into our work.

In the course of our three days together, the larger group struggled with big questions: What is a life narrative?[1] What use is there to studying life narratives?[2] Is there a place in my discipline for this kind of work?[3] Is there a place for me in my discipline?[4] We, the co-facilitators, struggled with smaller questions: Is it going well? Are people getting what they need from the group? Should we narrow the focus or leave it broad? Are people getting enough "down" time? At the end of our three days many individuals reported personal gains in clarity about a work problem, as well as a satisfying sense of having personally bene-fited from and contributed to the group project of helping one another think through problems in our separate projects. Someone suggested we should meet again next summer; everyone agreed it would be nice, but no one really thought it would happen.

A few months later Faye Crosby, the heart and soul of the Center for Feminist Conversation, asked us if we'd like to meet again—with some of the same peo-ple and, no doubt, some new ones. We worried that a replay is often a mistake, but a flurry of phone calls and emails reminded us that the "time out" we shared was restorative and we agreed to Faye's proposal. The following summer we re-converged on western Massachusetts, reconnecting with some "alumnae" and drawing a new circle to include the new recruits. We settled down to "work" with a little less anxiety and more clarity. After the first evening, we reviewed our thoughts and admitted to each other that a new and forbidden idea was germi-nating—an idea for a product. We'd undertaken the second session in the same spirit as the first. We knew that both we and the group participants suffered from having too many goals, too many tasks, too much to do. Part of the plea-sure of the venture was its very lack of instrumentality—the fact that it offered a much needed time out as well as the pleasures of the danger and creativity gained by engaging in a methodology and raising research questions considered "outlawed" in our respective fields of study. Despite our good intentions, in our second meeting we began to hear a theme that demanded our attention. As peo-ple told the stories of their projects and their problems, it became clearer and clearer that several of the participants felt that in their work they were hearing new stories, uncovering unfamiliar narratives, clearing space for women to recount their lives in ways that have not been heard before. There was great pas-sion and commitment in the researchers' stories of their projects; they felt an ur-gency and responsibility about their work precisely because they were the instruments of women's untold stories,[5] stories outside our culture's "master narratives."

In the next few months, encouraged by some of the participants and by Faye Crosby, we reviewed the projects we'd heard about during the past two summers and thought about other colleagues' projects we knew about from other sources. We decided to gather together a collection of this body of work. The fi-nal group of scholars represented in this book is drawn from our disciplinary backgrounds of psychology and sociology, as well as several other disciplines, in-cluding education, nursing, public health, justice studies, Chicano studies, and women's studies. Once more the Center for Feminist Conversation sponsored a gathering, this time in Ann Arbor. And this time we had a very clear goal and a task. We asked the participants—now book contributors—to join in the project of shaping this book. Everyone shared an early chapter draft with the entire group, and we all agreed to give feedback to one another. At the beginning of the three days we were all a little hazy about just what we meant by "untold stories" and stories that were "outside the master narratives." We felt challenged and frustrated by confronting narratives that did not neatly fit into either existing disciplinary or feminist frameworks. These were not stories of victims or heroines, but rather complicated tales of compliance and constraint, along with resistance and empowerment. As we discussed each paper and identified aspects of the story that were "untold" and outside master narratives, we gained clarity.

Our schedule was divided, as before, into one-hour sessions; however, this time we spent one hour on each chapter, offering suggestions and feedback, asking questions, and sharing admiration and criticism. Although the disciplinary divisions between sociology and psychology became more apparent, our commitment to feminist methods and research questions established a bridge and directed us toward an understanding of different perspectives. During the next few months, as revised manuscripts arrived to us in Arizona and Michigan—often before they were due!—we knew that our sense of collective understanding would bring together the diverse stories in this book.

TELLING OUR STORY

In one sense this is the official story, or master narrative, of this book. Yet, there are many other stories crowded out—stories of projects that did not fit into this theme but energized and captivated the group at one of the first two sessions; stories of individuals' private and professional pain and alienation that were often told in the large group or in small talks, stories of friendships made and renewed at one or another session, and stories of distances evaluated and maintained.

Why tell this story? Is it simply a story about coediting this book? We are moved to tell this narrative because it is an untold story in two senses. First, it's a recounting of the messy, organic process behind what we hope is now a constructed product, and those process-revealing stories are hardly ever told, in the same way that curtains conceal the backstage. Knowledge of what goes on backstage may, however, illuminate our understanding of what is on stage; in the hope that it might, we offer this backstage tour. Moreover, though ours is a story about an idiosyncratic and serendipitous process, we hope it might be useful to others. This book evolved in a way that was different from any book either of us has worked on before—as editors or contributors. We tell the story of this project's evolution partly because it offers a vision of another way to "do scholarship"—a way that felt more deeply collective than the other ways we've collaborated.

Though we recommend our process to others, we offer several caveats. It is a process that requires incredible generosity of the authors; they have to be willing to care enough about the larger project to take the time both to think hard about everyone's project and to find ways to offer meaningful feedback to one another. It is a process that requires resources: Someone must "host" the group, attending to the quotidian needs for food, rest, and comfort; funds must be found, by and from individuals or institutions, to bring everyone to a shared location; and everyone must have or make time to get together. The group must also be composed of people who understand how to be constructive group members, how both to shape and respond to collective work, and who see the value of finding a common project together, rather than defining (another) deliciously individual, private one. If all of this is possible, then a book may be born of the remarkably exhilarating, precious, and deeply political experience of creating knowledge as a group. We hope this book carries the mark of its birth.

WOMEN, STORIES, AND STORY-TELLING

Scholars have increasingly recognized the complex power of stories both to express and communicate experience and ideology and to mobilize action (see e.g., Menchu, 1983; De Chungara, 1978). Stories are economical vehicles of ideology, as well as powerful provocations. From the beginning of second-wave feminism in the United States, the power of women's storytelling to one another has been evident. Indeed, consciousness-raising as a political strategy provided a formal, collective, and instrumental structure for an activity—sharing personal stories—that without a feminist lens was often informal, individual, and enervating (Echols, 1997; hooks, 1989). By recognizing the power of the group to articulate the structural constraints concealed in a tale of personal woe, the women's movement not only created a tool for ideological transformation and political mobilization but also for the legitimation of new or untold stories. Part of the recognized work of consciousness raising was identifying the oppressive nature of certain familiar stories (Cinderella, Sleeping Beauty, La Malinche, Pocahontas, etc.), and reading their hidden ideological content. The other part was providing practice and help in reading the larger social systemic meanings in individual women's apparently "personal" stories. Serving as their own cultural experts and interpreters, women showed each other not only that cultural stories about women often had destructive effects, but also how their apparently private stories were filled with social meanings. Sharing stories allowed individual women to understand they were not alone in their inability to fit a cultural ideal. Storytelling moved out of the realm of gossip or futile "bitching" and into the realm of empowerment—socializing ourselves to the realities of a stratified system and creating counternarratives depicting difference in age, race, gender, class, sexuality, and physical abilities. Modleski (1998) points to the political importance of this kind of collective process. She suggests that "Women cannot afford to participate in the endless deferral of women's stories; they must instead become for each other . . . confidantes . . . engaging in their own confirmation process and

granting legitimacy to each others' stories in their sameness but also in their differences" (p. 28). As feminist scholars and writers created dreams of lives for
themselves very different from those of their mothers, they also reclaimed their
mothers' stories, recalling messages of resistance, survival, and identity (see e.g.,
Lightfoot, 1988; Brown, 1991).

During the past 30 years we have witnessed repeated calls to bring the silent
and silenced to voice, often through the vehicle of stories. Moreover, many different scholarly communities—women of color (see e.g., Hull, Bell Scott and
Smith, 1982; Moraga & Anzaldua, 1983; Anzaldua, 1990); critical pedagogy (see
e.g., Fine, 1992; Middleton, 1993; McLaughlin & Tierney, 1993); critical legal theory (see e.g., Kairys, 1982); critical race theory (see e.g., Crenshaw et al., 1995;
Delgado, 1995; Wing, 1997); gay, lesbian, and queer theory (see e.g., Plummer,
1995; Duberman, Vicinus & Chauncey, 1989)—have argued that naming and
defining experience, articulating and legitimating new and untold stories, and
making space for those stories in the wider culture, is crucial work of social
transformation. At the same time, we have heard increasing criticism of the divi-
sive impact of politicized identities narrated through particularized stories, of
the naivete of attributing social or other meanings to personal "experience," and
of the danger of personalizing and individualizing the social and political (see
e.g., hooks, 1989; Echols, 1997; Nussbaum, 1997). From our perspective, the object must be to maintain simultaneous focus on the individual and the collective,
to use the apparently personal story to understand the social structure that
shapes it, and to forward a liberatory political agenda both by articulating sup-
pressed and distorted stories and clearing space for new ones. This is not
straightforward work. As Modleski (1998) suggests, "On the one hand, feminism
can help grant legitimacy to women's tales, and by circulating them can continue
to alter our very experience of reality. On the other hand, feminism ought not to
affirm women's accounts simply because they are women's, for sometimes the
stories women tell . . . are intended to discredit other women's stories and to
shore up patriarchy" (p. 8). Recognizing that some women's untold stories are
not feminist, but rather are told *within* master narratives of gender, race, class,
and sexuality, is often frustrating; however, it brings us closer to understanding
how social structure, ideology, and culture constrain women's lives and stories.

MASTER NARRATIVES AND HOW THEY CONSTRUCT WOMEN

Our rich and complex culture offers many different narratives to women (and to
men), as tools for understanding themselves and others. These stories operate
as "master narratives" when they subsume many differences and contradictions
and restrict and contain people, by supporting a power structure in which gender, class, race/ethnicity, sexuality, and ability all define who matters and how.
"The dominant group creates its own stories, as well," Delgado (1995) wrote,

"The stories or narratives told by the ingroup remind it of its identity in relation to outgroups, and provide it with a form of shared reality in which its own superior position is seen as natural" (p. 64). The master narrative serves as a framework for the police, judge, and jury to interpret evidence and "transform meaning into law" (see e.g., Ikemoto, 1995; Ross, 1996; Crenshaw, 1995; Roberts, 1995), for the politician and political scientists drafting public policy (see e.g., Edin & Lein, 1997), and for film producers seeking a salable movie plot (see e.g., Lipsitz, 1997; Fiske, 1994). Master narratives are stories that are so familiar they seem inevitable and obvious in their meaning, even when they happen to us. Master narratives are the stories we were taught and teach ourselves about who does what and why. They are often elaborated, plot-filled stereotypes that tell us not only what someone is like but also where they've come from, what they're likely to do, and just how far they'll get. Those of us raised in the fifties knew, for example, the story about "fast girls"—they were from "bad families," they inevitably got pregnant, which destroyed their lives and ended their educations and life chances. It took several decades for us to learn that while this often truly was so, it was so because a sexist, classist, and racist society made sure that it was so, by structuring opportunities, alternatives, and sanctions that ensured that "fast girls" paid with their lives for violating gender norms. This particular classed, raced, and heteronormative master narrative not only controlled "fast girls" but also controlled girls who did not dare to be fast; in fact, that's what made it a master narrative. It supported dominant structures by mandating widespread sexual and reproductive ignorance in adolescence, legitimating the oppression of pregnant teenaged girls, requiring sexual self-denial of other girls, denying access to safe abortion, and encouraging redemption through mandatory motherhood.

Master narratives operate internally—we compare our lives to the stories we know. They also operate externally, in the ways other people interpret and understand our lives and reflect them back to us. They are, then, widely circulating in the culture, not only in obvious "story" forms (movies, literature, television) but also in our accounts of our own and each others' lives. They gain strength from repetition and mirroring; they accumulate familiarity and clarity while blurring and erasing plot elements that don't fit.

Women's stories cannot be fully comprehended without first considering the specific power structure (economic, political and social institutions, and dominant ideologies) in which they are constructed and told. Ignoring the context moves the reader toward misinterpreting, distorting, or simply not hearing the personal and social meanings conveyed in the stories. As Ken Plummer (1995) observes, "Stories are not just practical and symbolic actions: they are also part of the political process" (p. 26). For instance, three recent news events involving a man and a woman demonstrate the power of the master narrative in interpreting events and assuring that dominant cultural messages about race, class, gender, and sexuality are conveyed as the stories are told.

First we heard about Anita Hill and Clarence Thomas in the context of the Senate hearings about Thomas's confirmation as a Supreme Court justice in 1991. When Anita Hill's shelved FBI report of sexual harassment became public, the Senate Judiciary Committee debating Thomas's nomination was forced to hold a second hearing.[6] Many of us watching the hearings recall Senator Strom Thurmond peering down at Anita Hill and asking her if she was a "spurned woman," calling forth the master narrative used to discredit women who break silence about sexual harassment. In the end, Hill was "portrayed as a lesbian who hated men and a vamp who could be ensnared and painfully rejected by them" (Morrison, 1992, p. xvi). As Wahneema Lubiano (1992) explains, "[t]hat lesbian and spurned woman cannot be rationally linked together simply means that a debased discourse doesn't care whether the terms of 'othering' are logical or not" (p. 342).

Next we witness the story of Nicole Brown Simpson and her ex-husband, O.J., who had been one of America's best-loved black athletes and celebrities, until he was arrested and tried for the brutal killing of his ex-wife and her friend, Ronald Goldman. As the former wife in an interracial marriage, Nicole Brown Simpson's image was inevitably framed in the master narratives of gender and race. Simultaneously she was the white whore with a black man (see e.g., Frankenberg, 1993) and the battered white woman who provided evidence of the evils of "sexual threat posed by lusty black bucks [that also] serve[d] as the rationale for the rise of the Ku Klux Klan" (duCille, 1997, p. 298).

Finally, in 1998, after generations of denying legitimacy to the story about the paternity of Sally Hemings's children, DNA evidence was used to confirm that Thomas Jefferson fathered at least one of his former slave's children. Ignoring historical accounts of slave-master relations in the 1800s, editorials weaved "Romeo and Juliet" narratives into sound bites (e.g., "Jefferson and Sally Hemings, Together at Last"), refusing to recognize the implications of a former President owning and fathering slaves. Hollywood used the master narrative of Jezebel to depict their relationship in the film *Jefferson in Paris*. Contextualizing the DNA evidence within master narratives, the realities of black women in slavery in the United States were erased, particularly "rape . . . an uncamouflaged expression of the slaveholder's economic mastery and the overseer's control over Black women as workers" (Davis, 1983, p. 7).

In each of these news accounts, women's stories of rape, sexual harassment, and domestic violence were silenced, distorted, and discredited. Relying upon master narratives to make sense of historical and current events would ignore the significance of the political process and the narrative's ideological function to maintain compliance and social control.

COUNTERING MASTER NARRATIVES

Perhaps the best way to counter master narratives is to offer new, compelling and even more interesting stories—stories that sustain us, inspire others, and aim to subvert. Sometimes these stories are crowded out of public awareness by the dominance of the master narrative. For example, media discussions of adolescent pregnancy quickly developed a controlling image of teenage mothers as "babies having babies." Salome Chasnoff (1997) offered six teenage mothers a chance to tell their own stories on videotape. The girls rejected a stigmatized identity as "teen mothers" and dubbed themselves the "Fantastic Moms." In the video they created a collective narrative about choices, hope, and the pleasures of being mothers. "They looked straight at the camera and proclaimed, 'We and our children have a right to be here—as we are'" (p. 129).

Counternarratives arise both in autobiographical and in fictional accounts. For example, Toni Morrison's novel *Beloved* provided a counternarrative to the image of the promiscuous black woman as a breeder in slavery, by depicting how the horrors of slavery might lead a mother to kill her baby to spare the infant the experience of life in bonds. Anita Hill's book, *Speaking Truth to Power*, provides a counternarrative that breaks silence by presenting a black woman law scholar's voice about sexual harassment of women, the law, and legislation. Unlike master narratives, counternarratives can neither use a shorthand approach nor rely on sound bites.

In this book we will see how some women tell new stories about experiences we only thought we previously understood because of a master narrative that left this "new" story out. We will also see how some women directly challenge particular master narratives they find confining, distorting, or oppressive. And we will see how some women tell more complex stories than any master narrative can, thus complicating our understanding of experiences that have been portrayed in simple terms. In all of these cases, we recognize that the master narrative is often partially reproduced in the new narratives women construct, proving just how hard it is for women to articulate their stories in terms beyond the master narratives that construct them. In this volume, we have highlighted key aspects of these women's stories in three parts—breaking silence, talking back, and voicing complexity. Such a grouping does not imply that any of the narratives fit neatly or exclusively into these sections.

In the first section of the book, "Breaking Silence," we find stories that have been crowded out by dominant narratives. For example we present narratives of motherhood countering those produced by social scientists and many others as well as narratives about World War II contrary to those produced by academic and popular historians. Motherhood narratives are especially potent cultural forms, and only a few dominate the landscape. In the most popular account, every woman is a potential mother waiting to fulfill this role. How we become mothers and "do" mothering is culturally prescribed, although motherhood and mothering are written as "natural" phenomena; anything "different" is "unnatural." In this book, Rosario Ceballo tells the untold stories of two African American women's struggles with infertility, against the familiar backdrops of media coverage of prosperous white women's pursuit of medical interventions in their infertility and the stereotype of black women's natural propensity for producing offspring. Karin Martin and Lisa Kane Low offer the stories of two middle-class educated women's home births against the dominant story of sensible medicalized births, and the marginalizing story of "hippie" home births. Lora Bex Lempert provides the story of a mother who struggles with her daughter's disclosure of incest, to counter the images of a passive mother who colludes.

Our narratives about social historical experience are equally limited. While images of "Rosie the Riveter" romanticize expanding job opportunities and personal freedom, Janet Malley shows how little we know about the experience of housewives during World War II. Donna Nagata offers us the untold story of Japanese American women's experiences of internment, including the different recollections of younger and older adolescents and young women. Aída Hurtado presents the untold story of immigration as a process that can involve women as primary agents who maintain permanent ties in two lands. In all three of these cases we see how our understanding of American history, as well as of women's lives, has been impoverished by the dominance of simple, uniform accounts of complex experiences that varied for women of different ages and life circumstances.

In the second section of the book, "Talking Back," stories are told of women who felt the oppressive weight of certain master narratives and who made explicit and direct challenges to them. In the same spirit as bell hooks (1989) in *Talking Back*—"daring to disagree and sometimes it just meant having an opinion" (p. 5)—the stories in this section are narratives of women claiming an identity denied them in master narratives. These are narratives of women boldly engaged in storytelling that refutes master narratives used to distort and rename their experience.

PJ McGann shows how Erika, a "career tomboy," feels the weight not only of the master narratives surrounding traditional femininity but also those surrounding "tomboys." As a heterosexual adult tomboy, she confronts both narratives. Sandra Tangri and Joan Browne present the story of Laura, who challenges the master narrative of homelessness. As a middle-class, educated, suburban wife and mother, Laura both falls into and climbs out of homelessness, challenging narratives that emphasize "deviance" among the homeless. Mary Romero offers the story of Olivia, who resents the master's narrative that she and her mother are "one of the family" and exposes that narrative as both self-serving and oppressive. Equally, she shows that upward social mobility need not come at the cost of one's roots, but rather is compatible with a bicultural identity. Millie's story was written in part by herself in an effort to counter the master narrative of the female drug addict who is unworthy of the privilege of motherhood. As Marixsa Alicea and Jennifer Friedman recount, Millie simultaneously resists some narratives while adopting and internalizing others. Finally, Amy Schulz, Faye Knoki, and Ursula Knoki-Wilson collaborate in telling Faye and Ursula's stories of Navajo identity, language, and knowledge. They counter master narratives of Anglo knowledge dominance and Indian assimilation with a complex account of intergenerational continuities and changes in women's relationship to Navajo culture.

In the third section, "Voicing Complexity," authors explicate women's relationships to the public sphere in much more complex ways than master narratives permit. The first three essays examine women's participation in the political arena. Abigail Stewart presents the story of a white woman who participated in the national civil rights movement in the 1940s. Complicating our picture of white women's political activism, she shows that Noma Genné committed herself to a vision of racial equality and social justice in a period of relatively little public attention to women's political participation and in a person without any formal commitment to a feminist ideology. She shows that our master narratives about civil rights activism, women's political participation, and the relationship of feminism to the civil rights movement are seriously oversimplified. Joan Ostrove presents the outlines of two sixties activists' later life commitments, in an attempt to evaluate the master narrative of activists' later lives as "sell outs." She finds evidence for deep continuities in social and political commitments, even as the form of those commitments is transformed by the vicissitudes of adult development and social history. ThaoMee Xiong and Beverly Tatum examine the political activism of a Hmong woman, Mai, who is triply defined as politically inactive because of being an "Asian" woman, a Hmong, and a "model minority." Mai's bicultural identity as a political advocate offers her a complex solution to the problem of shaping a personal identity within the context of the cross pressures of master narratives.

The book concludes with two accounts of women's relationship to their work that complicate master narratives about working women. Anna Neumann explores the ways that a woman scientist's work is constructed around and through—rather than detached from—relationships. This narrative builds on our story at the beginning of this introduction, the story of how we engage in research and writing. María Soldatenko shows how Berta's career path from sweatshops to fashion showrooms cannot be contained by narratives that emphasize global industry or conventional accounts of Latinas in the garment industry. All of the narratives in this section articulate the richness and complexity of stories that do not fit the simple master narratives we have for women's public lives.

The untold stories presented in this book aim to empower women by breaking silence, talking back, and making visible the complexities of our lives. Naming identities and experiences makes women visible in historical events and confronts research, social policy, and laws that either ignore, distort, or simplify women's lives. Narratives that counter stereotyped images of poor women and women of color serve to confront the race-neutral stances of public policies based on master narratives of motherhood. Questioning the "natural" arguments about fertility and birthing serves to broaden our public discussion on health care and to present new alternatives. Counternarratives to assimilation and the Horatio Alger myth move us closer to a national race and class dialogue that not only addresses exploitation and oppression but also includes women's experiences as American immigrants and indigenous people. Incorporating women's stories as housewives during WWII, prisoners in the internment camps, activists and organizers in the civil rights and other social movements in the past and present, and as workers in industry and the academy, brings us closer to understanding U.S. history. In this book each chapter offers both new stories and analyses as part of the project bell hooks (1989) outlined: "To reaffirm the power of the personal while simultaneously not getting trapped in identity politics, we must work to link personal narratives with knowledge of how we must act politically to change and transform the world" (p.112).

NOTES

1. For related discussion, see Denzin, 1989; Plummer, 1983.

2. For related discussion, see Bloom, 1998; Personal Narrative Groups, 1989; McLaughlin & Tierney, 1993.

3. For related discussion, see Behar, 1996; Neumann & Peterson, 1997; Gordon, 1997.

4. For related discussion, see N. Aisenberg & M. Harrington, 1988; James & Farmer, 1993; Tokarczyk & Fay, 1993.

5. This commitment to women as a central feature in feminist methodology is well documented. However, narrative methodology brings the interviewee and interviewer in a particularly close proximity that involves trust and a sense of obligation to "tell her story" not found in other research methods. For related discussions of the complex issues raised by this close proximity see Oakley, 1981; Stacey, 1990; Bloom, 1998; Fine, 1992; Lykes, 1989; Behar, 1993; Personal Narratives Group, 1989.

6. In her article, "Hill, Thomas, and the use of racial stereotype," Painter also notes that Emma Mae Martin, Thomas's sister, was interpreted in the master narrative of the "welfare queen." Also see Lubianos, 1992.

REFERENCES

Aisenberg, N., & Harrington, M. (1988). *Women of academe: Outsiders in the sacred grove*. Amherst: University of Massachusetts Press.

Anzaldua, G. (Ed.). (1990). *Making face, making soul*. San Francisco: An Aunt Lute Foundation Book.

Behar, R. (1993.) *Translated woman*. Boston: Beacon.

_____(1996). *The vulnerable observer: Anthropology that breaks your heart*. Boston: Beacon.

Bloom, L. R. (1998). *Under the sign of hope: Feminist methodology and narrative interpretation*. Albany: State University of New York Press.

Brown, E. B. (1991). Mothers of mind. In P. Bell-Scott, B. Guy-Sheftall, J. Jones Royster, J. Sims-Wood, M. DeCosta-Willis, & L. Fultz (Eds.), *Double stitch: Black women write about mothers and daughters* (pp. 74–93). Boston: Beacon.

Chasnoff, S. (1997). Performing teen motherhood on video: Autoethnography as counter-discourse. In S. Smith & J. Watson (Eds.), *Getting a life: Everyday uses of autobiography* (pp. 108–33). Minneapolis: University of Minnesota Press.

Crenshaw, K. (1995). Mapping the margins: Intersectionality, identity politics, and violence against women of color. In K. Crenshaw, N. Gotanda, G. Peller, & K. Thomas (Eds.), *Critical race theory.* (pp 357–83). New York: The New Press.

Crenshaw, K., Gotanda, N., Peller, G. & Thomas, K. (1995). *Critical race theory: The key writings that formed the movement*. New York: The New Press.

De Chungara, D. B. with M. Viezzer. (1978). *"Let Me Speak" testimony of Domitila: A woman of the Bolivian mines*. New York: Monthly Review Press.

Delgado, R. (1995). Legal storytelling: Storytelling for oppositionists and others: A plea for narrative. In R. Delgado (Ed.), *Critical race theory: The cutting edge.* (pp. 64–74). Philadelphia: Temple University Press.

Denzin, N. K. (1989). *Interpretive biography*. Newbury Park, CA: Sage.

Davis, A. Y. (1983). *Women, race & class*. New York: Vintage Books.

Duberman, M. B., Vicinus, M., & Chauncey, G. (1989). *Hidden from history: Reclaiming the gay and lesbian past*. New York: NAL Books.

duCille, A. (1997). The unbearable darkness of being: "Fresh" thoughts on race, sex, and the Simpsons. In T. Morrison & C. B. Lacour (Eds.) *Birth of a nation'hood: Gaze, script, and spectacle in the O.J. Simpson case* (pp. 293–338). New York: Pantheon Books.

Echols, A. (1997). Nothing distant about It: Women's liberation and sixties radicalism. In C. J. Cohen, K. B. Jones, & J. C. Tronto (Eds.), *Women transforming politics: An alternative reader* (pp. 456–76). New York: New York University Press.

Edin, K., & Lein, L. (1997). *Making ends meet: How single mothers survive welfare and low-wage work*. New York: Russell Sage Foundation.

Fine, M. (1992). *Disruptive voices: The possibilities of feminist research*. Ann Arbor: University of Michigan Press.

Fiske, J. (1994). *Media matters: Everyday culture and political change*. Minneapolis: University of Minnesota Press.

Frankenberg, R. (1993). *White women, race matters*. Minneapolis: University of Minnesota Press.

Gordon, A. F. (1997). *Ghostly matters: Haunting and the sociological imagination*. Minneapolis: University of Minnesota Press.

Hill, A. 1997. *Speaking truth to power*. New York: Doubleday.

Hull, G. T., Bell Scott, P. T., & Smith, B. (1982). *All the women are white, all the blacks are men, but some of us are brave: Black women's studies*. Old Westbury, NY: Feminist Press.

hooks, b. (1989). *Talking back: Thinking feminist, thinking black*. Boston: South End Press.

Ikemoto, L. C. (1995). Traces of the master narrative in the story of African American/Korean American conflict: How we constructed "Los Angeles." In R. Delgado (Ed.), *Critical race theory: The cutting edge.* (pp. 305–15). Philadelphia: Temple University Press.

James, J., & Farmer, R. (Eds.). (1993). *Spirit, space, and survival: African American women in (white) academe*. New York: Routledge.

Kairys, D. (1982). *The politics of law: A progressive critique*. New York: Pantheon Books.

Lightfoot, S. L. (1988). *Balm in Gilead: Journey of a healer*. New York: Merloyd Lawrence Books.

Lipsitz, G. (1997). The greatest story ever sold: Marketing and the O. J. Simpson trial. In T. Morrison & C. B. Lacour (Eds.), *Birth of a nation'hood: Gaze, script, and spectacle in the O. J. Simpson case*. (pp. 3–29). New York: Pantheon Books.

Lubianos, W. (1992). Black ladies, welfare queens, and state minsrels: Ideological war by narrative means. In T. Morrison (Ed.), *Race-ing justice, en-gendering power* (pp. 323–63). New York: Pantheon Books.

Lykes, M. B. (1989). Dialogue with a Guatemalan Indian woman. In R. K. Unger (Ed.), *Representations: Social constructions of gender*. (pp. 167–85). Amityville, N.Y.: Baywood.

McLaughlin, D. & Tierney, W. G. (1993). *Naming silenced lives: Personal narratives and processes of educational change*. New York: Routledge.

Menchu, R. (1983). *I . . . Rigoberta Menchu: An Indian woman in Guatemala*. Translated by A. Wright and edited and introduced by E. Burgos-Debray. New York: Verso.

Middleton, S. (1993). *Educating feminists: Life histories and pedagogy*. New York: Teachers College Press.

Modleski, T. (1998). *Old wives' tales and other women's stories*. New York: New York University Press.

Moraga, C., & Anzaldua, G. (Eds.). (1983). *This bridge called my back*. New York: Kitchen Table Women of Color Press.

Morrison, T. (Ed.) (1992). *Race-ing justice, en-gendering power*. New York: Pantheon Books.

Neumann, A., & Peterson, P. L. (Eds.) (1997). *Learning from our lives: Women, research, and autobiography in education*. New York: Teachers College Press.

Nussbaum, M. C. (1997). Women in the sixties. In S. Macedo (Ed.), *Reassessing the sixties: Debating the political and cultural legacy* (pp. 82–101). New York: W. W. Norton.

Oakley, A. (1981). Interviewing women: A contradiction in terms. In H. Roberts (Ed.), *Doing feminist research* (pp. 30–61). London: Routledge.

Painter, N. I. (1992). Hill, Thomas, and the use of racial stereotype. In T. Morrison (Ed.), *Race-ing justice, en-gendering power*. (pp. 200–14). New York: Pantheon Books.

Personal Narratives Group. (Ed.) (1989). *Interpreting women's lives: Feminist theory and personal narratives*. Bloomington: Indiana University Press.

Plummer, K. (1983). *Documents of life: An introduction to the problems and literature of a humanistic method*. London: Allen & Unwin.

_____(1995). *Telling sexual stories: Power, change, and social worlds*. New York: Routledge.

Roberts, D. E. (1995). Punishing drug addicts who have babies: Women of color, equality, and the right of privacy. In K. Crenshaw, N. Gotanda, G. Peller, & K. Thomas (Eds.), *Critical race theory*. (pp. 384–425). New York: The New Press.

Ross, T. (1996). *Just stories: How the law embodies racism and bias*. Boston: Beacon.

Stacey, J. (1990). *Brave new families*. New York: Basic.

Tokarczyk, M. M., & E. A. Fay. (1993). *Working-class women in the academy, laborers in the knowledge factory*. Amherst: University of Massachusetts Press.

Wing, A. K. (1997). *Critical race feminism: A reader*. New York: New York University Press.

Breaking Silence

"The Only Black Woman
Walking the Face of the Earth
Who Cannot Have a Baby":
Two Women's Stories[1]

On February 16, 1998, National Public Radio's Morning Edition news program featured a story on the "Baby Business." "Millions of Americans are infertile," the story began, "and many are willing to spend tens of thousands of dollars on new high-tech treatments to help them have babies. New clinics are opening across the country to tap into that patient market" (Winters, 1998). In the past several years, journalists chronicled the stories of American couples desperately eager and able to spend tens of thousands of dollars on technologically advanced fertility treatments. The public image of infertility is one of a crisis facing predominantly older, financially solvent, white couples. The medical establishment, academic researchers, and the media simultaneously perpetuate a hegemonic view of infertility as a trauma solely afflicting affluent whites. In the public mind, the image of infertility almost never includes African American women or other women of color. On the contrary, the social stereotype of African American women depicts women with too many babies—certainly not too few.

Given our public image of infertility, it is not surprising that our attitudes toward fertility itself are just as heavily filtered by a racial lens. In November 1997, the nation embraced and rejoiced at the births of Kenny and Bobbi McCaughey's septuplets. These births were celebrated and featured on most major media outlets. Frequent news updates informed us of the babies' progress. Donations from around the country, both small and large, generously arrived for the family. Rooms filled with teddy bears awaited the children and corporate donations included a 15-seat van and a 16-year supply of apple juice and applesauce. Even President Clinton phoned the McCaughey's in Iowa with his personal congratulations. These events are in sharp contrast to the reception that Linden and Jacqueline Thompson received when she gave birth to their sextuplets, the first African American sextuplets to be born in the United States (Israel, 1998). (Unfortunately, one of their children, Alison Nicole, died in utero.)

Our society's lack of response to the Thompsons reflects a fear of African

American sexuality and fertility; many are dismayed by the possibility of many brown and black babies populating the country. In a story featured in the *New York Times Magazine,* Betsy Israel (1998) quoted Jacqueline Thompson, "'Oh, my, no, this is not about drugs. . . . This is most definitely a miraculous thing! . . . When I finally delivered, at 30 weeks, I was so weak. But forget me. The five were healthy. They fit right in our two-bedroom apartment. I come from a family of five, and my husband, he had 24 siblings—yup, all the same mom, with lots of twins and triplets. So we just did between us what we had to'" (p. 66). After the birth of their children, the Thompsons received no media coverage or large corporate donations until reports about the disparity between their experience and the outpouring of concern for the McCaughey's septuplets surfaced. Having many children or multiple births among African American women is not a celebrated event in our country. In contrast, white multiple births are hailed and marked as a national triumph, in keeping with the very public concern devoted to white infertility.

Many feminist scholars trace racist and sexist constructions of sexuality to long-standing historical antecedents. For example, Evelyn Brooks Higginbotham (1995) asserts that the continued rape of African American women after the abolition of slavery "underscores the pervasive belief in black female promiscuity" (p. 11). With a similar historical framework, Patricia Hill Collins (1990) identifies four socially controlling and oppressive images of African American women: the mammy; the castrating matriarch; the welfare mother; and the Jezebel. The fourth image, the Jezebel, is personified by the character of a sexually aggressive, African American prostitute who has given birth to many children for whom she has neither maternal nor nurturant feelings. Further, Hill Collins emphasizes that the underlying connection among all four of these images is "the common theme of Black women's sexuality. Each image transmits clear messages about the proper links among female sexuality, fertility, and Black women's roles in the political economy" (p. 78). The matriarch is an overly assertive and unfeminine woman who cannot adequately supervise her children because she is often not at home. The welfare mother has many children whom she cannot financially support. While the mammy also has many children, her preference is to nurture and care for white people's children.

Our public images of African American women rarely depict stories with childless female characters—despite whatever sociodemographic trends might actually exist in our society. Approximately 10 percent of couples in the United States are unable to conceive after one year of trying. The inability to conceive after 12 or more months of unprotected intercourse is the standard definition of infertility. Currently, infertility affects about 1 in 12 women, between the ages of 15 and 44 (Mosher and Pratt, 1990). While there has been no overall increase in the percentage of women with infertility, there are more childless older women with fertility problems and more women using infertility treatment services (Aral

& Cates, 1983; Mosher & Pratt, 1990). The changing demography of infertility may be a result of recent trends in delayed childbearing, entry of the Baby Boom cohort into the 25 to 44 age range, the availability of many new drugs and techniques to treat infertility, and increases in the number of physicians specializing in reproductive technology.

Similar to the journalistic coverage of infertility, most academic investigations regarding infertility are based exclusively on samples of white, middle- to upper-class women and men. Such couples are most likely to seek infertility treatments and thus make up convenient samples of patients who can be recruited for participation in research projects. In describing their sample selection procedures, which are quite typical of the literature, Abbey, Andrews, and Halman (1991) respectfully explained that "All study participants were married, white, middle-class, with no children by either member of the couple but a desire to have children. This is the sociodemographic profile of people most likely to seek treatment for infertility" (p. 299). Yet, this is *not* the demographic profile of couples who are most likely to be infertile in the United States. In fact, it is older, African American women who are more likely to struggle with experiences of infertility (Aral & Cates, 1983). Needless to say, this epidemiological fact runs deeply counter to social stereotypes, portraying African American women as "baby factories" and "reproductive machines." Thus, I propose that our society holds two inaccurate and rather unexplored narratives about women, race, and fertility. The first is that African American women are abundantly fecund and lead lives that are governed by the burdens of having too many children. The second is a story about the uniqueness of white women who bear the burden of infertility. Common stories about these women depict long, arduously painful paths pursuing many medical interventions, enormous emotional and financial sacrifices, and happy endings with a biological or adopted child. The voices in this chapter rise against both of these narratives as the only viable story.

In a study investigating the impact of infertility on African American women's socioemotional well-being and strategies for coping, I am using qualitative and quantitative measures to assess the role and impact of infertility on women's lives. Currently, 10 African American women have been interviewed as part of this ongoing investigation. These women were recruited through advertisements and announcements in community centers, churches, and adoption agencies, specifically catering to an African American clientele. In this chapter, I will highlight the experiences of two of the African American women in this sample. Their stories depict the period of time in their adult lives when a passionate desire and an overriding commitment to have children dominated their lives. A discussion of their strategies for coping with the pain of infertility will underscore their solitary resignation and self-reliance. Further, I posit that the need to cope in isolation is, in part, inherently related to a cultural silence around issues of infertility and to the internalization of racist assumptions regarding African

American women's reproductive abilities. Additionally, religious beliefs and values emerges as a source of strength that is of paramount importance in the lives of both women. I will begin by providing a brief account of each woman's struggle with infertility, covering the period of time in her life when these issues were most salient.

JOCELYN[2]: "I WAS MEANT TO HAVE KIDS"

Jocelyn is a 47-year-old, married African American woman who works in a management position at a large department store chain. While she does not have a college degree, she does have a certificate in business administration and currently makes a very respectable middle-class income. Jocelyn spent 11 years trying to get pregnant. She started trying to have a child when she was 23 but did not give birth to her son until she was 34 years of age. Jocelyn had always had painful menstrual periods. Before she started trying to get pregnant, her doctors dismissed the concerns she raised about her periods. After her first year of unsuccessful attempts to become pregnant, a doctor did an examination that revealed a number of uterine cysts. These cysts would rupture and cause Jocelyn enormous pain, resulting in scar tissue that ultimately glued her fallopian tubes to her uterus. After undergoing surgery for the removal of uterine cysts, her doctor told her, "You will never get pregnant. You will never have kids. As a matter of fact, by the time you're 35, you're going to have to have a hysterectomy, and you just might as well get used to that thought." Jocelyn was only 24 at the time.

Despite her doctor's negative appraisal of her ability to bear a child, Jocelyn did not let go of her personal belief that she would some day have a biological child. A year after her initial surgery, Jocelyn did become pregnant, but the pregnancy ended in a miscarriage. Jocelyn then decided to switch doctors in an effort to find a doctor who had a more empathic and sensitive manner. The next doctor recommended that she undergo a monthly procedure, a hysterosalpingogram, in an attempt to force her fallopian tubes open. Jocelyn described this treatment as an extremely painful and invasive procedure. After 8 months of treatment, Jocelyn again became pregnant but this time it was a tubal pregnancy. Her second pregnancy was yet another emotionally devastating and heartbreaking experience. Because of the tubal pregnancy, her doctor was forced to surgically remove her right fallopian tube. Afterwards Jocelyn reported, "My husband just said 'no more—no more pain, no more.' But I just felt that I was meant to have kids. And I didn't give up." In the face of overwhelming odds, Jocelyn refused to give up her dream of motherhood. As she recounted it, she gained strength from the dominant social script of motherhood for women. While some women find the compulsory expectation of motherhood to be constraining, Jocelyn relied on it as a source of hope and comfort for her quest. Her solace and perseverance were rooted in a belief that she was meant to be a mother.

When Jocelyn was 30 years old, her second doctor moved to another state, and she once again began investigating and searching for a new doctor. She was referred to one of the best fertility specialists in the state who turned out to be "the coldest person I've ever met in my life." Eventually, however, Jocelyn found an Arabic doctor with whom she felt comfortable and respected as an intelligent human being. After 9 years of trying to get pregnant, she underwent yet another surgery with this doctor. When this surgery failed to lead to a pregnancy, Jocelyn finally decided to end her pursuit of a biological child. She saw her inability to get pregnant as an act of God. "Lord, Thy will be done," she said and put to rest her attempts to fulfill her dream of motherhood. She had discovered a spiritual resolution to her crisis. Four years later at 34 years of age, she was joyously overwhelmed by the discovery that she was indeed pregnant. Her doctor declared that it was a miracle. Twelve years after she began her journey to have a child, Jocelyn gave birth to her son. Equally unexpectedly, she became pregnant again 6 years later. She was 40 years old when she had her second child, a daughter.

Jocelyn's attempts to become pregnant had relied heavily on consultations with medical professionals and medical interventions. Jocelyn's approach to the medical establishment was highly proactive. She read about different interventions, asked questions, investigated doctors, and even switched doctors when she felt she needed to do so. Initially, Jocelyn found and saw an African American doctor, believing that their racial similarity would produce a compatible and mutually comfortable working relationship. She was greatly disappointed by her first African American doctor, though, and surprised to find that it was a Jewish doctor and an Arabic doctor who treated her with the most respect and compassion. Due to her numerous experiences with doctors, hospitals, and medical staff, Jocelyn developed a cautious, healthy skepticism of the medical establishment. She relied on their knowledge and services but not without attending to issues of race and condescending paternalism.

AMANDA: "MINUTES OF EXCITEMENT"

Amanda is a 36-year-old, married, African American woman who works as a program coordinator in a small mental health agency. She was married at 29 to a 42-year-old man, and they started trying to have a child immediately. Amanda quickly began to fear that she might have difficulty getting pregnant because she is a recovering substance abuser. She first became sexually active at 16 and later exchanged sexual services for drugs from dealers in order to support her drug habit. Although she never had a sexually transmitted disease, she was concerned that the years of abusing her body may have compromised her reproductive abilities. She had been clean for 3 years at that point in her life. In addition, she knew that her husband's age might create difficulties in their attempts to have a child. During the next couple of years, Amanda enjoyed only "minutes of excitement" when she would miss periods and mistakenly believe that she might be pregnant. After 3 years she decided that she might be "trying too hard (and) maybe I just won't think about it, just kind of take it out of my mind." Four years after she began trying, Amanda discovered that she was indeed pregnant.

> So when I came home, I wanted to tell my husband—that's the person I wanted to tell; I picked up the phone to call my mother and I put it down. I'd pick it up again, and put it down. 'Cause he wasn't home when I got home. So I waited and I kept waiting. I couldn't even sit still, I was just so excited. So when he drove up—we park on the street; we don't have a driveway—when he drove up, I ran in front of the car, and he slammed on the brakes, and I hollered and screamed, "I'm pregnant! I'm pregnant!" So we both stood out in the middle of the street and hugged each other and cried.

In contrast to Jocelyn, Amanda did not pursue any medical interventions for her problems with infertility. Financial constraints were an important factor in her decision not to explore medical options. "I just knew I didn't have any money. If they could look and tell me what was wrong, I didn't have any money for them to fix it. So it didn't matter." Moreover, Amanda was further deterred from seeking medical attention by her past experience as a substance abuser. She knew that doctors would ask her many questions in taking a detailed history and she thought that they would not take her concerns seriously upon learning about her past. She explained:

> They [doctors] ask you all those questions and you feel obligated. . . . I wouldn't recommend that everyone go out and abuse drugs and become homeless . . . but I did it and it happened and I'm not ashamed of it. But I felt like I was crossing myself out by wasting my time if I go to a doctor and say, "Oh, I'm an ex-substance abuser." [The doctor would probably say,] "Oh, well, why are you wasting your time with me?"

Additionally, Amanda had no interest in adoption. "I didn't want to adopt. That's good for some people. However, I wanted my *own* baby. . . . I wanted her to come out of *me*."

Both Jocelyn and Amanda described the period in their lives when they were trying to have a baby as consumed by their passion to become pregnant. In listening to them talk about this part of their lives, there was little sense of balance or moderation. They were driven by one goal, and everything was viewed through the lens of this burning desire. Jocelyn remembered, "It was a long time. And everything else was on hold. Everything in my life was on hold. I could have accomplished so many things." She goes on to explain, "Everything. My energies were all focused on that [getting pregnant]." When I asked Jocelyn what things made her feel better when she was having difficulty getting pregnant, she replied, "Nothing. Nothing. Just praying. There wasn't anything, really, that made me feel better." There were no distractions, nothing relieved her from the pain of not having a child and there were no other equally important and satisfying pursuits. Similarly, Amanda reported that she could not find a sense of resolution with her struggle to conceive. Only a pregnancy would attenuate the emotional trauma of infertility. Predictably, both Amanda's and Jocelyn's pregnancies were fraught with worries and anxieties. Both women agonized throughout their pregnancy, fearing that something might go wrong.

THE SILENCE OF SELF-RELIANCE

Silence and isolation are a devastating characteristic of the emotional injury that African American women who struggle with infertility typically endure. Most of the women interviewed spoke about their effort to get pregnant as a lonely and solitary path. Jocelyn and Amanda were not exceptions. Both women reported that they went through the emotional journey of infertility predominantly alone. Jocelyn decided to share her story with me, in part, because of the profound loneliness she had experienced throughout those 11 years. She declared, "I will share my story with you because there wasn't anybody for me to share. . . . There wasn't anybody black to share with me. There wasn't anybody that understood." When I asked Jocelyn if she felt like she had gone through these experiences alone, she replied, "A large part of it, yes, I did. It was me and God." Jocelyn explains, "I felt like people tried but nobody understood because they hadn't been through it. They didn't know what it was like. . . . I didn't have anybody to share it with that understood what I went through." Amanda described the discrepancy between what she was feeling and what she would publicly reveal to others. She was feeling, "Why can't I? I'm married, I have a job, I'm clean now. I'm trying to be responsible. . . . Why can't *I* have a baby?" But she hid the pain and agony, even from her family. "I had a wall up to everyone else."

The sense of being alone pervaded most of their relationships with others, including their husbands, other family members, and friends. The emotional burden and isolation of having difficulty conceiving tore at the fabric of even their closest friendships with other women. Jocelyn's closest friend had a child in the same year that Jocelyn had her miscarriage. Her friend had planned a home birth that Jocelyn was supposed to attend. However, Jocelyn could not bring herself to be at the home birth, following her experience with the loss of a child. Afterward, there were so many hurt and misunderstood feelings between them that they ended their friendship entirely. Finally, one day after several years, Jocelyn's friend called and suggested that they meet at a hotel. "[We] hugged and cried and talked about what had been going on in our lives. And we swore never to do something like that again."

Jocelyn found it difficult to talk with her husband about her inability to get pregnant. He had a very different perspective on their situation. "His attitude was, 'If it happens, it happens; if it doesn't, that's all right. . . . Just don't worry about it. Just concentrate on me [your husband].'" Jocelyn pampered her husband, always trying to anticipate his needs. After awhile, other family members began to share her husband's perspective. They urged Jocelyn to abandon her attempts to conceive a child. This effectively meant that she could no longer share and talk with them about her thoughts, plans, and dreams. With her parents and other family members, Amanda never revealed a glimpse of her emotional struggle with infertility; nor shared any of her true feelings. As a defensive posture to hide her pain, she thoroughly convinced her parents that she did not want to have children and that she was too busy with her career to pursue motherhood. Her father was bewildered when Amanda told him that she was, in fact, pregnant. Amanda explains, "When I did tell my dad I was pregnant, that was the first thing he said, 'Oh, I thought you didn't want to have children.' It's like, 'No! That's what you say when things aren't going right, Dad!' You know, when you've been married a long time and you're 34 years old—that's what you say. You don't say, 'Well, I'm trying.' You say, 'No! I don't have time for that.'" Neither did Amanda talk about her experiences with other family members, co-workers, friends, ministers, or counselors.

Like Jocelyn, Amanda and her husband reached an unspoken agreement— they did not discuss their desire to have a baby and the difficulty they were having. "It was like an unspoken understanding. We never really sat down and discussed 'what.' We just kind of came up with our own assumptions, like I thought, 'Oh, well, he's old—there's something wrong with him.' And he probably thought, 'Oh, well, she's an ex–drug addict—there's something wrong with her.' But there was a shared understanding. We didn't talk about it a lot." Not surprisingly, most women interviewed reported that the years spent trying to get pregnant not only affected emotional closeness with their partners but also influenced their sexual and intimate relations. For Amanda, sex became a job, a mission, or simply a means to an end. She described her experience of sex saying, "Every time I laid down to have sex, I was thinking, okay, we've got to do this so I can get pregnant. That was on my mind. There was no enjoyment." More to the point, "Sex was a *job*. It was a job. It wasn't to show that we cared for each other or enjoyment; it was to make a baby. . . . Oh, he was a man. He enjoyed himself. But in my mind, I was thinking, okay, maybe I should turn this way because it would go further down." Jocelyn also remembered that during the most emotionally tumultuous time, she gained no enjoyment from their sex life.

Jocelyn and Amanda's discussion of gender differences in coping with infertility parallel the findings in the literature on white women's experiences with infertility. An abundance of clinical and empirical evidence points to the presence of dramatic gender differences in response to the stress of infertility (Abbey, Andrews, & Halman, 1991; Abbey, Halman, & Andrews, 1992; Andrews, Abbey, & Halman, 1992; Greil, Leitko, & Porter, 1988; Mahlstedt, 1985; Wright, Duchesne, & Sabourin, 1991). As compared to infertile men, infertile women are more likely to experience depression, anxiety, cognitive disturbance, anger, isolation, and negative self-esteem (Abbey, Andrews, & Halman, 1991; Wright, Duchesne, & Sabourin, 1991). Moreover, women tend to view the couple's infertility as a devastating life event and a catastrophic disruption of their gender identity. Men, in comparison, tend to view their infertility as an unfortunate event, but not a disastrous one (Greil, Leitko, & Porter, 1988).

INTERNALIZATION OF RACIAL STEREOTYPES

I contend that the ethos of self-reliant isolation and silence is, in part, attributable to African American women's internalization of social stereotypes that typically portray only white women as having difficulty conceiving. This self-imposed loneliness is magnified because many African American women believe that they are, in fact, alone—that there are no others who have similar experiences with infertility. To counter the emotional isolation that accompanies infertility, a fertility specialist recommended a support group to Jocelyn, but it was a group that met far from the city where she lived. Moreover, it included no other African American women. Jocelyn saw her experiences with infertility as fundamentally different from and not comparable to those of white women. She explained, "So to drive all that distance, and I didn't feel that it was the same experience. Their husbands didn't mind going through the tests. My husband was not going to go and pump semen into a jar. It just wasn't going to happen. And for so many of my sisters, it's just not a problem getting pregnant, you know. The problem is trying *not* to get pregnant. And that was just so hard to deal with." Jocelyn's assumptions of racial differences are supported by all of the women interviewed. With few exceptions, the women reported that their African American husbands would not undergo medical tests or procedures to identify problems that they might be contributing to the couple's infertility. As importantly, Jocelyn believed that she had no *sisters* who might, with guidance from their own similar experiences, help her through her present traumatic endeavors.

Many of Jocelyn's extensive experiences with medical professionals and hospital staff mirrored and confirmed racialized scripts and sexist narratives for African American women. Because she was an African American woman complaining about reproductive problems, doctors and other hospital personnel frequently imagined her to be an overly promiscuous, highly fertile, sexualized woman. She recounted one incident:

> I went through a lot because I used to have a lot of pain, and I'd have these—still have these cysts. . . . Sometimes I'd have to go to the emergency room, and they treat you like dirt because you're black. . . . One time I was at work, and I was in so much pain that I was on my knees. I was crying. And what it was was a cyst was rupturing. But I didn't know that that was what it was. . . . And I got to the emergency room, and this was a male doctor. He was Indian, and he examined me. And he said, "You sure you don't have gonorrhea or syphilis or something like that?" It's like, gee, you're black, you're female, you're young—you must . . . and I was a virgin.

At other times, medical staff refused to believe that she did not have any children or any previous abortions. The message was unmistakable: As an African American woman, her difficulty conceiving a child was unheard of. She was an anomaly.

Even as such stereotypes anger and offend us, a small portion of these messages can be internalized. Many women of color accept and believe unfounded, racist notions about African American fecundity. Amanda believed that she was "the only black woman walking the face of the earth that cannot have a baby." She further explains her thinking, "I thought this was, as the kids say, 'a white thing.' I thought it didn't happen to us. I was something abnormal." It is this fear of abnormality and of strangeness that so deeply stigmatizes African American women into a fortress of silence. Amanda did not know anybody in her extended family who had a problem having children. In fact, she explains, "I just assumed all black women have babies. I never met a black woman that had a problem getting pregnant. I've met a lot of white women. I've never met a black woman that had a problem getting pregnant. In my mind, our problem was having too many. Not knowing when to stop. I've never met a black woman that had a problem getting pregnant." The repetition in her explanation highlights the strength of these beliefs and the power behind our own acceptance of the process by which we are socialized to believe racial stereotypes.

Accordingly, it follows that social interactions with other African American women and their children are some of the most painful interactions to endure. The women interviewed frequently identified baby showers as one of the most trying social events they participated in. Rhetorically Jocelyn asked, "Do you know what it's like to go and sit at a baby shower, and hold babies, knowing you'll never have one of your own?" By the same token, questions about when they are going to have children pierce through their wounds. People would ask Jocelyn, "'Oh, you have any kids? Well, what are you waiting on?' You have to get used to having people say that to you and not crying your eyes out or being really mean to them.... Just to think about it now, I get tears in my eyes and I could just cry. . . . I can't tell you how many times people said to me, 'When are you going to have a baby?'" Because of her experiences, Jocelyn makes every effort not to ask such questions of others. "Sometimes, I find myself, when I say something like that, I say, 'I'm so sorry.' I try always to be conscious, never to say that to people because you don't know what their story is." Amanda also struggled with the anger provoked by pain and the desire to be mean to inconsiderate people. Amanda described herself as being angry with everyone and everything. "I was mad at God. I was mad at myself. I was mad at my husband—just the world in general. Mad at women that had babies. Mad at teenage girls that couldn't stop having them." In responding to people who asked her when she was going to have a child, Amanda quipped, "Why do you think all women have to have babies? I'm a career woman. I don't have time to change diapers!" Amanda's solace during the most difficult times was her job. She gained feelings of self-worth and value from her ability to help other people at work—that made her feel better. In sum, Amanda privately and silently negotiated a vast discrepancy between her highly defensive, public stance and her inner feelings.

There is an ethos of secrecy about sexuality and reproduction in the African American community; indeed, these are highly charged topics for many racial and ethnic groups. For African Americans, the code of silence is partially rooted in a historical legacy of racism and colonialism that condoned the enslavement and rape of African American women as well as the taking and selling of their children. Hill Collins (1990) posits that negative images of African American women's fertility provided a justification for the sexual assault endured by African American female slaves and a social labeling of African American women's fertility as superfluous and unnecessary. Consequently, the African American church tends to place enormous value on the generational continuation of families and culture through the arrival of children. Infertility is therefore unacknowledged and generally avoided in many African American churches. Undoubtedly, the cultural silence around infertility contributes to the isolation experienced by African American women who must cope with difficulty conceiving children. Jocelyn noted that her church was an exception to this standard and attributed this to the fact that her church has a female co-pastor. Sexuality and issues surrounding childbearing are easier topics to broach with the guiding presence of a female pastor.

STRENGTH IN RELIGIOUS BELIEFS AND FAITH

Most of the women interviewed spoke about their religious faith as the means by which they have endured their experiences and survived whole. Religious faith is an indispensable component of many African American women's arsenal for coping with infertility. It is important to note that this study's recruitment of women through African American churches may directly bias this sample in favor of women who tend to be more religious than women in the general population.

However, it is also worth noting that several recent empirical investigations have found that most African Americans believe the church is a beneficial social institution and demonstrate a high degree of religious participation (Chatters & Taylor, 1989; Levin, Taylor, & Chatters, 1995).

Jocelyn unequivocally identified her religious faith as the source of guidance that brought her through. "It [religion] was my comfort. It was my everything. . . . Even now, I can't make it without God in my life." Her faith in God even mitigated her feelings of isolation and loneliness. Jocelyn believed, "You can't go to anybody else with it, other than God." Indeed, when I asked her if she went through her experiences alone, Jocelyn replied, "It was me and God." She reported praying to God quite often. "I prayed a lot about it and just asked for direction. I had prayed and prayed and prayed." And one time, "The Lord just said, 'Go to [a local teaching hospital].'" This led Jocelyn to go sit in the emergency room of a local university hospital where she eventually asked an intern for a recommendation for a doctor. His recommendation led her to the kindest and gentlest doctor she ever found.

Ultimately, for Jocelyn, it was her religious faith that allowed her to reach a sense of resolution with her struggle to conceive. Resolution came when Jocelyn said, "Lord, Thy will be done. Not my will, but Your will. When and if You want me to, it'll happen. And I finally, finally just put it in His hands and let go. . . . Then I got peace. I had peace." Previously, Jocelyn admitted, she had tried to make "deals" with God. She would pray, "Lord, if you'll give me—if you'll let me, I'll do this. Oh Lord, if I get pregnant. . . . " When I asked Jocelyn what kinds of things she would promise God, she responded, "Oh, you wouldn't believe. The things you can think of. . . . 'If I could just have it [a baby] for a little while [we both gasp in pain].' What a concept! What a thing to think of! And then I'd think, 'What did you just say? How sick can you be?'" It is, of course, possible that Jocelyn's sense of resolution with God is more complete in retrospect than it was, in actuality, at the time. However, it is also conceivable that Jocelyn's recollection of her path to finding peace and resolution with God occurred exactly as she recounted it.

Amanda's route to religious involvement was not quite as direct and as unflappable as Jocelyn's. In the midst of trying to get pregnant, Amanda decided to start going to church. She reasoned that it probably would not hurt to throw "everything into the pot." She privately hoped that, in response to her new religious affiliation, God would make her pregnant. "I was hoping that a little more involvement on my behalf might usurp a few extra blessings [specifically a pregnancy]." Unfortunately, her underlying motivation for attending church made Amanda feel guilty. She sometimes wondered if God was punishing her for her past misdeeds and drug habit. Nonetheless, Amanda described her religious involvement during the most difficult times as a source of hope. Despite her early agenda for joining a church, Amanda's religious faith has become an important

and integral part of her life. She explained how presently, "It's [religious involve-
ment] becoming more a part of my everyday life. It's not just get up, get dressed,
go to church on Sunday. But I try to treat people a certain way."

INFORMAL ADOPTION ARRANGEMENTS

It was not uncommon for the women interviewed in this study to report that
their African American husbands showed little interest in adoption. Only one of
the woman interviewed was pursuing an adoption. Most often, the unpre-
dictability involved in adopting a baby—not knowing the child's genetic background—was cited as a main reason against adoption. In a study of the 1988 National Survey of Family Growth with a national probability sample of 8,450
women, African American women were just as likely as non-African American
women to have taken steps, at some point in time, to seek an adoption. However, it is noteworthy that for the African American women the experience of
seeking to adopt a child was not as closely related to an inability to have biological children (Bachrach, London, & Maza, 1991). In approaching this study, I assumed that informal adoption arrangements might be highly prevalent in African
American communities—that is, the "adoption" of children within extended
family networks, without any formal or official proceedings. Additionally, I expected informal adoption arrangements to provide a potential source of solace
and fulfillment to women who had difficulty conceiving a biological child. The
latter assumption is not entirely supported by the interviews. Such informal
adoption arrangements are filled with complex negotiations and unclear agree-
ments between family members. The most frequently reported challenge is dealing
with the paradoxical position of raising a child while having no legally recognized parental rights. Moreover, while many of the women reported that the role
of part-time parenting was enormously gratifying and fulfilling, it did not obviate
a couple's desire for their own biological child.

Jocelyn and her husband helped raise her husband's sister's two oldest children. Her husband's sister died after her fourth child was born. After she passed,
Jocelyn and her husband would take the two oldest children every weekend and
on holidays when Jocelyn could arrange her work schedule to fit school vaca-
tions. The children "completed my family. They were my family," Jocelyn explained. There was no ambivalence in the strength and conviction with which
Jocelyn assumed a parental role with these children. In speaking of them, she affirmed, "I love them. I raised them." The challenges in their arrangement, as she
described them, included, "the fact that they weren't mine and I didn't have the
ultimate say-so. That even though I took them every place, I did their laundry for
the week, that they did go home. We did have to take them home on Sunday
nights." In illuminating the fragility of informal adoptive arrangements, Jocelyn
described how quickly she lost the relationship she had spent years building

with these children. "I had raised them to be teenagers, and now all of a sudden, he [their biological father] wanted to be a dad, and he wanted them fully. So this was an opportunity for him to take them. . . . So I lost them for a few years, until they were older and now they're back. . . . They now have kids, so I'm like a grandma."

Conclusion

My hope in writing this chapter is that it might contribute to a process of making more visible the experiences of African American women coping with infertility—particularly to other African American women. This chapter depicts the lives of two African American women who struggled with infertility and its unrelenting pain. Religious faith and beliefs are highly salient in the coping strategies of both women. One of the women also relied on her role as a "parent" in an informal, adoptive arrangement within her extended family. Most striking about both women's strategies for coping, however, is their silence and emotional isolation. In the public mind, infertility evokes a social script of well-to-do, white couples. Consequently, this master narrative ignores and therefore silences the voices of women who do not fit within its domain. It is this hegemonic perspective of infertility and the internalization of racist assumptions about reproduction that contribute to African American women's desire to cloak their infertility in secrecy. African American women who have trouble conceiving can easily believe that they are alone in the world, estranged and different in their "flawed" uniqueness. Shame and guilt are embedded in the experience of stigmatization. And the implicit racial and class biase in the media coverage of infertile couples does little to assuage the pain.

Despite the self-reliance with which Jocelyn and Amanda endured the trauma of infertility, their advice to other African American women who undergo similar experiences included a strong encouragement to share, to confide, to talk with others. Jocelyn was particularly thankful that she had an opportunity to help a co-worker who was struggling with similar experiences of infertility. She was delighted by her ability to be there for other African American women, since she was not able to benefit from anyone's comfort herself. In describing the value of her experiences for others, she discussed the importance of "cry[ing] with somebody who knows what it's like and been successful. But even to cry with somebody that knows what it's like and not been successful. We do live through it." Additionally, Jocelyn was empowered by educating herself with information and an understanding of medical procedures. She used many means in her pursuit of a doctor with whom she could work and trust. Amanda offered similar advice to other women facing infertility, "I would definitely say talk with people. It's not a burden you need to carry all by yourself. There are other people out there that care. And not only people that care—people that care to help you."

Ironically, I believe that the richness and detail with which these two women shared their stories is greatly influenced by their outcomes. Both women eventually experienced successful pregnancies and are currently raising biological children. In fact, at the close of the interview, Amanda confessed that she would most likely never have talked to me if she did not have a child. According to her reasoning at the time of her infertility, there was no point in talking to anyone, for no one could change her situation. I choose to highlight these two stories, in part, because of the large quantity and richness of their interview material. In exploring these stories, I do not wish to give primacy to a "storybook ending" that values a pregnancy above all other outcomes. There are, of course, other resolutions to struggles with infertility. Some women pursue their dream of motherhood via the adoption of a child—through official channels or more informal ones—while others achieve a sense of resolution with not being a parent. It is imperative that we find and illuminate women's stories with different endings even as the master narrative makes this an especially difficult task.

In concluding this chapter, I would be remiss not to touch upon the politics of reproductive rights in the United States. Public policies are tied to the value of the nation's progeny. White babies are valued by our society; in fact, as I have noted, multiple white births are a highly celebrated national phenomena. Ample evidence testifies that children of color are not equally valued to white children. During the 1930s, the Public Health Service deprived African American men of the penicillin that would have cured their syphilis in order to conduct tests and observations of their deteriorating condition. As a consequence, many children were born into these families with a preventable disease. "Black women [partnered with men in the Tuskegee Syphilis Experiment] failed to receive so much as a pretense of protection, so widely accepted was the belief that the spread of the disease was inevitable because black women were promiscuous by nature" (Higginbotham, 1995, p. 12). More recently, an adoption agency published the following costs for adopting a child in 1990. In dollars and cents, the fees involved in adopting a white infant were $7,500; they were $3,800 for a biracial infant and $2,200.90 for an African American infant (Simon, Altstein, & Melli, 1993). Moreover, the infant mortality rate of African American infants is double that of white infants. After infancy, approximately one-half of African American children and one-third of Latino/a children live in poverty (Hill Collins, 1994). The relative value placed on children of different races is quite apparent.

Social values about race and reproduction are deeply rooted in public policies concerning reproductive benefits and insurance coverage of infertility treatments. Many state policies promote births among middle-class women while discouraging births among poor women. Thus far, 10 states have passed insurance mandates, providing some coverage of infertility treatments for employed women, typically excluding women in part-time or low-wage work and those on Medicaid who do not receive employer-sponsored health insurance

(King & Harrington Meyer, 1997). Likewise, our long history of limiting births among poor women includes forced sterilizations, family planning policies, and the recent retraction of any Medicaid coverage for fertility-related problems (King & Harrington Meyer, 1997). Indeed

> critics have charged that high-tech, hi-cost treatments were available only to middle- and upper-class married couples and inaccessible to the poor, racial and ethnic minorities, gays and lesbians, and unmarried women. Blacks have been particularly unlikely to gain access to infertility treatments given lower incomes, higher rates of uninsurance, and lower marital rates; this is especially troubling given the higher rates of infertility among African Americans. (p. 22)

Class biases and racial stereotypes shape public images and narratives about the value of reproduction among women of different races. Such values play a highly charged and influential role in (a) proclaiming a socially threatening fecundity among African American women, (b) silencing the infertility experiences of women of color, and (c) promoting state policies that support reproduction for middle- and upper-class women while discouraging reproduction among poor women.

NOTES

1. This research was supported by grants from the Michigan Initiative for Women's Health and the Office of the Vice President for Research at the University of Michigan. The author wishes to express enormous appreciation to all of the women who shared their stories for this study. Thanks are due to Debra DeFord for skillfully transcribing many interviews. I am very grateful to Antonia Abbey, Elinor Rosenberg, and Abigail Stewart for their keen insights and willingness to engage in endless conversations about these issues. Additional thanks go to all of the participants of a 1998 Ann Arbor Nag's Heart Conference who commented on an earlier draft of this paper. Finally, my greatest appreciation is reserved for Matthew Countryman and Abigail Stewart who continue to encourage and push me through the many challenges with this project.

2. Pseudonyms are used in place of real names and all identifying information has been changed to protect the identity of these two women.

REFERENCES

Abbey, A., Andrews, F. M., & Halman, L. J. (1991). Gender's role in responses to infertility. *Psychology of Women Quarterly 15*, 295–316.

Abbey, A., Halman, L. J., & Andrews, F. M. (1992). Psychosocial, treatment, and demographic predictors of the stress associated with infertility. *Fertility and Sterility, 57* (1), 122–28.

Andrews, F. M., Abbey, A., & Halman, L. J. (1992). Is fertility-problem stress different? The dynamics of stress in fertile and infertile couples. *Fertility and Sterility, 57* (6), 1247–53.

Aral, S. O. & Cates, W. (1983). The increasing concern with infertility: Why now? *Journal of the American Medical Association, 250*, 2327–31.

Bachrach, C. A., London, K. A., & Maza, P. L. (1991). On the path to adoption: Adoption seeking in the United States, 1988. *Journal of Marriage and the Family, 53*, 705–18.

Chatters, L. M. & Taylor, R. J. (1989). Age differences in religious participation among black adults. *Journal of Gerontology, 44* (5), S183–89.

Greil, A. L., Leitko, T. A., & Porter, K. L. (1988). Infertility: His and hers. *Gender & Society, 2* (2), 172–99.

Higginbotham, E. B. (1995). African American women's history and the metalanguage of race. In D. C. Hine, W. King, & L Reed (Eds.), *"We specialize in the wholly impossible": A reader in black women's history,* (pp. 3–24). Brooklyn, N.Y.: Carlson.

Hill Collins, P. (1990). *Black feminist thought: Knowledge, consciousness, and the politics of empowerment.* Boston: Unwin Hyman.

_____(1994). Shifting the center: Race, class, and feminist theorizing about motherhood. In *Mothering: Ideology, Experience, and Agency* (pp. 45–65). E. N. Glenn, G. Chang, & L. R. Forcey, (Eds.). New York: Routledge.

Israel, B. (1998). The babies boom. *New York Times Magazine, 66,* April 5.

King, L., & Harrington Meyer, M. (1997). The politics of reproductive benefits: U.S. insurance coverage of contraceptive and infertility treatments. *Gender & Society, 11* (1), 8–30.

Levin, J. S., Taylor, R. J., & Chatters, L. M. (1995). A multidimensional measure of religious involvement for African Americans. *The Sociological Quarterly, 36* (1), 157–73.

Mahlstedt, P. P. (1985). The psychological component of infertility. *Fertility and Sterility, 43* (3), 335–46.

Mosher, W. D. & Pratt, W. F. (1990). Fecundity and infertility in the United States, 1965–88. *National Center for Health Statistics: Vital and Health Statistics: Advance Data Reports, 192,* 1–9.

Simon, R. J., Altstein, H., & Melli, M. S. (1993). *The case for transracial adoption.* Washington, D.C.: American University Press.

Winters, C. (1998). Baby business. National Public Radio, Inc.

Wright, J., Duchesne, C., & Sabourin, S. (1991). Psychosocial distress and infertility: Men and women respond differently." *Fertility and Sterility, 55* (1). 100–8.

"Kind of Neanderthal"or "Perfectly Normal": Giving Birth at Home

THE MASTER NARRATIVE OF BIRTH in the United States goes something like this: A pregnant woman in her last month of pregnancy prepares a bag of things to take to the hospital when she gives birth. She has her first contractions at home but must monitor them closely so that she will arrive at the hospital at the "right" time—not too early or too late. A male partner/coach will drive her to the hospital and will be present with her throughout the birth. Nurses and doctors will monitor her progress through labor, will supply painkilling drugs if needed, will monitor the baby's heart rate, will speed up labor if it goes too slowly, will induce labor if it does not begin, will provide for every emergency, and if necessary will perform surgery to save the life of the mother and child. This narrative represents birth as an inherently unsafe, risky, painful event, normally requiring the use of technology (especially fetal monitors and epidurals), drugs (particularly Pitocin and Demerol), and often requiring surgery (cesarean sections in a quarter of all births).

There are some variations on this dominant narrative. Nearly 10 percent of women today have midwives, rather than doctors, who provide for them through the birth process. This represents a return to the way women today may express a desire for their birth to be "natural" and free of drugs, and therefore refuse painkilling medication. Some women have other birth attendants—mothers, sisters, and friends—along with male partners.

One thing does not vary, however, in this cultural story—the setting. *In the United States women give birth in the hospital.* This is the one of the most consistent aspects of birth in the United States, for even women who were influenced by the feminist self-help movement that transformed much of women's medical care in the seventies want to be at the hospital "just in case" something goes wrong (Davis-Floyd, 1992). Within the hospital setting, the "just-in-case" approach to giving birth is further institutionalized by having routine procedures for all women (such as the placement of an IV, not being able to eat, and remaining on a fetal monitor), when only a few may actually need these interventions. When a woman comes to the hospital to give birth, depending on the hospital, she may or may not be able to walk during her labor, she may be able to use the shower but only under set conditions, and even the number of people in the room during the birth is predetermined by institutional regulations, rather than her family size and comfort level. Hospital practices and policies determine what all women will experience rather than a woman's individual needs. In general, women comply with the authority of the hospital policies, nurses and doctors to assure the health of the baby because they believe that modern technology makes hospitals the safest place to give birth (Davis-Floyd, 1992; Murphy & Fullerton, 1998).

Given this narrative of birth, when we hear of a woman giving birth at home we think it must have been because some unforeseen predicament prevented the woman from getting to the hospital. It is assumed that no one would plan to give birth at home where it is unsafe and risky for the baby. We envision emergency calls to 911 and paramedics that save the baby and the woman in the nick of time. These stories of home birth are the ones that make exciting newspaper accounts, heroes of 911 operators, and thrilling television dramas. There is a secondary discourse about home birth as well. Some people hold vague notions of poor rural women, "hippies," or antimedical fanatics giving birth at home, but these narratives are not as developed in our dominant cultural landscape as the emergency home birth.

WHO GIVES BIRTH AT HOME?

Less than 1 percent of births happen at home in the United States, although the rate varies by region, with the highest rate in Alaska (2.47%), and the lowest rate in Rhode Island and North Dakota (0.24%) (Declercq, Paine, & Winter, 1995). This represents about 40,000 births annually, a number that has remained stable for the last several years (Murphy & Fullerton, 1998). Within the group there are two distinct sets of women who have home births—black, Hispanic, rural and/or low-income women, who may have unplanned home births; and well-educated, white women who have planned home births.[1] Both sets of women have home births in response to a medical system that controls pregnant and birthing women's healthcare choices. Black, Hispanic, rural and/or low-income women are often denied access to prenatal care and pregnancy and birth education. This lack of access and education leads to increased rates of unplanned home births and home births where the outcomes for infants are more negative than if the infants had been born in the hospital (Declercq, Paine, & Winter, 1995). These women best fit some of the dominant cultural narratives of having birth at home—home birth is an unplanned event, perhaps an emergency; home birth has negative outcomes for mother and baby; home births happen among rural women.

In response to the same medical system, some well-educated white women also birth at home. However, this group is not responding to a lack of access or education but to the set of controls that the medical system imposes on women's bodies, agency, and the meanings of their birth experiences. To escape these controls this small group of women chooses to have their births at home in order to regain control of the experience. These home births result in healthier than average mothers and infants (Declercq, Paine, & Winter, 1995). They also result in birth narratives that sound quite different from the narratives of these women's peers (other well-educated white women) who give birth in hospitals either with doctors or midwives.

The stories of home birth presented below come from this group of educated women who have home births. Their stories are outside both the dominant medical and cultural narratives of birth and outside the dominant cultural narratives of home births. These home births were planned, not emergencies; did not involve either rural women or "hippies" and were not "on communes." The women were not antimedical fanatics. These women do not describe their birth experiences as painful, risky, unsafe, sterile, or in need of technology, but as everyday (although not ordinary), domestic, safe, personal, and private. Finally, over the past 20 years, numerous studies have focused on the safety of home birth, but rarely on women's experiences of home birth (Bortin et al., 1994). We hope these stories will begin to fill this gap.

The Narrators

Amy and Jill were both interviewed about their birth experiences as part of a larger project that attempted to understand women's birth experiences, particularly their bodily experiences, from their own words and to counter the medical and practitioner accounts of birth that exist for training doctors and midwives. For the larger project (titled *Women's Voices: The Birth Experience*), 31 women responded to ads given to childbirth educators and placed at private prenatal clinics served by a tertiary care, university-based medical center that employed physicians and nurse-midwives. The women were pregnant when they agreed to participate in semistructured interviews that were then conducted in their homes within 1 week to 3 months after their first birth. Twenty-six women were interviewed in the larger sample; all were married except one, all were white except one, and all had some form of insurance coverage for medical care and had taken prenatal classes. Twelve of the women were attended during their birth by nurse-midwives, six solely by physicians, six by nurse-midwives and physicians, and two by direct entry or nonlicensed midwives. Finally, all of the women gave birth in a hospital or hospital-run setting except for two, Amy and Jill. Amy's and Jill's accounts stood out from the other interview subjects not only because they gave birth at home but also because their stories of giving birth sounded very different from the other descriptions we heard.

Jill is a married, 32-year-old teacher who grew up in the Midwest in a large family. Amy is a 40-year-old social worker. Her husband is a baker and part-time student. Her mother was a nurse and father a pediatrician. Neither narrator has a biography that makes them stand out from their peers in our larger sample. So why did they choose to give birth at home and how do their stories of birth compare to those of their peers who gave birth in hospitals?

CHOOSING BIRTH AT HOME

At 40 years old, most medical guidelines would place Amy at high risk for complications during pregnancy and birth, yet she chose a home birth anyway. When the nurse-midwife practice that she was using decided to close, Amy looked for an option that would allow her to control who attended the birth, would allow her privacy, and would allow her to control her bodily experience of birth as she wanted to. After investigating many options—other doctors, hospitals, and midwives—she chose to give birth at home. However, she did not tell her mother that she had made this decision until after the birth.

> Well, I didn't tell my mother, which is probably a good thing. I ended up not telling her 'cause I just couldn't deal with her anxiety during the pregnancy and she lives in another state. But my friends were real supportive . . . I told a couple of people at work that I was friendly with. Most people were ok but I did not tell everyone 'cause I knew I didn't want everybody's reaction. . . . I didn't tell everybody, I kind of took control of who I told.

Like Amy, Jill originally planned to have her baby in the hospital. She began thinking about home birth with the dominant narrative or "image" of home birth in mind. "At first we thought that home birth was, you know, people who live in communes, people who went around wearing those funny sandals. . . that kind of image, I thought it was more kind of a sixties thing." Jill says that she began to look into home birth seriously when she thought that her insurance would not cover the cost of a hospital birth. The more she read about it, talked to midwives who did it, and thought about what she wanted for her birth, the more she was convinced. Because home birth is outside the master narrative of giving birth in the United States, Jill suggests that she and her husband went through and continue to go through a process of "coming out" to friends and relatives about how and where their baby was born.

> I was apprehensive about telling my family, my sister had just come off of, like I said, an emergency C-section, very medical and stuff, so I was worried my family would go ballistic, cause there had just been that medical cesarean, but my parents were extremely supportive, and when my mom found out she could be here she was thrilled. My sister was like

are you sure it's safe enough? My brothers were like, well, that's Jill. . . . Derek's mother was like "what if something happens, are you close to the hospital?" but her daughter had had a traumatic birth, so she was panicked about it. . . . All Derek's fraternity buddies were like, gross, blood, gross, I hope you're gonna be drunk when you do it, man. . . . A lot of casual friends who we'd tell would say "We didn't think you guys were like that" referring to "we didn't think you guys were so hippie alternative." I said, "We're not, it's just a good choice for us."

Finally, Jill's "coming out" about home births led her to its history. She said, "I had never known anybody before coming to this city that had had a home birth, well my grandma, but I found that out when I told her and she said 'Oh you know Derek and Kim were born at home too.'"

From these stories of why they chose to give birth at home several things are apparent. First, neither Amy nor Jill fit the dominant image of who gives birth at home. They are neither rural, hippies, nor medical fanatics. In fact, striking in both Amy's and Jill's narratives is that both say they would birth in a hospital if they did not have the choice of home birth or if they thought it was medically necessary. Amy says, "If Kelly hadn't left [Hospital A], I probably would've had the birth in the hospital." Similarly, Jill says, "We will certainly have our next baby, if we have one, in a hospital if we don't have another option, and I have no problem with that." This part of the story makes another thing apparent—choosing to give birth at home requires having the option to do so. You must have the time, resources, and education to locate and explore home birth as an option. You must live in a community with midwives whom you perceive as safe and available to assist with your home birth; you have to be able to pay for it, as most insurance does not cover home birth. Most importantly, you must also have a tremendous amount of personal and social agency to challenge the dominant medical authority and the cultural standard of hospital birth that family, friends, acquaintances, doctors, and others will hold.

The Birth Stories

Stories of home birth challenge us to imagine birth as something different from the painful, risky, medicalized procedure that we usually imagine. Jill and Amy reference pain as work or labor, instead of as something dramatic, overwhelming, or to be survived. Jill's and Amy's stories were by far the most positive of the women interviewed for this project. Jill, referring to her friends' birth stories, captures this difference, "Let me say it this way, every woman I know who has had a birth in a hospital says, 'Oh the pain, the agony, trauma, I never want to do it again, it was awful, it was miserable, it was ugly.' I loved it! I wasn't in pain. It was exciting. It was exhilarating!" What strikes us is not so much the exhilaration and excitement of these births, but the way they are made ordinary and every-day by the context in which they occur.

Below we examine several aspects of the home birth stories of Amy and Jill. In contrast to the stories of hospital birth, these stories demonstrate how giving birth at home allowed these women control of their bodies and experiences. Every other woman in our sample faced at least one issue of control (whether over what position to be in, or whether or not to push when she wanted to, or whether or not to be given medication to speed up contractions) during their labor. To make the uniqueness of their stories more evident, we have included stories of two women, Kim and Terri, randomly chosen from and *representative* of the larger sample with which to compare them.

THE FIRST CONTRACTIONS

The first contractions for most women imply a sort of crisis or at the very least a signal that an important decision soon has to be made. As they go into labor, most women spend tremendous amounts of energy figuring out when it is time to go to the hospital. Practitioners give women guidelines for when to call the hospital, and when to go to the hospital—when their contractions are five min-utes apart and regular. Women must negotiate between this rule and their actual bodily sensations to decide when to leave for the hospital. Many women fear getting to the hospital too late, having the baby in the car on the way to the hospital, and yet they also fear the embarrassment of getting there too early, of being "wrong" about what they are feeling and experiencing. These are not un-realistic fears, but fears imposed by medical practitioners who treat women with standards developed from the population-based studies or "average woman's ex-perience." These practitioners follow these guidelines in caring for birthing women and are much less likely to listen to women's subjective knowledge of their bodies. Descriptions of anxiety and fear about having the baby at home be-cause she waited too long to go to the safety of the hospital were contrasted with facing embarrassment and frustration when told they were "overreacting" or were "too early" when they arrived at the hospital and had to make a humili-ating trip back home. Furthermore the focus was on how far dilated the cervix was rather than the woman's perception of her situation and/or need to be in the hospital for her comfort. We asked all the interviewees what it was like being at home when labor started.

Kim: Before we went to the hospital? There wasn't much time actually, be-cause when Jim came back to the bedroom and I told him I was, you know, I think I might be in labor, he called right away and we went in. So there wasn't much time.... And we had the bag packed and everything, but I just remember he was a little bit more nervous about getting to the hospital and about making sure we had everything than I thought. But it went pretty quick by the time I realized I was in labor until we got there. There wasn't that much time that we spent at home.

Terri: And I went into labor at like sixish in the evening . . . and the contractions were about 4 minutes apart for forever. And then I said I'm not going to the hospital, 'cause they're going to send me home. I'm staying home and I'm duking it out until I know I'm going to go. . . . So I called the hospital around one in the morning and talked to a nurse, and she was like, you know, take a hot shower, lay down, drink some water, see if it slows the contractions, did all that, breathing through the contractions every four minutes, breathing, breathing, breathing. And then finally about 6:00, they said, "Why don't you come on in and let us check you." Well, I had been at like 2 centimeters at the doctor's the night before, and I had already done 12 hours of breathing through contractions and I'm like we're going to be dilated to seven, we're going to pop this kid out, da, da, da. And it was 6:00 in the morning, and the resident came in and you could tell she was tired and she was in a crabby mood. And she checked me and she was like, "Well, you're only dilated to a two, and you're not even descended far enough to bother admitting you. And I'm like, "Excuse me, what does that mean?" "Well you can either go home or you can go walking" and I'm like, "Well, ok." So she leaves and I started to cry. I'm like, "I'm never going to have this baby." We haul the duffel bag and camcorder and everything back out to the car and started walking.

Jill and Amy's first contractions depict different experiences of the early part of labor. First contractions did not signal a decision to be made, and they were not assessed, evaluated, and judged by others. Rather, first contractions were incorporated into domestic routines and preparations for the baby's arrival. Also, note the different emotional tones of these narrators. Kim expresses some anxiety, Terri stoicism and a need to fight as she "dukes it out." Yet Amy and Jill meet their first contractions with calmness, a sense that what is happening is ordinary and will develop along its own course. These differences, we argue, are not due to personality but to contexts and discourses in which birth is taking place—a medicalized institution versus one that views birth as an ordinary, everyday, safe event.

Amy: That night my water broke at about five and I was doing some errands—I was kind of on my way out the door so I just kind of kept going. I thought, well, I need to finish this stuff. And then by the time I got to Toys R Us to return this Snugli, it was about 6:00 and I had my first contraction, which felt real different from the Braxton Hicks[2] and I definitely knew it was a contraction. And I was kind of squishing water, you know, still I was having surges every once in while or whatever. So I got home and I called my coach, a friend of ours who was going to come over, and I called my midwives and kind of said well, "I probably won't see you guys until later, probably early in the morning," thinking, you know, it would be a while. And my friend came over, she brought us dinner about 8:30 and I went for a walk about 9:15 and I was having labor pains, probably ten minutes apart, but during the walk it got to the point where I'd have to stop and it started getting serious, where I had to stop and just pay attention to them. We kind of walked for 20 minutes. So we came back and about 10:15, I thought I'd go to bed, but I got into bed and then they got really hard, and I thought I can't lay here with them. And my husband was supposed to go to work at 2 A.M., and so he was planning on doing that and being home probably in time for the birth. But between 10:15 and 11:00 they were 3 minutes apart already and 1½ to 2 minutes long. So we called our midwife back about 11:00, and she was kind of surprised, so she said "oh, I'd better come over."

Jill: We went into labor Wednesday night. I began to lose my mucous plug at about 9:00 at night, and I called my midwife right away, and she said, "Well, it could be tonight, it could be 3 days. You know just look for your contractions and when they get real consistent you'll know it's the real thing, and then call me and let me know." So we just kind of hung out. My husband was here and my husband's brother from out of state, who was visiting, expecting to see baby because she was 10 days late, but wasn't here yet, but he was here. And they were out having a beer, throwing horseshoes, and I walked out and said, "Derek, guess what, you know, I just lost my plug and I think things are going to start happening." And then we just kind of hung out, and the contractions didn't start to be real consistent until about midnight or 1:00, so we were able to go to bed, and I got some sleep and some rest and everything was fine, and got up about 1:00 and the contractions were definitely different than Braxton-Hicks and I knew that it was the real thing, so I was really excited and I was like, "wow, Derek, you know, this is it." Oh, it was really just so exciting because we had waited so long for this. So we got our birth kit out and we put plastic on the chairs and I made him vacuum the floor and I woke Rob up and I made him wash the kitchen floor, and we just got the house all ready. And I would do what I could. The contractions at this time were, you know, were nothing, they were just like, you know, I knew they were there and I knew it was different, that it was the real thing. But they weren't enough to hinder me from, you know, being involved in, you know, the getting ready for the birth. So we got the plastic on the bed and the sheets out and all the peripads and the pots and the herbs and all this kind of stuff. And then we were just kind of hanging out.

LABOR

As labor progresses for all of the women, the differences between hospital and home births continue to be evident. Terri's story of labor highlights pain and the use of medical standards over subjective bodily information to interpret and predict a woman's progress through labor.

Terri: And so my water broke . . . we discovered afterwards, he was on his side going in at an angle, so I had front and back labor. So forget all the stuff you learn in childbearing classes of walking and all those different position things, 'cause nothing seemed to help. . . . I was just; I was amazed at how painful it all was. I was a dancer and I've danced on second degree sprained ankles and I've got a really pretty good pain tolerance. It was just incredible. So it was like . . . occasionally it was hard to get on top of the contractions. And so the nurse would get right down in my face, come breathe with me, breathe with me. And she was just wonderful. Well then . . . she was-off duty at 11:00 at night and this was like 10:30 and my water . . . he would get to where the contractions were contracting and he would start to push against the contractions. And so it was like baby stop pushing, baby stop pushing, stop pushing. And then my water broke. And I had never had a problem with incontinence before, but I was like my water just broke, and I just peed in bed. I was all stressed and Kathy came back in, and she's like all right we're going to pop this baby out on time now, this is great, da, da, da, da. Because I guess generally speaking after your water breaks you're supposed to dilate a centimeter an hour. I didn't. I dilated one in 4 hours.

Terri measures herself against the medical standard. Jill, who also gets "puttsy" (slow), takes it in stride, as part of the process and does not measure her progress against an objective standard but her own feelings, wants, and desire, and without a worry for the safety of the baby. Jill also describes this stage with much greater detail and says almost nothing about pain. She also suggests that she is in control of what is happening to her, in contrast to Terri who emphasizes the nurse's role.

Jill: And then at about 3:00 they were getting strong enough that I felt like I wanted to go in the tub, so we went into the tub from like 3:00 until 6:00. And they were getting stronger, and Derek was sitting right with me, and he would time them, and I really was introverted. . . . I was one of those that wanted it absolutely quiet. . . . I just didn't want anyone to touch me. And so whenever I would feel a contraction starting I would hold up my finger and Derek would just be absolutely still and absolutely quiet, and I would just kind of go inside myself and really, really relax and kind of hum through the contraction. And I was in the tub, so it was buoyant, it was warm, it was comfortable. So they were really, really easy. At 6:00 in the morning I was still in the tub. They were getting close enough together that we felt we should call our second coach, my friend Christine, the midwife, and my mom, because my mom was going to fly out and try to be here for the birth. So we called all those three people, and Rachel said when your contractions are 1 to 2 minutes apart and you know, 60 seconds long, call me again. And we told Christine to come over at about 9:00 or 10:00, and mom said I'm on the first flight there. So then from 6:00 until 9:00 I kind of transferred between the tub and the bed and I just kind of hummed through my contractions, you know, they were getting fast and furious and they were like a period cramp intensity, more like a band, but nothing that was unbearable at all. And you know, as long as it was quiet, I had my music on in the background, but Derek would just chill and wouldn't touch, wouldn't move, wouldn't do anything. And he would take cold rags in between and wipe off my face, and that was a real revitalizer. So you know, we just kind of hung out and just kind of blew through that part. And Rachel got over here at about 9:00, and she just kind of watched me for a couple of contractions and said I was doing really, really well. And Christine showed up she was amazed at how well everything was going. And I think she had kind of expected the scream and the torture and that kind of stuff. . . . So then, yeah, Rachel was here and Christine was here, and the contractions kept coming. But once Rachel got here they kind of spaced out a bit, which kind of bummed me out, because I was thinking I'll just keep chugging along and then I'll have my baby here in an hour. Well, it didn't happen that way obviously. I mean it's like I had performance anxiety. This is what Rachel said. She said you should expect this, you know. When it's just you and Derek and things are going great, then when you've got people introduced, you know, we don't mean to be a stress but we can be. And there is just this lull. So we kind of went into this lull phase from 9:00 to 11:00. . . . And then at about 11:00 Rachel asked if I would like to have an internal to find out how far I was dilated. And I said sure. And that was the first internal we had, and I was almost 8 centimeters already. So I was really happy about that. I thought, you know, I'm not in any pain, these contractions are so easy, I'm only at 2 centimeters, so when she said 8 I was very excited and very happy. And so then from like 11:00 until 2:00 we just kind of continued to go through the contractions spaced farther apart. But it was the last bit of cervical stretching that had to happen and at 2:00 the contractions changed and I started to feel like I had to push a little bit. . . . So Rachel asked if she could check again to make sure that I was fully dilated, because she didn't want me pressing against a less than fully dilated cervix. So she checked again and I was fully dilated except for a small lip. And so she said "just try to work with a few more contractions, Jill." So we did that but the contractions were still real far apart, which I was kind of surprised about. And then came—this is the one hard part about the labor and the birth experience—was that from 3:00 until 8:00 at night I was like in this puffy, puffy push stage. I would get contractions that were totally painless like once every 15 to 20 minutes. And I would just push with all my heart, because I wanted to see my baby, and I was so excited to see my baby, and I wanted so badly to just have my baby. But it wasn't the overwhelming need to push. . . . And it was just like I went "puttsy" stage and that was frustrating and I'm sure that my tension didn't help at all, because even though I tried to be real mellow and cool about it, I was like, you know, I really want my baby and what's taking so long. But, you know, Rachel said, "just chill and things are happening, as they should. The baby's descending down the birth canal. You can feel her, you know, when you do push, things are happening. . . ." And she was right. . . . I was just like, I want my baby, I want to hold my baby and that was why I was frustrated. But, medically, I never once had anxiety because I thought, you know, something's wrong that my baby's taking so long to come. And then at 7:30 or 8:00 Rachel said, "you know, your waters haven't broken yet. I think you're pushing and the water is going against your cervix and not your baby's head and that's why it's taking so long." So she goes, "if you'd like, we can break the water. If you don't want to, we don't have to because it's not medically necessary. But if you want to speed things up we can." And Derek and I decided we did. We did want her to break the bag of waters. So at one of the next contractions she stuck this really cool amnio-hook between her fingers and she inserted that very gently inside me, and then she snagged my waters during a contraction, and then after that things really started to happen. And it was exciting because there was a difference.

Amy: And I labored for about 4 hours, really intensely, at least that's what it felt like to me. I don't know it's the first time. Some of those contractions were right on top of each other. I didn't have a break in between. And then Barb, my coach, kept me on top of the contractions. . . . I was having a real sudden peak and then a down, so she helped me to kind of get on top of that and be breathing through them. I did this kind of moaning, oohing through them to just keep myself slowed down. And a few times I felt like I was panicking and she would say you're breathing too fast. And I could really feel myself getting kind of panicky, but they just kept me kind of focused. And my husband was there . . . . I remember he rubbed my feet, and he was just there. They sent him on little errands for things, and he wasn't sure whether he was going to be able to stay through the whole delivery, and he did.

Pushing

As their stories continue, the hospital births begin to look even more different from the home births. Kim receives pain medication, and she talks about herself as an object that things are done to by others. She is not doing them herself. For example, she says, "They tried laying me on my side" whereas Amy says, "I was on my hands and knees" and Jill says, "I was sitting and squatting."

Kim: I just can't describe how bad the pain was. And again it was all back pain. And I remember when I started to push, the nurses came on and wanted me to start pushing, I would try and just right before I'd do the pushing, to try and relax and try to do some visualization and all that, but it just didn't work. All I can remember about it is the intense pain, the back pain, and even, you know, they'd come in and they'd give me a little extra boost of the epidural and it just didn't help. And they tried laying me on my side and it wouldn't help, and nothing just seemed to, toward the end, get rid of the pain [Q: At the end?]. At the end, yeah. Because they backed off a little bit on the epidural and then just what they thought was just my anatomy and the way she was lying was just putting a lot of pressure. And truly, all I can remember is the intense pain. I remember the shakes, too. I remember having extreme shakes. That caught me totally off guard, and I thought, "oh, my gosh, you know, I'm septic or something." Because I just remember, just being under the covers and just shaking uncontrollably. That's something nobody ever told me would happen. That, I forgot about that, but, yeah, that was very pronounced, I had that frequently.

Amy: I just felt like my uterus was squeezing like a tube of toothpaste, you know, somebody had grabbed the top. Instead of this like waves, you know, the contraction with a lot of pain, there wasn't any pain, it just felt different. It was like all of a sudden someone was squeezing it to squeeze the baby out. And then they got more intense, you know, well, now I'm pushing—went from the contractions to pushing. That's what that was about. And they'd be in waves, like after I got going, like three or four were just a push and then a period of time in between. So I don't know if that's pretty normal? . . . But yeah, it definitely just felt real different. And through the whole thing I was on my hands and knees most of the time that was the position that was comfortable for me. And then at one point for about eight contractions I got really bad back pain, which was probably the baby coming around the, they told me later like the back, I forget what they told me, but . . . It made sense and Barb had to like—she kind of knuckled in in a spot [pushed her knuckles into the spot] and that really helped. But yeah, it was just different. And then I would kind of sit up through the pushes, they said to get gravity. I was kind of on my knees and . . . then when I finally delivered, I got down on my side and delivered that way. And she was doing hot compresses on that. I didn't tear at all, which I thought was also pretty amazing.

Jill: It's like all of a sudden I really had to push and the contractions started coming a lot faster, they were not painful at all but they were just now let's get down to business. So when they would come, I was sitting on the chair in the other room in a squatting position so I could hold onto the side of the armchair and just push down, and I would push, and push, and push with all my heart and it felt so good. And I remember Derek saying, "OK, I just saw her head." So her head was showing and that was just like this huge landmark for me. I was like, "wow, it's finally happening." So that was just really exceptional. And when that happened—when we started seeing her head—we transferred from being out in that room in the chair to the bed. And my husband and I, we felt like a rowboat, I had my hands in his hands, he was across from me and I had my feet under his butt. So whenever I would have the need to push or a contraction, I would rock myself up and just use him as a lever, and I would just really, really pull against him and push down. So for like the next hour and a half incredible progress was made. I could feel it. Everybody around could sense it. The baby's head would show a little bit and then peek back, and show a little bit and peek back. And then finally it showed and stayed, and then it got a little bit bigger, and a little bit bigger, and a bit more and a bit more. And it was just, I mean I was working so hard, but I knew.

BIRTH

The stories are different as well when the babies are actually born. Terri, like a quarter of all women who give birth, had a C-section. Kim, like many women and most doctors, focuses her story on the outcome of the birth—the baby, and says very little about the process. Amy's and Jill's stories are both unusual as both narrate the actual birth itself with great detail. For example, Amy touches her baby's head before it is born, and Jill depicts the moment of birth as celebratory, like "a champagne cork popping."

Kim: Let's see what else? . . . Um, the best part was after she was born they put her up on my stomach and let me hold her and tell her how much we loved her and how glad we were that she was here. I told my husband I felt kind of bad because I kind of hogged her for myself then. You know, he was right there and he had helped me through the labor and everything, but I don't remember trying to include him in that process and I felt a little bit bad about that afterwards, but I think I was just so excited she was here and so enamored with the whole thing that I didn't think to include him, and I felt kind of bad about that. And I was really glad I had that period because she needed to get antibiotics, so they took her away for awhile. And so I was really glad that I had that time to be with her and to bond with her a little bit before they took her away. She was only gone 3 hours but it's a long 3 hours to have her gone. I can't think of anything else off the top of my head. It was a good experience. It hurt more than I wished, though but it was a good experience.

Jill: We had a mirror right between Derek's legs so I could see what was going on, and it was so exciting. She had fuzz black hair and Rachel was sitting behind me supporting me, and it was a good situation. And then at about 10:00 my bottom was starting to get sore because the softness of the mattress was bothering me, so we shifted to the floor. . . . And we were sitting down there for maybe 10 minutes and at our Bradley classes we had learned that whenever you push and you feel burning that you should stop and try to pant through the contraction because your perineum hasn't stretched enough and you'll probably tear, so just try to pant through the contractions so that your perineum naturally can spread with baby's pressure and gravity working with you. So I was pushing and pushing and pushing, and at one contraction I felt the burning. And I said, "uh oh, uh oh, I feel the burning," so I laid back and I panted through it and everything was great. And Rachel said, "you're doing wonderfully, Jill." That's exactly what you should do because you could just see the perineum stretching with just the force of gravity without me having to push at all. So we had a few more contractions like that where I would get halfway through the contraction and I would feel this burning, so I would lean back. My friend Christine was behind me at this point in time and Rachel was down there with Derek, and then I would lean back and pant my way through the rest of them. And then at like 10:30 I had that same sensation. I sat up and I was pushing really hard, and I said oh, "I'm burning again." And I leaned back and I started to pant and all of a sudden, pop, and baby came out—head, shoulders, knees, and toes. And she projected two feet across the room and landed in my husband's lap. And it was the most incredible—I thought my bag of waters had broken. I just thought, oh, my back waters have broken, because I felt this gush. And then I looked down and there was a baby on me. I was like, "oh my God, my baby came out." I couldn't believe it. It's like I wasn't pushing, we weren't expecting it, and it happened so fast. I thought well, her head is going to crown and then her head will be born and then the shoulders and the rest will slither out, and it will take awhile. And she was just like a champagne cork popping—I mean the whole baby just came out. And Rachel, my midwife, afterwards said that . . . I mean she has given birth to almost 200 babies—and she has never seen anything like it. . . . So then my baby was on me and I was holding her and she started to nurse right away and we were just talking, and my mom was just crying and Christine was like, "wow, I can't believe it just popped out like that and it was so fast after all that pushing." And Derek turned around and we were talking and I said, "do you want to hold your baby," and I gave the baby to Derek . . . and her cord was still attached, and Derek gave her back to me and we were just hanging out and talking to her and Rachel was checking to make sure that everything was okay, and I thought for sure that I was just shrapnel down there because of the rate at which she had come out. So I said, "oh Rachel, did I tear, I just can't believe that she came out so fast." And Rachel looked and said that I had a little tiny like first-degree tear on the bottom of the perineum. . . . And then, yeah, we were hanging out and the cord stopped pulsing, and so Rachel and Derek tied off the cord and Derek got to cut it. And about a half an hour after baby was born the placenta came out. . . . I was feeling contractions but they weren't strong or anything cause I was with baby and I was more wrapped up in her obviously than anything else. . . . And then about 45 minutes after that I got really light-headed and I had not been drinking like I should have been drinking in the last part of my pushing stage. So I was getting really light-headed from dehydration, so my mom took the baby into the other room, and Rachel gave me some oxygen so that I could just kind of get my bearings, and I drank like ten gallons of Gatorade and then everything was fine. So that's how it happened. And it was wonderful and it was so exciting the way it finally ended up happening. Because I had pushed so long and I waited so long and all of a sudden she just joined us. And I love, you know, my husband says his analogy is like a zit popping, but I prefer to say a champagne cork popping. It was just so exciting. So that was my birth experience and it was everything I thought. Quite a bit less as far as the pain element and quite a bit more as far as just the whole surrealism, just the feeling, just the emotions of looking down and I thought I had broken my waters and then there was a baby on me and that was so exciting, it was just overwhelming. So that was it.

Amy: Again, it was happening so fast. I remember thinking now where is this baby? I was thinking what place is it now? It felt like she just came so quickly in a sense. I'm trying to remember. I didn't really feel it. I just felt like that urge to push all the time. I mean as she got closer to the end I definitely felt as her head started to crown. You know you feel that burning sensation. I really didn't have a sense of it to tell you the truth that I can think of. I just remember thinking that I had to keep pushing and to try to get with the pushes so I was putting all my voluntary energy behind what was happening involuntarily. And they did show me when she started to crown, they showed me her head, and I could see her. You know I touched her head once. At the very end too I was surprised I didn't realize where she was and I felt like I jettisoned her out of me, because they told me they were going to ask me to stop pushing and to puff and when they did that I was in the middle of a big push, and I couldn't stop it and all of her came out. You know, her head wasn't out yet, so head, shoulders everything, just the whole baby came out in one push, and so that was unexpected to me that that would happen. I thought it would be little by little. So I guess I was lucky, as I said because I didn't tear.

Conclusion

Finally, we asked all the interviewees how their birth experiences influenced their lives. The women's answers echoed the types of births they had. Kim and Terri both discussed the influence of the baby on their lives, focusing, like doctors do, only on the outcome and not the process of birth. Speaking about the other/baby with little regard for themselves in the process. Kim said, "It's just, you know, when you're pregnant you know there's this baby, but it just isn't that real, and when you actually give birth, it's like this is a person. It's just incredible, and it just gives you respect for human life in general." Similarly, Terri said, "that I had a healthy baby, I mean, I remember thinking how terrible it would have been, you know."

Amy's and Jill's answers focused not only on the outcome—the baby—but also on the process and what it meant to them. Amy said, "Well, I feel more confident that I did it, you know, I remember thinking before I just wasn't sure how I was going to handle it. Could I really do it? But I just feel confident about that I did do it. And I feel like, you know, I wasn't a parent before and now I am. I kind of crossed this line and I have a daughter." Jill said, "Certainly it's empowered me. I feel like I did it. I did it without drugs. I did it the way I wanted it to be done, and that's empowering, and that's, you know, . . . that empowerment just kind of carries above and beyond in your everyday life, you know, just going back into the world saying I had a baby, I did it, you know, and that's a good feeling."

In sum, the stories of home births presented here do two things; they high-light that birth is not inherently medical and show how some women integrate it into ordinary everyday domestic life. They reveal how medical institutions have captured the site and meaning of birth—a high-risk event that needs to be con-trolled by professionals. Hospital birth becomes an event that is regulated by ex-ternal measures and institutional policies for the safety of the baby, rather than a woman-centered, bodily experience that has multiple dimensions including the well-being of both the woman and her baby. They also highlight that stories of birth usually are stories of pain gotten through to achieve a successful outcome and rarely are about the process of birth. Yet despite the challenges they entail to dominant models of understanding women's bodily experiences, these stories of home birth are also stories of privilege. They are the stories of white, well-educated women with the time, resources, and education to spend planning their home births. The dominance of hospital birth is so strong that the legal, structural, and economic barriers to the option of a home birth are substantial. Finally, they are also stories of resistance. To make the choice to give birth at home is to choose against the incredibly powerful master narrative of birth in the United States. It is a choice both of these women made in order to claim con-trol over their bodies and entire birth experiences.

Notes

1. Since birth certificates do not make a distinction between planned and unplanned home births, there are not good data to suggest the proportion of these within the 0.6 percent of births that happen at home.

2. Braxton-Hicks are early contractions that many women feel before labor. They tend to be shorter, irregular, and not painful.

References

Bortin, S., Alzugaray, M., Dowd, J., & Kalman, J. (1994). A feminist perspective on the study of home birth: Application of a midwifery care framework. *Journal of Nurse-Midwifery, 39* (3), 142–49.

Davis-Floyd, R. (1992). *Birth as an American rite of passage*. Berkeley and Los Angeles: University of California Press.

Declercq, E., Paine, L., & Winter, M. (1995). Home birth in the United States, 1989–1992: A longitudinal descriptive report of national birth certificate data. *Journal of Nurse-Midwifery, 40* (6), 474–82.

Murphy, P. A. & Fullerton, J. (1998). Outcomes of intended home births in nurse-midwifery practice: A prospective descriptive study. *Obstetrics and Gynecology, 92* (3), 461–70.

"An Unbelievable Kind of Thing":
A Mother's Response
to the Disclosure of Incest

> She blames me for not knowing. I should have. . . . I was the
> mother, I was the wife, and I should have known the father, the
> husband. . . . I will never make up, I mean, you know, I could
> live to be 200 years old and I could never make up for it.
> —Sarah Alexander, 1997

SARAH ALEXANDER (her chosen pseudonym) is a friend of mine. Sarah is black;
I am white. We do what friends do, that is, we play together and we talk.
On one such play night, Sarah shared the story of her daughter's incest.

There were five women present that night—three African Americans and
two whites—friends from an amusement activity to which we are all committed.
Over shared pizza in a conversation about relationships with men, Sarah asked,
"Do you want to know why I got a divorce?" And then the story of her daughter's incest spilled out.

Several days after the dinnertime disclosure, Sarah, who is aware of my previous research on abused women, approached me and said, "You should write
about me." Her suggestion underscored a tension inherent in interracial friendships in a race conscious society like our own. For Sarah, an African American
woman, chose to include me, a white woman, in the disclosure of her personal
and painful story of paternal incest. She then trusted me to use my privileged
position as an academic to write that story for the edification of interested others. Sarah and I are friends, but our friendship is situated within broader social
contexts that are quintessentially "raced" (West, 1995) and that create an invisible backdrop to our personal lives. This paper is the consequence of my friend
Sarah's request.

Although the events recounted and the process of telling did and do occur in
racialized social contexts, the story that Sarah tells is foremost the story of the
mother of an incested daughter. Incest supersedes race in saliency in Sarah's nar-

rative, although race remains the unspoken context within which the incest occurred and within which Sarah tells her story of disclosure.

WAYS AND MEANS

Sarah's fully explicated narrative evolved from several informal discussions, two lengthy, open-ended taped interviews, as well as her comments, or lack thereof, on interview transcripts. Although her story, as told and analyzed, is in many ways individual and compelling, the process of personal narrative construction necessarily draws upon and is embedded in the social discourses and ideologies of the dominant society (Richardson, 1997). Incest is, by definition, rooted in social and cultural mores. If ideological mores fashion our personal narratives as Richardson (1997), Plummer (1995), and Gergen (1992) argue, then a woman's construction of herself as the mother of an incested daughter can be analyzed as an example of social ideologies that are individually appropriated. I argue here that Sarah Alexander's retrospective reconstruction of her life experiences prior to and shortly after the disclosure of incest reflect her struggles to resist the master narratives available to her as the mother of an incested daughter and therefore connect her experiences to public forms of social organization (Lempert, 1994). I further argue that, although the myth of the oversexed black male and its corollary the promiscuous African American female (Chafe, 1995; Davis, 1983; Hall, 1992) is one ideological frame against which Sarah constructs her narrative, it isn't her most salient narrative frame. A woman whose daughter has been paternally incested focuses on resolving the ambiguity and confusion resulting from the allegations (Elbow & Mayfield, 1991). If able, she may also resist the mother-blaming interpretations that follow such disclosures. The immediacy of these tasks appears to attenuate contextual issues of race.

By examining Sarah's story of disclosure, that is, *what* she said about her daughter's allegations and her own innocence of knowledge about the incest, the resulting grounded theory analysis (Glaser, 1978; Glaser & Strauss, 1967; Strauss, 1987; Strauss & Corbin, 1990) simultaneously focuses on *how* Sarah tells her story, how she retrospectively reconstructs the actors and their interactions through the narrative process. By attending to the content of Sarah Alexander's story, it is possible to explore the ways that she appropriates, uses, and resists the master narratives of race and mother-blame.

Although the analysis of Sarah's narrative is presented here in linear form, as recounted in the interviews, her recollections and reconstructions were partially formulated and episodic. While Sarah began conventionally by temporally ordering her narrative, when she began to relate the incest allegations and her responses to them, her story became more fragmented. She continued in her attempts to impose a sequential order on the emerging inconsistencies and ambiguities, while she simultaneously constructed her narrative montage of allegations, denials, demands, and uncertainties. My analytical telling of her story necessarily reflects some of these narrative disjunctures.

SHOULDS AND OUGHTAS: SARAH'S FAMILY OF ORIGIN

Sociologists agree that the first and most important agents of socialization are the child's parents and family. Through words and gestures, parents and family members interpret their particular culture and society for their children. These interpretations are internalized when parental caregiver expectations become part of the child's own thought processes (Hess, Markson, & Stein, 1996). By contextualizing Sarah Alexander's formative years, it is possible to trace her construction of the incest within her personal and social history and to examine *how* these early sociocultural assumptions saturated her adult sense-making resources. Seeded in Sarah's account of expectations in her family of origin are the later manifestations of image making, management, and maintenance; of gender rules, roles, and responsibilities; and of the shattered dreams of self and family with which she attempted to reconstruct her life. The processes through which her personal experiences are linked to underlying master narratives of women, wives, and mothers that present the mothers of incest victims as dependent, collusive, dysfunctional, and/or absent (Cohen, 1983; de Young, 1994; Elbow & Mayfield, 1991; Faller, 1988; Green, 1996; Johnson, 1992; Tinling, 1990) becomes more salient through analysis of her narrative.

Now a 55-year-old professional, Sarah grew to maturity as one of several daughters in an "elite" black family in a burgeoning postwar community in middle America. "We were considered, you know, among those who have. The elite. I mean my parents were educated. They had [several] really pretty girls who made it through school." Her father had earned a bachelor's degree, which was "incredible for two reasons. One, just doing that [going to school full time and working full time]. And number two, being a black man. I mean that was just not heard of." Her mother's post–high school education was "in the area of secretarial or that kind of thing." Sarah grew up in integrated postwar subsidized housing. Because her father "would have been concerned about, you know, his daughters," Sarah and her older sister attended a private, predominantly white, elementary school.

Perhaps as an antidote to sociocultural images of African American families as "pathological" (Moynihan, 1967, 1990), pride in family was an axiom of the Alexanders. "If you did anything wrong or bad or not the right things, [it reflected badly] on the Alexander name. I mean it was just never. . . . Image, image was just so incredibly high on the family list. I mean you wouldn't believe, I mean it was probably at the top. . . . Because of evolutions in my life, I'm not saying it's not important, but it isn't there [at the top] anymore."

In high school, Sarah "was known because I was so and so's sister. And I was also known because I was black." Sarah described herself as not "student minded," as more involved in social than in academic activities. It was an event in this active social life that brought her together with her husband, Jack. Their first formal date grew out of some class plans for a holiday celebration. At the time, Sarah was dating a young man "whose mother was a teacher, father was a [city employee]. I mean one of these, you know, the right thing." But this young man was in college and he was unable to come home for the party. Sarah, who "sort of knew [Jack] but didn't," called him and asked him to take her to the party . . . all of my friends just *loved* him." Although her parents also approved of him, they were less enthusiastic. "It was OK with my parents. At that time his mother was a teacher. His dad, however, was a [day laborer]." Jack himself was a senior in high school. "He was a nice gentleman, very nice, polite gentleman up until actually this whole incest. He really was respectful of both of [my parents], of me, of his parents." Jack was offered some college football scholarships, but he didn't "follow through." And while he attended college for a year and a half, he didn't do well academically.

"When we started dating, I never thought the Vietnam War would have a direct effect on me." Jack, however, knew he was going to be drafted, so he enlisted. Sarah went away to college. By this time, the couple had become sexually active and were talking about an engagement and marriage. "Jack had always made it perfectly clear, even in high school dating, that he didn't believe in going steady. He didn't date one person at a time. I knew perfectly well that we might go out on Friday night and he might go out on Saturday night with somebody else and Sunday with somebody else. . . . Although I didn't like it, there was nothing I could do about it. . . . The one thing is that Jack was perfectly honest about it." So Sarah accepted Jack's terms. But Jack refused to be engaged while Sarah was away at school, so Sarah came home to be with him. "I gave up something I was thrilled to death to have." Shortly thereafter, she became pregnant. "That's where the family name, the family image, just all of that, was just terrible."

Having grown up with dreams of a formal wedding as a bride with "all the trimmings," Sarah's romantic dream was shattered. "My parents let me know after I got pregnant that they were not going to pay [for a wedding or for college] anymore. . . . They were so unhappy with what I'd done. . . . I was going to tarnish the image." Jack, however, was elated. "From the minute he found out that I was pregnant, I mean he just thought that was a man thing." The young couple was married by Jack's minister in the backyard of Jack's parents' home. "Jack didn't quite meet up to the standards of who I would like to have married probably because he didn't have a degree. I mean he speaks well, does well with people . . . physically he was attractive."

Their daughter, Michelle, was born 6 months after their marriage. "Right before I went into the delivery room, you know, my mom would say, 'We'll just tell people she was three months early.'" The first time Sarah told anyone about being pregnant before her marriage occurred when her daughter was 11 years old. "I felt that much shame, that much embarrassment." Image maintenance continued to frame Sarah's social encounters.

Sarah and Michelle lived with Sarah's parents until Sarah finished college and Jack's tour of duty in Vietnam was over. At that point, Sarah and Jack left her parents' home to live together as a married couple. Within 2 years, the couple had a second child. Sarah completed her undergraduate work and followed a consistent professional-career trajectory. While always gainfully employed, Jack had a series of career starts and stops; he returned to college at various times but never completed a degree program. Sarah and Jack maintained an active social life and the appearance of middle-class success, respectability, and happiness. "The family really liked him. . . . I did a really good job on the surface as a wife and mother. . . . I can bake the cookies and make the clothes and Jack and I can go to social events . . . that kind of thing." Such unwavering commitment to and construction of the image of "happy family" contributed to Sarah's inability to detect underlying family fissures.

Although Michelle alleges that the abuse began when she was 5 years old and continued until she was 20 years old, Sarah eschewed any knowledge of the sexual interactions. Even in her retrospective account, she maintained complete ignorance: "I went through the family album, I was . . . going through looking, you know, looking in her face. I mean, going back to the early days and just seeing if there was just a difference in her expression, a different kind of smile. . . . I couldn't pick up anything."

The ideological frame of the master narrative of mother-blame invites questions: How is this possible? How could a "mother" not know? How could a "mother" live in the intimate circumstances of a nuclear family and be totally unaware of sexual interactions between a father and daughter? Sarah Alexander's narrative is rife with the ideological formulas that structured her world and formed the lenses through which she interpreted all interactions. Paternal incest is incomprehensible to a woman enacting an American Dream life who has no reason to suspect, who has faith in her husband, and who believes in the inviolability of the incest taboo (Elbow & Mayfield, 1991). This framework constrained Sarah's ability to detect interactions, like incest, that were incompatible with her ideologies of love and family.

Sarah grew up in an African American family concerned with their social image and their external presentations of self (Goffman, 1959), a concern perhaps born out of centuries of vilification (Hine, 1989). Violations of carefully cultivated images that could sweep the family into denigrating cultural stereotypes of African American families, such as Sarah's premarital pregnancy, were either denied or reconstructed in conformity with the Alexanders' public presentations. Foundational to both making and maintaining image and the roles and responsibilities of gender was the ideological frame of family as the context for "happily ever after." "Happily ever after" never includes paternal incest.

While a life predicated on sociocultural ideologies may be a condition for ig-norance of incest, it is not a sufficient condition. Sarah's ignorance was also se-cured by the ambiguity of the disclosed sexual interactions between her husband and her daughter, that is, the allegations and the denials, the lack of physical evidence, the retrospective constructions, the personal histories of all parties, and her own lack of suggestive cues or insights, even retrospectively, in more than 20 years of marriage. Ambiguity and image were interpenetrating constraints in Sarah's life.

MOTHERS IN "INCEST FAMILIES"

For the girls and women in "incestuous families," disclosure or discovery of pa-ternal incest turns private troubles into public woes (Mills, 1959). For African American women, incest disclosure may also result in feelings of community jeopardy for while the personal lives of the girls and women involved are opened for public scrutiny, the public nature of the disclosure of incest may also feed the stereotypes of "pathology" (Moynihan, 1967, 1990) in African American families (personal communication, Rev. Benjamin Baker, 1998).

In child sexual assaults by strangers, the criminal justice system, the thera-peutic establishment, and the popular media conventionally hold the adult per-petrator individually accountable for acts committed against the victim (Clark, 1993); the mother of the abused child generally is not held accountable. But be-cause incest occurs in familial contexts where both normative and aberrant be-haviors are simultaneously enacted and where intimacy is the norm, disclosures of paternal incest secure father, daughter, and mother in a tangled web of public denials, guilt, and blame (Elbow & Mayfield, 1991). For better or worse, women's lives are situated inside relationships (Fine, 1989), and it is from these social lo-cations that the mothers of paternal incest victims become central figures in the abuse.

Master narrative images of the "good mother" demarcate a contextual frame within which mothers of incested daughters are frequently blamed for overtly or collusively causing the abuse (Breckenridge & Baldry, 1997). Because mother-blame assumes maternal or spousal inadequacy, mothers are retroactively con-structed as actively or passively collusive, as submissive, dependent, enabling, and/or abandoning (Cohen, 1983; de Young, 1994; Elbow & Mayfield, 1991; Faller, 1988; Green, 1996; Johnson, 1992; Tinling, 1990). Such denigrating char-acterizations of the women who are the mothers of victimized daughters as well as the wives/partners of incest perpetrators remove them from broader social contexts and render invisible the patriarchy, hierarchy, and sexism that struc-tures their lives (de Young, 1994; Green, 1996; Solomon, 1992). Conceptualizing mothers as central in the pathology of incest undergirds the unchallenged assumptions of master narratives by deflecting attention away from the perpetrators and by minimizing the responsibilities in choice and action of fathers who commit incest (Breckenridge & Baldry, 1997; Elbow & Mayfield, 1991; Green, 1996; James & MacKinnon, 1990; McIntyre, 1981; Wattenberg, 1985).

Sarah Alexander's "personal experience narrative" (Plummer, 1995) of incest disclosure problematizes conventional mother-blame discourse. In addition it underscores the master narratives of race and gender that contribute to the social silences surrounding African American women's experiences (Collins, 1990, 1998). Stories like Sarah's have been invisible for incest and mothers' stories of incest are taboo (McIntyre, 1981; Plummer, 1995) and therefore unspoken and unknown.

By focusing research attention on the narrative of the disclosure of incest to Sarah, a mother whose daughter was paternally incested, generic constructions of mothers of incested daughters can be destabilized. Sarah's account is a challenge to the culturally circumscribed master narrative of mother-blaming that surrounds revelations of incest. By analyzing the ways that Sarah's fierce enactment of cultural and ideological images of "good wife" and "good mother" blinded her to the social processes that ensnared her, I demonstrate how the cultural resources available to reconstruct events, family, and self after disclosure of incest fail to capture the ambiguity and complexity of the experience.

Constructing Mothers of Incested Daughters

The vast majority of literature on women whose daughters have been incest victims consistently identifies them in their social locations as "mothers." The women are only nominally presented as wives of incest perpetrators and are never (to my knowledge) presented simply as women who might be ancillary to their daughters' sexual victimizations.

Much of the research literature on mothers of incested daughters has been written since the 1970s and has blamed the mothers for not "protecting" their daughters and/or for "allowing" the abuse to occur (Elbow & Mayfield, 1991; Johnson, 1992; Meiselman, 1978; Stark & Flitcraft, 1996; Tinling, 1990). In numerous studies, victimized daughters themselves blame their mothers for the sexual abuse perpetrated by their fathers (Herman, 1981; Jacobs, 1994; Meiselman, 1978). Several analytical explanations have followed, including denial and lack of maternal support that sometimes accompanies disclosure (Jacobs, 1994), mother's collusion in the abuse (Cohen, 1983; Wattenberg, 1985), the mother's dysfunctional personality (Cohen, 1983; Tinling, 1990), the mother's co-victimization (Herman & Hirschman, 1981; Stark & Flitcraft, 1996), domestic violence within the family (Jacobs, 1994; Johnson, 1992), and the child's perceptions of the mother's omnipotence (Chodorow, 1978; Jacobs, 1994). In all of these analyses, the central focus is on the familial role of "mother." Women are judged—by their children and by society—as good or bad, competent or incompetent, on their enactment of the normative sociocultural expectations of "mother" (Chodorow, 1978). Embedded in these judgments are assumptions that good mothers will be aware of everything that happens to their children and that they can stop anything that is wrong (Breckenridge & Baldry, 1997; Johnson, 1992). These unacknowledged cultural images have resulted in an individualistic research bias that "extracts women (and men) from their social contexts" (Fine, 1989, p. 551) and that consequently obscures ideological narratives of gender and motherhood.

Family systems theorists have offered an alternative explanation that views incest as an aberration particular to patterns of interaction within dysfunctional families where all family members are implicated (to greater or lesser degrees) in the incest behaviors (Cohen, 1983; Giaretto, 1982; Ribordy, 1990). While capturing the interplay among family members, family systems theory unfortunately also obscures the gender politics involved in incest, as well as the hierarchical power relations within the family and between the family and the wider society (James & MacKinnon, 1990).

Feminist theorists have challenged these incomplete formulations and have instead described the family as a system characterized by inequity, conflict, and contradiction (Butler, 1985; de Young, 1994; Elbow & Mayfield, 1991; Green, 1996; Jacobs, 1990; Herman & Hirschman, 1981; Solomon, 1992; Stark & Flitcraft, 1996), further arguing that explanations of mother/family pathology mask the sexual politics in which the women are held culpable and thus appear as villains rather than victims (Stark & Flitcraft, 1996). This research suggests that neither term is apt.

AMBIGUITY AND IMAGE: SARAH'S ACCOUNT OF DISCLOSURE

Disclosure of paternal incest shatters the taken-for-granted social world of the family unit. The impact of such devastating news on a woman, who had no previous inkling of sexual contact between her husband and daughter, might well be shock and disbelief. Yet, in the throes of processing claims that render their worlds meaningless, mothers are frequently criticized for their responses to the revelations (Elbow & Mayfield, 1991; Green, 1996), for not immediately protecting vulnerable daughters, for not immediately leaving the perpetrator, for not immediately filing criminal charges. In short, women who have simultaneous identities as wives and mothers (as well as workers, friends, colleagues, aunts, cousins, and so on) are expected to enact only the identity of the ideological "good mother," that is, the source of childhood protection and nurturance (Breckenridge & Baldry, 1997). If they don't respond to such ideological expectations, then they are blamed for not believing, and consequently not protecting, their daughters.

Yet the daughters' allegations might be delivered with more ambiguity than clarity (Elbow & Mayfield, 1991). For Examplel, Sarah's 22-year-old daughter, Michelle, made her allegations during her third, lengthy, therapeutic hospitalization for an emotional disorder, a context that contributed to the uncertainty of Sarah's initial reactions. Here Sarah provides a fragmented account of her experience of Michelle's disclosure and of her own vacillation between belief and uncertainty:

> She said, "I've been abused." And maybe that's what she said first because it was kind of like, "What?" You know, like "you never had any broken bones or black eyes" or you know, and again, maybe it was like that was, that was as far as I could think in terms of abuse, you know. And then it was, "No, I was sexually abused." It's like "What?" I mean again it was the, you hear it and you don't. And you certainly don't want to believe it. . . . It's kind of an unbelievable kind of thing. And then it's like, you know, there's like no reason for it not to be true. I mean, you know, I never witnessed anything. I never caught anything. I never, you know, it's not like, "oh yeah, god, I remember, you know, seeing something."

Sarah's immediate reaction to her daughter's revelation of "sexual abuse" was shock. At the time of disclosure, she was completely unable to integrate the message. The poignant expression of the gap between Michelle's allegations and Sarah's ability to understand them is discernible in her disjointed narration:

> Whether it was the next week or that session, [Michelle] said it was her dad. . . . I heard but, of course, I didn't want to believe it. He vehemently denied it. . . . I didn't yell. I didn't, I think I just went inside. I mean I just couldn't manage it. And Jack was the one doing all of the, you know, "You're wrong. I don't know where you're coming from." You know, that kind of thing. And I do remember coming home [from Michelle's therapy session] sitting on the [bus]. I mean, I don't know if I was in shock. I wasn't talking. And it wasn't, "Oh my god, I knew there was something going on between she and her dad or anything like that." And Jack was the one saying things like, "She is really sick. She is getting these ideas from everybody else when they have the group sessions."

For Sarah, there were no longer any sureties. The disclosure contradicted all the information that she had previously relied upon to make sense of her world. Sarah's ideological center crumbled as she struggled to work through her disappointment and betrayal. Her social location as wife and mother trapped her in a he-said/she-said Gordian knot. Michelle accused; Jack denied. Accustomed to a definitional gender hierarchy, Sarah retreated emotionally to process the new information and to assess the conflicting accounts. The lives and identities that were formerly understood and predictable became chimerical and nonexistent for Sarah.

At the outset, Sarah resisted the definition of the situation that Michelle's disclosure imposed. Her resistance was supported in the expanded story of the second, more detailed, allegation in which Sarah also adds her own pointed denial of knowledge of the abuse. Incest is the story, but Sarah's claims support the authenticity of her resistance and her ignorance. Sarah tells the story of a clueless mother and an incested daughter.

In conventional interactions, the actions of the participants are understood as flowing from the nature of the situation and the conventional actions embedded in routine realities. Most aspects of interaction are taken for granted. These were the routine schema within which Sarah began interpreting her daughter's claims. But neither Michelle's emotional disorder nor her allegations of incest were conventional interactions. Both were problematic and both dramatically ruptured the taken-for-granted flow of interactions, as well as Sarah's carefully cultivated images of family. As Sarah went on to describe the painful, incremental process of her own acceptance first of Michelle's emotional disorder and then later of her revelations of paternal incest, she also again displayed the interpenetration of ambiguity and image that dominated her narrative: "I felt like I sort of went through a variety of losses with this emotional disorder. I mean, one the emotional disorder, that was a family embarrassment again and that kind of thing. And then I had this kid in a hospital and you know. But then it also became apparent that she was not going to return to university, she was not going to be a [performer]. I was just, it was just painful for me." The public disclosure of Michelle's hospitalizations for an emotional disorder had already forced Sarah to reconstruct aspects of her old definitional frame, which included her images of self, family, and motherhood. The additional impact of Michelle's disclosure of paternal incest required that Sarah reject both her recent reconstructions and her original definitional frame, including her ideologies of love and family. Initially, Sarah denied and normalized the discrediting information, reverting to previously cultivated images:

> I guess it was maybe the way I was raised or how I felt. . . . I actually know that when [Jack and I] got home, although, you know maybe for that weekend or for a few days, I was really bothered inside. I just buried it. I couldn't deal with it. On the surface, it was like "Michelle are you gonna come home for the holidays?" "No, nope." But I just couldn't feel. And people would say, "How is Michelle?" "Oh, OK," or "It was a rough meeting but we'll get through it. . . ." You know, [there] wasn't anybody I could talk to. I mean, I didn't feel like there was anybody. I

mean, what do you say? I had a hard time with the emotional disorder. So now I say damn. Just an emotional disorder was real easy.

Sarah did not know how to characterize Michelle's claims within her own operable social constructions. She was alone with the ambiguities and she wrestled alone with the uncertainties. She continued the routinized pattern of her life concealing the incest allegations from others. But her image making was again ruptured by a solo session with Michelle and her therapist told in the fragments characteristic of her narrative montage:

> It was like rub your face in it. I mean, they were just rubbing my face in it. And it was, "Don't believe her if you can't believe her." [They argued that Michelle was] telling me the truth, you know, "get some help in order to deal with this." At the time that session, which was probably two hours long, was over with, and again, you know, it wasn't like she said "Remember when?" And the only thing she said was, "Remember when you guys bawled me out royally for burning the rug with the curling iron?" I said, "Oh yeah." You know, that's when she's just barely old enough to have a curling iron, whatever age that would have been. And she said, "I didn't burn the carpet with my curling iron." I said, "Oh." "I burned it with matches. I was trying to burn a pair of underwear." Again, I mean, it's not like I missed that pair of underpants in the laundry or saw them burned in the trash. . . . Then I think we ended it with: "So what are you gonna do, Mom? What are you gonna do about this?" And it was like, "I guess I better get some help."

Mother blaming has a long history in both research and popular literature on child sexual abuse. Mothers are blamed for causing the abuse and for inadequate responses when the incest is disclosed (Green, 1996; Jacobs, 1994; Johnson, 1992). "It cannot be overemphasized that in a therapeutic setting, a lack of support is a subtle form of blame" (Green, 1996, p. 340). Within this social context, it is not surprising that Michelle and her therapist want Sarah to "get some help in order to deal with this." Implicit in the suggestion is the assumption that such "help" would support Sarah's acceptance of Michelle's claims. If therapy is, in some measure, a process that assists clients in constructing, or reconstructing, coherent life stories, then Sarah needs therapy to reassemble the pieces of her shattered ideological center. Michelle's hospitalization for an emotional disorder had already precipitated one ideological reconstruction. To accomplish another Sarah needed cues, clues, and evidence; she needed proof of the veracity of Michelle's claims.

The material evidence Michelle offered was an anecdotal story. Although Sarah recalled the incident, she used the narration to highlight the ambiguity that she experienced. Sarah actively constructed an image of herself as lacking knowledge of the clues that would, presumably, have led her to question her daughter. Lacking more definitive evidence, the allegations remained he-said/she-said conflicting versions of reality. Sarah was caught between the proverbial rock and a hard place. If she believed her daughter, then she lost her husband; if she believed her husband, then she lost her daughter. Sarah's familiar and familial ideologies offered her no stable interpretations and no resolution of the ambiguities. For multiple reasons, Sarah reluctantly accepted Michelle's account:

> I think I went from I'm not gonna deal with this, I mean, I'm simply not gonna deal with this. I simply shut it right out, to pretty much believing it. . . . I guess for all practical purposes I had to make a choice. I mean if I had chosen him, if I'd chosen our marriage, I wouldn't have either of the kids. . . . I've always dearly, truly loved my kids, and I think, you know, it just wasn't the same [feeling] for Jack. It wasn't, you know, we just weren't that happy. It just wasn't that good anymore. And I don't even know whether it was really ever that good. I think I was just hanging in there, you know, two kids, husband, [pet], two cars, you know, that image. . . . I don't know whether it's [that I] believed her more, it's like what she said and how she said it made me a believer. He didn't do anything that made me believe him.

As Sarah confronted the "truth" of the incest, she also confronted the "truth" of her marriage. She reinterpreted the history of her marriage in a cost/benefit analysis and she chose to continue her relationship with her daughter.

DISCUSSION

The master narratives available to women whose daughters are incest victims are inherently contradictory. As mothers, women are conventionally expected to be nurturing, loving, and virtuous. Once incest is disclosed, however, the same women are blamed as complicit, collusive, and pathological (Cohen, 1983; de Young, 1994; Elbow & Mayfield, 1991; Faller, 1988; Green, 1996; Johnson, 1992; Tinling, 1990). Women are silenced by this either/or, dual-nature dichotomy, which underscores a cultural script that blames the mothers of the victims, limits the kinds of stories women can tell about themselves in relation to the incest, and shifts responsibility from the father to the mother.

Sarah Alexander's narrative reflects both resistance to these cultural scripts and her initial, unsuccessful attempts to synthesize the mother-blame dichotomy after Michelle's disclosure. Sarah's long personal and familial history of image making and her own image maintenance of herself as a "good mom" and of her family as "happy" began to dissemble with Michelle's hospitalizations for an emotional disorder. It was completely shattered by the allegations of years of incest. At all levels of social and cultural interaction, incest is socially stigmatizing. For Sarah it was also an ideological disruption that forced her to ask the prevailing mother-blaming questions of herself: How could I (a "good mom") not know? How could I fail so profoundly at protecting my daughter?

"The disclosure of incest differs from other family crises in that the mother is asked to believe something she may not want to believe, to interpret something that is at best difficult for her to comprehend, and to resolve the conflict between her roles as central support figure to both her child and her male partner at a time when her own social, emotional, and economic supports may be at risk" (Everson et al., 1989, p. 198). Elbow and Mayfield (1991) assert that when incest is disclosed, a mother faces simultaneous and overlapping tasks: (a) assessing the accuracy of the information; (b) determining the meaning of the incest to self and family; (c) deciding what to do with the new information; and (d) locating and using resources. All these tasks are cognitive, rational, based in the sociocultural frame of woman as mother and protector. The underlying "emotion work" (Green, 1996; Hochschild, 1983) that mothers of incest victims must also accomplish is absent from the list. Disclosure of paternal incest thus generates an additional task for women, that is, a reevaluation and reconstruction of themselves as women, wives, and mothers.

To those outside the interactional frame, incest may seem unequivocal (Elbow & Mayfield, 1991). However a woman who has heretofore had no reason to suspect her partner and who has had no previous monitions from her daughter, it is highly ambiguous. The ambiguity begs for interpretation. Sarah says there was "no reason for it not to be true," but there was also no evidence of its truth. "You hear it and you don't." Michelle's initial allegations didn't comport with Sarah's personal experience of her husband or her daughter. And Michelle initially chose to couch the incest in the euphemisms of "abuse" and then "sexual abuse." Such euphemisms create ambiguity for mothers in situations of initial disclosure as they are disguised, generic descriptors that lack specificity and are, consequently, open to a wide range of interpretations (Canavan, Meyer, & Higgs, 1992).

Even researchers of familial adult-child sexual conduct have difficulty defining the terms of study. Finkelhor (1984), for example, defines sex between adults and children as "activities, involving the genitals, which are engaged in for the gratification of at least one person. Thus, 'sex' is not limited to intercourse" (p.14). While Canavan, Meyer, and Higgs (1992) define incest as "sexually oriented physical contact between family members which must be kept secret" (p. 129). Thus the range of behaviors covered under the research definitions is wide—fondling, genital exposure, oral sex on adult or child, digital penetration, vaginal penetration, anal penetration, and/or intercourse—and each distinct behavior has a subjective, and differentially interpretable, range of harm/abuse (Canavan, Meyer, & Higgs, 1992). The difficulty researchers experience in operationalizing terms is compounded for a mother hearing the allegations for the first time.

How could a mother not know? The answers contained in the cultural scripts available to mothers of incest survivors are all denigrating: the mother colludes in the abuse; the mother is physically or emotionally absent and/or abandoning; the mother is herself a victim of abuse and unable to protect; and the mother, for any number of reasons, is incompetent and the daughter assumes family caretaking responsibilities (Cohen, 1983; de Young, 1994; Elbow & Mayfield, 1991; Faller, 1988; Finkelhor, 1984; Green, 1996; Herman, 1981; Herman & Hirschman, 1981; Jacobs, 1994; Johnson, 1992; Meiselman, 1978; Stark & Flitcraft, 1996; Tinling, 1990; Wattenberg, 1985).

Sarah's narrative is the "Catch 22" of mothers of incested daughters. If she declares her innocence of any knowledge of the sexual activity, then she completely fails as the ideological "good" mother. If she is a "good" mother, then she would have been aware of the mythical danger of the black male, would have suspected and would have protected. Sarah can't be both a good mother *and* be innocent of knowledge, for these are mutually exclusive categories in the cultural script for mothers of incested daughters. No synthesis of these bivalent scripts is possible. As the mother of an incested daughter, Sarah Alexander unwittingly drew upon the cultural models—of women, mothers, and African Americans—for both the form and content of a narrative through which she could symbolically construct meanings and interpret the incest events. Sarah actively resisted the stereotypical and stigmatized identities available to her, as she ultimately assigned meanings to the events that reflected her own understandings of the sociocultural assumptions permeating society.

References

Breckenridge, J. & Baldry, E. (1997). Workers dealing with mother blame in child sexual assault cases. *Journal of Child Sexual Abuse, 6* (1), 65–80.

Butler, S. (1985). *Conspiracy of silence.* San Francisco: Volcano Press.

Canavan, M. M., Meyer, W. J. III, and Higgs, D. C. (1992). The female experience of sibling incest. *Journal of Marital and Family Therapy, 18* (2), 129–42.

Chafe, W. (1995). Sex and race: The analogy of social control. In P. S. Rothenberg (Ed.), *Race, class, and gender in the United States,* (pp. 417–31). New York: St. Martin's Press.

Chodorow, N. (1978). *The reproduction of mothering: Psychoanalysis and the sociology of gender.* Berkeley and Los Angeles: University of California Press.

Clark, C. C. (1993). Child sexual abuse. *The CQ Researcher 3,* (2), 25–48.

Cohen, T. (1983). The incestuous family revisited. *Social Casework, 64,* 154–61.

Collins, P. H. (1990). *Black feminist thought: Knowledge, consciousness, and the politics of empowerment.* New York: Routledge.

———(1998). *Fighting words.* Minneapolis: University of Minnesota Press.

Davis, A. Y. (1983). *Women, race and class.* New York: Vintage.

de Young, M. (1994). Immediate maternal responses to the disclosure or discovery of incest. *Journal of Family Violence, 1* (1), 21–33.

Elbow, M. & Mayfield, J. (1991). Mothers of incest victims: Villains, victims, or protectors? *Families in Society: The Journal of Contemporary Human Services,* CEU Article #9, 78–84.

Everson, M. D., Hunter, W. M., Runyon, D. K., Edelsohn, G. A., & Coulter, M. L. (1989). Maternal support following disclosure of incest. *American Journal of Orthopsychiarty, 59* (2), 197–207.

Faller, K. C. (1988). The myth of the "collusive mother." *Journal of Interpersonal Violence, 3* (2), 190–96.

Fine, M. (1989). The politics of research and activism: Violence against women. *Gender & Society, 3* (4), 549–58.

Finkelhor, D. (1984). *Child sexual abuse.* New York: The Free Press.

Gergen, M. (1992). Life stories: Pieces of a dream. In G. C. Rosenwald & R. L. Ochberg (Eds.), *Storied lives: The cultural politics of self-understanding,* (pp. 127–44). New Haven: Yale University Press.

Giaretto, H. (1982). A comprehensive child sexual abuse treatment program. *Child Abuse and Neglect, 6,* 263–78.

Glaser, B. G. (1978). *Theoretical sensitivity.* Mill Valley, CA: The Sociology Press.

Glaser, B. G. & Strauss, A. L. (1967). *The discovery of grounded theory.* New York: Aldine de Gruyter.

Goffman, E. (1959). *The presentation of self in everyday life.* Garden City, NY: Doubleday Anchor Books.

Green, J. (1996). Mothers in "incest families"—A critique of blame and its destructive sequels. *Violence Against Women, 2* (3), 332–48.

Hall, J. D. (1992). "The mind that burns in each body": Women, rape, and racial violence. In M. L. Anderson and P. Hill Collins (Eds.), *Race, class, and gender,* (pp. 397–412). Belmont, CA: Wadsworth.

Herman, J. L. (1981). *Father-daughter incest.* Cambridge: Harvard University Press.

Herman, J. & Hirschman, L. (1981). Families at risk for father-daughter incest. *American Journal of Psychiatry, 138* (7), 967–70.

Hess, B. B., Markson, E. W., & Stein, P. J. (1996). *Sociology.* Boston: Allyn and Bacon.

Hine, D. C. (1989). Rape and the inner lives of black women in the Middle West: Preliminary thoughts on the culture of dissemblance. *Signs: Journal of Women in Culture and Society, 14* (4), 912–20.

Hochschild, A. R. (1983). *The managed heart.* Berkeley and Los Angeles: University of California Press.

Jacobs, J. L. (1990). Reassessing mother blame in incest. *Signs: Journal of Women in Culture and Society, 15,* 500–14.

_____1994. *Victimized daughters.* New York: Routledge.

James, K. & MacKinnon, L. (1990). The "incestuous family" revisited: A critical analysis of family therapy myths. *Journal of Marital and Family Therapy, 16* (1), 71–88.

Johnson, J. T. (1992). *Mothers of incest survivors: Another side of the story.* Bloomington: Indiana University Press.

Lempert, L. B. (1994). A narrative analysis of abuse: Connecting the personal, the rhetorical, and the structural. *Journal of Contemporary Ethnography, 22* (4), 411–41.

McIntyre, K. (1981). Role of mothers in father-daughter incest: A feminist analysis. *Social Work, 26*, 462–66.

Meiselman, K. (1978). *Incest: A psychological study of causes and effects with treatment recommendations.* San Francisco: Jossey-Bass.

Mills, C. W. (1959). *The sociological imagination.* New York: Oxford University Press.

Moynihan, D. P. (1967). The negro family: A case for national action. In L. Rainwater & W. L. Yancey (Eds.), *The Moynihan Report and the politics of controversy,* (pp. 41–124). Cambridge: MIT Press.

Moynihan, D. P. (1990). Families falling apart. *Society 27,* (5), 21–22.

Plummer, K. (1995). *Telling sexual stories: Power, change, and social worlds.* London and New York: Routledge.

Ribordy, S. C. (1990). Treating intrafamilial child sexual abuse from a systemic perspective. *Journal of Psychotherapy and the Family, 6,* 71–88.

Richardson, L. (1997). *Fields of play.* New Brunswick, NJ: Rutgers University Press.

Solomon, J. C. (1992). Child sexual abuse by family members: A radical feminist perspective. *Sex Roles, 27,* 473–85.

Stark, E. & Flitcraft, A. (1996). *Women at risk.* Newbury Park, CA: Sage.

Strauss, A. L. (1987). *Qualitative analysis for social scientists.* Cambridge: Cambridge University Press.

Strauss, A. L. & Corbin, J. (1990). *Basics of qualitative research.* Newbury Park, CA: Sage.

Tinling, L. (1990). Perpetuation of incest by significant others: Mothers who do not want to see. *Individual Psychology, 26* (3), 280–97.

Wattenberg, E. (1985). In a different light: A feminist perspective on the role of mothers in father-daughter incest. *Child Welfare, 64* (3), 203–11.

West, C. (1995). Foreword. In K. Crenshaw, N. Gotanda, G. Peller, & K. Thomas (Eds.). *Critical race theory,* (pp. xiii–xxxii). New York: The New Press.

Life on the Home Front:
Housewives' Experiences of World War II

*T*HE PICTURE IS SO CLEAR in my mind I don't need to go to the family album for verification. My parents are standing hand in hand outside the small stone church where they were just married. He is in his crisp white naval officer's uniform and she is in a long, lace gown. They are smiling, ready to pass through the arch of swords presented by the attending naval servicemen, into their new life together. It was the summer of 1945 and the war was coming to a close.

While this image of my parents' happiness and hopefulness in the midst of international warfare may seem paradoxical, in fact, my parents' experience was not unique. During the 1940s marriages took place in record numbers and the birth rate increased significantly (the genesis of the baby-boom generation) (Hartmann, 1982; Sealander, 1991). The war, coming on the heels of the country's most serious economic depression, produced significant, if in some instances transitory, changes in American society.

Collective understanding of home-front life during the war is generally encapsulated by a few widely accepted views or narratives about the period; two prominent master narratives are almost always associated with World War II. One is the view that this was the "Good War" (Terkel, 1984), undertaken for noble and moral causes. United against a common enemy, all citizens took pride in their ability to do their part to win the war. These efforts are most clearly exemplified by the second master narrative—the one that pointed to the influx of normally at-home mothers and wives into nontraditional work to support the war and was embodied in the image of Rosie the Riveter. These widely held views about the war are certainly consistent with my own perception of my family's early life during this time as evidenced in the family photo. However, I was forced to seriously reconsider them after I had an opportunity to speak with several women who experienced, firsthand, home-front life.

In 1996 my colleague Jacquelyn James and I were engaged in a research project for which we interviewed several women who were young mothers during World War II. We were principally interested in learning of their experiences raising families in the 1950s and 1960s and what the longer-term outcomes of these experiences were for them and their children. These women, drawn from a population of families in two white working- and middle-class suburban Boston communities, participated with their children (all in kindergarten) in an earlier 1951 study by Sears, Maccoby, and Levin, in *Patterns of Child Rearing*.

Since the initial research project the children have continued to be studied well into their adulthood (most recently in 1988); however, no efforts were made to recontact the mothers until we began to do so in 1996. Ultimately we located 78 mothers who agreed to engage in lengthy, face-to-face interviews and to talk with us in some detail about their lives during the intervening 45 years. While the original researchers asked only about the mothers' parenting attitudes and behaviors, we broadened the scope of our study to explore other aspects of the women's lives (e.g., work and leisure activities, health, and attitudes about social issues). In the course of these interviews we asked the women about their early family life. While we did not specifically ask about their lives during the war, three women in particular provided impromptu detailed descriptions of their experiences of home-front life. Like all the mothers from this sample, they raised families in the suburbs during the 50s and 60s and were married with at least one child during the war; nevertheless, their individual life experiences were also quite divergent.

Mary[1] was one of the youngest women in our sample. She was born in Canada, the youngest of nine children. By the time she was 12 both her parents were dead and she was sent to live with relatives in Central America. Her strongest memory of that time was the lack of any physical affection or love from her new family. It is perhaps not surprising that she left high school to marry in 1943, at age 17, and had her first child within a year. Three additional children were born in the next 13 years. Mary spent most of her adult life at home, raising and caring for her children.

Both Pat and Hannah were older than Mary. Pat grew up in an upper-middle-class New England family and followed family expectations by pursuing college and graduate training at prestigious institutions on the East Coast. After her schooling she held several professional jobs before she met Bob, whom she married in 1941 when she was 25. The oldest of their two children was not born until 1946. Pat continued to work throughout her adult life, believing, unlike Mary, "that every human being who is healthy and within all the norms of good health and so forth needs to go beyond [home]. That doesn't diminish the importance of staying home, but we have to have some extensions of that."

Hannah was born in the Midwest, but left as a young adult to attend school in the east; after completing her schooling she became a social worker. She didn't work after she was married, endorsing, like Mary, the traditional view that "it's terribly important to take care of your family." However, she also felt it was her responsibility, "especially with the training I had . . . to help and that's why I continue to do volunteer work at the hospital and help with senior citizens group and whatnot." She and Charles married in 1932, when Hannah was 27.

Their oldest child, Joanie, was born in 1942, and Charles was called to serve in the armed forces not too long after. Their second child, Peter, was born after the war was over, in 1946.

These three women's stories, offered quite spontaneously and vividly recalled more than 50 years later, suggested to me that there may be another narrative about women's experiences of the war, perhaps less well articulated and certainly less well known than either that of the Good War or Rosie the Riveter. I was intrigued by this possibility and sought out other accounts of women's experiences during this time. I was surprised to find many other stories similar to those recounted by Mary, Pat, and Hannah. All these narratives caused me to reexamine critically my view of what life was like then—a view that had been substantially shaped by the lore of Rosie the Riveter and the Good War.

THE GOOD WAR

In the 1940s the United States was coming out of its worst economic depression, stimulated by increased productions to support the war overseas. By 1944 the U.S. unemployment rate had fallen to a remarkable 1.3 percent (O'Brien & Parsons, 1995) and real wages grew from an average of $754 in 1940 to $1,289 in 1944 (Hartmann, 1982). Because most of the eligible male population enlisted or was drafted into the military, the government turned to the remaining civilian population, including women, to take their places on the production lines, as draftsmen, welders, factory workers, pilots, riveters, and a host of other, often well-paying, jobs not previously open to women. These increased job opportunities and recovering economic conditions were a welcome relief after years of economic depression and imparted a renewed sense of optimism in much of the country.

The resulting financial advantages associated with this economic boom even reached many of those for whom employment opportunities were historically limited as a result of racial and sexual discrimination, particularly those living in urban areas. Although working conditions did improve for considerable numbers of marginalized populations, their overall level of job attainment did not reach that of their white counterparts. Minorities continued to face significant racial discrimination and segregation in the workplace (Hartmann, 1982) and women were often paid materially less than their male counterparts for similar work.[2]

The general economic prosperity of the time was coupled with a seemingly united consensus among the citizenry about the need for the country to join the conflict overseas. Early resistance and fear of reliving the First World War virtually disappeared with the bombing of Pearl Harbor (Hartmann, 1982). World War II became the Good War (Terkel, 1984), the morally right thing to do. In recalling that time, a school music teacher remarked, "We were stopping Hitler. . . . We were saving the world. . . . When it started out, this was the greatest thing since the Crusades. The patriotic fervor was such at the beginning that if 'The Star Spangled Banner' came on the radio, everybody in the room would stand up at attention" (pp. 117–18).

This apparent eagerness for the war seemed to persist despite (or because of[3]) severe shortages of material goods brought on by the intense war production. In fact, even in the face of these shortages, the standard of living at the time was much improved over what it had been during the Depression years (Lingeman, 1970). Most important, experiencing daily hassles as well as more serious hardships allowed those left on the home front to feel a part of the war and the struggle against Hitler. As one young woman wrote to her soldier husband, "It seems to me, Dear, we are doing our share for the defense business. Look at all the stamps we buy—have bought and will buy. There's a lot of money. And we're separated in part and that's worse, so I feel real patriotic" (Litoff & Smith, 1991, p. 19). Similarly, a mother cheerfully wrote to her son overseas, "We still are having fun getting our food. Meat seems almost nonexistent. . . . Potatoes have entirely disappeared and we are substituting macaroni, rice, and very often R. I. Johnny cakes but nobody seems to mind" (Litoff & Smith, 1991, p. 186). Certainly wartime hardships faced by those at home as well as on the front lines were not always that easy to solve. Nevertheless, the generally accepted "rightness" of the war effort seemed to make any difficulties more palatable. The patriotic fervor of the times is captured in a wife's letter to her husband on learning that the war was over:

> One thing I AM sure of—a thing this war has taught me—I love my country and I'm not ashamed to admit it anymore. . . . I know I am proud of the men of my generation. . . . [They have] shown the world that America has something the world can never take away from us—a determination to keep our way of life. . . . That is why, tonight, I am proud to be an American, and married to one of its fighting men. (Litoff & Smith, 1991, pp. 276–77)

The Good War narrative, then, can be understood in large part as reflecting the rapidly growing economic prosperity that benefited large segments of the population, combined with an easily recognized, immoral enemy against whom the citizens appeared to be united.

ROSIE THE RIVETER

The new working woman, engaged in serious war work and embodied in the Rosie the Riveter master narrative, is also a well-worn image of women of this time. Wise and Wise (1994) describe the traditional women at home as a critical "third force" in the wartime economy, stepping in to take on war-generated business and production jobs left unfilled by men mobilized by the armed conflict. In 1944 more than 18 million women participated in paid employment, more than a 50 percent increase over 1940 figures (Campbell, 1984). Many were single women already in the work force; in addition to helping the war effort, they saw these new jobs as opportunities to develop skills and advance in careers normally not open to women. (Campbell, 1984; Wise & Wise, 1994). Margarita Salazar McSwayn, a young woman living in Los Angeles at the time, recalled:

> I quit [my beauty shop job] and went to work for defense. I could see that I wasn't going to make that much money working as an [beauty] operator and the money was in defense. Everybody would talk about the overtime and how much more money it was. And it was exciting. Being involved in that era you figured you were doing something for your country—and at the same time making money. (Gluck, 1979, p. 85)

Some housewives, who normally left paid employment when they married and had children, also began to work outside the home to supplement family incomes decimated by the depression; by the end of the war 25 percent of all American wives had paying jobs (Hartmann, 1982), representing an important shift in social views about appropriate behavior for women (Chafe, 1990). They hoped to benefit from the career opportunities the war brought to work in nontraditional jobs and were also attracted by the financial rewards. A woman who worked as a coppersmith and welder during the war remembered:

> I got comments [from male colleagues at work] like "What are you working for, a new fur coat?" Actually I was working for a new house. You couldn't get housing at the time. If you had a child, no one would rent to you. . . . I went to work to get a house, and also because they had asked all of us to help out. (Wise & Wise, 1994, p. 55)

In addition to the career and financial dividends associated with wartime employment, these two women also articulated another important explanation for women's increased job participation at this time. The government was eager to maximize production at home, linking it directly to the country's ability to win the war, and saw unemployed women as the obvious source of that essential "manpower." To lure them out of their homes and into roles normally considered inappropriate to their gender, women were bombarded with billboards, flyers, magazine advertisements, and Hollywood movies exhorting them to fulfill their patriotic duty by taking up war work (Hartmann, 1982; Honey, 1995; Koppes, 1995) and depicting them in strikingly atypical ways.[4] Stories and advertisements in women's magazines portrayed working women as ostensibly like men—reliable, capable, and patriotic. Norman Rockwell, for example, created an illustration for the cover of the *Saturday Evening Post* Labor Day issue of a "woman dressed in red, white, and blue coveralls, rolling up her sleeves and striding purposefully toward a distant goal while loaded down with the bric-a-brac of defense work—air raid warning equipment, a wrench, and a service hat" (Honey, 1995, p. 91). A *Ladies Home Journal* article from January 1943 reported:

> American women are no longer bystanders of war. They're in it—up to their ears. . . . Not all are in uniform, but all are earning their stripes. It may be unbrave, sweaty ways like welding, driving mild wagons. . . , riding cranes in a shipyard, or the less spectacular job of being mother and father to tomorrow's children. . . . All of these things American woman does proudly. . . . It's her war. Her men are sacrificing their lives for everything she loves and believes in, for the way she wants life to be for herself and her loved ones. (p. 63)

The chance to contribute to the war effort through employment was attractive to many. One young woman, recently graduated from high school, decided to become a nurse after learning of Pearl Harbor, "That was the fastest thing I could do to help our boys. . . . I wanted to really have something to do with the war. . . . [I remember] the kind of person I was, a little hayseed, with all this altruism in me and all this patriotism" (Terkel, 1984, pp. 129–34).

This period, then, saw a sizeable increase in the number of women in the labor force, many even engaged in jobs typically reserved for men, in response to the government's need for war-industry workers. To support this apparent shift in women's social roles, white women were characterized in the media as strong, independent, and capable of men's work, an image remarkably different from the normative view of womanhood held at the time. It has been argued (e.g., Polenberg, 1972) that encouraging citizens to engage in productive work for the war effort fostered a sense of well-being and unity in Americans. Clearly, both the Good War and Rosie the Riveter master narratives endorse this generally held view of home-front life.

A DIFFERENT NARRATIVE

Adams (in O'Brien & Parsons, 1995) counters that this optimistic picture of home-front life during World War II, "everyone was united: there were no racial or gender tensions, no class conflicts. Things were better, from kitchen gadgets to public schools. Families were well adjusted; kids read a lot and respected their elders" (p. 4) is a myth—a myth that continues to be galvanized by the notion of the Good War, in which everyone did his or her part for the common good, including Rosie the Riveter. The stories told by Mary, Hannah, and Pat, as well as other women, about their lives at this time support Adams's contention that our collective account of this time is not consistent with the reality for many women on the home front.

Mary's Story

While her husband served in the war, Mary describes her life at home as very traditional, contrary to the image of Rosie the Riveter, and also marked by the isolation of a new life totally separate from old family and friends. She told me how she met her husband, Joseph, in Central America, where he was stationed during the war. They went to Canada, where her siblings still lived, to be married. However, immediately after the wedding Joseph returned to the service and Mary went to live with his family, whom she'd never met, in a small apartment in Massachusetts. Home life there was entirely different from her earlier experiences. She recalled the day she arrived at their front door, "There were three or four of his aunts . . . his mother, I think 10 of them [living in the apartment]. . . . [And I remember the day I arrived] all of them going down the hallway to the kitchen. And one of them turned around and said, 'Oh, we left her.' And I was still standing at the front door."

This large, warm, and exuberant Italian family was far different from what Mary had experienced in her own family. And, while her in-laws were very welcoming of her, Mary found it difficult to adjust to this new home environment.

> I was in another world, a completely different world than I had ever seen before. I was accustomed to a life that was a little conservative. . . . I didn't know where I was, what I was doing there. . . . I just kept quiet until they talked. When they talked to me, I was all right. I don't think I looked like or acted like a dope, but I just went, like they say today, with the flow and just blended in wherever I was supposed to.

Young, unemployed military wives, relying on their husband's stipend, rarely had sufficient financial resources to maintain private residences; hence, it was not uncommon for them to move in with relatives during the war years. Moreover, with the influx of new workers into urban areas in response to new job opportunities, housing shortages increased significantly across the country forcing families to double up or take in boarders (Crawford, 1995; Hartmann, 1982). Mary remembers her own circumstances, living in an apartment with 10 new relatives and sleeping on a cot in the dining room. Her situation, while possibly extreme, was not unusual.

Perhaps if she had been employed outside the home Mary would have been less unhappy with her living situation. However, over the course of her adulthood Mary maintained the traditional role of homemaker. While she did not fit the stereotype of the Rosie the Riveter narrative, she was by no means unique. Despite the widely held view of a major shift in women's traditional role from homemaker to that of working women capable of "men's work," the reality of women's employment experiences during this period was far more complex. Campbell (1984) notes that while, in general, women increased their overall level of paid employment during this period, more than half were not employed;[5] and the patterns of employment for those with jobs was typically irregular and inconsistent. Most employed women worked part time, especially those with jobs in the service industry; they also tended to work sporadically, moving in and out of jobs in response to family needs and constraints (Campbell, 1984).

Housewives, particularly mothers of young children, were less likely to have paying jobs. The extra demands of homemaking in the face of critical shortages of food, clothing, and household goods resulting from war demands, as well as husbands' preferences for them to maintain their traditional homemaking role, kept many wives out of the labor market. In fact, it was not uncommon for the demands of housework to increase during this period. To extend the life of the few resources that were available to civilians, the government encouraged housewives to apply very high standards to their home-maintenance efforts by appealing to their patriotic duty. The *Seattle Times* noted, "the kitchen and the sewing room are the housewife's battleground" (Anderson, 1981, p. 87).

Thus, Mary's experiences as a young war bride were quite similar to many of her peers and contrary to the Rosie the Riveter narrative. If her financial need had been greater, then perhaps she would have taken on paid employment. However, like many of her contemporaries, Mary held very traditional views about her role as a wife and mother and her need to be at home for her family. "I just thought that was it; you're not supposed to go to work when the children are young."

However, Mary found her efforts to sustain the traditional housewife role in her in-laws' home and without her husband increasingly stressful. She described to me the event that ultimately pushed her to change her circumstances,

> [O]ne day, two or three letters came [from Joseph], and they were all air mail; they were censored. And in one letter he said he just found out he was being shipped to Europe. . . . And I just felt that he wasn't *ever* going to be around. I went into the bathroom with the letter, and I think I cried. Then there was a knock on the door, and it was one of my sisters-in-law. And I said, "Joseph is going to go away again. I don't know where he's going." She said, "I know, I read the letter." And it didn't hit me then because I was upset. It was much later [I understood] she must have opened all my mail.

While trying to "go with the flow" in this new environment, Mary was horrified to learn the extent to which her privacy had been invaded. Ultimately she felt compelled to use her limited funds to rent an apartment nearby. While the move improved her situation, it did not completely insulate her from her in-laws. "This was the first time I was ever by myself and I liked it. But they were down every day, somebody came down every day. And the live-ins started then. A younger brother-in-law and his wife got married and my mother-in-law asked if they could stay with me for a few weeks. They came and stayed with me [for several years]." Despite the tremendous sense of violation she initially felt at having her letters read by her sister-in-law, Mary's anger did not persist. She understood that the crowded living conditions provoked the situation [and may have also realized that her sister-in-law's behavior reflected her genuine concern for her brother's well-being], and was grateful to her in-laws for taking her in. Over time she came to see them as her own family. "I grew up with them," she told me. Thus, while at the time extremely uncomfortable, Mary's earliest experiences with her in-laws, propelled by the exigencies of war, ultimately gave her the family life she lacked from her own family.

Pat's Story

In contrast to Mary, Pat's story appears, at least on the surface, to exemplify the Rosie the Riveter story since she worked in an ammunitions factory during the war. However, her experiences, as well as those of her female co-workers, did not conform to this new, independent and capable image of women, but rather confirmed the traditional subordinate position of women in society. Pat's story demonstrates how, in a period of ostensible gender-role flexibility, traditional gender stereotyping was, in fact, further entrenched.

Not long into their marriage Bob, a medical technician, was needed by the military. "I was married for a very short time when Pearl Harbor happened. And as a doctor, . . . he was called up very early." She described that initial period of marriage before Bob's departure as fairly pleasant:

> We were together for about a year before Bob was drafted into the medical corps. I went with him to New Jersey and lived with my brother and Bob was able to commute to Fort Dix. Then he was put on alert, which meant he couldn't come home. But he was allowed to make one outgoing call a day. . . . And one night he called and said he was being shipped out, but didn't know where. But before he was shipped out he was sent to Camp Carson. So we went out to Colorado. . . . It was a wonderful experience for both of us—with this thing about the war over our heads, but we didn't know what it meant.

Pat, who had lived in New England all her life, developed a strong social network at the time. She recalled, "We had a wonderful house and very interesting and different friends," which made her separation from her husband more tolerable than Mary's. When Bob was shipped overseas, Pat lived at her family's summer home and worked in a factory making weapons. She chose this work, discrepant with her professional training, not because of any sense of patriotism, but rather to fill a void. "I [had] nothing to do, and the part that was awful were nights, so I took the shift that went from 3 to 11."

Pat's wartime work experience differed considerably from the conventional Good War image of everyone pulling together for the common good. In fact, she describes the company she worked for as "a really down and out exploitative factory." She continued:

> I worked with . . . women usually, the men were gone. These were all women out of poverty with no education . . . and the men who owned the factory were totally exploiting us. . . . They had minimum bathroom facilities, and never had toilets that worked. They never had toilet paper. The supervisors ran car pools because . . . gas was very hard to get. . . . So the supervisors had car pools that would overcharge these workers . . . And they would give us 15 minutes for lunch. They were absolutely breaking any labor law that existed. The conditions were horrendous.

Although she had significantly more years of education than her co-workers, Pat deliberately presented herself as working class to them. "I swapped cars with a neighbor so that I had a very minimum looking car. I didn't want to show that I was a different class. I was very conscious of that, and I was very accepted, and I got to be one of them." This strategy allowed Pat to operate as a spokesperson for the women factory workers, a role consistent with her lifelong view of herself as a pioneer and architect of change:

> I was almost like an organizer. I gave these women a voice. . . . [When] I found out about the carpooling I would pick them up for 25 cents—they were charging a dollar each way, and I charged 25 cents round trip. So then the supervisors found out about it, and they fired me for that reason. And . . . even then I protested, and I said, "I know you're firing me for that, and you'll get into trouble if I tell anybody about it," so they kept me on. But they were worried about me.

While not fitting the Good War scenario, the exploitation she and her co-workers experienced was, however, not inconsistent with the government's true orientation toward women and work. The new image of women promoted by the government was designed not only to urge them into nontraditional work roles but also to engender a more general acceptance of this expanded role for women across society. It was essential both that women moved into the workforce and that their potential male employers were willing to hire them. However, economic need, rather than any changes in social views about men's and women's roles, was the real motivation behind the Rosie the Riveter story, and society was ultimately not prepared to abandon long-established segregated sex roles. The message, therefore, was mixed and these new representations of women still reflected an essentially feminine creature (Honey, 1995). For example, a magazine ad for electric power described a female machine operator:

> five feet one from her 4A slippers to her spun-gold hair. She loves flower-hats, veils, smooth orchestras—and being kissed by a boy who's now in North Africa. . . . How can 110 pounds of beauty boss 147,000 pound of steel? . . . through the modern magic of electric power. The magic that makes it possible for a girl's slim fingers to lift mountains of metal. (Honey 1995, p. 93)

Understanding this double message—women can do the work the country needs them to do to support the war effort and still maintain their feminine, and vulnerable, position in society—casts Pat's experience in a new light. Coupled with the overt racist, sexist, and class-conscious tenor of the 1940s, the mistreatment of Pat, her co-workers, and other women factory workers for economic gain, is inconsistent with the Rosie the Riveter story and not surprising.

The calculated use of women workers was ultimately self-evident when victory was at hand and the government's need for them ended; almost overnight women were laid off from their jobs. Pat recalled, "When the men came back all those women were fired." It was assumed that as men returned to resume their place in the work world, women would return to their homes, restoring the natural social order. Rosie the Riveter was fundamentally a temporary aberration, exemplifying the sacrifice women were willing to undertake, in the short-term, to support the war effort. Thus, she was not the harbinger of important changes in women's social roles, but rather represented their traditional standing as nurturer and ultimate caregiver. As the war came to a close, the more normative aspects of women's character were reemphasized in the media. These later ads depicted a new Rosie—"Rosie the Housewife"—war weary and eager to return to her life of domestic paradise and leisure (Honey, 1995).

While many women willingly relinquished their jobs to returning soldiers and more traditional roles, others did not. Margarita, the beautician, was disappointed, but resigned to losing her job, "Occasionally I did worry about what I'd do when the war ended. I could have enjoyed an assembly job. I could have gone on and made a career of that. But I didn't think that there was anything like that available for women. It was just an emergency that they hired women in, and I didn't figure that there was enough chance finding anything to bother trying to keep in that line" (Gluck, 1979, p. 88). Still other women, like this wife who wrote her husband the following note, were transformed by their work experience:

Sweetie, I want to make sure I make myself clear about how I've changed. I want you to know *now* that you are not married to a girl that's interested solely in a home—I shall definitely have to work all my life—I get emotional satisfaction out of working; and I don't doubt that many a night you will cook the supper while I'm at a meeting. Also, dearest—I shall never wash and iron—there are laundries for that! (Litoff & Smith, 1991, p. 157)

Like Mary's, Pat's experiences, although including defense work employment, do not fully correspond to the Rosie the Riveter characterization. Nor was her sense of marginalization and exploitation consistent with the notion of the Good War.

Hannah's Story

What is particularly striking about Hannah's story is how her wartime experiences served to intensify her traditional gender role expectations as wife, mother, and family caretaker, rather than providing opportunities for role expansion. Her account does not engender that sense of camaraderie and unity of purpose articulated by the Good War scenario, but rather documents her extreme loneliness and desperation as well as her feelings of powerlessness to improve circumstances.

It was a terrible time. I grew up in the Midwest, and my family was all out there, and I was in Massachusetts. And we had bought this big old 17-room house. We had to buy it when Charles bought the doctor's practice. . . . I was in this big old 17-room house with Joanie and with my family all out in the Midwest, and no money to travel back and forth, and oh, it was awful. It was a terrible time. I don't think I would have existed, but the minister of our church and his wife had been very fond of my husband and then were very fond of me, and they were very good. They had no children, and they lived just a couple of blocks away. So I know I just couldn't have existed if it hadn't been for their goodness. But oh, those days were terrible.

In fact, loneliness was a serious problem for war wives (Campbell, 1984), many of whom like Hannah and Mary came to live in their husbands' communities, away from their own families and social networks. Although, nationwide, very few women were married to servicemen, these young wives were especially likely to be separated from their husbands for a prolonged period of time (Anderson, 1981). For Hannah, the separation lasted for 4 years.

The emotional and practical difficulties of such long separations are self-evident. Women who subscribed to the accepted division of family roles of the time and relied on their husbands to make important family decisions as well as to attend to difficult home repairs, were often left to manage on their own. Some blossomed under these opportunities for self-sufficiency. One young war bride wrote to her husband, "If you could see me now, pleased as punch because down in the cellar the fire is burning and it is of my creating. I am determined to master that imperturbable monster" (Litoff & Smith, 1991, p. 11). Others seemed unable to cope with the added demands and loneliness, like this wife who confessed to her husband, "That blue letter I wrote last night—I am afraid this one won't be much better. I've been about as low in spirit the last few days as I have been at any time during our separation. My financial worries keep my mind in a torment, and added to the strain of missing you, it seems pretty hard" (Litoff & Smith 1991, p. 104).

In addition to the new tasks and responsibilities normally assumed by their husbands, war wives also struggled with raising children and maintaining a normal family life, sometimes for several years, while a key family member was absent. Hannah, whose daughter was 2 when Charles was first called up, believes Joanie was permanently scarred by the long-term absence of her father at such an early age.

> When he came back she was almost afraid of him, because she hadn't seen him all those years. I think when he first came home from the war, he was such a physical wreck, to have a little kid climb up on his lap and muss up his hair—he was patient about it, but at the time he just couldn't [handle it]—I think it distressed him when Joanie would climb up on his lap and want to muss up his hair and things like that.

Hannah noted that, in contrast, Charles's relationship with his son, born after he returned from the service, was particularly close.

Pat also recalled the difficulties of preserving family life while her husband was in the service.

> After [he was wounded and] he got better, that's when we decided to have a baby and I became pregnant. In my ninth month he was sent to Kentucky. They wouldn't let me go with him because there was no maternity facility in that particular place. That was a very big trauma in my life. He went to Kentucky and I went home. I stayed with Bob's brother and sister-in-law, whom I didn't like very much, waiting every day to have the baby. . . . When I went into labor my sister and her husband drove me to [the hospital]. The conditions were such that there were a lot of women having babies and no husbands around. And so you had to make reservations. I had no reservations, so they put me in a corridor; as soon as a room was open, or part of a room, they put me in there. And my husband wasn't there, my family wasn't there—my sister drove

me in and left me, they couldn't wait. So I actually had the baby alone. When I woke up, I had a baby and nobody was there.

One can only imagine the desolation of starting a new family under such conditions; but perhaps Pat's feelings were comparable to another young woman, in similar circumstances, who wrote to her husband after giving birth to their first child, "Reading between the lines, you might get the idea that I'm lonesome. Strange, isn't it? Well, I am lonesome—so lonesome for you that I could cry until I died!" (Litoff & Smith, 1991, p. 106).

While husbands and fathers were missing from day-to-day family life, their wives worked to keep them present and to protect children from their own fears that their husbands might never come home. Hannah recalls how "if the tears got me I tried to escape to the closet or something so Joanie wouldn't see me." Like Joseph's family, Pat also remembered how worried she was for her husband's physical safety once he was shipped overseas. "the mail was very infrequent, and I heard from the Red Cross that Bob was wounded, but they never told me where it was. You know, that kind of thing was horrible." Pat then described for me what happened to Bob:

He was put right into the most incredible invasion of Sicily in a field hospital, and he was bombed. So he wasn't in the fighting very long. He was taken out as a patient and sent to North Africa, and then sent back to this country eventually.

Hannah recounted an even more distressing story. Charles was part of a mobile surgical unit that followed the front lines for 4 years, often in enemy territory. During those years he and Hannah were only able to communicate through letters that were censored and erratic. Hannah remembers those times as "awful years. Weeks and weeks would go by, and I wouldn't hear and I wouldn't know if he was alive." For a time Hannah even believed Charles had been killed.

Along about the third year of the war, I got a package and a beautiful letter from a nun in Germany. His plane had been shot down, and she found his things and thought he was lost. So she wrote me a beautiful letter saying how awful war was, and she sent me back all the pictures that were with his stuff. For eight weeks I thought he was dead, and then I finally got word that they had escaped and were back at the lines. . . . My family was clear off out [west], and oh I don't know. Those years took a lot of strength.

As Hannah's story illustrates, despite a media blitz declaring a new, Rosie the Riveter woman promoted by the government, the normative expectations

for women to preserve family life and care for its members, frequently under extremely difficult circumstances, persisted. Moreover, women had very few resources available to them to actively provide that care and often found
themselves, like Hannah, relying on their inner strength to sustain the family.
Throughout the war, wives were counseled to cheer their soldier husbands on
from the sidelines as the men got on with the task of winning the war. They were
encouraged to write letters to their husbands but were advised to keep them up-
beat and positive. The *Ladies Home Journal* (January 1943) cautioned, "Don't wait
for an answer before you write a second letter. Our fighting men are busier than
you are, and your biggest war job is to keep writing the right kind of letters.
Every wail by mail telling of home troubles or business worries means a psychological setback to a service man" (pp. 10–12). Consistent with normative gender
roles, men were recognized as the family champions and their wives were given
the unsympathetic task of caring for them. A handbook for servicemen's wives
suggested that in writing letters to their husbands, wives should:

> leave out all personal upheavals. Did you run into a bit of in-law trou-
> ble? You have before, you know, and will again. Why mention it? Are you
> feeling lonely and upset and vaguely suicidal? Don't put it into written
> words unless you are prepared to jump out of the window. . . . This has-
> n't been an easy time, and some days are worse than others. But on pa-
> per it has a permanence that lasts until your next letter arrives, and even
> though your "blue" mood has long since passed, you're inflicting it on
> someone as if it were a thing of the present, filled with present con-
> cerns. . . . If you get a gloomy, depressed letter from him, you say, "Poor
> darling, I wish I could help." Then you fold it away and get back to all
> the million and one things you have to do that are part of his life too.
> But if he gets a dejected letter from you, he can't slide back into the
> details of your common life to refresh his memory that not all is as black
> as you paint. . . . One of the minor messes [resulting from war] is the
> need for women to stay at home and wait and work and keep things
> going. There is no use fidgeting in a letter about it. (Gorham, 1942,
> pp. 187–91).

The message to wives was clear: as the family caretakers, they were ultimately
responsible for their husbands' well-being, and men's problems took precedence
over women's. Now, though, women's emotional and material hardships during
the war, described quite vividly by Mary, Hannah, and Pat, should be understood
more fully. It may have been advisable at the time to focus all our attention and
concern on those in the armed forces. However, the war is long over and continuing to be so single-minded serves no useful purpose and effectively silences the
expression of these other, equally valid, experiences.

No doubt emotional strength and fortitude, as Hannah described, did help. But, surely Hannah was not able to simply respond with a "Poor darling, I wish I could help" when she learned her husband's plane was shot down in enemy territory. It also appears, at least from the accounts of these three women, that having family and friends close by provided important support during these stressful times. Hannah, the most isolated of the three, clearly understood how critical the friendship of the minister and his wife was to her ability to persevere. Perhaps of equal importance, these women had the ability to draw on their husbands for support. While the magazines cautioned not to burden husbands with home-front troubles, many women, as evidenced in some of the letters quoted here, did not always follow that advice.

CONCLUSION

During World War II housewives remained at home to manage civilian life independent of their soldier husbands; they took on tasks and responsibilities normally fulfilled by their spouses and worked to maintain a semblance of family life in the face of the prolonged absence of husbands and fathers. At the same time the government provided unprecedented support for women's employment in jobs typically reserved for men. These phenomena suggest a period of important change in social values and attitudes about women's roles and are reflected to a large extent in the era's two master narratives: the Good War and Rosie the Riveter. While the Good War narrative supports the notion of women's independence from constricting social roles more globally, that is, everyone working together to do what was necessary to combat the common enemy, Rosie the Riveter provides a more specific image of women's changing role from family caretaker to accomplished working woman.

However, a deeper analysis of the experience of some women during this time suggests that these changes were more cosmetic than real and that traditional gender roles were still intact at the end of the war. Most obviously, as a significant proportion of women were not employed during this time period (and those who did have paid employment often worked in traditionally female occupations), the Rosie the Riveter image only applied to a limited number of women. More seriously, while the overt depiction of Rosie is of a woman able to take on a man's job, the underlying message sustains her fundamental femininity; Rosie was not so much a new role for women, but rather the same role of nurturer and caretaker in new circumstances.

While World War II received considerable public support, the notion of the Good War belies the societywide discrimination and exploitation experienced by minorities and white women. In addition, the social pressures on women to minimize their problems in favor of their husbands' is inconsistent with this vision of a united whole fighting against a common evil.

By perpetuating these two master narratives, wives' true experiences of the war have been forced into the background—a phenomenon not inconsistent with the silencing of the women in the initial 1951 study, which asked them only about their parenting role. Thus, it is not surprising that the image of home-front America is one of relative optimism and tranquillity and that the stories of Mary, Hannah, and Pat, as well as many more women like them, have not been heard. While the sacrifices made by servicemen (and women) should not be minimized, it is also important to recognize and understand the hardships endured by the women left at home.

NOTES

1. All names of participants and particular details of their lives have been changed to preserve their confidentiality.

2. It should also not be forgotten that Americans of Japanese ancestry suffered serious emotional trauma and significant material loss as a result of their forced internment by the government (see Donna Nagata's chapter in this volume).

3. Some (e.g., Friedel, 1995; Polenberg, 1972) have argued that many of the shortages experienced during this time were manufactured by the government to ensure that a war fought overseas would not be lost from public awareness. This perspective coincides with some, at least retrospective, accounts of the time, as reflected in this further comment from the school music teacher, "I suspected the ration system was a patriotic ploy to keep our enthusiasm at a fever pitch. If you wanted something you didn't have points for, it was the easiest thing in the world [to get it]. . . . Almost everybody had a cynical feeling about what we were told was a food shortage" (Terkel, 1984, p. 120).

4. It should be noted that consistent with the overt racism of the times, these depictions were about and directed to white women. Minority women continued to face discrimination and segregation from both employers and fellow male and female workers.

5. In 1941, prior to Pearl Harbor, 57 percent of women were housewives; by 1944 that number had decreased only slightly to 55 percent (Campbell, 1984).

REFERENCES

Anderson, J. (1981). *Wartime women: Sex roles, family relations, and the status of women during World War II*. Westport, CT: Greenwood Press.

Campbell, D. (1984). *Women at war: Private lives in a patriotic era*. Cambridge: Harvard University Press.

Chafe, W. H. (1990). World War II as a pivotal experience for American women. In M. Diedrich & D. Fischer-Hornung (Eds.), *Women and War: The Changing Status of American Women for the 1930s to the 1950s*, (pp. 21–34). New York: St. Martin's Press.

Crawford, M. (1995). Daily life on the homefront: Women, blacks, and the struggle for public housing." In D. Albrecht and M. Crawford (Eds.), *World War II and the American dream: How wartime building changed a nation*, (pp. 90–143). Cambridge: MIT Press.

Friedel, R. (1995). Scarcity and promise: Materials and American domestic culture during World War II." In D. Albrecht & M. Crawford (Eds.), *World War II and the American dream: How wartime building changed a nation,* (pp. 42–89). Cambridge: MIT Press.

Gluck, S. B. (1979). *Rosie the Riveter revisited: Women and the World War II work experience.* New York: New American Library.

Gorham, E. (1942). *So your husband's gone to war!* Garden City, N.Y.: Doubleday, Doran & Co.

Hartmann, S. M. (1982). *The home front and beyond: American women in the 1940s.* Boston: Twayne Publishers.

Honey, M. (1995). Remembering Rosie: Advertising images of women in World War II. In K. P. O'Brien & L. H. Parsons (Eds.), *The home-front war: World War II and American society,* Westport, CT: Greenwood Press.

Koppes, C. R. (1995). Hollywood and the politics of representation: Women, workers, and African-Americans in World War II movies. In K. P. O'Brien & L. H. Parsons, (Eds.), *The home-front War: World War II and American society,* (pp. 25–40). Westport, CT: Greenwood Press.

Lingeman, R. R. (1970). *Don't you know there's a war on? The American home front, 1941–1945.* New York: G. P. Putnam's Sons.

Litoff, J. B. & Smith, D. C. (1991). *Since you went away: World War II letters from American women on the home front.* Oxford: Oxford University Press.

_____(1997). *American women in a world at war: Contemporary accounts from World War II.* Wilmington, DE: S. R. Books.

O'Brien, K. P. & Parsons, L. H. (1995). *The home-front war: World War II and American society.* Westport, CT: Greenwood Press.

Our Girls in Uniform (January 1943). *Ladies Home Journal, LX* (1), p. 63.

Polenberg, R. (1972). *War and society: The United States 1941–1945.* Philadelphia: J. B. Lippincott Co.

Sealander, J. (1991). Families, World War II, and the baby boom (1940–1955). In J. M. Hawes & E. I. Nybakken (Eds.), *American families: A research guide and historical handbook,* (pp. 157–81). Westport, CT: Greenwood Press.

Sears, R., Maccoby, E., & Levin, H. (1957). *Patterns of child rearing.* Evanston, IL: Row, Peterson & Co.

Terkel, S. (1984). *The good war: An oral history of World War Two.* New York: Pantheon Books.

Wise, N. B., & Wise, C. (1994). *A mouthful of rivets: Women at work in World War II.* San Francisco: Jossey-Bass.

Your Men in Uniform. (January 1943). *Ladies Home Journal, LX (1),* 10–12.

Expanding the Internment Narrative: Multiple Layers of Japanese American Women's Experiences

𝒯HE STORY OF THE WORLD WAR II internment of more than 120,000 Japanese Americans remained outside the master narrative of American history for more than 40 years. It was not until 1980 that the Commission on Wartime Relocation and Internment of Civilians (CWRIC) conducted an extensive investigation of the wartime incarceration and concluded that the internment had been a "grave injustice" (CWRIC, 1997). Nearly a decade later, in 1988, the U.S. government agreed to issue a formal apology of wrongdoing and $20,000 monetary redress to each surviving internee.

The forced removal and internment of all persons of Japanese ancestry (two-thirds of whom were U.S. citizens) from the west coast of the United States mainland began just 10 weeks after Japan bombed Pearl Harbor. The government, concerned that Japanese Americans were potentially disloyal because of their ancestry and proximity to Japan, claimed mass internment was a military necessity. Yet U.S. intelligence sources at the time did not see a need for such action, and Hawaii, which was significantly closer to Japan, interned less than 1 percent of its sizeable Japanese population. Also striking is the fact that even though the United States was at war with Germany and Italy, neither German Americans nor Italian Americans were subjected to mass internment (CWRIC, 1997).

Often with only 6 days' official notice of their removal, and taking only what they could carry, Japanese Americans suffered tremendous economic and personal losses (CWRIC, 1997; Morishima, 1973; Nakano, 1990). Tens of thousands were forced together in crowded, degrading conditions, initially in horse stalls or livestock pavilion assembly centers and later in more permanent barrack-style camps where they lived for up to 4 years. Communal meals, toilets, and bathing made privacy nearly impossible, while the barbed-wire fences and armed guards surrounding the camps served as daily reminders of the Japanese Americans' lost freedom.

THE EXCLUSION OF NISEI WOMEN'S NARRATIVES

Most written materials on the internment fail to focus on women's experiences. "When one scans that literature," notes Nakano (1990), "one finds that it is . . . a record almost exclusively about men . . . skewed, imperfect, devoid of an account of half the people who lived in it" (p. xiii). With a few exceptions (e.g., Matsumoto, 1984, 1989; Nakano, 1990), academic descriptions of women interned during the war are rare. Why have women's experiences remained so absent? The absence of interned women's stories can perhaps be understood in relation to three types of internment narrative: (a) one that justified the internment and minimized its significance; (b) one that has emphasized male, rather than female, internee experiences; and (c) one that has depicted the internment as a monolithic, rather than diverse, experience.

In the first type of narrative, the internment was portrayed as necessary to protect the United States against potential acts of espionage or sabotage by individuals of Japanese ancestry. At that time, it was an argument readily accepted by a public that held long-standing prejudices toward Japanese immigrants and were outraged by the bombing of Pearl Harbor. Following the war, this narrative of military necessity remained unchallenged for decades. Because the internment was justified, it remained absent from U.S. history books and national discourse: mainstream society saw no need to address it. This "internment-as-justified" narrative minimized the significance of the incarceration experience and, as a result, reduced the likelihood that women's lives from that time would be examined. The emphasis on military necessity also led to the neglect of women on another level. Because Japanese American men were viewed as the greatest threat to national security, Japanese American women and children remained largely invisible in a narrative that focused on military matters.

A second form of narrative described the internment from a male-gendered perspective. Media accounts of the incarceration have often centered on men's experiences from that time highlighting, for example, the bravery of the all-Nisei (second-generation Japanese American) combat troops that included young men who volunteered out of the camps. Attention also has focused on the court cases brought by three Nisei men who challenged the government's evacuation and curfew orders. These experiences are clearly important in telling the internment story. Nisei men faced unique challenges under internment, forced to confront the government's military draft, witnessing their fathers' loss of male status as primary providers, and assuming major responsibilities as the oldest sons in families whose fathers had been arrested. Nisei women, however, also experienced unique challenges that have been less publicized. Young mothers struggled to care for infants and young children under adverse camp conditions (Matsumoto, 1984; Nakano, 1990). Others witnessed severe changes in their roles as women when mess halls replaced home-cooked meals and the kitchen, previously the "literal and symbolic center of family," was lost (Nakano, 1990, p. 146).

The prominence of male perspectives in the internment narrative may stem from an emphasis within American culture on male dominance as a master narrative in itself. Nisei women born in the United States lived in a bicultural-bilingual world, guided by male-dominant American values along with traditional Japanese values that also stressed male privilege (Nakano, 1990). Japanese American women were sheltered, expected to marry early (Yoo, 1993) and be silent (Smith, 1990), and sons were favored over daughters when it came to educational opportunities. In the context of both American and Japanese emphases on male dominance, Nisei women's stories during the internment remained obscured.

A third form of narrative has portrayed the internment as an historic injustice perpetrated against an entire ethnic group. This narrative is critical in calling attention to the racially based violation of civil rights that took place. However, descriptions at this level can create the impression of the internment as a monolithic story without focusing on the diversity represented in individuals' stories. Most accounts of the incarceration do not examine gender differences and this has limited our understanding of Nisei women's experiences.

LOOKING AT THE NARRATIVES OF NISEI WOMEN

The present chapter challenges traditional narratives surrounding the internment by exploring the experiences of five Nisei women who were interned during the war. All participated in a recent, large-scale research project. (Note: Pseudonyms are used and details of the cases have been altered). In listening to their narratives, the reader is encouraged to consider how these women's stories enrich our understanding of the internment. Through their comments, we see the internment as a tremendous injustice that had far-ranging and varied effects on women's lives.

All interned women suffered the loss of freedom and home and the denigration of their ethnic heritage. The stories described here, however, were selected to reflect a diversity of internment experiences. Of primary focus is the degree to which they reflect a range of ages during the incarceration period (from 9 years to 23 years). This age range will illustrate how developmental stage and gender interacted to shape individual women's perspectives. The women also differed in their level of experienced trauma. Two had fathers arrested and separated from the family, and one woman was deported from her homeland in Peru to be incarcerated in a U.S. camp. These narratives show different ways in which Nisei women responded to their internment experiences after the war. At the same time, within the diversity we witness the strength with which these Nisei women have coped.

THE PAIN OF LOSING A FATHER

Kay, who was 12 just before the war, grew up happily in a predominantly white California community. Everything changed just days after the Japanese attacked Pearl Harbor. The FBI raided Kay's home, reading her sister's love letters, and dismantling or confiscating any object they considered suspicious. After questioning her father briefly, they took him away. Kay recalled the trauma of his arrest, "It was the most painful thing. No time for anything. Just a knock at the door. . . . I still feel that was the most traumatic part of my life. It was so humiliating. How *dare* they take him, when he didn't do anything wrong!"

It was 3 years before Kay's father rejoined the family. By that time Kay, her mother, and siblings had spent several months in an assembly center and were living in an internment camp. Her father, who had grown ill during his separation, died shortly after his release. Kay was forced to cope with the repeated loss of her father, first when he was taken so suddenly from the home, second through his years of absence, and finally when he died. "I was too young to know what was going on," Kay recalled. "I just felt the pain of losing my father. I couldn't understand. . . . I knew it was wrong that we should be treated so harshly, but I wasn't aware enough to do anything about it."

While the incarceration had tremendous negative effects, Kay did identify a positive postwar impact in her family. Her older sisters were among the many Nisei who, after taking a loyalty oath and gaining government clearance, left the camps and went east for college before the war ended. For Kay, this was an important positive result since such an educational opportunity would never have been available to Kay or her sisters had they remained in their small prewar California community.

After camp, Kay returned to the West Coast where she eventually married and raised a family. Yet, her incarceration experiences continued to be a part of her life, shaping her approach to parenting. "We raised them [our children] to be white so that they will be accepted in the mainstream and not be discriminated against . . . to grow up straight and tall without all the sadness, [without] branding them they are different."

Kay has not attended camp reunions, noting "I'd rather forget that time," and was initially undecided about the movement to seek redress for former internees, concerned that there would be a backlash of anti-Japanese hatred. "I certainly didn't want to be isolated again and pointed at!" she explained. However, Kay was very happy that redress did succeed. "It was the right thing when you think about all the losses that everybody had." At the same time, she felt that it would have been more meaningful for the Issei, her parents' generation, who suffered most from the internment but died before the legislation was passed.

POSITIVE NEGATIVES

Betty was also 12 years old when the attack on Pearl Harbor took place but had a very different internment experience and reaction than Kay. Betty's family lived on a farm near a primarily white community where "[w]e knew we were second-class citizens." Living in a rural environment, Betty had few contacts with other Japanese Americans. While Kay experienced positive interrelations with the white community before the war, Betty encountered hostility and rejection. These negative experiences contrasted greatly with the positive contacts she eventually made with other Japanese Americans during her internment. The struggle to find a social group for the sensitive preteen girl proved painful before camp. "From seventh grade . . . that's when you had gym classes and I think that was my biggest shock. Suddenly I found out that I didn't have friends and nobody [white] wanted to be my partner because you would shower together."

The Japanese attack on Pearl Harbor brought even greater rejection from non-Japanese. People immediately stopped buying her father's produce. Kids she had grown up with pointed at her, calling out "Jap!" With three days' notice of their removal, Betty's family had no choice but to give away their valuable farm equipment and belongings. While fortunate to have her entire family intact when they were taken to an assembly center, the forced evacuation nonetheless created tremendous anxiety, and Betty recalled her father thinking they were going to be slaughtered in camp.

The family lived several months in horse stalls at the assembly center, then spent more than 3 years in an internment camp. Like Kay, who was also 12 when first interned, Betty felt that her youth shielded her from the more dramatic losses that older Nisei encountered. She noted that she was not burdened by an immediate disruption of career or the responsibility to care for elderly parents. For her, "[i]t was kind of a like a fun, scary experience."

Among her clearest memories was the frustration and embarrassment from the lack of privacy, something that was especially important to her as a 12 year old entering puberty. "The building was constructed with cheap lumber so they had a lot of knots in there. Men would pop the knots so you'd always see some eye looking in peeking at you. . . . Taking showers where they used to wash horses. . . . They put this middle divider which went up about ¾ or ½ way up. And the boys would always climb up that wall and be looking at you." Communal conditions also meant that preteens like Betty were suddenly exposed to the bodies of other women. "For the first time, seeing a pregnant woman [naked]," she remarked, "That was shocking!" This could be especially unnerving for young girls who were aware that they would likely become mothers in the future, yet had never observed so intimately the extreme physical changes that accompany a pregnancy.

Like many other Nisei, Betty initially sat with her family in the mess hall for meals but eventually chose to sit with her friends. Rather than seeing this as a loss of family structure at the time, Betty noted, "No, it felt like freedom . . . it was a positive negative." Another "positive negative" was Betty's peer relations in camp. She enjoyed being surrounded entirely by other Japanese Americans and relished the fact she no longer stood out as different. "It was boy meets girl. . . . For the first time . . . not being rejected, not feeling like a second, not feeling insignificant." Betty also felt that her postcamp relocation to the East Coast after the camps closed was positive. "It opened us up to a world which we never would have been exposed to."

Yet there were costs as well. Betty noted that she had felt like a second-class citizen before the war, but "[i]t [the internment] really confirmed, really emphasized that I didn't belong in this country. That my face, my yellow face, made the difference and I will never belong." In addition, while Betty did not lose her father, as Kay did, she witnessed her parents' loss of dignity and self-determination. Both ended up working in menial jobs following their release from camp, having lost everything. Betty lost her educational future as well. She expected to go to college, but schooling in camp was substandard and after the war everyone needed work to help support the family. To this day, she dreams of getting an advanced degree.

Betty favored the push to seek an apology and monetary redress but acknowledged mixed feelings about it. "One [reaction] was, 'Oh wow, we sure could use the money,' and the other was 'Hey, does this begin to compensate us for what they did to us? . . . What about the emotional loss, the trauma?' You can't put a dollar sign on that." Like Kay, she was also sensitive to the potential reactions of non-Japanese Americans. "They [non-Japanese Americans] feel that the Nisei Japanese have money. They feel they're [the Nisei] comfortable, but that's not the issue. So I really don't talk about it." Unlike Kay, Betty attends camp reunions and enjoys socializing with other Nisei who were interned with her.

I Might as Well Learn Something

At 20 years of age, Jane was significantly older than Betty and Kay and just finishing high school when the internment began. Jane's father ran a business in a community comprised largely of Chinese and Japanese Americans. Like Betty, Jane immediately felt rejection and ostracism following the Pearl Harbor attack, recalling, "They [non-Japanese Americans] started to get very cold to us."

Fortunately, Jane's family had several months before being interned. Because they by-passed going to an assembly center, there was time to sell belongings in preparation for the move to a camp. Once inside camp, Jane decided to make the most of her situation. She was upset over the injustice of being incarcerated but decided, "I might as well learn something. . . . I didn't waste any time." While

Kay and Betty were required to attend middle school in camp, Jane had already finished her high school degree and had more freedom in choosing her activities. In her 3 years of incarceration, she worked various camp jobs, organized club activities, and became involved in Japanese language and culture.

While Betty saw her education in camp as detrimental, Jane saw her education in camp as a positive and, after the war, used her Japanese language and cultural skills in the workplace. Part of the difference between Betty and Jane's educational experiences may relate to their age differences. At 20, Jane was able to pick the classes she wished to take. Betty, on the other hand, who was only 12, had to take a set curriculum for junior high school students and was in no position to choose her subjects.

In contrast to both Betty and Kay, Jane did not identify a sense of loss or sadness about her camp experience. She recognized that many of her friends suffered negative effects, but could not think of any personal ill effects. Describing her own life she responded, "It [the internment] gave me more incentive to stand up, as a Japanese American. Sort of the prestige, the honor of becoming Japanese American because of what we went through but still we survived. So that's a positive." She actively attends camp reunions and speaks in the public schools about her experience to educate others.

Like Betty, Jane valued the success of the redress movement but felt the monetary award was small compared with the actual losses of Japanese Americans. Also, like Kay, she expressed sadness that her parents and other Issei did not live to receive their redress.

I'M NOT THAT KIND OF PERSON

Kiyoko was 23, living on her own and working when the war broke out. Concerned about the uncertainty of her family future, she soon returned to her family's farm. Although her closest neighbors were Japanese, there was little contact with them due to the long distances between farms in the area. Unlike Betty who also lived in a rural community, Kiyoko did not feel increased discrimination or rejection after Pearl Harbor. The FBI raided her home and interrogated her father but fortunately, in contrast to Kay's story, agents did not arrest him.

The family had very little notification of their removal. Because she was the oldest child and her parents did not speak English, Kiyoko had to dispose of the family's farm equipment and household furnishings. This was an especially difficult position for a young Nisei daughter who grew up in a patriarchal and male-dominated Japanese culture. Suddenly she was propelled into a major decision-making role regarding her entire family's possessions.

Upon arriving at the assembly center, Kiyoko confronted temperatures so hot that the tar melted on the floors of their barracks. "[It was] hotter than blazes, always dry and I remember that in order to dig they were using a jackhammer!"

After 3 months, she and her family were transferred to an internment camp.

Like Jane, Kiyoko responded to camp life by keeping productive. She focused her attention on learning clerical skills, rather than Japanese culture or language, explaining, "I wasn't the type who liked to do cultural things. I'm no good at flower arranging. Give me business things!" Like Betty, Kiyoko applied the skills learned in camp to her career after the war. These skills and her exposure to diverse life experiences after relocating out of camp were positives she identified.

Kiyoko viewed her reaction during the incarceration in terms of her particular personality. "I don't have strong feelings because I'm not that kind of person. . . . I'm pretty calm and collected." Part of this reaction might also be attributed to Kiyoko's Japanese upbringing and her role as the oldest sibling. "As the oldest one," she explained, "My parents [would say] 'Win by losing.' I heard it constantly because I'm older. In other words, if you have a fight with younger siblings, you give up, let them have their way." This philosophy, she indicated, guided her behavior at the time of the internment.

When asked about the negative effects from camp, her response was "[o]ther than losing that time, I can't say." Yet, Kiyoko also revealed that her father died only a few months after being released from camp. "It [the internment] was really hard on him. . . . My dad was married to the land. . . . It was so sad for him to see how it [the farm] got so overrun. . . . He couldn't accept it and died."

The government apology accompanying redress was especially important to Kiyoko. For her, the increased publicity about the internment has been critical in marking the historical significance of the incarceration.

ANOTHER LAYER

Kay, Betty, Jane, and Kiyoko were all born in the United States and were among the 120,000 Japanese Americans interned during the war. Most people are unaware that more than 2,000 Latin Americans of Japanese descent (approximately 80 percent from Peru) were also deported to the United States to be interned at that time. The U.S. government held the Latin Japanese in internment camps due to fears that Japan might attack the Panama Canal and hoped to use them as prisoners to exchange for American citizens held in Japanese territories (CWRIC, 1997; Gardiner, 1981).

Born in Lima, Peru, 9-year-old Haru was the Japanese Peruvian daughter of a business merchant in 1941. She lived with her family in a Spanish Peruvian community attending private Japanese schools and a Japanese Christian church. Tensions had always existed between the Spanish Peruvians and Japanese Peruvians and relations deteriorated quickly with the outbreak of the war. "The Peruvian government didn't like Japanese being established, being successful," Haru explained. "They were jealous of Japanese. They wanted to get rid of all Japanese. . . . We were brought here [to the United States] because of prisoner of war exchange." Like Kay's father, Haru's father was abducted abruptly and taken to jail. More than a year passed before the family was reunited in a detention camp in the United States.

After her father's arrest, Haru's family waited anxiously in Peru. "One by one we started hearing that he's gone, they're gone (as families were deported)." When it was her family's turn, Haru recalled thinking they were "just going on a trip, . . . like we were going on a big ship." But the trip was difficult. Haru and her siblings suffered seasickness for more than two weeks as they made their way to the port of New Orleans. She recalled terrible food and cramped conditions, traveling with her family of 6 in one tiny room. Haru played with friends to pass the time, but she was always aware of her mother's continuing worries about their future in a strange country.

Once they arrived at New Orleans, Japanese Peruvians underwent interrogations and group showers. "It was terrible. All the family," she recalled, "All the girls on one side and all the men on the other side. I don't know why, but . . . everyone in one great big shower." From there they were taken by train to Crystal City, Texas, where the Department of Justice established a special camp to detain enemy aliens, including Japanese, Germans, and Italians. Haru and her family spent the next years living together in a tiny plywood hut.

Haru recalled that both Japanese Peruvians and Japanese Americans lived in Crystal City, but they did not associate much with each other. Japanese Americans spoke English, while the Japanese Peruvians spoke Japanese. Japanese Peruvians referred to the Japanese Americans as "Tairiku" [from the continent] and Haru sensed that there may have been some tension between the two groups. "We used to say they [Japanese Americans] lived in a better home . . . and they left camp before we did because we didn't have any place to go." After the war, the Peruvian government initially refused to readmit the deported Japanese Peruvians. An inability to speak English made adjustment to postcamp life in this country especially difficult. The only employment Haru's parents could get was working as domestics. Japanese Peruvians like Haru lived in limbo for years, unable to return to Peru and ineligible for citizenship in the United States. It was not until the early 1950s that U.S. citizenship was possible, and Haru eventually became a naturalized citizen.

Haru minimized her own level of suffering from the incarceration and deportation. "I think we felt lost," she remarked, and then added, "It's our parents who suffered so much." She has attended Japanese Peruvian camp reunions but keeps conversations about her incarceration to a minimum saying, "It's just part of my life; it just happened." Haru supported seeking redress for Japanese Latin Americans even though more than 50 years had passed. Just this year, the U.S. government agreed to a formal redress settlement. However, they approved maximum individual redress payments of only $5,000 for Japanese Latin Americans, far less than the $20,000 provided to Japanese American internees and only if funds are available. The final outcome of Japanese Latin American redress remains to be seen.

LEARNING FROM NISEI WOMEN'S NARRATIVES

The narratives of the Nisei women presented here help to illustrate the roles of age and gender in shaping their internment experiences. Younger internees felt somewhat shielded from the incarceration's negative effects because they were too young to help the family cope with the disruption of uprooting or to fully comprehend the injustice of their situation. At the same time, sibling position could affect women's experiences. Daughters who were the oldest children in their families (like Kiyoko, for example) could suddenly be required to take on responsibilities that countered traditional gender-role expectations.

Age also appeared to influence the degree to which women's opportunities were disrupted. Inadequate schooling in camp undermined Betty's later goals, making it even more difficult for her as a Nisei woman to overcome the preferential treatment given to males seeking an advanced education. In contrast, Jane and Kiyoko felt their later careers benefited from what they learned in camp. This difference, as noted earlier, may be related to the fact that while Betty had little choice in her middle school curriculum, Jane and Kiyoko had already graduated high school and chose the classes and skills they wanted to learn.

Age may have affected the ways in which the internment shaped Nisei women's sense of identity as well. For older internees like Jane, a personal sense of ethnic identity was more likely to have already been shaped before the war. However, younger internees like Betty were in the midst of developing a peer-group identity. The placement of young Nisei in the all-Japanese environment of camp may actually have provided a context for shaping a Japanese identity more strongly than before the war for individuals like Betty. Ironically, this contrasts with the fact that one of the working assumptions guiding the camps was that they "could speed up the assimilation of Japanese Americans into the dominant pattern of American life" (James, 1987, p. 38).

The lack of privacy in camps also had important effects related to developmental stage. Nisei women were raised to be modest in public and at home. Yet during their incarceration they were physically exposed through group showers, communal toilets, and shoddily constructed walls and fences. This stress was especially significant for young preteen girls such as Betty, who were entering puberty at that time and self-conscious about their physical appearance.

The diverse postinternment reactions of the Nisei women to the internment are instructive. For some, the negative effects of the forced uprooting and incarceration are clearly articulated. For others, few ill effects are reported. Jane strengthened her ties to the Japanese culture during and after camp, while Kay avoided references to Japanese culture following the war and raised her children to be "white." Responses to redress reflected the greatest similarity in postwar reactions. While some women expressed concerns about a potential backlash against Japanese Americans, the success of redress was valued by all the interviewees, perhaps because they were united in their view that they had indeed been treated unjustly by the government.

The narratives suggest that there are actually many layers to being "outside" the most typical internment narratives. Haru's story as a Japanese Peruvian woman shows that the Latin Japanese experience remained outside the larger internment narrative that has gradually gained greater representation in American history. Rejected from both her native country of Peru and barred from citizenship in the country of her imprisonment, she saw her family's treatment under incarceration as inferior to that received by Japanese Americans. This sense of exclusion has been reinforced by the recent decision to award far less redress monies to Japanese Latin Americans than was awarded to Japanese Americans. Clearly, Haru faced challenges that differed significantly from American Nisei women. Here we see that what is "outside" is not simply defined by Japanese American/Caucasian American dichotomies but also by Japanese American/Japanese Peruvian dichotomies.

Another layer to what is "outside the internment narrative," is what might be seen as a striking omission of openly expressed anger or suffering within the women's stories. Betty, Jane, Kiyoko, and Haru emphasized that others suffered much more than they during the internment. These women tended to identify positives from their experience. In contrast, a preliminary examination of the narrative accounts in our research suggests that Nisei male participants were more likely to express negative effects and emotions. It is possible that, as a group, Nisei women experienced fewer or less intense negative effects from their incarceration than did Nisei men. However, it is also possible that the Nisei women did not report negative effects partially because of gender-role expectations that women should not show anger or negative affect.

Another possibility is that these women may be describing negative internment effects but in indirect ways. While they typically denied personal trauma, other comments signaled that they have felt negative impacts. Betty, for example, reported no ill effects from her internment yet described her pride in being a Japanese American "because of what we went through but still survived." The latter portion of her response references hardship and suffering although it does so indirectly. Similarly, Kiyoko's response to being asked about negative internment effects was "[o]ther than losing time, I can't say." The loss of several years of one's life hardly seems a minor issue, although she minimized its importance.

The process by which the Nisei women shared their stories reflects what might be seen as another layer of being "outside" the common internment narrative. In many of the interviews, the women articulated reactions and memories for the first time since their internment. Most Nisei have remained silent about their internment (CWRIC, 1997; Miyoshi, 1980; Nagata, 1993), and it is interesting to consider how the interview process altered this long-standing silence by changing an internal "internment narrative" of noncommunication for these women. There may be important ramifications of such a change not only for the women but also for those around them. One woman, for example, commented that after her interview she hoped to share more with her children about her experiences. In doing so, she will not only have changed her own silence but also the silence within her family. This could lead to even greater revelation and remembrance over time.

The material presented here represents only a small sample of experiences related to Nisei women's internment. Yet even within this small sample we can appreciate significant diversity. The stories challenge previous narratives that omitted the perspectives of Nisei women and point to the contributions of gender and developmental stage in shaping individual experiences and responses to wartime incarceration.

REFERENCES

Commission on Wartime Relocation and Internment of Civilians (CWRIC). (1997). *Personal justice denied.* Washington, D.C. and San Francisco: Civil Liberties Public Education Fund; Seattle: University of Washington Press.

Gardiner, C. H. (1981). *Pawns in a triangle of hate: The Peruvian Japanese and the United States.* Seattle: University of Washington Press.

James, T. (1987). *Exile within: The schooling of Japanese Americans 1942–1945.* Cambridge: Harvard University Press.

Matsumoto, V. (1984). Japanese American women during World War II. *Frontiers, VIII,* 6–14.

_____(1989). Nisei women and resettlement during World War II. In Asian Women United of California (Ed.), *Making waves: An anthology of writings by and about Asian American women* (pp. 115–26). Boston: Beacon.

Miyoshi, N. (1980). Identity crisis of the Sansei and the American concentration camp. *The Pacific Citizen 91* (Dec. 19–26), 41, 42, 50, 55.

Morishima, J. K. (1973). The evacuation: Impact on the family." In S. Sue & N. N. Wagner (Eds.), *Asian Americans: Psychological perspectives* (pp. 13–19). Palo Alto, CA: Science and Behavior Books.

Nagata, D. K. (1993). *Legacy of injustice: Exploring the cross-generational impact of the Japanese American internment.* New York: Plenum.

Nakano, M. (1990). *Japanese American women: Three generations 1890–1990.* Berkeley, CA: Mina Press Publishing; San Francisco: National Japanese American Historical Society.

Smith, J. (1990). Living in the U.S.A.: The troubled love story of American women of Japanese ancestry and the country that betrayed them. *The San Francisco Examiner,* (Feb. 11), Image, 9–17, 32, 34–35.

Yoo, D. (1993). "Read all about it": Race, generation, and the Japanese American ethnic press, 1925–1941. *Amerasia Journal, 19,* 69–92.

Cross-border Existence:
One Woman's Migration Story

ROM THE VERY BEGINNING, as I got to know Inocencia's life, I was constantly struck by how she did not fit many of the categories and frameworks I had studied in the social sciences. She lives in a small border town in South Texas—a predominantly Mexican American area—known for its agricultural produce and the geographical area that produced Selena, the slain singer who popularized Tex Mex music. In spite of Inocencia's rural surroundings and limited English skills, Inocencia is a sophisticated, cosmopolitan, woman who kept track of national and international issues. During our interviews she would often weave her own personal narrative with what was going on in the popular media, both in the United States and Mexico. One of her favorite Mexican movie stars is the aging actress Maria Felix who lives half the year in Paris and the other half in Mexico City with her much younger lover, who is a painter. She admired Maria Felix's independence and ability to rise above normative restrictions imposed on women to create her own life. Inocencia lives in a humble house of only four rooms in the heart of the Mexican barrio. Yet, she paints her home once a year and takes great pride in decorating by sewing her own curtains and making tablecloths out of material she buys in the wholesale fabric store. Her home is filled with fashion magazines where she copies the latest fashions and takes them across the border where her favorite seamstress makes much cheaper versions of the latest styles. She gets her hair dyed often and splurges once in a while and also gets a manicure. Her lack of money does not dictate a stark existence or a depressing one where there is no attention to aesthetic values. Her humor, conversation, and critical engagement with the public world is not what we read about in the social science literature when poor, immigrant, Mexican women are described. So it was with great anticipation and excitement that I got to know this woman and her amazing story of pain but also of survival.

WOMEN'S IMMIGRATION AND MASTER NARRATIVES

Most master narratives on immigration have focused on men, while women are introduced as wives or as part of the families that men bring to the United States

(Gordon, 1964; Portes & Rumbaut, 1990). In contrast, feminist writers address the differences in the immigration process for women, especially when they come as unskilled workers and their labor upholds particular industries (Hondagneu-Sotelo, 1994; Repak, 1995; Tiano, 1994). I follow this line of inquiry by presenting Inocencia's story as she struggles to come to the United States by herself and begins her life here as an undocumented worker then quickly strategizes how to become legal and bring her family into the country. I relate her life's story not to study particular labor markets, but rather to illustrate her struggles as a single woman who always took major responsibility for her family—a situation common to many immigrant women (Ruiz, 1998; Weber, 1994).

Studying women's immigration patterns is important because the obstacles and restrictions they experience are different from men (Ruiz, 1998). For example, as a woman, Inocencia violated many of the expectations placed on her to forge her way in this country. The restrictions placed on her came from her family, culture, and structural position, as well as from racism, sexism, and from her workplace. There were very few contexts in which she did not experience restriction. Yet her story is about using her wits, talent, and courage to not succumb to these restrictions. Her struggles were not only because she was an immigrant and poor but also because she was a woman. To be sure, Inocencia is one of many immigrant women who have had to navigate all of these restrictions, sometimes successfully, sometimes not so successfully. Inocencia's experiences have remained largely outside the "[male] master narrative" of the immigration research. Inocencia's life, as well as the lives of many other women, have remained undocumented and, therefore, underground, not informing how gender influences the process of immigration (Arguello & Rivero, 1993; Ruiz, 1998; Weber, 1994; Zavella, 1994).

I use Inocencia's life history as a case study to focus on four subnarratives that flow from the master narrative of immigration, which has not conceptualized the immigration process as a "gendered transition" (Hondagneu-Sotelo, 1994). I address the notions that (a) most immigrants from Mexico come from rural areas where many generations of their ancestors have resided and that their journey to the United States is not only their first migration but also their first transition to urban settings; (b) immigrant men's networks give them better access to job mobility and stability than women's networks; (c) men are principally responsible for bringing their families to the United States from Mexico; and (d) once in the United States, individuals have less and less contact with Mexico and eventually their families become disengaged from interaction with their home country. Several researchers have studied "circular migration"—the periodic return to Mexico for extended periods of time (Sánchez, 1993; Zamora, 1993). Addressed less, however, is the issue of a *cross-border existence,* that is, when individuals literally live in one country and work in another, thus negotiating the cultural and political border on a daily basis.

The data for this chapter come from a variety of sources. First and foremost are the transcripts of the interviews I conducted with Inocencia during a 2-year period. I also interviewed her daughters, siblings, and other family members. In addition, her children and family members generously provided letters that Inocencia had written throughout her life, which elaborate many of the events Inocencia spoke about in her interviews.

INOCENCIA'S MEXICAN MIGRATIONS

Inocencia comes from a long line of migrants. Both of her parents arrived from the rural areas of Mexico to the metropolitan city of Veracruz in the state of Veracruz. Inocencia's mother came from a small village in the state of Veracruz, and her father came from Guanajuato, another economically depressed rural area in central Mexico. Whereas Inocencia's mother came from the lush Caribbean part of Mexico where indigenous religious beliefs predominate, her father came from the central area, which is arid and deeply Catholic—antithetical to the tropical climate of Veracruz. All of these migrations were in search of a better economic life and material survival.

Inocencia's life was also composed of many migrations in search of economic success and social survival. Her first migration occurred in 1952 at the age of 21 when against her parents' wishes, she married Agustino, a young man from her neighborhood who had a third-grade education and was decidedly the most handsome bachelor around. They got married in full regalia—white dress, Catholic Mass, *damas* (bridesmaids)—the bill footed by Inocencia's father. Immediately, the newlyweds moved to Poza Rica (literally meaning "Rich Well"), a small village 4 hours from Veracruz so that Agustino could work in the Pemex's oil fields (Pemex is the national oil company of Mexico).

After a few months in Poza Rica, Agustino and Inocencia were forced to relocate to Mexico City because Agustino was not a permanent employee (*no es de planta*) and was the first to be laid-off when the oil wells slowed down. In Mexico City, Agustino worked as a doorman in a residential building. He and Inocencia were forced to live in little more than a doorway barely covered by a flimsy door next to the building's entrance, this spot facilitated their availability 24 hours a day to open the *portal* (large door) for the building's residents. Life in Mexico City proved too harsh for Inocencia and Agustino, and they migrated back to their families in Veracruz.

Once in Veracruz, Inocencia was persuaded by her father to continue her studies in nursing and midwifery:

[M]i papá quería que estudiaramos. Dijo [su papá] "Lo único que les puedo dejar es un título, no les puedo dejar dinero." Yo estaba para pasar a tercer año de enfermeria, y me casé. Dejé de estudiar hasta que

Gabriela tenia un año, y luego de ver tanta pobreza, me metí a estudiar otra vez porque se enfermaba Gabriela y tenia que ir con mi papá a perdirle medicina y todo. Me hechaba mis frijoles porque nunca quisieron a Agustino. Me dijo [su papá] "Usted tiene que volver a estudiar. Yo le voy a pagar los libros, los uniformes y todo." Y fue como entré a estudiar otra vez. Ya casada con Gabriela chiquita, entré al tercer año de enfermeria. Luego terminé y segui con el primer año de partos y ya no queria yo, porque estaba embarazada de Fernando y me dijo [su papá] "No, usted tiene que seguir." Tenia una camionetita y cuando podia me llevaba hasta al hospital. Y asi empujandome el, empujandome el.

[M]y father wanted us to study. He said "The only thing I can leave you is a diploma, I can't leave you any money." When I got married, I was about to go into my third year of nursing. I stopped studying until Gabriela was 1 year old, and after experiencing so much poverty, I started studying again. Gabriela would get ill and I had to go and ask my father for money to buy medicine and everything. He wouldn't miss the opportunity to rub it in because they [her parents] never liked Agustino. He [her father] told me "You have to continue to study. I'm going to pay for your books, your uniforms, and everything." That's how I got back into school. I was already married and Gabriela was quite small. I started my third year of nursing and then I finished and I started the first year of midwifery. I didn't want to continue because I was pregnant with Fernando and he [her father] told me "No, you have to continue." He had a little truck and whenever he could, he'd drive me all the way to the hospital. He [her father] pushed me, he pushed me.)

Inocencia's father and her husband's support of her educational achievements are in direct contradiction to the master narrative that Mexicans do not support women's education. This further underscores the necessity of taking seriously Castañeda's assertion that Mexico needs to be studied as a heterogeneous nation not as a monolithic society (quoted in Zavella, in press).

Inocencia finally finished her degree while pregnant with her second child and soon found work in the local hospital. Agustino, on the other hand, was unable to find any kind of employment. The combination of economic stress and Inocencia's family's dislike for Agustino resulted in divorce.

Inocencia began yet another migration shortly after her divorce. Her younger sister Lupe was pregnant, and her father threatened to beat her and throw her out of the house. The family was shamed by the youngest daughter's unwed pregnancy, especially after the two older daughters left the paternal home *de blanco* (dressed in white). Inocencia took her two children, her pregnant sister, and the few belongings she had, and headed for the border. It was 1957 and

Inocencia was 26 years old. They arrived at the border city of Reynosa, Tamaulipas, 6 hours away from Veracruz. Inocencia's plan was to work as a midwife while her sister took care of Inocencia's two children until her own baby was born. Inocencia failed to find a job in Reynosa and quickly went to Matamoros, a neighboring border city about an hour away. She has better luck in Matamoros where she found a nursing position in a local clinic. She also found an apartment, furnished it, and moved her sister and her children to Matamoros from Reynosa.

All went well for a few months until, to Inocencia's great surprise, her sister, by sheer coincidence, encountered on the streets of Matamoros, Rodolfo, the father of her child. As a midwife, Inocencia's job required her to live in the clinic so she could be on 24-hour call for deliveries. Inocencia, therefore, was rarely at home with her children and her sister. This allowed Rodolfo to move in without Inocencia's knowledge or consent. Inocencia found out through a neighbor and was beside herself with anger that her sister would even consider the man who abandoned her as soon as he found out about her pregnancy. Inocencia continued to support her sister, but the presence of Rodolfo created distance between them. Rodolfo, who for all practical purposes lived with Lupe and Inocencia's children, did not contribute to the support of the household.

Inocencia continued to work until the closure of the clinic was unexpectedly announced by its owner, who no longer liked Matamoros and decided to return to his hometown of Guadalajara, Jalisco. Overnight, Inocencia was without a job and had her children, her sister, and her sister's live-in boyfriend to support. Feeling defeated, Inocencia rode the bus home. En route and by a stroke of luck, she met a former nursing student who told her of a job in Mercedes, Texas, a small town across the border from Matamoros. Inocencia only had a *tarjeta* (card) that allowed her to go shopping over to *el otro lado* (to the U.S. side); she could not to stay for more than 3 days and could not go to work without the threat of deportation and possible jail time. She nonetheless took the risk, sent her children to live with her mother in Veracruz, and moved in with the former fellow student who had told her about the job.

WOMEN'S NETWORKS FOR SOCIAL AND ECONOMIC SURVIVAL

Women's previous migrant and work experience, together with their education influences the type of networks they develop. The fact that Inocencia had migrated within Mexico for better job opportunities influenced how much she stayed in one particular job sector. In Hagan's (1998) study, Mayan women immigrants to Houston, Texas, worked almost exclusively as maids, which might have been influenced by their lack of previous migratory experiences within Mexico as well as by the fact that most had a ready-made Houston community from the same village where they had grown up. Zavella (in press) quotes Mexican scholar

Xóchitl Castañeda, who urges us to conceptualize Mexico as a diverse society, as diverse as the United States, so we can better understand all social phenomena "one should take into account of the heterogeneity of the country [Mexico], the particular circumstances of place and the different sectors of the population, and especially gender inequality. The historical, economic, and social processes engendered by globalization have varied significance in different regions of the country." Hagan (1998) also notes that immigrants' networks in the United States can both help and hamper immigrants and that these networks can change over time. In Inocencia's case, her skills acquired through her training in nursing and midwifery helped her obtain her first job in the United States. The working conditions were exploitative, but she was able to obtain employment. Furthermore, some of her friendship networks were instrumental in helping her forge ahead; however, individuals within the same job network were very willing to report her to the Immigration and Naturalization Service (INS) as an undocumented worker. In Inocencia's words, "Antes se delataban mucho. Entonces me dijo mi amiga, 'fijate que hay rumor que te quieren reportar.'" ("At that time people would turn you in a lot. So my friend told me, 'there is a rumor going around that they [co-workers] want to report you [to the INS].'")

Laura, the same friend who alerted Inocencia to the possibility of deportation by fellow workers, also helped her find another job at a neighboring clinic. Furthermore, Laura also let Inocencia know that if she played her cards right, the owner of the clinic (Dr. Pierce) might help her obtain her U.S. residency. According to Inocencia, Laura told her, "'[Te] voy a recomendar, con un Doctor Pierce en Mercedes . . . y el te arregla el pasaporte, nomas que no digas nada hasta que a el se le ocurra.'" ("'I'm going to recommend you to a Dr. Pierce in Mercedes'" . . . and he'll get you your passport [green card], but don't say anything to him until he mentions it.'") Inocencia indeed obtained her legal residency through the advocacy of Dr. Pierce, but she was constantly exploited in that job, in fact, she became the all-around-handy-person:

> Allí trabajé como cuatro meses, pero encerrada de dia y de noche me tenía allí. Cuando yo fuí allí, había sido una clínica muy famosa, y el [Dr. Pierce] se traia enfermeras de Monterrey y les arreglaba un dos por tres. Era [clínica de] partos—operaciones no—partos, inyecciones, radiografias, laboratorios. Pero cuando yo fuí, ya estaba en decandencia. Entonces me tenian allí encerrada. Tenia que andar limpiando todo, los zoclos, y todo. Si faltaba la cocinera me metian a la cocina. Atendía partos y lavaba las sabanas. Y, de todo hacia, verdad? Y este llegaba una inyección, corria y dejaba el delantar, me ponia el gorro y iba a inyectar.

> (I worked there for about four months, but I was locked up day and night. When I went there, it had been a very famous clinic, and he [Dr.

Pierce] would bring nurses from Monterrey [Mexico] and he would fix their papers right away. It was [a clinic] for deliveries—not operations—deliveries, injections, x-rays, lab workups. But when I got there it was already in decline. So, they had me stay there day and night. I had to clean everything, the edges of the tile floors and everything. If the cook didn't come in, they put me on kitchen duty. I assisted deliveries and I would have to wash the sheets. I had to do everything, see? Then someone would come needing an injection, I would run and leave the apron and put my nurse's cap on and give them the injection.)

Inocencia found this job very difficult because she had to stay at the clinic on 24-hour call. She could only go see her children during the weekends. Nonetheless, she continued to work until the clinic closed down because of alleged illegal drug activity, a situation unknown to Inocencia.

Again, through her friendship networks Inocencia learned that she could earn much more in "*el norte*" (When Inocencia is in Mexico, she refers to "the north" as the United States. When Inocencia is in the United States, she refers to the north as the northern part of the United States).

Una de las afanadoras de donde trabajaba en Mercedes [Texas] me dijo, que iban para "el norte," y que ganaban mucho dinero, pero pues eran familias grandes y que saben manejar la tierra, verdad? No pues dije, "yo me voy." Y fue como fui a dar por alla; en esas circumstancias.

(One of the women janitors where I worked in Mercedes [Texas] told me they were going to "the north," and that they would earn a lot of money, but they were large families and they knew how to work the fields. So I said, "I'm going." And that's how I ended up over there; under those circumstances.)

Using the above information, Inocencia surmised that she could find more economic stability and less exploitation if she joined the seasonal migrant stream. She left with her two children, who at the time were 5 and 7 years old. Together with another 50 individuals, they boarded a bus leased by the company to drive them to Fostoria, Ohio, to work in the fields and packing operations of the firm.

Her arrival in Ohio was not auspicious. The bus unloaded close to a small cluster of buildings made out of corrugated metal. These buildings constituted the "labor camp" where all of the workers were housed. Inocencia was assigned a smaller unit because, unlike other families who had as many as 15 family members, there were only three in her family. She walked into a hangarlike structure that had a cement floor and no internal walls.

Fuimos a dar a Ohio. Total habia mucho frio. Y nos dieron un cuarto grande, bien helado, y una estufita de petroleo, y una cama, y dos sillas y por cierto que se mojaba allí cuando llovia, y el baño estaba afuera y no había agua caliente, había que calentar en una cubeta. Y nos ibamos amaneciendo porque estaba lejos la labor. Y allí me los llevaba [sus hijos] a uno pegado asi, arrinconados con mucho frio iban los dos aquí [points to her side]. Y allí ibamos a la labor. Gabriela [Inocencia's eldest child] tenía cinco años.

(We ended up in Ohio. In fact, it was really cold. They gave us a large room, really freezing, with a small petroleum stove, one bed, two chairs, and as a matter of fact, the roof would leak when it rained, and the bathroom was outside and there wasn't any hot water, you had to heat up water in a bucket. We used to go off to work at sunrise because the fields were really far away. And I used to grab my children close to me on my side, cornered on my side because they were very cold. We would all go to the fields. Gabriela [Inocencia's eldest child] was 5 years old.)

Inocencia's greatest shock, however, came when she started farm labor, which she did not expect or know how to do. Every morning at 6, the company trucks would arrive to pick up the workers—men, women, and children. They would pile up in the back of these trucks and drive to the different fields, there they would weed (*deshaijar*) with a long-handled hoe the rows of cucumber plants. Most of the families employed in the labor camps were skilled at this type of work and one family could finish a field within a few hours. Inocencia was essentially by herself and had never handled a hoe before. She recounts how her lack of agility with the hoe forced her to take an inordinate amount of time with each *surco* (furrow). She cried when she realized she was getting paid by the amount of work, not by the hour.

Deshaijar es quitar la yerba de donde plantaron; quitar la yerba para que la deje crecer. Como [yo] no sabia manejar el asadón, tumbaba las yerbas tambien. Entonces Gabriela iba atras de mi plantandolas para que no se dieran cuenta que las tumbaban.

(We were brought in to weed; to remove the weeds from the other plants; to take the weeds so the plants could grow. Because I didn't know how to handle the hoe, I would also take the plants down together with the weeds. Gabriela would walk behind me re-planting so they [the field foreman] wouldn't know what I had done.)

While her oldest child, Gabriela, seeing Inocencia's distress, would replant the cucumber plants, because Inocencia would often miss the target with her hoe, her little boy was younger than Gabriela and would get distracted from the work. He would simply try to find a tree by the side of the field and sleep as much as possible.

Immigrants' networks are gendered, that is, men befriend men, and women befriend women and families. Feminist writers have been influential in bringing to light how women's friendships are an important part of women's work and social lives and are especially influential in politicizing women to participate in union organizing (Weber, 1994; Zavella, 1985). Inocencia's economic survival, especially as a single mother, was very dependent on her women friends and their families, who helped Inocencia during especially difficult economic times and also helped her move from job to job in search of greater economic stability. Our understanding of immigrant women's economic life is incomplete without analyzing their social networks (Ruiz, 1998; Weber, 1994). For example, Inocencia worked extremely long hours during her entire summer at the Green Giant Company. However, she could barely make ends meet. Inocencia often relied on the network of families working with her in the fields when she ran out of groceries at the end of each month. Also, it was Inocencia's women friends that introduced her to Max and Chora, a Mexican family who lived close to the Green Giant labor camp. Max and Chora invited Inocencia to come live with them and their 12 children when seasonal work ended in September. Inocencia was extremely grateful and helped with all of the household chores. Inocencia continued to work in the fields during the week as the fall harvest began. On weekends, Inocencia would do the laundry, cook, and clean for the entire family. In return, she was allowed to sleep in the living room with her children. This arrangement worked well because she liked both Chora and Max and they got along.

Soon after, another friend of Chora's, Velia, worked in a Catholic hospital in the neighboring city of Toledo, Ohio. She assured Chora that she could find Inocencia a job, and Inocencia agreed to go with Velia and temporarily leave her kids with Chora and her family until she got settled. The job turned out to be a dream come true. The nuns, who ran the hospital, were incredibly understanding and gentle with Inocencia's almost nonexistent English. They also provided her with the opportunity to use her training in nursing. She was hired as a staff member not as a nurse, because her Mexican credentials did not meet U.S. requirements and she did not speak English. But as usual, Inocencia distinguished herself for her indefatigable energy and commitment to work. She seemed to be at all places at one time and had a very pleasant professional demeanor, especially in her rapport with patients. She immediately began English classes in the evening and tried her best at her job. She saved enough money within 6 weeks to rent an apartment right across from the hospital and brought her children from Fostoria. She enrolled them in school, and they began their stable life in the United States as a "documented" family. Unlike most patterns of immigration where women are dependent on the more advantageous opportunities provided to men in the labor market, Inocencia was the one in her family who was the main breadwinner and who pushed for the economic betterment of her family.

REUNITING FAMILIES

After living in *el norte* (the north) for a period of time, Inocencia had various romantic relationships, one of which resulted in her having a third child. Inocencia eventually moved back to her parents' home in Veracruz, Mexico, and after 10 years of divorce, she and her ex-husband Agustino reunited.

Inocencia felt that economic opportunities were very limited in Veracruz and insisted that Agustino and the three children, the two oldest were teenagers, move to Matamoros, a town next to the Texas border. With all of her family in Matamoros, Inocencia's goal was to stabilize their economic situation by using her own social networks. She quickly contacted old friends to find out the process by which her husband could become a temporary worker in the local Pemex oil company—the best paid unskilled labor around. (Pemex has an elaborate union system that gives its workers lifetime guarantees.) Inocencia obtained the number of Agustino's *ficha* (union credential) from their days as newlyweds in Poza Rica and approached union officials. The union in Pemex is an elaborate patronage system in which union officials give their friends first dibs on 30-, 60- and 90-day contracts in return for *regalitos* (small gifts), which amount to kickbacks. Agustino, although he always accompanied Inocencia, was too ethical and shy to approach and insist on meetings with union officials. It was Inocencia who would push, cajole, charm, and simply insist on meeting the appropriate authorities. She also realized that, although she had a *planta en el Hospital del Seguro Social*—a permanent job in the hospital providing socialized medicine—the rate of pay was not comparable to the local Pemex hospital. She eventually obtained a position as a *enfermera transitoria* (a temporary nurse) in which she was eligible for 30-, 60-, and 90-day contracts at a time. In order to obtain these contracts, however, like Agustino, she had to pay patronage gifts to the union representative, Chole, the head nurse. The greater the gifts, the longer the contracts:

> Las [trabajadoras] transitorias [teniamos que] darle muchas cosas a la que nos daba los contratos, que era Chole. Le compramos un comedor. Eramos tres transitorias las que mas nos fregaba, una que es comadre mia, Norma, que le ayudó mucho, que esta muy pobre. Era comedor, televi-sion, máquina de coser, el baño. Era Norma, Julia Herrera, una señora grande, y yo, las tres que nos fregaba mas. Incluso Agustino le llevaba

[ropa] a la tintoreria, y luego ya pues no pagaba, teniamos que sacarla nosotros. O cosas que apartaba alla en Brownsville [Tejas], nomas nos daba los esos [stubs], nomas los enganchaba y nosotros teniamos que sacarselos. Nos explotó mucho, mucho, pero teniamos el trabajo.

(The transitory workers had to give a lot of things to the person who gave us the contracts, in this case it was Chole. We bought her a dining-room set. There were three transitory workers that she abused the most, one is my *comadre* [godmother of my child], Norma, who was the one who helped her out the most, she's currently very poor. Things like a dining-room set, a television, a sewing machine, a bathroom [built an addition]. It was Norma, Julia Herrera, an older woman, and me, the three of us, we were the ones who were taken advantage of the most. In fact, Agustino would take her clothes to the dry cleaners, and then she wouldn't pay, we had to take it out for her. Or things she would place in layaway in Brownsville [Texas], she would give us the stubs, she'd only put a down payment, and we would have to take them out for her. She [Chole] exploited us a lot, a lot, but we had a job.)

Inocencia did not only want to reunite her family but she also wanted them to succeed. She was very willing to take the initiative to insure that all of her children would obtain the educational opportunities that the United States had to offer. Agustino was not convinced. Inocencia argued that it was better that she and Agustino commute to work on the Mexican side. All of the family was "legal" with the exception of Agustino. That meant that he ran the risk of harassment and possible imprisonment for living in the United States even though he worked in Mexico. Earlier, Inocencia had convinced Agustino to marry her again in the United States and she quickly applied for citizenship papers. Within a year, through arduous study, Inocencia passed the naturalization test and Agustino went into the queue of U.S. spouses—a quicker avenue to become legalized.

But still the pressure was enormous because Agustino did not like legal hassles and it had always been his pride that in spite of his poverty he had always worked and abided by the law. Now Agustino had to deal with the border patrol on a daily basis. Agustino and Inocencia were temporary workers in Pemex, and were at the bottom of the totem pole, assigned to work the night and afternoon shifts. In Agustino's case that meant he would finish his shift at either midnight or eight in the morning—both dangerous times to cross the border. In the evening, it was dangerous because of the obvious association with illegal activities, and in the morning because that's when undocumented day workers cross the border for work. Agustino often slept in his car until it was late enough that he could pass as a "day shopper," simply coming to the Unites States *de compras* (to shop). Inocencia was also in the same situation in her temporary job at the

Pemex hospital, consequently, when their shifts did not coincide, they did not see each other for days.

The transition to the United States was very difficult for Agustino. Although he had only a third-grade education, he was an extremely articulate and social man who made friends easily, which was hampered in the United States by his lack of English skills. Moreover, Inocencia felt that Agustino lacked her drive and fearlessness. He hated the aggressiveness and lack of gentility in the United States and was often at a loss for how to elbow his way into the low-paying, competitive, unskilled jobs that his qualifications restricted him to. Inocencia's assessment of Agustino's "drawbacks" did not take into account that he was an older worker with fewer skills and education than her own. Nonetheless, Agustino found a semipermanent job in Brownsville, Texas, in a vegetable-packing shed where he worked 8 months out of the year and was laid-off and collected unemployment the rest of the time. Agustino remained at this job for the next 18 years, never receiving pay above minimum wage, no medical care, no retirement package, no vacation time, and no other benefits. Agustino remained loyal to this job and never missed a day. The only advantage to this job was that during the summer months when he was laid-off, he could take care of Lupita, the child he and Inocencia had in their forties. He loved taking care of the baby and it helped them economically by avoiding childcare costs. He also provided Inocencia and his children with the stability they never had before because once settled, he refused to move. Instead, he managed the family's money so wisely and with such discipline that eventually he and Inocencia were able to buy the humble three-room house they had first rented when they came to live in Brownsville.

As historian Vicki Ruiz (1998) states, "The experiences of women who journeyed north alone or only in the company of their children have received scant scholarly attention" (p. 11). She continues by stating that she and other researchers, however, have found "numerous examples of women, like Pasquala Esparza, who arrived *al otro lado* on their own" (p. 11). In Inocencia's life, she was the one who originally came to the United States and who insisted on having her children be part of the package when Dr. Pierce offered her to help with becoming legalized. Again, when her family was reunited, she was the one who urged them to move to the United States to take advantage of the educational opportunities for the children. Her husband took a backseat to many of these decisions, and it was she who was instrumental in reuniting her family on "this side of the border." As Weber (1994) suggests, oral histories allow us to examine "the relationship for Mexicanas between the economic system of agriculture and community, politics, familial and cultural life. Oral histories help answer (and reconceptualize) fundamental questions about class, gender, life and work, cultural change, values and perceptions neglected in traditional sources" (p. 395). The life experiences of women like Pasquala Esparza, Inocencia, and many other women who took primary responsibility for their families, have not informed the master narrative on immigration.

CROSS-BORDER EXISTENCE

Inocencia's skills acquired in Mexico facilitated her integration into a difficult job market in the United States. At the same time, the fact that her job skills and education acquired in Mexico were not fully recognized in the United States eventually led her back to seeking employment in Mexico and simultaneously she and her family still took advantage of resources in the United States. She chose a cross-border existence to maximize the opportunities she and her family could obtain from both countries. She and Agustino made this adaptation out of a rational weighing of their options and restrictions because of lack of English skills and, in Agustino's case, lack of education. When I asked Inocencia why she didn't seek employment as a nurse in Brownsville, she replied:

> Yo ganaba mas que lo que ganaba Agustino en la bodega en ese entonces. Estaba el dolar muy bajo. Entonces nunca me interesó trabajar en Brownsville porque, bueno, como enfermera me hubiera convenido, pero tendría que aprender inglés y todo eso y yo estaba ganando bien.

> (I earned more than what Agustino was earning in the packing shed at that time. The value of the dollar was a lot lower. So I never became interested in working in Brownsville because, well, if I had worked as a nurse it would've been worth it, but I would've had to learn English and everything else and I was earning quite well.)

In spite of the economic advantages, it wasn't an easy existence, especially with the commuting. Also, her "transitory" status in Pemex, which lasted 12 years and ended in 1983 when she obtained her *planta* (permanent position), consigned her to the swing shift. At times, especially during holidays, Inocencia had to work double-shifts as permanent employees were granted "vacation days" for the holidays. The commuting especially took its toll:

> Nomas que iba y venia, casi fueron 18 años, ir y venir. Habia una sola [carretera], no como ahora que hay doble carretera por un lado y hay dos puentes. Era un solo puente. Por ejemplo salia a los ocho de la mañana iba a dar a las once. En diciembre que hay mucha gente, a las once, tres horas de camino a la casa, y llegaba desvelada. No llegaba a dormir, llegaba a hacer de comer, a ir por la niña a la escuela. Fue cuando fuí por Lupita con el camisón puesto y el pantalon abajo. Con el medio camison arriba porque andaba siempre a la carrera. Entonces ya me dormia despues de que iba por ella que llegaba Agustino a comer y todo, me dormía alla como a las seis, siete. Y luego ya cuando agarraba padre el sueño ya tenia que levantarme para irme otra vez.

(I had to commute, almost for 18 years, going back and forth. There was only one [lane], not like now where there is a highway with two lanes and there are two bridges [to cross to Mexico]. There was only one bridge. For example, I would get out [from her night shift] at eight in the morning and I would get home at eleven. In December when there's a lot of people [shopping in the United States], at eleven, three hours on the road to get home, and I would get home really sleepy. But I wouldn't get home to sleep, I would get home and make lunch, go pick up my little girl at school. There was one time when I went to pick up Lupita with my slip over my pants because when I changed, I forgot to take the slip off, I was always in a hurry. Then I would finally go to sleep, after I had gone to pick her up, and after Agustino would get home and we would eat together, then I would go to sleep around six or seven in the evening. And then just when I was really getting into my sleep, then I had to get up and start all over again.)

In addition to working in Matamoros and living in Brownsville, Inocencia and Agustino did most of their grocery shopping in Matamoros, thus stretching their resources, especially raising four children with very modest means. Agustino and the children had no health benefits in the United States; this became especially important when Agustino was diagnosed as diabetic at the age of 50. As a spouse of a Pemex worker, Agustino had all of his health care needs met through Inocencia's employment. This also included their four children. In fact, when Lupita was born in 1971, they could not afford to have her in Brownsville; instead she was born in Matamoros under Inocencia's health plan. Lupita, as a daughter of a United States citizen, automatically qualified for a permanent resident visa as soon as she crossed the border with her parents at the tender age of 4 days.

Agustino and Inocencia also had a very lively social life with longtime friends, many of whom Agustino knew from his days in Veracruz and who had also migrated to Matamoros to work in the oil fields. Inocencia was very popular with her coworkers at the Pemex hospital. The two were often guests and *padrinos* (godparents) at weddings, baptisms, and other celebrations. Neither Agustino nor Inocencia really connected socially with many people on the U.S. side of the border. The only exception was Inocencia's initiative to befriend the women in her neighborhood. She often delivered their children for very little money, or gave their children injections as well as referrals to cheaper health care services in Mexico. Overall, though, their social existence was in Mexico, and they often included all their four children in social events.

In addition, they kept close contact with their families in Veracruz and often spent Christmas or New Year's with their parents. Their children spent entire summers with their grandparents and since neither Agustino nor Inocencia felt comfortable with English, their children grew up speaking only Spanish at home and English in school or with their friends. By the time their children were adolescents, Inocencia and Agustino took great pride in the fact that their children were not only bilingual but also bicultural and could function well on both sides of the border. In fact, they insisted in having Lupita's *quinceñera* (a traditional Mexican celebration when a young woman turns 15) in Matamoros so that their friends and relatives would not be excluded because of the lack of the necessary documents to cross the border to Brownsville.

This cross-border existence worked well for Inocencia and her family. She often commented that having the best of both countries was how she and Agustino eventually had a very successful marriage. Their language, social, and cultural needs were met in Mexico. Their children grew up with many of the same values Inocencia and Agustino's parents had instilled in them. Inocencia had no desire whatsoever to ever move beyond the 11 miles from Mexico where she still lives.

Inocencia became a widow when Agustino died unexpectedly of a heart attack at the age of 59. Today, at the age of 68, she lives alone in the same house she and Agustino bought when they first arrived in Brownsville almost 30 years ago. She is economically self-sufficient from the social security payments she receives and from the small amount she gets in retirement from her job in Mexico. She owns her car and her home. She has a large network of mostly women friends whom she visits on a regular basis. She still enjoys going across the border from Brownsville to Matamoros to do her grocery shopping, make doctor's visits, and socialize. She also continues to take trips to Mexico to visit her sisters whom she helps with clothes and money. Her brother lives a mile away from her in Brownsville. She brought him and his family, illegally, into the United States and then helped them get their "green cards." To this day, she occasionally delivers babies in her home to make extra money, especially for women who come across the border to have their children so they can be U.S. citizens in the hope that they will have a better economic future.

Inocencia's children are now grown and have families of their own. They live in various parts of the United States, and Inocencia visits them once or twice a year. She loves them dearly but has never quite felt comfortable not being in charge or having something to do. She also misses the border where she can exist in two cultures.

IMPLICATIONS OF EXCLUDING GENDER IN IMMIGRATION NARRATIVES

There are many areas where our understanding of the immigration process can be enhanced by including gender. In particular, Toro-Morn (1997) indicates that the new scholarship that focuses on gender and development "suggest[s] a paradigm shift from seeing 'women as victims' to seeing women as actors and agents of change." Throughout Inocencia's narrative during the 2-year period I interviewed her, I was consistently struck by how much she assumed responsibility and took action in all of the problems around her; whether with problems in her family, like her husband's inability to fight as hard she did in the economic realm, to helping her sister during her unplanned pregnancy, to pushing her children through school. In the case of her eldest child, Gabriela, who finished high school with honors but could not attend college, Inocencia, known in her family for her flair in writing letters, took the initiative and contacted her state representative. She reasoned that his Mexican American background would help him understand the importance of sending another Mexican American child to college. She related how she wrote a letter to Representative Kika de la Garza and his response:

> Cuando Gabriela estaba en la high school, no teniamos para que siguiera estudiando, yo le escribí a Kika de la Garza. Le mandé sus calificacciones. Allí tengo dos cartas de Kika de la Garza donde me respondió que ya no me preocupara. Hay las tengo guardadas, estan en la casa. En otra [carta] me respondió, luego, luego. El habló y ya Gabriela se abrió paso en la universidad. En la otra [carta] le mandamos un gallito de esos que compra uno en Matamoros. Eso le mandamos Agustino y yo, y nos mandó otra carta donde nos da las gracias por el. Ya se retiró Kika de la Garza.

> (When Gabriela was in high school and we didn't have any money so she could continue studying, I wrote to Kika de la Garza. I sent him her grades. I have two letters from Kika de la Garza where he responded, he told me not to worry. I have them saved at home. In another [letter] he responded right away, right away. He called and then Gabriela was able to make her way in the university. In the other [letter] we sent him a little rooster that you can buy in Matamoros. That's what Agustino and I sent to him, and he sent us another letter where he gives us thanks [for the present]. Kika de la Garza already retired.)

One of Representative de la Garza's assistants contacted the local "Upward Bound" program dedicated to recruiting talented minority students and that's how Inocencia and Agustino were able to help their child continue her education.

Obstacles never stopped Inocencia from assuming she could do something about them. She also did not express regret or see herself as a victim. In narrating her life, Inocencia recounted events and traumas as part and parcel of what every individual experiences; her goal was to negotiate all that life handed her. There was a total lack of self-pity in recounting her life history.

The master narrative of immigration assumes that indeed Latina women comply with male-dominated cultural norms and that when they come to the United States they become more "liberated." Without bringing Latina women to the center in immigration research, it is not possible to study the full range of adaptations to patriarchal cultural norms. Certainly many women comply, as they do in most cultures; but there are many that resist. In fact, many Latina women who immigrate have often questioned and resisted patriarchy in their native countries before they arrive in the United States (Ruiz, 1998; Zavella, 1994). One could even argue that the resisters are more likely to venture away from the security of their homeland. In this case it is not that the women arrive "meek" to the United States and then become liberated as predicted by the assimilation framework (Hurtado, 1997). This was certainly not the case with Inocencia. Even though Inocencia existed within a very well developed patriarchal structure, she did not comply to its strictures at all times. She was especially susceptible to her father's influence and judgment, but ultimately she always rebelled. She did marry Agustino against her father's wishes, although later she succumbed to the pressure to divorce him. However, this was not all of her father's influence. Inocencia repeatedly mentioned in the interviews that during the early part of their marriage, Agustino lacked the ambition to find a better situation for his family and felt comfortable letting Inocencia take the initiative. This evaluation changed in the latter part of their life together as Inocencia began to appreciate Agustino's ability to support and encourage Inocencia's "nontraditional" behavior. Inocencia also violated her parents' wishes when she remarried Agustino and certainly having a child in *el norte* without benefit of marriage were not in compliance with her parents' and community's normative standards. In fact, Inocencia was perceived by her entire family as being a "difficult" person, who always got her way and never let any barriers discourage her from her objectives. She was not perceived by anybody in her family as complying with family restrictions.

Another important dimension of immigrant women's resistance to patriarchy is that such resistance is accomplished in the context of allegiance, rather than in isolation from their families and their communities. For example, Inocencia always helped family members, and still does. When her father became ill after a long battle with diabetes, he lived with Inocencia and her family in Brownsville. By this time, her father was a shell of his former self; he suffered a leg amputation and slowly lost his mental faculties. Inocencia hired somebody to help her take care of him while she worked, but it was she who was responsible for bathing him, feeding him, and taking him to the doctor. This all transpired in the midst of a troubled period in her marriage, and while raising her teenage children. Again, her loyalty and commitment to her immediate as well as extended family has never wavered.

Finally, Toro-Morn (1997) also feels that the challenge to include women's voices in immigration research has prompted researchers to expand their methodological approaches and to "show signs of maturation in the variety of

and combinations of methods—interviews, surveys, oral histories, ethnogra-
phies—employed to understand the complexities facing women, men, and families in the core, semiperiphery, and periphery" (p. 1020). To include women in
immigration narratives has benefited the field not only in content but also in
method. As more women's stories push against the "immigrant master narrative"
we will know more about this "gendered transition" that is such an integral part
of this country.

NOTES

1. The names of the respondents and places have been changed to protect the privacy of all individuals in this chapter.

REFERENCES

Arguello, L., & Rivero, A. (1993). Violence, migration, and compassionate practice: Conversations with some women we think we know. *Urban Anthropology, 22* (3–4),
259–75.

Gordon, M. M. (1964). *Assimilation in American life: The role of race, religion, and national origins.* New York: Oxford University Press.

Hagan, J. M. (1994). *Deciding to be legal: A Mayan community in Houston.* Philadelphia: Temple University Press.

_____(1998). Social networks, gender, and immigrant incorporation: Resources and con-
straints. *American Sociological Review, 63* (1) (Feb.), 55–67.

Hondagneu-Sotelo, P. (1994). *Gendered transitions: Mexican experiences of immigration.*
Berkeley and Los Angeles: University of California Press.

Hurtado, A. (1997). Understanding multiple group identities: Inserting women into cultural transformations. *Journal of Social Issues, 53* (2), 299–328.

Portes, A., & Rumbaut, R. G. (1990). *Immigrant America: A portrait.* Berkeley and Los Angeles: University of California Press.

Repak, T. A. (1995). *Waiting on Washington.* Philadelphia: Temple University Press.

Ruiz, V. L. (1998). *From out of the shadows: Mexican women in twentieth-century America.* New
York: Oxford University Press.

Sánchez, G. (1993). *Becoming Mexican American: Ethnicity, culture, and identity in Chicano Los
Angeles, 1900–1945.* New York: Oxford University Press.

Tiano, S. (1994). *Patriarchy on the line: Labor, gender, and ideology in the Mexican maquila industry.* Philadelphia: Temple University Press.

Toro-Morn, M. I. (1997). Gendered transitions: Mexican experiences of immigration, by P.
Hondagneu-Sotelo. *Signs: Journal of Women in Culture and Society, 22* (4), 1020–25.

Weber, A. D. (1994). *Raiz fuerte*: Oral history and Mexicana farmworkers." In V. Ruiz & E. C.
DuBois (Eds.), *Unequal sisters: A multicultural reader in U.S. women's history* (2d ed.) (pp.
395–404). New York: Routledge, 1994.

Zamora, E. (1993). *The world of the Mexican American worker in Texas.* College Station: Texas
A & M Press.

Zavella, P. (1985). "Abnormal Intimacy": The varying work networks of Chicana cannery workers. *Feminist Studies, 11* (3), 541–57.

_____(1994). Reflections on diversity among Chicanas. In S. Gregory, & R. Sanjeck (Eds.), *Race* (pp. 199–212). New Brunswick, N.J.: Rutgers University Press.

_____(In press). Chicanas and Mexicanas talk'n sex: Theorizing silence and sexual pleasure.

Talking Back

Skirting the Gender Normal Divide:
A Tomboy Life Story

Snips and snails and puppy dog's tails,
that's what little boys are made of.
Sugar and spice and everything nice,
that's what little girls are made of.

I'M SURE YOU KNOW HER. You've seen the one: wears jeans and tennies, sweatshirts and grass stains? Wouldn't be caught dead in a dress? Or worse, playing Barbies? Even within the confines of a private school *dress*code she still, somehow, manages to look and act "like a boy." Despite differences of race, ethnicity, religion, class, even venue—in the city she climbs fire escapes, in the country, trees—since at least 1592 (*Oxford English Dictionary*) she has gone by one name: Tomboy, a culturally masculine girl.

Tomboy lore and imagery are widespread in North America, Britain, and the English-speaking Caribbean. Whether framing a story of lifelong female resistance or telling a transformative tale of the former tomboy who (thankfully!) "blossoms" into a beautiful lady, "the Tomboy" is a useful biographical trope.[1] The Tomboy narrative is also a frequent plot device, as in the film *Fried Green Tomatoes*, the novel *Little Women*, and the sitcom *Roseanne*. Sometimes tomboys even appear in social-scientific research. There though, as in academic psychology, "tomboyism" is depicted as anomalous, at times as pathological, always from an outsider's point of view (cf. Green & Goodman, 1982; Rekers, 1992; Zucker & Green, 1992). Both folk and formal knowledge, then, provide glimpses of the Tomboy. Yet actual tomboy lives, especially as told from the point of view of the tomboy, are rarely the focus—or origin—of such tales.

Regardless of its (in)accuracy, the Tomboy narrative is a useful resource for the construction of personal identity and the interpretation of that of others. "Everybody knows," after all, what a tomboy looks and acts like! Implied in images of what a tomboy is are messages of what a normal girl is *not*; thus the Tomboy narrative also demarcates the limits of acceptable girlhood. As such, the figure of the Tomboy works as a sort of "text" of the gender order, "readable" for the cultural assumptions regarding sex, gender, and desire embedded within it.

How do individuals construct identities and lives in and around, against and alongside of, narrative presumptions of what they should look and act like? What they should do? Who they should *be*? As exploration of these questions, I present the topical life story of Erika, a 30-year-old white heterosexual performance artist. Although Erika has been a tomboy since childhood, the meaning of her tomboyness, to others and to herself, shifted throughout her life. In adolescence Erika faced increasing pressure to become traditionally feminine, pressures she sometimes succumbed to—given her crushes on boys. By adulthood Erika had so often been falsely presumed to be lesbian that she entertained the only other available explanation of her gender misfit: transsexualism. Erika now describes herself as "in recovery," flirting with a return to the gender fluidity that marked her early tomboy identity.

In what follows I mostly tell Erika's story from her perspective using her words. At times I interrupt her voice to comment and compare, to explore connections between everyday experience and the larger social forms that shape it — in this case, cultural Tomboy imagery and the actions of others as informed by these images. Told in this way, from the inside out, I present a lived tomboy perspective in hopes of correcting the distortions of the master narrative. Such attention to the intersection of individual biography and cultural forms suggests the constitutive power of narrative. In this regard master narratives comprise the scaffolding of identity, the frameworks around which individuals assemble identities by bringing shared gender symbolism to bear on the particularities of their lives. With this in mind, I close by considering how the telling of individual stories collectively—as in this text—not only helps (re)shape a master narrative but also may transform private troubles into public issues. First though, a mention of method.

LISTENING TO TOMBOY VOICES

"Every life story is a multiplicity of stories that could be told" (Denzin, 1989, p. 72). The topical life story I present here was collected as part of a larger study of the gendered identity development of 35 individuals who were tomboys as kids (McGann, 1995, forthcoming). The participants of that study varied in terms of age, race, class, ethnicity, national origin, childhood location, religion, and sexual identity. Despite this diversity, for all "Tomboy" was a *lived childhood social identity.* That is, the interviewees were not merely "tomboyish" kids. Nor did they simply look back as adults and claim a tomboy identity retrospectively (Thorne, 1993). Rather, as children and adolescents (and sometimes beyond) they were known by others—family, friends, neighbors, teachers, and the like—as *being* tomboys.

The taped interviews lasted from 2 to well over 6 hours in length. After basic demographics I asked the participants to tell me in their own words "what it was like to grow up as a tomboy." This opening elicited story upon story, allowing me to mostly listen and follow the narrator's lead, here and there posing basic questions to clarify autobiographical detail (Plummer, 1983). I then asked open-ended in-depth questions in hopes of discovering—rather than imposing—topics of relevance. Even so, this is no neutral telling.

Erika's voice, like that of the other tomboys I spoke with, was shaped in a particular context, one framed largely, at least initially, by me. Although my aim was to be inclusive while producing a grounded theory style analysis (Glaser & Strauss, 1967; Strauss, 1987), my starting point was my own identity. Thus the analysis reflects an interaction of my embodiment with that of others. I sought to be aware of and observe this influence throughout the research process; even so, my "biographical presence" in this text shapes it (Denzin, 1989). Hence, I should confess: I'm a misfit. A physical laborer turned intellectual. A kid who played with—and as?—the boys. A queer in a straight world. A white feminist scholar who saw/sees neither her present self nor her tomboy past in feminist models of female development (McGann, 1995, forthcoming).

Just as Erika told her life in relation to, sometimes in contradiction of, the master Tomboy narrative, my (re)presentation of Erika's story is likewise a form of "back talk."[2] In my case, however, I speak not only to the master Tomboy narrative of everyday life. I also address feminist depictions of girls and women that represent *feminine* development as female development. Because these multiple and malleable gender meanings shape Erika's life, identity, and desire, I begin with hegemonic Tomboy imagery.

GENDER AND CULTURE: THE MASTER TOMBOY NARRATIVE

> Tomboy. 1. A rude and boisterous boy. 1553; 2. A bold or immodest woman. 1579; 3. A girl who behaves like a spirited or boisterous boy; a wild romping girl; a hoyden. 1592. (OED)

> There are statistics that say that 100 percent of women who cross dress are lesbians. Well, they're wrong. Here's one right here. There's a lot of statistics out there that totally marginalize me—and others. (Erika)

The master Tomboy narrative is part of a larger Western *gender culture:* the totality of socially constructed and shared—though not necessarily uncontested—meanings relating to sex (femaleness and maleness), gender (femininity and masculinity), and sexuality (heterosexuality and homosexuality). Although socially constructed and historical, standardized story lines like Tomboy tend to be experienced as natural in everyday life. When coupled with dualistic constructs of sex and gender—that which is female is feminine, not male/masculine—this naturalization adds a moral tone to gender conventionality and deviance (McGann, forthcoming). In effect, then, narratives like the tomboy demarcate a gender normal divide: a line distinguishing presumably naturally occurring, hence normal, embodiments of gender from those thought unnatural, hence pathological. Gender narratives thus bespeak the moral boundaries of gendered and sexualized bodies (McGann, 1995).[3]

"Tomboy" is derivative of the more desirable "normal girl" narrative—though "normal" is usually unspoken. (Normal) girls prefer "feminine" attire, exhibit "girls'" interests and desires, play "girls'" games with "girls'" toys, and do so with other girls. (Normal) girls are easy to find. There she is in pink and pastel on the doll boxes piled floor to ceiling in the toy aisle of any North American department store. There she is smiling sweetly in a TV ad for a Playskool kitchen. There she is in a Disney movie, waking gently from Prince Charming's tender kiss. And there she is learning to be attractive to boys, as she looks back at herself thumbing through the pages of *YM, Seventeen, Cosmopolitan, Chatelaine*.

Though less prevalent, the Tomboy also comes easily to mind. There she is wearing "boys'" clothes, playing with "boys'" toys, playing with boys. It seems she wants to be a boy. (Boys, after all, have more fun.) Sometimes she even *says* she wants to "be a boy" or, worse, insists she *is* or will become a boy. Because they do not look or act like feminine girls, in everyday life such tomboys are thought to be "masculine." Because they transgress the "natural" gender binary, in discourses of medicine and psychiatry tomboys are thought to be "cross-gendered" (APA, 1994).

Although traditional femininity is preferable, tomboyness is *sometimes* acceptable—provided it is properly phased and not overly intense. In fact, young tomboys are frequently thought of as "special girls," popular with classmates and teachers alike (Martin, 1990). This "garden variety tomboy" (Green, 1975, p. 91) has many culturally boyish qualities. Yet at times she will, albeit reluctantly, wear "girls'" clothes and participate in "girls'" activities. When doing so, however, the Tomboy most likely "enacts the male role in play" (APA, 1994). Unlike her male counterpart, the "Sissy," the Tomboy is neither punished by her parents, nor teased or beaten up by other children. And neither is the Tomboy forced into gender-typed appearances and behaviors by well-meaning adults—not, at least, according to the master narrative.[4]

They may do so at different times, but acceptable tomboys eventually "grow out of it," gradually becoming traditionally feminine. Tomboys who do not abandon their "boyish" ways are suspect; those who do not rescind their tomboyness in adolescence skirt the gender normal divide. They, along with "too tomboyish" tomboys, risk slipping from the realm of the acceptable into that of the pathological. Folk and formal knowledge story lines converge on this point, linking overly intense and improperly phased "tomboyism"—as the psychological syndrome is known—to future lesbianism (Green, 1974; Green, Williams, & Good-man, 1982). This link of tomboyism, mannishness, and inversion is long-stand-ing; "Tomboy" was used in newspaper accounts as a link to active lesbian desire as early as 1892 (Duggan, 1993). The association persists in contemporary les-bian lore, where a tomboy past is seen as proof of authentic lesbian identity (Boston Lesbian Psychologies Collective, 1987; Cahn, 1994; Faderman, 1991; Phelan, 1993). More recently the mannishness story line has been elaborated as "gender dysphoria," a supposed precursor to adult transsexualism (APA, 1994). Consequently, from a medical-psychiatric point of view therapeutic intervention is necessary to derail possible lesbian, transvestite, or transsexual outcomes (Rekers, 1992; Zucker & Green, 1992).

In sum, according to the master narrative tomboys are girls who not only act like boys, but also wish they were boys, perhaps even going so far as to say so. As part of the legacy of inversion, such "mannishness," especially in girls who do not *naturally* grow out of it, may indicate future lesbian sexuality. Today such a statement—a girl saying she wants to be or is a boy—may be taken as evidence of gender identity disorder, proof that the tomboy thinks she *is* a boy (McGann, 1995;1999). Of course, not all tomboy lives fit the pathological caricatures of the master narrative. Yet all tomboys are, at least at times, constrained by its shad-owy images of tomboyism gone awry: inversion, mannishness, and transsexual-ity. And all must somehow navigate the malleable gender normal divide.[5]

IN THE SHADOW OF MANNISHNESS: ERIKA'S STORY

Girls will be boys? Erika's life does not mirror the standard story line: She did not rescind her tomboyness, and she is neither lesbian nor transsexual. Still, the contours of her identity and biography reflect the influence of the master Tomboy narrative. Erika grew up in Nova Scotia in a "very religious home, very Christian home," surrounded by working-class laborers and their families. With-out any "specific gender expectations in the family," she grew accustomed to seeming contradictions early on. Though well-educated, her family was poor: "We lived in the country with no electricity, with a hole in the ground outside for a toilet, but we also had a maid!" The youngest of four children (two nontomboy sisters and a brother), early on Erika was raised mostly by her minister father. At 6 or 7, her parents divorced. She then lived with her mother, a painter, a woman Erika described as "feminist." At 10 years old, Erika was converted from funda-mentalist Christianity to B'Hai.

As a "career" tomboy, she did not rescind her tomboy appearance or identity at puberty.[6] When we met, Erika wore sturdy black jeans, a black shirt with a col-lar, black Converse tennies, and a heavy men's leather biker jacket with buckles and wide-toothed zippers. Her black hair was flecked with just enough silver to pick up that of the hardware on her jacket, not to mention the multiple thin chains around her neck and wrists. Short and spiky, her hair drew attention to her unmade-up face and sparkling, confident eyes. Her stride was both graceful and strong. She carried her bike helmet so casually it seemed a part of her.

Erika didn't always look this way. As a young child her gendered appearance and interests were more diverse: "I even liked girlie clothes when I was real little. But I didn't care if I got 'em dirty. My tendency was to like get a pretty dress and go climb trees in it! That didn't seem to be a conflict early on. I had long hair, and I liked having long hair. . . . I always liked my little shiny black church shoes, too!"

As with her clothing preferences, Erika's early play activities were an eclectic blend of feminine and masculine. She loved cooking and *Star Trek* and adored the *Galloping Gourmet*. Sometimes she even played with "girlie" toys: "I had a thing about dolls: I took them apart to see how they worked. I had one doll that I played with that was—I often wonder why I particularly played with that doll." Dolls though, did not hold Erika's interest for long. "I played dolls when girls would come over and they would play with dolls. But as soon as they were gone I would put them back." Erika responded similarly to other nonactive toys: "I didn't like stuffed animals, to the point that I put them all in the back of my closet and told everybody that they were hibernating. 'Thank you for giving me a Teddy Bear. [laughing] Now it's going to go hibernate with the other ones!'" Erika even tried her hand at that quintessential girls' pastime, playing house: "My sister was blond and cute and cooked and cleaned and had dolls and a tea set. Whenever we played house she was the mother and I was the father. . . . But I didn't like tea parties. I didn't like any of that stuff. I didn't like having to play with her—and she didn't like having to play with me."

As it turned out, once she got older Erika realized she also "didn't like girls very much." But not because of their gender, or because Erika thought she was or wanted to be a boy. Instead, she said girls "were BORING. They didn't do any-thing—well, my idea of doing anything." Active toys and games were more Erika's style. She "liked outdoors things, shells and rocks and natural things were my toys. Marbles. Legos. I loved Lego! Legos and marbles. Marbles—I would cre-ate games with the marbles. I was pretty attached to marbles." Erika was also fond of stereotypically masculine toys, like her BB gun. Her favorite toy though, as with nearly all the tomboys I spoke with, was her bike. "My bike was always one big toy that was great. If my parents wanted to ground me, the only thing they could really do was take away my bike for a week. That was like HELL. The bike meant FREEDOM. Yeah, freedom. Getting out of there. Getting away." One wonders: Getting away from what? Freedom from what? Erika explained:

> I hated the lack of freedom that I had as a girl child. Although I just made myself have freedom—did a lot of things independently. Just being able to go off alone. It just didn't seem like it was cool to go off, like on your bike for example. You know it probably wasn't so cool for a

little boy either, but there was this sense that I—as a girl—might get hurt. And ahh, that pissed me off!

Correctly or not, Erika suspected that she—*as a girl*—faced restrictions she otherwise might not. This suspicion that her treatment was gendered soon led Erika to think differently about things "female." "I don't remember, it must've been probably around 8 years old, sometime in there, that I stopped liking girls' clothes. But I couldn't tell you why—probably because they were restrictive. I kept getting told, 'Now don't get that dirty!' Because I was so active, that was a problem. I thought, 'Well, I won't wear it if I can't get it dirty.'" But the restrictiveness of femininity entailed more than clothing style. Though she did not yet understand how or why, "appearing" as a tomboy somehow signaled a further dimension of rebellion:

> When I was 7 or 8 I was the cutest girl. The cutest boy in the class was supposed to go out with me. I thought, "OK. I guess I'm supposed to do this. Right?" So Kevin and I dated you know at whatever kind of ridiculous age we were. In those days I had my long hair and I wore my little dresses and everything. Then—I remember this day very clearly. We were out somewhere and I had this friend who was not well thought of, came from a poor family. Her cat had just had kittens. I was going to go over and see her kittens. Kevin was like, "You're not going to go over and see her kittens." I said, "What?! You're telling me what to do? Excuse me!" Of course, I broke off with Kevin instantly. I realized then that men were stupid and that they actually thought that they could tell you what to do! . . . I remember that moment and I think that may have been the beginning of my dress-changing habits, making a statement to the world.

Illustrative of the intertwining and co-construction of sexuality and gender, in Erika's experience simply *being* a girl entailed restriction. Wearing girls' clothes led to further limitations. In the end femininity, restriction, and passivity seemed to be the same, with all three symbolized by clothing: "It's this whole thing that I associate little girls with—soft, stupid. Unfortunately I had attached those soft [feminine clothes] to stupid and frivolous and things like that." With this fusion of restriction and femininity, the motivational logic of Erika's tomboy identity changed. At first she seemed to choose clothing, toys, and activities based on their *intrinsic* interest to her—sometimes wearing girls' clothes and doing girls' things, other times not, depending on her assessment of "fun." The older she got, however, the more often Erika faced gendered restrictions. In response her tomboyness became more a *reaction* to imposed meanings of femininity than an expression of her felt authenticity. Erika then became committed to avoiding "girlie" things for their own sake: "My real tomboy days were between 10 and 13 . . . at that period of time I was very male identified. I dressed only in guys' clothes and called myself Rik, and did not like being called Erika. . . . I was a tomboy before that, but it wasn't—I didn't dress like it."

Erika's clothing preferences quickly distinguished her from other girls. Early on this tomboy difference was viewed positively; Erika seemed to be a special sort of girl. However, contrary to the master narrative's account that tomboyness is valued while sissyness is not, the meaning of Erika's tomboyness shifted subtly the older she got. Soon enough, Erika noticed that not only was she different from other girls, but that her difference was devalued:

> It was mostly at school, where the pressure was. . . . Certainly watching television tells you that there is something wrong with you. I would look at that and just go "hmmmm." Which is why I think the media is such a destructive thing. So, if there hadn't been television, even though we didn't watch a lot of television, I think that I would've barely noticed—other than at school.

At school and other sites of kid culture, Erika no longer fit into the increasingly dualistic gender order. This misfit increased as the meaning of her tomboyness changed. In response, Erika started spending more time alone. But her solitary days weren't wholly negative. "Bored by everybody," Erika sought mastery and high adventure on her own:

> My big thing would be to find something really hard to do, do it until I could do it, then challenge people to do it. One of my favorite activities was jumping off this, the local gravel pit. It was quite high and it was a stupid thing to do—so it was perfect! I did a lot of jumping into the gravel pit and challenging others to do it. I always practiced, rehearsed. But I came down in the equivalent of mountain biking now, biking down rough terrain. Skateboarding, too. A lot of high-risk things.

For a time "doing her own thing" worked. Yet the older she got, the more dramatically Tomboyness shifted from asset to liability. By middle school Erika was routinely teased, sometimes to the point of tears: "I remember being called 'tomboy' and 'gorilla woman.'" Fortunately for her, unlike many of the other tomboys I spoke with, Erika's "parents were pretty cool about it," providing a respite from, rather than an application of, gendered social control. "They were more interested in me having a good time than in looking right."

But the good times didn't last. Erika, like the other tomboys I spoke with, experienced the definitional shift in Tomboy from positive to negative difference as a sudden and jarring collision with mysterious "new rules": What was cool became uncool, what was once thought lame was valued. Overnight, or so it seemed, the world changed, pulling the rug of self-confidence from under Erika's feet. Then, just when she had accommodated to the teasing, it suddenly grew worse: "In high school I got some real strong terms. 'Macho girl.' I got some unpleasant TITLES, not just nicknames or name calling."

In response, Erika tried to follow the mandatory but unwritten new rules. The baseline seemed easy enough, given her attraction to boys. Yet the invisibility of her heterosexual desire to others meant she still did not quite "fit."

I had boys I liked a lot. I had crushes on them but my relationship to them was like, let's go biking or something. Which meant I became one of the guys. Which never quite worked at that age cuz you can't really be one of the guys. There's always the problem of, "but she's a GIRL!" You know? It was always frustrating to me that I couldn't just hang with them without it being "Erika likes John!" That kind of thing getting in the way. Now that was maybe usually true, but my approach was to just hang with the guys.

Kid culture changes profoundly at adolescence. Teen bodies and psyches are sexualized (Thorne, 1993)—or, more correctly, *hetero*sexualized. With the more explicit expansion of heterosexual meanings into teen culture and onto teen bodies, the safe space once allotted to childhood "cross genderism" shrinks. Although children (and many adults) experience the shift as a sudden one, the heterosexual meanings of gender were always already there. (Think, for example, of the prevalence of greeting cards depicting children dressed up as grooms and brides.) Looking back, Erika recalled suffering early on for violating heterogendered (Ingraham, 1994) expectations, beginning when she broke up with Kevin. "From that point on I became unpopular. Because you didn't break up with Kevin. So, umm, I think something started going wrong there, when I started having options."

As adolescence nears, tomboy identity becomes increasingly problematic. In fact, many tomboys "reform" at or near puberty—coincidentally the same time that the association of persistent tomboyism and lesbianism congeals. Reformed tomboys renounce their tomboyness, often over the summer, reappearing as (normal) girls in the fall. Reformed tomboys thus venture near the contaminating meanings of mannishness. Yet they blossom in the end. Traversing the gender normal divide, reformed tomboys return safely to the realm of normality. Others, like Erika, take a different tomboy trajectory.

Erika's persistent tomboyness led her in the other direction across the gender normal divide. As a career tomboy, Erika dwelled in the dangerous realm of pathology. There Erika endured various attempts by others to "police" her gender. Attempting to sidestep antitomboy sentiments while also avoiding the restrictions and objectification that accompanied femininity, Erika became a full-fledged loner. Ironically, her flight rigidified into a caricature straight out of the master narrative. She adapted to gendered social control by restricting her tomboyness to a locale "conveniently in another town over" that she biked to. There, Erika became Rik, the go-cart king:

> For a period of time I was very much the tomboy, to the extent of calling myself Rik and going to a go-cart [raceway]. . . . So I called myself Rik and I hung out at this go-cart park where I was the go-cart king. I looked just like a boy—I was so psyched! I dressed only in guys' clothes and called myself Rik, and did not like to be called Erika. Really liked getting away with being called Rik. At this go-cart place they just thought I was a guy. They didn't know that I wasn't a guy.

For Erika, passing as male was about interests and privileges—about a gender *style* known as masculinity—not sex. Sex though, would soon enough intervene in gender. Given her age, Erika's clandestine tomboy activities could not last. When puberty hit and her breasts developed she "just stopped going [to the go-cart park]. I just dropped off the face of the earth and reappeared as a woman. So yeah. It was a tough transition for me. Not one that I ever really made."

After her body changed, Erika returned to the school and neighborhood social scenes and tried again to fit the gender order of teen life. But the "the boy-girl thing" was still confusing. She sought clues and strategies from other girls, then watched distastefully as they simpered. Erika was trapped in a paradox. Adhering to the new rules undermined her tomboy dignity and self-assertiveness. Avoiding them, she was invisible: "I did not make myself a sexual object. So I was NOT a sexual object." She tried again to "hang with the guys," a strategy that exacerbated her frustration:

> ASK ME TO THE DANCE! Don't tell me who you're going to ask to the dance. Ask ME to the dance! There's a very cheesy Hollywood film that made me cry my eyes out because it was the story of my childhood. What was it called? *Pretty in Pink*? It was the typical kind of friendship between the young guy and the girl. It's very typical. This guy really has this crush on this girl and of course his best friend who is coaching him is a girl. And of course she likes him. In the end he gets a clue. Which doesn't usually happen in real life, but it was nice in the movie! That's been the story of my life, being the coach when I really wanted to be asked out.

While lesbianism was hinted at in some of her childhood teasing, as she passed through adolescence into adulthood the shadow of the invert loomed larger over Erika. Eventually her continued tomboyness led to such blatant lesbian presumption that she was excluded from the heterosexual economy. In response, now and again Erika went into "femme phases" in her style of dress, "thinking it was going to get me a man." Because Erika was uncomfortable in such self-consciously "performed" femininity, each femme phase never lasted long: "As soon as I had a solid relationship, phoom, back to myself." For Erika "doing gender" (West & Zimmerman, 1987) engendered painful feelings of feminine incompetence: "I feel awkward and unattractive and like I'm failing. I'm failing in the *Cosmopolitan* image. I could never do it, so why bother? I'm a failure, so NEVER MIND. I will wear my black jeans anyway. I have gone through a couple periods of time where I tried, but I walk around pretty miserable so I just decided to skip it." Erika's femme phases and resulting gender self-consciousness continued through her college years. In time though, the persistent gender trouble became more than a liability; it also inspired Erika's study of theatre and dance. Both provided Erika new means to explore issues of bodies and movement. Then, one day, a door to insight suddenly opened. In a reversal of a long-standing theatrical tradition of men playing women, Erika was cast in a male role.

A lot of the phase I went through in my adult life, the struggle with gender identity, was after putting on a man's suit and feeling at home for the first time. Umm, and that really didn't fit, because my father didn't wear suits. So it's like, "What the fuck is this?! This is just as destructive as the feminine side. This is not a positive." I didn't see it as a positive thing, but I felt COMFORTABLE. So I explored that for a long time. I think that I felt comfortable because suddenly the way that I moved— which has always been very "masculine"—became, it made sense. It looked like suddenly you were supposed to FIT in the world. I put this suit on and I was perceived as a man in a man's suit and the way that I moved was finally fine.

Shocked but intrigued, Erika continued to explore the implications of her theatrical transgender experience. And as the line between male and female, masculine and feminine blurred, so too did the distinction of personal gender issues and professional interests fade. Erika then became a professional performance artist. Her early works were occasions to sort out the entanglement of sex, gender, and desire her life had become. "For a while I dressed as a man. Then it just became part of my work. I wore a man's suit around for a short period of time." She continued, "When I am performing as a man I just love it. I LOVE IT! It's not a sexual thing. It's a total identity thing." Thus, in the normal course of her life Erika stumbled upon a core tenet of much recent gender theory: sexuality and gender are not the same thing; gender is not inherent but enacted; the seeming naturalness of femininity and masculinity is, at least in part, sartorially produced. Erika explained, "Putting on a man's suit and being PERCEIVED, actually going out in the world and having people assume that you are a man—is very different from being a woman and being perceived as if you're either a lesbian or rejecting the traditional female role."

Unfortunately for Erika, the audience doesn't always get this. Instead they maintain the commonsense conflation of "cross-gender" appearance and desire: "When I perform I get love letters from women coming out to me. 'Thank you for opening me up to my lesbian tendencies.'" I say, "I'm happy for you—but don't call me!" Even Erika's long-term lesbian friends dwell in the invert's shadow. In a nod to the usual interpretation of Tomboy style as sign of lesbian desire, they jokingly call her the "undercover heterosexual." Intentional or not, as with many jokes the frivolity of "undercover heterosexual" works as social control. In this case the moniker patrols the gender normal divide.

> I mean, I haven't gotten a lot of flack, but some of my lesbian friends I know sit around and say, "She's a dyke. She's a dyke." That, frankly, pisses me off. I don't sit around and think, "Oh, she's straight.". . . I don't assume every time that one of my lesbian friends puts on a dress that she is not lesbian anymore. But if I dress like this it is assumed I am lesbian. I don't like to be assumed. I like pointing it out to people because I don't think it's necessary to assume that.

Erika attributes lesbian presumption to her "political stance and performing as a man"—both of which, of course, are given meaning using the resources of the master narrative. In the wake of lesbian presumption, Erika's heterosexual desire gasps for breath and nearly drowns. She laments, "It's been confusing in my love life. Definitely. Plenty of situations where men just assume that I am lesbian and don't even ask, don't even consider that I might not be." This disappearance of desire is compounded by Erika's understandable penchant for dressing up in what she feels best in. "Whenever I'm sexually attracted to a guy I put on my best male stuff. Yeah! It doesn't work. It does when I find the *right* guy, but, it's been an interesting challenge." She explained:

> I still for a long time had that battle with a man: Are we friends or are we lovers? That question has been a fight for me for a long time. Liking someone, working my way into his life, then having him say things to me like "Oh, it's so nice to have a woman I don't have to be sexual with!" And I'm going, "Oh no, not again!" And then being hit on by another woman. And trying to explain, to justify once again, "Yes. I am heterosexual. No. I don't need to go through this again. Yes. I have considered the possibility—" So that's been a real issue for me.

Erika's struggles with lesbian presumption and her professional insights into the performative nature of gender led her to others who also critique gender binarism: transvestites and transsexuals. At first, the trans community provided an oddly familiar way of attributing gender. "I think it was very comforting when I was going to the transsexual community because there they confirmed 'you are your identity.' You internally identify as male, you are male. External reality is different, but you are male. That point of view was what I needed to hear." In time, though, Erika fit less easily within trans discourse. She embraced Tomboy as the core of her being, but her life did not follow a one-dimensional trans mapping of her "cross-gendered" trajectory.[7] Erika explained:

At first it was a release. But then it was, you know, I left one bad situation for another. . . . One of the reasons I started hanging out with them, one to get political about it, two to get community, and three because they were very attached to calling yourself Erik. They would call me Erik. Or Rik. They were attached to labeling things that way. That's what woke me up to well, if this is a problem, I don't have to suddenly become a man in my life to experience these things. I do not have to dress in men's three-piece suits—which represent things that I do not necessarily respect—to reclaim and own what my true identity is. This is going in the wrong direction. This is maybe how they have to deal with it because of the way the outside world is fucked up.

From Erika's perspective, the transsexual story line fell into the same dualistic gender trap as did the master narrative, albeit with a twist. In both narratives masculine gender style occurs only with a male body. According to this either/or construction of gender and sex a person is either masculine or feminine, and either male or female, never both (and certainly never neither!). Following a principle of consistency, this dualism of gender and sex extends to desire, with the effect that sexuality is gendered. Thus, masculine male bodies "naturally" desire feminine female bodies (and vice versa). When they don't, something is awry. Yet even deviations from the binary are understood using its logic, leaving little room for a person like Erika. No wonder she could not find herself within the trans and master narratives! Erika experienced herself in another locale—beyond the binary. "But in rejection of that, I just reject the gender thing altogether. . . . So, it's that re-thinking of it. And yes, it's been both a political effort and also personal in trying to reclaim that whatever I do is female because I am female. Some of it is CATEGORIZED as male, but it isn't masculine, just categorized." Outside gender once again, Erika found herself. At last she could articulate: Gender was not the essential core of her being.

As far as I am concerned it is irrelevant. Not totally irrelevant, but it is a less important aspect of my being. That's one of the gifts of being a tomboy or being someone that had done a lot of gender work is that you free yourself up from that attachment. We are, from some of the gender identity research that I've done, I think overly attached to our sex identities. I think this is extremely unfortunate.

Despite the joyous return to her early childhood gender fluidity—before female-ness meant femininity and femininity meant restriction—Erika encountered a new ambivalence:

Sometimes I don't like ["Tomboy"] because my whole thing is that what I did was what I did and I was a girl so it has nothing to do with being a "boy." I don't like the association. . . . I sit like this because it's comfort-able, not because it's masculine. That's only been attributed to male. The same way with "tomboy." A lot of what I do was attributed to masculine being so therefore it was tomboy. I don't like the term because I was a girl. I was a biological female. I just did those things that happened to be attributed to a biological male. So it's not like the term never did any damage to me. Cuz once I used to plug the term, I thought the term was cool. It was hip to be a tomboy. But now I don't like referring to the things that are so-called masculine in myself even as masculine.

Erika bolstered her theoretical gender critique with practical attempts to "recover" from her more rigidified tomboy identity and appearance. She contin-ued to wear "masculine" clothing but also dabbled now and again in feminin-ity—with mixed results.

When I put it on I feel vulnerable and decorative. When I put it on the feminist side of me takes a stance against it. And then there's the per-sonal side that has a repulsion towards it. Then there's another side of me that likes it. So I have to have these little conversations inside me before I decide what to do about it. I'm kind of at peace with the femi-nist aspect of it. The repulsion side is still there sometimes. I'm trying to understand that at this point.

As with any skill, consistent practice helped Erika better "do" her gender, allevi-ating her feminine incompetence. At the same time, her redefinition of feminin-ity as a literal performance helped decrease her self-consciousness:

Usually the times when I am comfortable with [femininity] are the times that I'm able to think of it as being in drag. And the more I think of it as my drag—a lot of my male friends who are gay and do drag have helped me with that. "Just enjoy it as drag," they say. "So you feel like a man in drag! We have fun in drag, can't you?" Actually, the most help I've gotten with it has been with my male friend who walks better in heels than I ever will.

Still, Erika's feminine incompetence and associated anxiety sometimes pose difficulties. Erika's roommate "is this blond jazz singer, total babe, feminine thing." They're "tight" now, but this wasn't always the case.

It's been tough though, because the feminine women push all my buttons. They're everything that I'm supposed to be but that I'm not! And they get relationships with men because they're everything that I'm supposed to be and I'm not. Very little self-esteem with my so-called feminine allure, whatever that's supposed to be. Feeling mostly incredibly unattractive. Feelings about just being ugly. And not being attractive to the opposite sex. And being with someone who is confident with their female sexuality and how to use that—my roommate is the EPITOME sometimes. You know, we talk about it. We joke about it. But it also means that I have to work hard for me to be comfortable.

As she became more comfortable with feminine attire, Erika started to reconsider her childhood fusion of femininity, restriction, and passivity. The last time I saw her, her hair was thicker and longer, down to her shoulders, parted neatly in the middle. She wore no jewelry or makeup. Her black tennies—now intentionally speckled with multicolored paints—coordinated well with her purple tights and black bike shorts. Both were covered somewhat by a billowing purple and turquoise shirt. And of course, her leather jacket. She explained that her new look was about "letting myself be the little girl I never got to be." "But," she said, "I think I will always be in my Converse sneakers. There will always be that little part. I don't think I WANT to leave my so-called tomboy; I like being gender confused, gender neutral."

BUSTING BINARIES

> The implication of the word tomboy is that an active, inquisitive, energetic girl acts like a boy, not a girl. In other words, she is abnormal for one of her sex. (Miller & Smith, 1980, p. 121)

Erika's story, as retold here in relation to the master Tomboy narrative, helps illustrate the constitutive power of narrative: how socially shared story lines of identity provide the symbolic resources for the construction and interpretation of individual identity. The widespread availability of the Tomboy narrative—in books and magazines, on TV, in folk knowledge—locates Erika in gender culture, allowing her to "come to terms with herself." At the same time, the Tomboy narrative provides others with a means to understand and respond to Erika. Early on this constitutive process was mostly positive; the tomboy label referred to Erika's status as a special sort of girl. Later though, as the negative meanings of Tomboy came to the fore, so too did the disciplinary quality of narrative: Tomboy became code for mannishness, a boundary marker of (normal) girlhood.

Necessarily general, narratives of identity like the Tomboy flatten variation, overtaking lives lived following less-common pathways. Certainly Erika, who ventured away from a femininity she found tainted with messages of passivity and restraint, disappeared in the contours of the master narrative. Throughout her life, Erika skirted the malleable gender normal divide. As she did so her childhood tomboy identity shifted from gender fluidity to rigidity. At the same time, the negative meanings of tomboyism helped forge the parameters of Erika's heterosexuality, rendering it mostly invisible to others, at times liminal to her. This disappearance of desire led to Erika's encounter with the most recent elaborations of mannishness in the master narrative: the transvestite and the transsexual.

Such were the personal consequences of Erika's confrontation with the disciplinary dynamics of Tomboy. Beyond shaping individual lives, master narratives are also constitutive in a wider sense: they express and reproduce broader cultural assumptions. In this regard, Erika's story may be read for the meanings of sex, gender, and desire embedded within it, providing insight into the gender order. As for sex, there are two. Only two. As for gender, there are also two, only two, mapped onto sex such that normative femininity and masculinity entail heterosexual desire. The world of gender possibility is thus cleaved in half, leaving one side conventional and normal, the other deviant and abnormal. By demarcating a line of gender cleanliness and contamination in this way, the master Tomboy narrative helps constitute our larger gender culture.

A devalued—and feared—homosexual image hovers over this gender normal divide, spooking those who would venture too far past the socially constructed dualisms of supposedly natural femininity and masculinity. The spectre of lesbianism is a potent agent of control; the costs of gender difference increase dramatically when mannishness becomes prominent over the gender normal divide. Then the pathological tomboy is the one whose gender choices challenge the socially constructed naturalness of the heterogender system, while the acceptable tomboy is the one whose gender choices fit the practical and aesthetic contours of heterosexuality. Erika's embodiment—a so-called masculine woman who desires men—disrupts these interconnected dualisms of sex, gender, and desire.

The haunting of the gender normal divide works, in part, due to a conflation of sexuality (desire-based identities and acts) with gender (social and historical meanings and embodiments of sex). Heterosexuality is "unremarkable" all the while: Taken for granted as natural, it tags along with gender but goes unspoken. In this silence the dangerous meanings of tomboyism gone awry—the incipient bull dyke, the transsexual—noisily mark the limits of normal femaleness. Seemingly neutral, the conflation of sexuality and gender known as traditional femininity is defined as such *by its relationship to* the abnormal. The abnormality of Tomboy thus holds heterosexuality in place.[8]

TELLING STORIES ABOUT STORYTELLING

> The life I am trying to grasp is the life that is
> trying to grasp it.
> —R. D. Laing

We think through words. How we think, how we talk, are applications of power. I have struggled here, through narrative, to show how the social shapes the personal. "The constitutive power of narrative": a dense phrase that attempts my summary of the narrative production of identity. There is, of course, more to the story since storytelling is a performative self act. As well, narrative shapes the *telling* of a life. And the telling of a life in turn shapes narrative—at least sometimes. Regrettably, not all narratives are equally valued. Some are disguised or otherwise hidden from view. Others are disqualified as inadequate, naive, or unscientific. Though "subjugated" (Foucault, 1980) in this way, narratives like Erika's have a transformative potential. Written as it is from the point of view of lived tomboy experience, Erika's story modifies the master narrative—depending, of course, on how it is read.

The narrative changes resulting from this telling extend further, deeper than this. This inquiry—*my* inquiry—began in my own embodiment: my gender deviance, discomfort, dis-ease. As I spoke with other tomboys my personal sense of misfit lessened. After talking with Erika I wrote in my notes: "I felt deep resonance with her words. I felt she was speaking my life." This feeling increased the more I listened across the many stories of tomboy lives. With the privilege of seeing how individual lives intersect with and reflect larger social processes my edginess eased even more. More important, for me as for those I spoke with, I then saw too how individuals resist and, in this resistance, remake social processes.

Telling a life story in relation to history and social structure provides a means to link that life to those of others. The life-story method is thus well suited to a feminist sociological praxis. With such a telling, what seems at the outset to be individual and idiosyncratic is instead revealed to be social and patterned. With such a telling, private troubles are politicized, transformed into social matters. In this case the movement from individual to social afforded by looking back changed the lived meanings of tomboyness—for the narrators and for me. Rather than potential pathology, might tomboyness be *resistance* to a restrictive gender order? And so we're back to back talk. In this collective (re)telling, out of tomboy as gender misfit arises an incipient gender warrior.[9]

NOTES

1. When referring to the master narrative, I will capitalize Tomboy; when referring to actual girls and women it will be written in lower-case.

2. I here use "back talk" both as vernacular and as reference to the critical tradition of afrocentric feminist theory. In everyday life back talk refers to the words of the less powerful as spoken in response to those with more power. Back talk is thus political speech: speech that, by intention or not, challenges the point of view of those with more power. In this spirit, bell hooks (1984, 1989) back talks when assessing hegemonic white feminist thought from her standpoint as a black woman.

3. Gender narratives, like gender itself, are also racialized and classed.

4. I am here describing the master narrative. My empirical work debunks these myths. Tomboys *are* subject to a variety of social control techniques, ranging from verbal teasing to physical punishment and aversive reconditioning therapies. In this regard, other children, siblings, parents, teachers, clergy, and psychiatrists act as "femininity police," enforcing the binaries of the Western sex/gender/desire system (McGann, 1995, forthcoming).

5. Although not the focus of this analysis, an interweave of specificities of race, class, and age shape which Tomboy stereotypes are brought to bear on particular tomboys. As suggested in the OED's hoyden reference, tomboyness is often linked with working-class embodiments of femininity (cf. Duggan, 1993). Many "tomboy novels" use classed and animalistic imagery to police nonbourgeois femininities when describing tomboys (McGann, 1995, forthcoming). "Tomboy" has been used as a class-based slur to indict female athletes' violations of (white) middle-class standards of femininity (Cahn, 1994). The master tomboy narrative is also racialized. The presumption of whiteness in Tomboy renders white as unmarked and seemingly neutral—a conceptual move that supports racism by constructing white people as not "of color," hence also without race. Thus, in addition to lesbian presumption, some tomboys face a matrix of classism, racism, and xenophobia as they negotiate the negative meanings of Tomboy. The parents of African American tomboys, for example, are anxious that their daughters "look like junkies." White upper-class and wealthy parents fear their tomboys "look poor" or "common." Parents of immigrant tomboys fear their tomboy daughters do not "look American" (McGann, 1995, forthcoming).

6. I develop the notion of the "career tomboy" (and other grounded conceptualizations used in this chapter) elsewhere (McGann, 1995, 1999).

7. Erika's understanding of the group's transsexual discourse is not necessarily representative of all transsexual discourse. Not all transsexually identified folks conceptualize or experience gender and sex in this binary fashion (cf. Rubin, 1999).

8. The "holding in place" language is broadly poststructuralist and underlies much

queer and postcolonial theory. Poststructuralism also has an affinity with feminist theory. DeBeauvoir's (1961) depiction of woman as Other vis-à-vis man, for example, is post-structuralist in spirit. Similarly, feminist critiques of the valuation of masculinity at the expense of femininity highlight the dangers of "co-constructed" hierarchical dualisms (cf. Miller, 1976; Gilligan, 1982). Rich's (1980) articulation of the grounding of compulsory heterosexuality in the invisibility of lesbians is compatible with another poststructuralist theme: silences, spaces, and other disappearances are powerful forces constructing the Natural. For Rich, the "lesbian invisibility" in analyses that purport to be about *all* women reinforces the naturalness of heterosexuality.

9. "Gender warrior" is Leslie Feinberg's (1996) wonderful term.

REFERENCES

American Psychological Asociation. (1994). *Diagnostic and statistical manual of menian disorders* (4th ed.). Washington, D.C.: APA.

Boston Lesbian Psychologies Collective. (1987). *Lesbian psychologies.* Urbana, IL: University of Illinois Press.

Cahn, S. (1994). *Coming on strong.* New York: Free Press.

de Beauvoir, S. (1961). *The second sex.* New York: Bantam.

Denzin, N. K. (1989). *Interpretive bioigraphy.* Newbury Park, CA: Sage.

Duggan, L. (1993). The trials of Alice Mitchell. *Signs 13* (4), 791–814.

Faderman, L. (1991). *Odd girls and twilight lovers.* New York: Oxford.

Feinberg, L. (1996). *Transgender warriors.* Boston: Beacon.

Foucault, M. (1980). *Power/knowledge.* New York: Pantheon Books.

Gilligan, C. (1982). *In a different voice.* Cambridge, MA: Harvard University Press.

Glaser, B. G. & Strauss, A. (1967). *The discovery of grounded theory.* Chicago: Aldine.

Green, R. (1975). Adults who want to change sex: Adolescents who cross-dress and children called "sissy" and "tomboy." In R. Green (Ed.), *Human sexuality: A health practitioner's text* (pp. 83–96). Baltimore: Williams & Wilkins Co.

Green, R., Williams, K., and Goodman, M. (1981). Ninety-nine "tomboys" and "non-tomboys." *Archives of Sexual Behavior 11* (3), 247–66.

hooks, b. (1984). *Feminist theory: From margin to center.* Boston: South End.

_____(1989) *Talking back: Thinking feminist. Thinking Black.* Boston: South End.

Ingraham, C. (1994). The hetrosexual imaginary. *Sociological Theory 12* (2), 203–19.

Martin, C. L. (1990). Attitudes and expectations about children with non-traditional and traditional "gender roles." *Sex Roles 22* (3/4), 151–65.

McGann, PJ. (1995). The ballfields of our hearts: Tomboys, femininity, and female development. Doctoral dissertation, Brandeis University.

_____(1998). Academics and jocks. In revision for *Gender & Society).*

_____(forthcoming). *The ballfields of your hearts.* Philadelphia: Temple University Press.

Miller, C. and Smith, K. (1991). *Words and women.* New York: Harper.

Miller, J. B. (1976). *Toward a new psychology of women.* Boston: Beacon.

Oxford English Dictionary (1987). New York: Oxford University Press.

Phelan, S. (1993). (Be)coming out. *Signs 18* (4), 765–90.

Plummer, K. (1983). *Documents of Life.* Boston: Allen and Unwin.

Rekers, G. (1992). Developmental problems of puberty and adolescence. In E. Walker & M. C. Roberts (Eds.), *Handbook of clinical child psychology* (pp. 607–22). New York: John Wiley.

Rich, A. (1980). Compulsory heterosexuality and lesbian existence. *Signs 5* (4), 631–60.

Rubin, H. S. (1999). *Always already men*. Chicago: University of Chicago Press.

Strauss, A. (1987). *Qualitative analysis for social scientists*. New York: Cambridge.

Thorne, B. (1993). *Gender play*. New Brunswick, NJ: Rutgers University Press.

West. C. & Zimmerman, D. (1987). Doing gender. *Gender & Society 1* (2), 1215–51.

Zucker, K. & Green, R. (1992). Psychosexual disorders in children and adolescents. *Journal of Child Psychology and Psychiatry and Allied Disorders 33* (1), 107–51.

Climbing out of the Pit:
From the Black Middle Class to Homeless and (Almost) Back Again

*W*HAT IS OUR IMAGE of homeless people? That they are dirty? Lazy? Aimless? Do we think that if only they had tried harder, been more careful, planned better, perhaps been more adaptive, they would still have their home and family about them? Beyond these personological attributions, the master narrative about homeless people also carries marks of race, class, gender, and sexuality. In spite of recent attention to emerging data that show otherwise, the generic homeless person is still generally assumed to be male, single, nonwhite, lower class, and either asexual or promiscuously heterosexual. Against this narrative, Laura's story stands in strong contrast. This chapter describes how Laura became homeless, which she refers to as "the pit," how she survived the degradations of homelessness, and how she ultimately moved beyond it. The chapter ends with a discussion of why the master narrative is constructed the way it is, and why we are reluctant to revise that narrative in ways that would more veridically reflect the experiences of women like Laura.

Much of Laura's life has been lived straddling various borders: between security and insecurity, between white and African American society, between victim and survivor. To Laura, the focal point of her story is how she climbed out of the pit of homelessness. Therefore, we begin with some background on homelessness in the United States.

HOMELESSNESS IN THE UNITED STATES

According to Burt (1992), homelessness arises from no single factor, but is instead perpetuated by pivotal interactions between external social and economic conditions and personal vulnerabilities. In the United States, there are four major events that trigger homelessness: family breakup (true of one-third of homeless persons); eviction (applies to a third of homeless persons); job loss (true for 29 percent of homeless persons); and relocation (true for 24 percent of homeless persons) (Legal Services, 1991). Laura experienced the first three of these and each contributed to her homelessness. Two other important factors that can push an individual into homelessness are mental illness and chemical dependency (Burt, 1992). Burt (1992) reports that 27 percent of homeless single women have been hospitalized for mental illness, and 59 percent scored above the cutoff point on a standard measure of clinical depression (pp. 22–23). The incidence of addiction among the homeless is disputed (National Coalition for the Homeless, 1998). Laura suffered two "nervous breakdowns" on her way to homelessness and several hospitalizations for alcohol poisoning.

Violence against women and poverty also play a role. One study found that 50 percent of homeless women and children were fleeing abuse (Zorza, 1991). Laura was beaten twice by her husband, and her psychological abuse was fairly constant in the last 10 years of her marriage. Poverty is also a major contributor to homelessness in the United States (Burt, 1992; Liebow, 1993). The U.S. poverty rate is two to three times that of Australia, the United Kingdom, Canada, Germany, Norway, Sweden, and Switzerland, and poverty rates have always been higher for African Americans than for whites or Latinos (Legal Services, 1991). While poverty has been growing in the United States (Legal Services, 1991), low-rent and subsidized housing for poor people has been shrinking. Fewer than half of those who qualify (9.6 million) for housing subsidy from HUD actually receive it. Laura is now living in a subsidized apartment with her grandson. Thus, there is nothing remarkable about the basic facts of Laura's path into homelessness, yet her story departs in many significant ways from the pictures in our heads of homeless people. Perhaps we ought to question the accuracy of those pictures.

HAVING IT ALL, LOSING IT, TRANSFORMATION, AND RECOVERY

Laura was not always poor, and even while homeless could charge purchases to her credit card. Although she was born to an unwed mother in 1947, she was raised from the age of 3 months by her maternal grandparents who were solidly working class or lower middle-class. Her grandfather, "Daddy," was a mechanic who occasionally owned his own business and whose own father had owned a very successful blacksmith business. Her grandmother, Laura reports, "quit her job the day after he asked her if she would be willing to raise me. So she was home with me all the time." Laura was not a "latchkey" child and enjoyed the luxury of having a stay-at-home parent at a time when high proportions of African American mothers were in the labor force.

More significant to her was the fact that this grandmother was a "generational Washingtonian," and so is she. "It's a little different from someone coming to the city, or someone whose parents come. Being a generational there was a certain set of social things established that Washingtonians didn't do . . . like . . . sitting on the front stoop in a kitchen chair. That was a no-no. You don't take kitchen furniture out in the front." Being a Washingtonian is clearly a class marker by rolling migratory status into class.

In high school Laura developed an interest in animal psychology and had her sights set on college. Her grandmother had hoped schools would be desegregated in time for her to go to a nearby "white" school, but they weren't and she went instead to a "Black" school "which was quite a walk," but Laura "thought nothing of it." She realizes now that she was "sort of sheltered a lot. . . . I didn't know that much about segregation, per se, until I started seeing it [the civil rights movement] on television."

What she did become aware of early on was sexism. As a child, Laura describes herself as a "tomboy" who hated to wear dresses. She recalls:

> I was the best boy in the neighborhood. I was the competition. . . . I had my gun and holster set. My grandmother used to buy me all girl toys, and my grandfather got me an erector set when I was 4 years old. He would take me on his little repair jobs on the weekends . . . that's where I got my mechanical attributes, because I was always under the hood with "Daddy."

But this exuberance about who she was did not last:

> I think I first started not liking myself as a female in junior high school. We had to take an aptitude test. This was to help us decide whether to go into the academic track, business, or—I don't remember the other one. My highest score was in the mechanical aptitude and the math side. I remember the female counselor looking at my scores and shaking her head and said "I don't know what to tell you to do, maybe you could learn how to sew." And I can still remember how I felt.

Instead of rebelling against the gender norms that she felt diminished her, she tried to live by them. She was an avid student and attended a Georgetown University college preparatory program during two summers and a semester. This helped her to get four scholarships upon graduation from high school. Her grandparents were set on her going to college. Instead, she fell in love and, much to their chagrin, married a white man 3 months before she graduated from high school at age seventeen. She had her first child, a son, later that year. Her daughter was born 3 years later, in November 1968. Although her family encouraged her to continue her education, Laura had to go to work. But with a high school diploma and no work experience, opportunities were limited. Her first job was at a soda fountain at a drugstore. Later she worked in various positions, from an apprentice lens grinder with an optician, to running an offset printing press in a government office. With her mechanical aptitude and strong desire to learn, she developed solid mechanical and computer skills, which were highly marketable as organizations rapidly converted to computer-based operations.

Her marriage lasted from 1965 to 1990. This was not an easy time to be in an interracial marriage in Washington. But other than some stories about neighbors and family moving their attitudes around, co-workers' resentments (". . . working with a group of black men . . . having a white husband was a threat to them. It was like a slap in the face"), and her fear for her husband's safety during the riots of 1968, this does not weigh heavily in her narrative: "We weren't the typical couple of Capitol Hill—he was white, I was Black . . . but we just took it in stride." In fact, it was the apparent success of this life that gave rise to the question that sounds like the classic "problem that has no name" (Friedan, 1963): "I had the symbols. . . . I had the three-bedroom house in the suburb, I had the camper, had the new car and the new truck. . . . I had the American Express card, the Optima card, you know, the Diner's Club. I was making about $40,000 a year. . . . And I would look around and say 'but why am I unhappy?'" The difference between her situation and that of the white women that Friedan wrote about, however, is that Laura was working full time, taking university classes, and her children were grown. This was probably the period of Laura's greatest "success" in the terms that are commonly taken to stand for success. But these did not prevent her "fall from grace." Her attempt to adapt to society's gender and class norms contributed to her sense of failure as a woman when her marriage fell apart.

Losing It

The lifestyle she and her husband had built became more and more expensive to maintain, because her husband simply did not keep up his end. The responsibility of maintaining it was more and more on Laura's shoulders. So she began working the night shift because it paid more. Her husband reacted to this by becoming involved with a younger woman, but he did not lessen the financial burden on her. Laura coped with both problems by working more: She had one full-time job, one part-time job, and was also attending school while raising her two children.

> I was moving all the time. . . . It was very hard for me to relax. So I drank and I used my tranquilizers. When I would come home from the part-time job, if I got home at four I had to be able to get up at 7:30 in order to go to work, so I had to have a drink and a tranquilizer to hurry up and sleep so I could go to work. I had to hurry up and do everything. Then I had coffee on the way to work.

At the time she graduated from high school Laura thought she could do anything; now she found herself unable to cope with a slow-growing despair. In this context her daughter's premarital pregnancy triggered her first nervous break-down: "And there was nothing I could do. . . . You know, it was too late to get an abortion. I couldn't fix it. . . . I didn't know what to do to fix it. . . . It was out of my hands. I guess I just went into the hospital for a rest."

Both her daughter's pregnancy and her own breakdown violated standards of respectability that were central to the "generational-Washingtonian" code of behavior, creating a crisis in self-definition that had been long in the making. Looking back at that time, she reflects on the loss of self that accumulated over the years of her marriage and the behavior that was a symptom of that:

> I got lost between [ages] 17 and 30, or almost 40. . . . I had nothing to hope for. I was stuck. . . . I felt so empty inside, I used to buy two and three of everything, in case something broke. When my girlfriends came over and had a yard sale for me, they took so many things out of the attic that were in boxes. . . . But that's how empty I was . . . I just, I just . . . I just gave up. . . . There was always something going on, something I was trying to fix.

Among the things that needed "fixing" as she turned 41 were her husband's increasing belligerence, his flaunting a girlfriend in front of her, his unpre-dictable temper and occasionally violent and menacing behavior (she finally put a lock on her bedroom door; "I was like a battered wife"). Also, her son had moved in with them after returning from a military stint in Germany and was abusing alcohol and possibly other drugs. Her daughter ceded the custody of her out-of-wedlock son to Laura and Laura's husband when the boy was 5 months old. Too many things were going wrong that she couldn't fix. Each one assaulted, in large or small measure, her concept of who she was and what her life was sup-posed to be like. Her attempts to "fix" the story line of her life could not keep up with the barrage of insults to it. Those efforts dissolved in an anesthetic of alco-hol, tranquilizers, and withdrawal. "And without seeing that the person that needed fixing was me. . . . My husband used to joke about trading me in at 40. Escape was alcohol, tranquilizers, and staying out of the house in a productive way [working and taking classes]. . . . I was trying to be respectable. But I was still trying to escape. . . . I even started keeping food in my room so I wouldn't have to go downstairs and see anyone."

When she turned 41, her world crashed: Her beloved grandmother died in March; her favorite uncle died in May; her husband left her in July.

> You know, men joke about that: "I'm going to trade her in on two 20s." Well, lo and behold, the eve of my 41st birthday, he says that he's in love with a 20-year-old African woman, and he wants to have her and me, and if he can't have both of us he's gonna leave. Well, is that a joke? So

> it came to pass. . . . Here I am, all of a sudden I'm feeling, "I'm all washed up. . . . As a woman . . . I'm all washed up. I'm over 40." He said he was going to trade me in, children don't need me anymore, I can't take care of anything, I was done for, I was nonexistent.

In addition, her son was "putting [her] through a whole lot" with his alcohol problem, including "two or three" attempts to commit suicide. After several trips with him to the emergency room she asked him to move out, for which she says he has never forgiven her.

> You know, all that was like boom, boom, boom, boom. And then I had to do everything. I was left with all the bills and complete responsibility for [my grandson] and then, after we separated, [my husband] was coming in [to the house] after I would leave for work and doing things . . . [until] I changed the locks. . . . I was just scrambling trying to hold on to everything. . . . Then February of '89 . . . I was getting backed into a corner.

Her ability to cope, including her ability to work, was then further derailed by her husband's physical abuse and its psychological as well as physical impact on her. After their separation she visited him in the hospital after he had eye surgery: "I went over to see if we could just liquidate everything and make a clean break of it. Before I realized it he had knocked me to the ground and he was stomping on me. . . . He fractured my knee. . . . It had to be completely reconstructed. . . . And he wasn't going to give [my grandson] back. . . . That was one way to get my attention." She spent a week in the hospital having reconstructive surgery on her knee; the initial injury has left her permanently disabled. When she got home from surgery, her drinking got worse and she was using tranquilizers: "I used the alcohol to regulate the tranquilizers." Her work suffered, she was fired from her government job (she sued to have her discharge changed to "disability"), and was fired from a subsequent part-time job as well. She was hospitalized several times for alcohol poisoning. She became more and more withdrawn and her behavior became somewhat bizarre. Finally, when she found herself playing with the gun she owned, she reached out for help and got it. "It was so strange . . . everything was just way away and I was just functioning." She was in the psychiatric ward of the hospital for 3 weeks:

> So that was that, and I am glad I was in there. . . . I said God must have wanted me to be here, because it's a scary place to go . . . to a mental ward . . . to be there a second time, and seeing others there that were also there a second time. It was really strange me being there. . . . You know my spirituality really grew . . . my belief in God grew during my

trials and tribulations. My condition was such that I was considered a candidate for electroshock.

While she was in the psychiatric ward this time (in June 1990), her home was auctioned off because the mortgage wasn't being paid. Nevertheless, she was able to continue living there for a year after being released from the hospital. After 6 months at home, in December 1990, she stopped drinking. Finally, in June 1991, she was evicted, spent a few nights at various friends' houses, and started her life in various homeless shelters for women. She eventually entered the Dorothy Day Shelter where she stayed for just over a year (from June 1991 to August 1992). This was rock bottom for her, "the pit." "You know, when I lost everything, for me, that was the bottom of the barrel. And after I was sober, too. So I know God wanted me to be sober to go through all this."

In this account of Laura's path to homelessness we see in vivid detail the meaning of Burt's (1992) statement that homelessness results from pivotal interactions between external conditions and personal vulnerabilities. Perhaps the absence of any one factor—her daughter's pregnancy, her husband's infidelity, her son's suicide attempts, or her shame about any of these, or the unwitting collusion of a nonattending physician and unaware pharmacist that kept her supplied with tranquilizers—could have spared her from descending into "the pit."

Surviving and Climbing out of the Pit

Homelessness is destructive. That anyone survives is near miraculous, according to Liebow (1993):

> And yet, there is something about these women that makes them seem larger than life. This is certainly not because poverty ennobles us or because people at the bottom of society are stronger or more virtuous than others. What sets these homeless women apart is that, sane or crazy or physically disabled, they are all engaged in a titanic struggle to remain human in an unremittingly dehumanizing environment. Most of them are successful, and it is in this sense—the sense of remaining full and complete, even ordinary, human beings—that one can say that they are "making it." (p. 222)

How did she survive the pit? For Laura, survival in and departure from homelessness required twinned struggles to remain fully human while homeless and to claim or reclaim an identity that did not rest on the pillars of "generational-Washingtonian" respectability, even while that standard served as an effective foil to further losses of self-esteem.

Part of Laura's self-definition included her refusal to identify with other homeless people (referred to as "distancing" by Snow & Anderson, 1987, p. 1348) whose response to the dehumanizing nature of homelessness she understands from the inside. She considered herself lucky that she wasn't on the street, where she thinks she wouldn't have survived:

> I started thinking . . . [what happens] when a person can't take a shower, brush your teeth. So then you get anxious. But you can't stay anxious, so you learn to live with it. And when you have to wear the same dirty, tattered clothing. After a while you have a chip on your shoulder. You are daring anybody to say anything about it because you're defending yourself. You can't do anything about it. . . . They'd be defiant. Just dare you to say anything. That's what happens. Your humanity is plucked away, like plucking a chicken, one feather at a time.

Asked what was the most powerful experience that contributed to her climbing out of the pit of homelessness, she said: "Being in the shelter, there is a whole subculture . . . that was really weird to me, really scary. They were comfortable. . . . These people just gave up trying to move out, because it seemed hopeless. *I didn't want to become part of this, where it didn't matter anymore.*"

The contrast with what she had known was motivating:

> Having less than I had, the status and respectability of being married, having two children, three-bedroom house, 2½ bathroom detached house, the camper, new truck, new car. I had all the status symbols, I had the credit cards. Having lost all of this, I had to come to terms with that. But then I had to come to terms with . . . I didn't want to stay where I was. . . . Seeing the difference between the two worlds, and realizing *I didn't want to stay in that world. I didn't want to give up.*

She had strategies for surviving homelessness, including both instrumental and expressive behaviors. She went to Mass in church every morning when she left the shelter, to get herself centered for the day. And she carried all the information she would need on a computer disk and hard copy:

> my health insurance numbers, OPM [Office of Personnel Management] numbers, lawyers' numbers, addresses, the information that is needed when you go for an initial interview for services.

> I had an agenda every day. . . . The weekends were the hardest because there was very little open until after ten [NB: residents could not remain in the shelter during the day]. . . . I had something to do on Saturdays and Sundays. I would get [my grandson] and take him out to various things.

To combat the dehumanizing treatment accorded to the homeless, she would use her credit cards in a department store just to hear a sales clerk say, "Thank you, Mrs_____. . . . " She ordered a "Learn by Phonics" video for her grandson COD: "You know, I had to laugh at myself. Here I am in a shelter, and I'm ordering things." Becoming known to the "regulars in the church" was "another way of becoming a person rather than a faceless there."

But the shelter experience also brought her a crucial realization about herself: "When I was homeless was when I realized that as long as I attached myself to external symbols, I wasn't going to move." She realized that having material things would no longer suffice as a way to define herself. Losing everything—which is to say all the externals, the material possessions and relationships that had defined her "success"—made possible the transformation that changed her life: "Being in the shelter with women and seeing some of the things that those women went through, is when *I realized that I had to define myself from the inside out. All before it had been from the outside in.*"

Transformation

"The pit" meant hitting bottom. But the "pit" turned out not to be not a "trap," because losing everything also meant losing the constraints of the "generational—Washington" wife and mother roles where norms of race, gender, class, and sexuality all intersect. This new and painful freedom from the various master narratives to which Laura had heretofore subscribed also gave her a new freedom to explore a self worth constructing.

While in the hospital Laura took advantage of every service that was offered: groups for depressives, groups for substance abusers, psychodrama, and so forth. She took charge of her own treatment, deciding each day what activities she would and would not participate in, and got the staff to allow her to do as she saw fit:[1] "After the first or second day when I was a little more cognizant, I was choosing my own program and I didn't realize that not everybody did that. . . . I said 'No. Let me tell you what I'm going to do.'" This reversed her slide into helplessness and passivity. It was at this point that her naturally assertive personality—buried under years of marital "adaptation"—began to reassert itself: "But I was just coming back into it. It was buried so long during my marriage."[2]

After leaving the hospital, while living in the home that had been auctioned off, and then throughout her year-long stay in the homeless shelter, she continued to seek out services and self-help groups that she felt she needed, including AA groups, group therapy, Emotions Anonymous, daily Mass at church, talking with a nun at the shelter who gave her a lot of support, and visiting the social service agencies. She was also consulting lawyers (who worked on a pro bono basis or were from Legal Services) about her divorce, her disability suit against the federal agency where she'd been fired, and about getting herself qualified for Medicare.

She also started attending a variety of gay meetings related to alcoholism: gay Al-Anon, Gay AA, adult children of alcoholics, and a four-step workshop on Saturdays. Her exploration of these groups was not motivated by a discovery or reclamation of homosexual desire, but by her dissatisfaction with the other groups. In the heterosexual AA group, she found the women vapid and the men looking for a pickup, which did not interest her. In a gay-male group, on the other hand, she found the members more serious, more honest, and she felt "safe": They weren't going to hit on her. "Those people in the [gay] meetings were being a lot more honest with themselves, than the people in the world that I was no longer in, that I was alienated from. . . . I needed hugs, but I didn't want someone to think that the hugs were going to lead somewhere. And the safest place was in an all-male gay meeting. That was safety." She completed the year-long Whitman Walker Alcohol and Substance Abuse (WW) program: "It's a very intense program, over a year. There's a lot of soul-searching involved."

But it was in the Lesbian group where she finally experienced empowerment and was able, at last, to stick with the program.

The inspiration [to climb out of the pit] I got from the gay community. And I didn't even entertain the thought of being a Lesbian until I filed for divorce. . . . It was really, just, I got strength from being in the community. . . . Going to St. Mary's [Friday night meetings for gay women] was a big step for me because I had all the myths in my head about Lesbians not being wanted women. Also it would put me in the same situation as in the straight meetings. . . . I needed to talk, and I needed to listen. And lo and behold . . . I think about four women came over to me after the meeting at St. Mary's and said to me, "We'll love you until you can love yourself." I felt, well gee, I didn't know I was lovable, because I didn't love myself.

I can remember when I first went to the Black Lesbian Support Group, and they were having the editor of *Essence* [as speaker]. She'd done an article on "coming out." The power I felt walking into a room full of women, and they were talking about something interesting, that was exciting! I can truly say that was the first time I enjoyed being around women. . . . I usually had a hard time getting along with women.

Laura's account of discovering Lesbians does not resemble any of the familiar master narratives about "coming out." It centers much more on discovering community than on sexuality. How this aided her growth into a self she could love, and how this in turn aided her transformation from being "socially defined" to "self-defined" (Stewart, 1978) is described below.

Breaking the Glass Slipper and Stepping through the Looking Glass

Finally, she had to redefine her relationships to her significant others, beginning with her husband. This had actually started as her marriage was foundering, as she began re-asserting herself in small but significant ways.

> I started doing things for myself more. And he [husband] wanted to pressure me, put me back into that so-called wife role, which I was resisting more and more. And then, with my grandmother's death, he figured he'd lost control. When I would talk to her, I would get in line again. . . . The last couple of years, my girlfriends kept telling me, over and over again, I could do it [leave him]. I was too dependent to do anything. And so [he] saved me by leaving.

We might note, however, that he did not leave until she got herself into a hospital, so we might ask who left first?

But even more significantly, she had to change her relationship to her parents, both her birth mother, who she saw only occasionally and not happily, and her grandparents. The defining moment in relation to her birth mother came after her grandmother died, on the day of a nephew's funeral, when she realized both the price and the return for being the "good girl" she had been trying to be. It happened to be the same day for which she had made a prior commitment to go to her first Passages Conference with a new friend from one of the Lesbian groups. Passages is an annual regional community conference "for, by, and about Lesbians," that offers a wide range of workshops on topics and issues that affect Lesbians. Her mother and son pressured her to come to both the funeral and the wake, which would have caused her to miss the conference.

This day turned out to be a pivotal one for Laura, forcing her to choose between her newfound sense of self and the demands of her family. Negotiating this boundary, represented by the conference, on the one hand, and the funeral, on the other, was enacted by splitting her time between the two events. Even this was considered an inadequate demonstration of loyalty to the family. "My son called me and I could tell he was drunk. Apparently [my mother] had been crying to him. He was going to straighten things out. He could handle me. Everyone could handle me before! I was the scapegoat, the rug, the doormat." On the pay phone at the shelter, she listened to her son say, "Well, if you can't make it . . . for the whole day, don't ask any of the family for any help!' And that hit me. I stood there and I looked around at the walls of the shelter, and when I went back to the phone, he'd hung up. I think he realized what he'd said!"

On the day of the funeral she went first to the conference in the morning, "still sort of unsure of my sexuality," and the first workshop she attended was on changing sexuality "which was something I hadn't even thought about." The main thing she got out of that discussion was "that you don't have to be sleeping with women in order to be a Lesbian. It's more a way of thinking and being in the world."

From there her friend took her to the funeral and her unanticipated big test: "I was face to face across the aisle with my mother. She looked so miserable. . . . I was getting ready to take a step toward her, and it hit me that if I do this, I'll be hooked. So I stepped back, and I let the usher handle her. . . . And I would say that's when I became a true member of Al-Anon. That's when I became a person and started to do things on my own, instead of being pulled in." We might say it was also an act of rejecting the gender norm that requires women always to be responsive to others' needs first, regardless of their own needs. It was certainly her first conscious step away from requiring herself to be the "fixer" in a situation she felt would trap the fixer.

After the funeral, she and her friend returned to the conference and the next workshop she attended was on the transpersonal approach to death and dying. What she remembers from that is "that you don't have to be forced into emotion that you don't feel, for show. It was perfect for me." She thought about all the discussions she'd been hearing in the various gay groups about how difficult it was for them to go home for the holidays, and realized:

> Here I was in the area with the nucleus of my family, and I didn't want to be around them. But it's a guilt trip because society tells you you're supposed to want to be around your family at holiday. And I didn't want to be near them. So I had to come to terms with that. And to terms with myself and society. Because so many of the things were the opposite of the things I was supposed to want. . . . So it was a lot of realization.

A realization, in other words, that another socially constructed expectation about family may not be for her own good. Finally, at the conference dance at the end of the day, revelation came:

> The first record they played was "We Are Family." And then it hit me that I had a larger family, and I didn't have to depend on my nuclear family. . . . I said to [my friend], "You know, that's what my life should be like." Everything in its time and place. And the next time I went back to the [WW] clinic . . . I said, "OK [counselor], I know what I am now. I'm a Lesbian. I'm going to need a therapist, I'm going to need. . . " He said, "Whoa! whoa! Coming out is a process not an event! Slow down." So that was the beginning of my coming out. Especially when I realized that you don't have to sleep with a woman to be a Lesbian. And you see how hung up I was on the myths, and what those feed on. I think that was the turning point.

Her process of redefining herself ("from the inside out") began with actively rejecting the very norms that helped her to land in "the pit," and that simplistic prescriptions for homeless women would have them adopt: be nice, be responsible (for others), go back to your family, be a good (heterosexual) wife. And above all, don't be a deviant! She decided to "be" a Lesbian because that community felt like it met a need to belong somewhere after her alienation from "the world that I was no longer in."

Perhaps most painful was the reassessment of her relationship with her beloved grandparents. Of these, her reflections on her relationship with her grandmother reveal the greatest reinterpretation. In describing the importance of her grandmother to her in her childhood, Laura remembers shopping trips, "hours and hours reading to me or playing games with me," going to museums and movies. "Mommy" hadn't believed in physical punishment, she believed in talking. Her grandmother also protected her: "I did a lot of little mischievous things and my grandmother would back me up. Yeah, she was my backup." Her grandmother was also the peacemaker in the family, getting Laura to wear a hated dress that her mother had bought her for graduation and to apologize for having disrespected her mother on another occasion. It was her grandmother who paved the way for the rest of the family's acceptance of her husband by working on her grandfather, who then insisted that they both come to the family dinners so the rest of the family would get to know him. "My grandmother . . . was just a cushion for me. She was everything between me and the world." She now realizes "this gave her psychological control too. That wasn't bad, that was good," referring to her child-rearing style. But in referring to this relationship during the trials of her marriage, she says, "I know when I would call my grandmother when I would get so mad at [my husband], she would say, 'Well, when you get married, it's for better or worse.' I think that's what kept me there so long. I think [my husband] had to get out while he could 'cause with my grandmother gone, his control was gone. When I would talk to her, *I would get in line again.*"

Much the same kind of reassessment is revealed in her descriptions of her grandfather: When she was a child he would brag about her mechanical aptitude, and when times were good when she was a teenager, he would "toss me a hundred dollars and say, 'Go buy yourself something.'" They would play games that involved some form of competition, often about outsmarting each other. But when she married a white man, her grandfather expressed his displeasure by asking her to not come home. So she moved out. Again, her grandmother brokered a reconciliation.

After her grandmother died, Laura tried to do for "Daddy" what "Mommy" had done for him, cooking, and so forth, for him on her lunch hours and evenings. But "he was playing his games, too. He wanted to control everything.

And I said, 'Daddy, I don't have time to play the games anymore.' He knew one way of relating to people, and we didn't have Mommy for the cushion anymore." When he first learned that her husband had left her, her grandfather said, "'He wasn't worth anything. You need to forget him and go on with your life.' And Daddy expected me to just turn and go. . . . 'Maybe you'll have more time for me.' And I said, 'Daddy, it doesn't work that way.'"

Other elements in their relationship were revealed when she was in the "mental ward." He came with her mother to visit her, but they spent the whole time berating her for not doing what they thought she should have been doing: "If I would go to church I wouldn't be in there, and I just wanted sympathy, and they weren't going to give me any sympathy." That was the last time they came to see her while she was there. Although her mother did most of the talking, her grandfather was a silent partner to this put-down.

Before she went into the homeless shelter, a friend talked Laura into asking her grandfather if she could stay with him for a few days. He stalled, wanting to ask the resident manager, because of the rules for the senior citizen's housing where he lived. She interprets this as "his chance to get me where he wanted to. So that I would be grateful. It was a controlling thing. . . . I just didn't want to have to listen to that all the time. It's sort of like, 'I got myself into this, I have to get myself out' was more or less the way I felt." She told him to just "forget it." Thus the family was both cushion and chain. As Liebow writes about the women that he met in the shelters: "Family relationships are almost as likely to be sources of pain and rejection as pleasure and support . . . relationships with parents are often unsatisfying, even destructive. . . . Anger and resentment appear to be the basic stuff of these relationships; power, control, and sometimes money are the major issues" (Liebow, 1993, p. 112).

Near the end of our interview, Laura said "I went through a transformation. That's the process that I went through." To us (the authors), Laura's story suggests a leap from a familiar cushion that has chains attached, to an unknown and possibly unchained new cushion. We all need cushions. The question is, "At what cost?" For most of us, the fear of abandoning the rules we grew up with, even when they don't serve us well, prevents us from trying to find new ways to live. Laura used her fall into "the pit" to begin this process of reinventing herself and the rules she would live by.

Within 3 years after leaving the shelter (in 1992), Laura won her disability case, got into a subsidized apartment, won back custody of her grandson, completed her AA degree at Montgomery County College, entered the BA program at the University of Maryland with a double major in psychology and computer science, and started volunteering at the Whitman Walker Clinic and at the Passages Conference. She has also testified before the state legislature on homelessness and has been invited by several organizations to speak on the topic. She thinks she may want to become a WebMaster.

DISCUSSION

The path from middle-class security to homelessness and back is not unique to Laura, but often it is overlooked. Why is that? And why is the master narrative constructed as it is? We propose some possible answers.

The construction of a master narrative serves a social purpose; A social construction such as the master narrative about homeless people can serve several purposes. One is to demarcate the boundary between the acceptable and unacceptable; *una frontera* (a border) that threatens to close behind you should you lose your way and blunder over to the wrong side, however inadvertently that may happen. This narrative helps to keep people "in line," in lives that help maintain the illusion of social order and justice. A narrative like that also provides a priori assumptions that undergird the politics and policies of homelessness. If homeless people are without homes because of their psychological, intellectual, and characterological flaws, then their thinking and perceptions about homelessness can be discounted. They need not participate in the public dialogue about finding solutions to homelessness, and their priorities or perspectives would not carry any weight if they were heard. Thus, policies on homelessness can be formulated from the perspective of those who are not homeless; This perspective will be influenced by a domiciled self-interest—and the interpretation of the electorate's interests—as much as the interests of homeless people. Thus, we need to be aware of who the stakeholders are in the perpetuation of the master narrative about homeless people.

If stories like Laura's are not unique, then why do we not hear them? Do people who are not politicians, not bureaucrats, and not social workers have a stake in maintaining the master narrative? If so, one reason may be that a story involving a "fall from grace" is threatening to all whose sense of security is predicated on the belief that "it can't happen to me." Thus, it is easier to believe that those who suffer drastic drops in status must somehow have brought it on themselves, than to believe that it could happen to anyone, and therefore to oneself. Homeless women are aware of this dynamic. As one homeless woman told Liebow (1993) about the people who work in the shelters:

> Staff people and volunteers are scared of us. They think they have a decent life because they are decent people, because they're clean and honest and hardworking. [To them] homeless women are homeless because they're the opposite—dirty and dishonest and lazy. But most of us don't look like that, are not like that, and that really scares them. . . . What makes them so scary is that the people in them are so ordinary and look like everybody else. . . . The staff were afraid that they themselves were not as far from being homeless as they would like to be. (Liebow, 1993, p, 129)

Another said, "There was this general consensus, that if you were homeless, you must have caused it to happen" (Liebow, 1993, p, 137).

This phenomenon of thinking in terms of a just world has been documented in the social psychological literature. The "just-world" myth—not only do people get what they deserve but also they must have deserved whatever they got—is harder to sustain in the face of a story that demonstrates that the same individual who "fell from grace" can also recover, go to college, successfully raise a child, and take an active role in community affairs.

It may also be that most of the women who experience this loss of status do not particularly want to reveal what and how it happened. If they buy into the "just-world" perspective, then they may see it as shameful, thinking that somehow they were to blame. To acknowledge this part of their history might be experienced as a further loss of status. It may be that most women who have this experience wish to deny it.

Also, most of the sociological literature on homelessness focuses on:

> the characterological problems the homeless are thought to have (e.g., cultural deprivation, genetic inferiority, and mental depravity), the problems they are thought to pose for the larger community (e.g., crime, contamination, demoralization, and welfare), or the problems associated with their material survival (e.g., food, shelter, and clothing). Their inner life . . . is rarely a matter of concern. (Snow & Anderson, 1987, p. 1337)

Although written in 1987, this statement remains mostly true. Elliot Liebow's (1993) recent book, *Tell Them Who I Am,* is a notable exception. The stories, however, are there for the telling: stories about the strength, courage, determination, resourcefulness, and mutual concern of people without homes who wage a daily struggle to remain fully human.

Finally, this is a story of redemption through transformation. Although it may be the case that this is not the master narrative for all women, the redemption story is a central narrative for some people whose lives are distorted by poverty, prejudice, and other social ills, whose lives are constrained and bent out of shape by a social system designed to advance the interests of some at the expense of others.

NOTES

1. "A very few women were able to make this transition [from homelessness to a place of one's own] entirely on their own efforts. More women made this transition with the assistance of subsidized housing. Unfortunately, very few homeless women can expect to get jobs that will allow them to support themselves, and very few can expect to

come to the top of the list for housing assistance" (Liebow, 1993, p. 231). In both these respects, Laura is unusual.

2. See Hancock (1990) and PJ McGann (1995) for expositions of this process.

REFERENCES

Burt, M. R. (1992). *Over the edge: The growth of homelessness in the 1980s.* New York: Russell Sage.

Friedan, B. (1963). *The feminine mystique.* New York: W. W. Norton.

Hancock, E. (1990). *The girl within.* New York: Fawcett Columbine.

Legal Services. (1991). Poverty comes home: Women and children in the 90s. Special Issue of *Clearinghouse Review, 24* (4).

Liebow, E. (1993). *Tell them who I am: The lives of homeless women.* New York: The Free Press.

McGann, PJ. (1995). *The ballfields of our hearts: Tomboys, femininity, and female development.* Unpublished doctoral dissertation, Brandeis University.

National Coalition for the Homeless. (May, 1998). *NCH fact sheet #3.* Washington, D.C.: author.

Snow, D. A., & Anderson, L. (1987). Identity work among the homeless: The verbal construction and avowal of personal identities. *American Journal of Sociology, 92* (6), 1336–71.

Stewart, A. J. (1978). A longitudinal study of coping styles of self-defining and socially defined women. *Journal of Consulting & Clinical Psychology, 46,* 1079–84.

Zorza, J. (1991). Woman battering: A major cause of homelessness. *Clearinghouse Review, 25* (4).

One of the Family, or Just
the Mexican Maid's Daughter?:
Belonging, Identity, and Social Mobility

> "We just love her! She's like one of the family and she just adores our little Carol! We don't know what we'd do without her! We don't think of her as a servant!"

$\mathcal{T}$HIS QUOTE FROM ALICE CHILDRESS'S BOOK *Like One of the Family . . . Conversations from a Domestic's Life,* depicts a common theme found in domestic service—the faithful old servant taken care of in his or her old age, or the domestic marrying into the employer's family, are versions of the rags-to-riches stories found in domestic service. Even though the soap-opera romances and inheritances are unlikely occurrences in the United States, the lore is so embedded in the narrative of the immigrant maid that even her daughter is confronted by questions of belonging and identity. Is she indeed "one of the family" or does she remain the Mexican maid's daughter?

Assimilation and the assumption of sameness lie at the core of the master narrative that outlines a one-directional journey of integration and eventual success of immigrants in the United States. According to the master narrative, the script rationalizes hard work with economic upward mobility, while the transformation from immigrant to a member of the American family occurs through equal opportunity and a democratic process within a social structure of meritocracy. While numerous social scientists (e.g., Mills, 1943; Omi & Winant, 1987; Steinberg, 1981; Winant, 1994) have challenged the basic assumptions supporting an assimilationist framework and have pointed to the serious limitations for analyzing a gendered, racialized ethnic and class-based immigrant experience, mainstream academics continue to argue its legitimacy. Even the master narrative for European immigrants has been challenged by both social scientists and historians researching *whiteness* (Frankenberg, 1993; Feagin and Vera, 1995; Ignatiev, 1995) and gender (Hondagneu-Sotelo, 1994). In his book, *The Ethnic Myth,*

Steven Steinberg (1981) calls into question the stock story of the successful immigrant experience in the United States:

> In the first place, the problem is stated falsely when it is assumed that all immigrant groups started out on the bottom. In point of fact, ethnic groups in the United States come out of very different historical and material circumstances, and therefore different outcomes may only reflect different beginnings. Secondly, depending on the time of their arrival and the patterns of settlement, immigrant groups encountered different opportunities, as well as different external obstacles to their economic advancement. The experiences of the immigrant generation, furthermore, tended to establish a foundation that placed next generations at greater or lesser advantage.

Despite important critical scholarship, the master script remains essentially unchallenged in the public mind. The basic themes of assimilation, acculturation, melting pots, and salad bowls are widely purveyed by popular culture, particularly in literature and movies. The mass media and the education system echo and reinforce the master narrative, scripting a story that serve the interests of politicians, opponents of affirmative action and bilingual education, and provides ideological sound bites and slogans that shape the thinking and decision making in key equal protection legislation.

This chapter draws from the narrative of a young Chicana woman who experienced life as a Mexican maid's daughter while living in her mother's employer's home. Although her life story could easily be "read" through the lens of the master narrative on immigration, she offers a counternarrative that rejects assimilation and embraces biculturalism, retains family and community ties in her journey toward social mobility, points to white privileges gained from oppressive working conditions, and questions the adage that she and her mother are "just like one of the family." Before turning to her story of a specific incident that revealed the tensions and contradictions of belonging, identity, and social mobility, an overview of the master narrative applied to the Mexican American experience is presented.

BARRIOS AND BORDERS IN THE CONSTRUCTION OF THE MEXICAN EXPERIENCE

Currently, there are two popular Mexican American accounts of the master narrative: The first is contained in Richard Rodriguez's autobiographical memoir, *Hunger of Memory*. The son of Mexican immigrant parents, Rodriguez began school in Sacramento, California, knowing little English and triumphing as a scholarship student. He characterized his life as a journey from a socially disadvantaged child to a middle-class American man (Rodriguez, 1982). Assimilation frames the entire account and justifies his turn away from his mother tongue, Mexican culture, and eventually from his parents. The second is Linda Chavez's book, *Out of the Barrio* (1991). The leading spokesperson for the neoconservative perspective on Latinos, Chavez characterized the barrio as self-imposed segregation by which Latinos, especially Mexican Americans, have been duped by Latina and Latino politicians, activists, and academics (which she refers to as power brokers in an attempt to appropriate and distort Acuna's critique of party politics).

"Out of the Barrio" is a metaphor used to represent the cultural, social, and economic move out of ethnic neighborhoods, organizations, and political alliances and into what Chavez referred to as "the mainstream" by which she clearly means white neighborhoods, white organizations, and white-dominated political alliances. Like other neoconservatives who claim ethnic minority roots, such as D'Souza (1991), Sowell (1983), and Steele (1990), programs, facilities, institutions, and businesses that are controlled or owned by Latinos, Blacks, Native Americans, or Asian Americans have been redefined to mean "separatism," while "integration" apparently refers to white-owned and -controlled "mainstream" businesses that are "inclusive" of nonwhites as clients and employees.

Chavez and Rodriguez are important spokespersons scripting the master narrative for Latinos, precisely because they have gained tremendous "visibility" as Latinos. Even though Rodriguez has been widely criticized, and a 1992 issue of *Hispanic Magazine* described Chavez as "the woman everyone loves to hate," their positions have been bolstered by Anglo journalists and writers pursuing Latino themes. These include recent books on the "Hispanic experience" by Ilan Stavans (1995), Earl Shorris (1992), and Peter Skerry (1993) that employ similar constructions of the master narrative. Chavez (1991) argued that Mexican Americans and other Latinos are no different from European immigrants "(w)hose appearance, culture, and language set them apart from previous groups that settled in the United States—[and] had gradually been accepted into the social and economic mainstream" (p. 2). But they went wrong because—unlike the French, Italians, Greeks, and Jews—Mexican Americans have insisted that they are a permanently disadvantaged minority in need of civil rights, including the Voting Rights Act, bilingual education, and affirmative action. Chavez strongly opposed civil rights for Mexican Americans and other Latinos on the basis that assimilation is the road to economic and political salvation not government policies advocating special entitlement.

Herein lies the significance of the notion "out of the barrio." The "barrio" was once seen as a residential area, produced by Anglo exclusionary practices, populated by poor and working-class Chicanas and Chicanos over generations, where one found Mexican curio shops, bakeries, restaurants, and other Mexican-owned businesses, as well as Catholic and Evangelist churches offering bilingual services; and where we would expect (or at least hope!) that the residents were represented on the local school board, city council, and among city employees, including teachers, police officers, fire fighters, and managers. This barrio has been distorted by conservative social scientists pushing rational choice theory, the culture of poverty, economic theories of middle-class flight, sociobiological and IQ theories. In the neoconservative revision, the barrio is indicative of a "ghetto mentality" produced by illegitimate demands for civil rights, affirmative action, and economic access.

In the following section, I present a counternarrative to the immigrant experience contained in the "out of the barrio" and "hunger of memory" metaphors. The excerpt that follows is part of a larger narrative of the life that a Mexican maid's daughter lived with her mother in the employer's home. Her narrative is focused on her experiences growing up in the intimate space of an upper-middle-class Anglo family in Los Angeles in the 1970s and her struggle to claim an identity and sense of belonging as she moves back and forth from the social world of the Mexican immigrant worker and their employers. Unlike the Mexican immigrant workers in the community who toil as maids, gardeners, or valets at the local country club, the maid's daughter has the opportunities to gain access to the employer's family—eating dinner with them at the dining-room table, going to school with their children, and attending events at the country club. Her recollections of growing up in the employer's home capture complex and seldom explored issues of belonging, culture, identity, and social mobility that are glossed over and submerged by the assimilationist master narrative of the immigrant experience. The setting facilitates a microanalysis of issues that occur nationally at a macrostructural level, including the tension between maintaining ideas of family/peoplehood while socially located in different positions of privilege and power. The counternarrative challenges the master narrative's persistent emphasis on assimilation, rather than "integration," "incorporation," or "inclusiveness" in the political, economic, and social life in the United States. As the maid's daughter moves between social worlds, rather than rejecting her Mexicanness and becoming assimilated, she challenges notions of "out of the barrio" by linking privileges and oppression in the same neighborhood and society.

I met Olivia María Salazar Gomez[1] after a conference presentation I made in El Paso, Texas. She told me that her mother, Carmen, was employed as a live-in domestic and thus she wanted to know more about my research on Chicana private household workers. The following year we met again, and our conversation that afternoon became the beginning of a decade-long life-story project about Olivia's life as the maid's daughter. The narrative has now filled more than two dozen tapes and consists of more than 500 pages of transcription.

At our first formal interview session, Olivia began her narrative with the story of how Carmen began working as a domestic for a middle-class family in Juarez, Mexico, earning about eight dollars a week when she was 15. Lured by the potential for making higher wages, Carmen crossed the border and became a live-in maid in the country club area in El Paso. In her late twenties she accompanied other Mexican women and their male cousin to Los Angeles to find better-paying jobs. She found employment in the garment industry but quickly left the sweatshop and sought employment in domestic service through an employment agency. She was immediately hired as a live-in maid in a very exclusive neighborhood in Los Angeles. After Olivia was born, Carmen returned to Juarez with her baby. Carmen retained her network in Los Angeles and returned a few years later. She arranged for a live-in position in Los Angeles that accepted her 3-year-old child in the household. During the next 15 years, Olivia and her mother lived with the Smith family. During this time, Olivia spent her summers in Mexico with her extended family and during the school year had regular contact with her mother's friends living in San Fernando and with the other Mexican immigrant women employed as live-in maids in the same neighborhood.

Olivia and her mother shared the maid's quarters, a room that was located next to the kitchen. Although Carmen had originally negotiated a live-in arrangement with the Smiths, their financial situation changed and they were no longer able to offer her full-time employment. While living at the Smiths, Carmen began doing day work throughout the neighborhood. Carmen worked every Saturday for the Smiths, as well as doing daily chores such as picking up, doing dishes, and ironing every evening when she returned from her day work. Instead of paying her a weekly salary, the Smiths offered to enroll Olivia in the same private school as their daughters and to pay the tuition. Even though Olivia did not attend the elite private schools past grade school, the Smiths and Carmen never renegotiated the terms of their relationship. The requests Mrs. Smith made as an employer were not distinguished from those made as a friend and Carmen's wage labor became diffused with the labor of love. Mrs. Smith continued to include Olivia in her annual shopping sprees for school clothes and Christmas and birthday presents. Everyday life with the Smith family blurred Carmen's boundaries between work and family life, and Olivia was frequently caught straddling the two worlds.

Carmen continued to work a combination of live-in and day work throughout the 15 years that Olivia lived with the Smiths. Consequently, Olivia became known throughout the neighborhood as the maid's daughter. Carmen's relationship with her employers shaped their families' interaction with Olivia. As Olivia got older, her mother increased her working hours, leaving her daughter alone with the Smith family. Olivia's involvement with the Smith family broadened to include dinner with their friends, attending the country club, and inclusion in a middle-class lifestyle unknown to her other family members. However, Olivia was not always included and did not receive the same opportunities as the Smiths' own children. Olivia understood that the additional time her mother spent working for employers was time they were not able to spend together. When the Smith children did not pick up their dishes, clothes, and left trash,

Olivia remained conscious of the fact that her mother was expected to pick it up. Even though Mr. and Mrs. Smith referred to Olivia and her mother as "one of the family," Olivia knew they were not.

In organizing the transcription into a coherent and readable narrative, I have identified several reoccurring themes in the construction of her life as the maid's daughter: belonging, identity, culture, and social mobility. Learning the rules that designate her place in social situations is a theme that looms large in Olivia's early memories of entering into the employers' world. These rules defined where she sat, what she played with, what language she spoke in, and the limits of her activity within an employer's home. The classic adage found in domestic service, "just like one of the family," was applied to the maid's daughter, and Olivia was expected to juggle the inconsistent message of behaving like one of the employer's children without having all the privileges, as well as knowing when she was expected to assume the mannerisms and place of the maid's daughter. However, the employer's insistence that Olivia and Carmen were "just like one of the family" posed the additional challenge of maintaining their own family relationships of daughter and mother. Throughout Olivia's narrative are accounts of incidents in which mother and daughter felt devoured by the demands of the employer's family and the constant fear that each would lose the other to the employer's family—Carmen accusing Olivia of wanting to be the Smiths' daughter and Olivia accusing her mother of preferring the companionship of the employers to spending time with her own daughter. Issues of identity and belonging emerged throughout her life as Olivia learned the educational and cultural skills necessary to function successfully in the employer's world and yet tried to maintain her cultural skills and community ties to her family in Mexico and the Mexican immigrant community in Los Angeles. Olivia's desire for social mobility was structured around her commitment to retain a Mexican identity, Spanish language competency, and a Chicanismo perspective that advocates collective struggle through ethnic politics.

SOURCES OF TENSION IN THE COUNTERNARRATIVE

The maid's daughter is faced with the Americanization process that every immigrant encounters yet her narrative differs dramatically from the Latino male story by Richard Rodriguez who constructed his autobiography as the classic Americanization process that requires separation from family and culture. Despite superficial similarities—both were children of Mexican immigrants, graduated from prestigious colleges, enjoyed successful careers, achieved middle-class success, and described the high price of "making it" in middle-class America— Olivia's narrative would not be characterized as "the poignant journey of a 'minority student' who pays the cost of his social assimilation and academic success with a painful alienation—from her past, parents, and culture."[2] Rather than concluding that estrangement from family and community is inevitable, Olivia's narrative locates sources of tension in contradictions between an ideology of assimilation and social, political, and economic practices that exclude Mexicans and limit both their access for resources and their feelings of acceptance and sense of belonging as Americans. Unlike Rodriguez, who attacks bilingual education, affirmative action, and ethnic studies, Olivia advocates ethnically based collective action, as well as government programs and legislation aimed at structural issues rather than finding solace in individual change and personal transformation.

As the daughter of a Mexican immigrant employed as a live-in domestic, Olivia was exposed to the master narrative of the successful immigrant in her school and home environment. However, she was simultaneously immersed in the stark realities of the Mexican immigrant workers employed as live-in maids, nannies, and gardeners throughout the upper-middle-class neighborhood where she lived. Interaction with Mexican garment workers living in San Fernando exposed her to evidence counter to the ethnic myth and social mobility. This unique position within the employer's home and neighborhood clearly afforded her the opportunity for developing double consciousness: "It is a peculiar sensation, this double-consciousness, this sense of always looking at one's self through the eyes of others, of measuring one's soul by the tape of a world that looks on in amused contempt and pity" (Du Bois, 1903, p. 3). Her continued participation in a Mexican immigrant community enabled her to juxtapose firsthand knowledge about the lived experiences of Mexicans working and living in the United States. Unlike Richard Rodriguez, Olivia does not internalize contempt or self-pity but constructs a life incorporating both her experiences and knowledge about white upper-middle-class family life and working-class Mexican-immigrant family life in the United States. She acquired cultural competence in the middle-class without developing a "hunger for memory" or desire to get "out of the barrio." She remains part of her community of origin.

Olivia's narrative describes an ongoing negotiation of place and belonging in the social world of her mother's employers while working to maintain an ethnic identity based on Spanish language competency and meaningful interaction with the Mexican community. A major source of struggle throughout her story is the blurred boundaries between employee and employer family. As their interaction with the Smith family develops, the employer's claim that Carmen and Olivia are "just like one of the family," and mother and daughter fear losing each other to the employer's family. On the one hand, Olivia has to compete for her mother's time, attention, and energy against the endless demands and needs of the employer's family. On the other hand, Carmen fears that Olivia is ashamed of being the maid's daughter and really desires to be the Smiths' daughter.

I have selected an excerpt from the transcript that captures the tensions created in the "like one of the family" relation of domestic service. The incident that Olivia describes takes place when she is away at college and no longer living with the Smiths. The excerpt is Olivia's narrative account of a fight between Mrs. Smith and Carmen over work arrangements. Finding herself with the additional work and responsibility of caring for her grandchildren, Mrs. Smith gives Carmen an ultimatum to increase her work hours or vacate her room in their house so another live-in worker can be hired. However, Mrs. Smith does not offer to increase Carmen's pay or to compensate her fully for the loss of wages she is currently making as a day worker in other employers' homes. The disagreement concludes with Carmen quitting her job and moving out of the Smiths' house. The incident establishes the class issues that underline the illusion that Olivia and her mother are "just like one of the family." When the employers attempt to continue their fictitious familial relationship with the maid's daughter in the absence of her mother's employment, the ambiguous and blurred boundaries between family and worker become sharply and clearly defined. The incident unleashes concealed feelings and attitudes about the paternalistic nature of the mistress-maid relationship, particularly when the same action results in an employer's expectation of gratitude and the employee's accusations of exploitation. The fight becomes a significant point in Olivia's relationship with the Smiths as she questions the realities of family belonging and identity represented in the adage "just like one of the family."

I got so pissed off when my mother told me she had this fight with Mrs. Smith. I rushed home and took everything out of the closet. I moved her. Mr. Smith came home. I remember the disgust I felt towards Mr. Smith when we were moving out of the house. I just remember seeing Mr. Smith get out of his fucking Cadillac, come in, and say hello to me. I didn't even answer him. David (employer's son) was so upset that he was crying. Jane (employer's daughter) was crying. David left and didn't come home for a week because he was so disgusted about this fight and my mom leaving. David more than anybody was upset about it.

When my mom told me about this big fight with Mrs. Smith, I said, "The bottom line is that Mrs. Smith thinks that you are her servant."

My mother said, "Oh no! They don't. They love us."

She even tried to separate us and said, "They may not love me as much as they love you." When I was critical of the Smiths, my mom agreed with me most of the time. She never really protected them. But she always said, "Oh, Mrs. Smith really cares about you."

I said, "That's irrelevant. She cares about me because she failed as a mother. All her kids aren't doing shit so she's got to have pride in someone. So it doesn't have anything to do with me—my personality or who I am. It has to do with her. Her inability to be a good parent. So she's got to take credit for something. So she might as well take credit for me."

I discussed the racist comments the Smiths made with her and said,

"They don't love me. This is what they really think. They think they are always doing me a big goddamn favor and they are not doing me any favors. You have earned everything that I am. They haven't given me an education. They haven't given me shit. You got cheated for it."

When I told my mother that, she started crying. She felt that I was the big bad guy. I was insensitive and that I didn't realize that she was doing this all for me. She felt I should have realized that.

Mr. Smith called me at my dorm on campus and asked me to lunch. He called because Mrs. Smith was really upset because I hadn't come home and didn't call. She saw my car at home in Liberty Place. She knew I was coming home but I didn't go to her house.

Mr. Smith picked me up in his fucking Mercedes. Here I was involved in MEChA at the university and involved in all this political activity and I think, "Oh my god, get out of my life." We went to the BelAir Country Club for lunch and he explained how Mrs. Smith was really sorry.

I got into it with him and told him I didn't give a shit. He tried to tell me that my mother and Mrs. Smith were friends forever. They had been best friends. Mrs. Smith talked to him about this friendship that she had with my mother. Like all friends, they had gotten into an argument. This was just one of their arguments.

I said, "Well, I don't think it's some little argument! And it affects me! You guys are all a bunch of liars. You tell me that this is my home and that you all love me very much. But then I'm away at college, where I'm supposed to be doing well, and I turn around and hear this happening. I have to come home and move my mother out."

He tried to tell me how I needed to understand that their house was always going to be my home. "Mrs. Smith doesn't want you to feel like you don't have a place to go and you don't have a home. You have to understand that they are going to get into arguments. It was just a matter of business and you have to separate the business from the emotion."

I said, "She is my mother and nobody's going to take that away from me."

He told me, "I understand that your mother wants to make money. But you need to understand that Mrs. Smith felt really abandoned."

I said, "Wait a minute. My mother is like below the poverty line. And you're trying to tell me that my mother, who is 50, should not be interested in making money? Is that what you're saying to me?"

He was just taken aback. Mr. Smith never dealt with me on an intellectual level. We always had one-sentence conversations. It was never a conversation. He never heard me put together more than one or two sentences. So it was really devastating for him to see me be articulate whatsoever. He was just really surprised.

I remember him just being more shocked and saying, "Well, what does your mother need the money for?"

I said, "What do you need your money for?"

I said, "My mother has just as much right as you do to provide for the future for herself and for retirement. She's never had social security."

That was the issue. They didn't feel she needed it. What was the purpose? She could always retire with them—like that's what she really wanted. Mr. and Mrs. Smith were pathetic. "Oh yes, Carmen and you are just going to get old and live out your life in this house with us." They made it seem as if it were this lifelong affair. I really resented that they had made a decision about what my relationship was going to be with them. I had no intention of it being that way.

I was really pissed off that my mother humored them that way. My mother never gave them any sense of having another life: "No. I'm going to have a life for myself and I'm going to retire with my sisters in Mexico." I think she put too much emphasis on the differences between her and her sisters and how accustomed she was to life in LA. This only set her up to be exploited even more because the threat of her leaving was not prevalent. I mean it was just nonexistent. She never said, "Oh, I'm going to leave." She always encouraged them to think that she would be with them forever, "Oh yeah, we'll stay together and drink wine till we're eighty. Sit in the Jacuzzi in the evenings."

The argument between Mrs. Smith and Carmen stripped away the facade of familial relationships and placed class issues at the center of their relationship. Carmen's position as the domestic (not a family member) precipitates the move out of the Smith house. The family analogy is completely disassembled in Carmen's decision to move out of the maid's quarters in order for Mrs. Smith to hire another live-in worker. A family member cannot simply be replaced by another individual, but workers are routinely replaced; and in this case one domestic is replaced by another Latina immigrant woman. Mr. Smith's representation of the conflict between Mrs. Smith and Carmen as an argument between friends indicates the degree to which the economic realities of domestic service have been made invisible. Mrs. Smith does not consider the option of offering Carmen additional pay for additional hours because the familial characterization of their relationship has erased the labor involved in household work. Like many employment situations that are characterized in familial terms, Carmen finds herself faced with an employer's request that has blurred her job description and confused paid labor done as an employee with unpaid labor done as a friend. The informality of the terms of employment is further aggravated when familial terms cloud the boundaries of time on and time off, as well as labor of love with wage labor. In the process of redefining her work from wage labor to labor of love, Carmen's manual labor becomes invisible. The personalism embedded in the characterization of the work relationship in familial terms assures that the labor will not only remain shadow work but also unpaid labor. "Personalism camouflages work conditions which become distorted and unintelligible within the context of the interpersonal relationships between domestics and employers. Employers' refusal to relate to domestics' concerns as workers' rights distorts the real conditions of their inter-action" (Romero, 1992, p. 123). Carmen experiences her labor interpreted through a sexist lens that challenges housework as "real" work.

The invisibility of Carmen's paid labor is further manifested in Mr. Smith's question about Carmen's financial needs. The question captures a popular gen-dered narrative of immigration that denies the presence of Mexican women as immigrants and as workers. Mr. Smith's question appears absurd because Car-men is an immigrant women in her fifties with no social security benefits, a sin-gle mother, helping to send Olivia to college. However, Mr. Smith does not perceive Carmen as an employee selling her wage labor, but rather as a servant under his care. The promise to care for Carmen after retirement is consistent with the reported behavior of past employers in domestic service and fits into the larger practice of characterizing domestics as family. Images of master-servant and mistress-maid legacies depict the faithful old servant taken care of in old age or the young, single, attractive domestic marrying into the employer's family. Promises of economic security and advancement are so common that the "rags-to-riches" stories are part of the folklore in domestic service. Although the promise to care for her in old age appears inappropriate, Olivia concludes that he actually does believe that Carmen will be with the Smith family for the rest of her life, retiring with him and his wife. But this is a fantasy. The United States is not a feudalistic society but a capitalistic one. Employers are not masters re-sponsible for their serfs and servants in their old age. As a wage laborer, Carmen is responsible for her own livelihood. "Under capitalism, employers' gifts or promises of a reward for employees' loyalty are not the same as the obligation a master had to care for his servants. The employee's involvement in the interper-sonal relationships is a gamble" (Romero, 1992, p. 122). Olivia not only chal-lenges his "promise" to care for Carmen in her old age but also points to the fact that he is not currently demonstrating good faith because he does not pay social security or provide health benefits.

Like similar reported systems of gifts and obligations operating between employers and domestics, the pattern operates as a strategy of oppression (Co-ley, 1981; Rollins, 1985; Romero, 1992). In Carmen's situation, the system of gifts and obligations in domestic service not only involves the everyday interaction between Carmen and Mrs. Smith but also involves Olivia. Carmen's strong sense of obligation and loyalty to the Smiths was the result of gifts and promises made during the 15 years that Olivia lived in the Smith household, attending the same schools as their children, and in many ways was included as one of the family. While Carmen may still have strong feelings of obligation and debt, the reciprocal nature of favors is no longer present. The Smiths have not been paying Olivia's tuition for several years now and she no longer lives with them. Carmen's rejection of Mrs. Smith's request that she not only continue doing the same amount of household labor but increase her work without pay is not surprising. The inequalities in the relationship between Mrs. Smith and Carmen are central in the exchange between Olivia and Mr. Smith.

Although Olivia is away at college and is not currently living with the Smiths, she refuses to separate herself from her mother's plight and becomes involved in moving her mother out of the Smiths' house. Mr. Smith claims the fight has nothing to do with Olivia; however, she is not only implicated in the system of gifts and obligation but is expected to participate. Past arrangements to pay Olivia's grade school tuition in lieu of a salary served to decommercialize the Smith relationship and create an appearance of familial exchange. Olivia was expected to assume some of the debt of obligation and loyalty, not by doing manual labor but in emotional labor. Pressure to do emotional labor is obvious in her mother's comment, "Mrs. Smith really cares for you." Olivia also experiences direct pressure from the employers. Mr. Smith's advice that Olivia not get involved in the fight between Mrs. Smith and Carmen is a call for her loyalty to the Smiths. His request that she separate the emotional from business, requires Olivia to manipulate her personal feelings in order to make Mrs. Smith feel good about herself and her relationship with the employee's family.

However, Olivia's allegiance is with her mother. She is unwilling to engage in the emotional labor required to accept Mr. Smith's request to frame the argument as a disagreement between friends. Instead, Olivia argues that the fight is between employer and employee. Making it a labor issue lifts the veil from the fictitious familial relationships, and Olivia is able to name the paternalism and exploitation involved in the relationship. She feels the inequalities of the system of gifts and obligations and refuses to engage in emotional labor. By refusing to visit the Smith's, she acts out her rejection of the familial definition of their relationship. Unwilling to attribute her educational success to her relationship with the Smiths, Olivia calls attention to the hard work and sacrifices Carmen has made in establishing particular working conditions and relationships in order to gain access to middle-class opportunities otherwise unattainable to an immigrant Mexican working woman. In doing so, Olivia refuses to erase her mother's physical and emotional labor done as wage labor under the employment of the Smith family. In her refusal to express gratitude to the Smiths, Olivia denies them the emotional labor necessary to affirm and enhance their image of themselves as generous, nonracist, egalitarian employers, and helping the less fortunate. The refusal is also a rejection of the image of herself as needy and obliged.

Implications of the Counternarrative

In my previous research on domestic work (Romero, 1992), I explored the master narrative of the immigrant experience as it is embedded in theoretical conceptualizations of the service occupation and characterizations of workers. Maintaining myths about social mobility, the American Dream, and an American claim to meritocracy, traditional and popular writings concerning maids and madams placed assimilation at the center of the analysis. Early sociological writings on domestic service classified it as a "bridging occupation" or transitional occupation to upward mobility (Katzman, 1981; McBride, 1974; Stiger, 1946). The argument characterizing domestic service as a bridging occupation claimed that domestic service provided the work experience that rural ethnic immigrant women required to be introduced to white middle-class family life—and thus, the skills and values to assimilate and move on to higher-paying skilled jobs. Although recent research on women of color domestic workers has shown that domestic service is more accurately characterized as a ghetto occupation (Glenn, 1986), employers today still continue to rationalize the low pay, long hours, and lack of benefits as trade-offs to the Americanization that occurs within their homes.

Juxtaposing Olivia's narrative with the master narrative of immigration/assimilation identifies important conceptual issues that appear in the national dialogue on race. The ideology that shaped Mr. and Mrs. Smith's relationship with their Mexican immigrant household worker and her daughter, is the same one that informs popular opinion: If immigrants will just give up their old ways and culture, then they can become "just like one of the American family." The feelings of betrayal, anger, and abandonment that the incident between Mrs. Smith and Carmen unleashed, highlight the paternalistic nature embedded in the act of ignoring different positions of power and in attempting to create a sense of family or "oneness" without a redistribution of resources and addressing fundamental issues of autonomy or equality. The unspoken (and sometimes spoken— "America, love it or leave it" slogan) expectation of gratitude highlights important social distinctions of rights and privilege.

Unwilling to frame the fight in a familial context rather than an employer/employee dispute, Olivia was also rejecting the unconditional terms for defining her relationship with the Smith family. She refused to accept the fictitious family relationship when it involved ignoring her mother's concrete economic situation. Instead of accepting the conditions for continuing as "one of the family," Olivia responded to the Smiths with accusations of exploitation. The complex set of arrangements that developed between worker and employer reveal everyday practices in which systems of domination are embedded as well as the use of ideological constructs in maintaining illusions of meritocracy and equality in an American Dream. When these ideologies are challenged and contrary evidence is presented, members of marginalized groups are attacked as ungrateful or accused of demanding special entitlements that previous immigrants did not receive. The different economic, political, and social conditions that structured the entrance of ethnic racial groups remain absent in this ideology of the level playing field. The accumulation of wealth from past privilege is ignored.

The process of Americanization and assimilation involves an important indoctrination—not an indoctrination of the ideology and belief system, but rather the indoctrination that we can explain the distribution of resources and privileges with these concepts. In the case of Richard Rodriguez, he can blame the lack of social mobility among Mexican Americans on their unwillingness to become competent monolingual speakers, to take a public voice, and to define themselves as American men and women rather than Mexican Americans. In his narrative, Rodriguez affirms and enhances the master narrative. However, Olivia refuses to ignore the economic realities that are inconsistent with the ideology.

Although Olivia is in college and well on her way toward economic success, she refuses to break the ties with her mother. She still accepts her mother's perspective and rejects the Smiths' explanations for the disagreement. This decision to choose between family of origin and the dominant society is similar to the circumstances that many children of immigrants find themselves in as they begin to experience social mobility. As they begin to share in the privileges of the middle class, racial ethnics experience strong pressure to accept an assimilationist model attributing economic success solely to rugged individualism and denying the sacrifices made by family and the collective struggle that made new opportunities available. Acceptance of the dominant ideology provides a master narrative that places individuals as the root of social problems and assimilation as the solution.

Olivia has acquired all the cultural trappings of assimilation but chooses to retain her culture and community, thus having the bicultural abilities to function socially in more than one stratum in the United States. She is uncomfortable with being defined as a success story in the terms of the master narrative. She does not want the Smiths to be credited with her success because to do so would erase her mother's hard work and sacrifices. However, there is another important reason found in her response to Carmen's claim that "Mrs. Smith cares about her": "She cares about me because she failed as a mother. All her kids aren't doing shit so she's got to have pride in someone. So it doesn't have anything to do with me—my personality or who I am. It has to do with her. Her inability to be a good parent. So she's got to take credit for something. So she might as well take credit for me." Olivia understands that Mrs. Smith's interest in her is not her biculturalism or ties to the Mexican community, but rather her competency in white culture and success in mainstream society. Olivia is aware that Mrs. Smith knows little if anything about her extracurricular activities in MEChA and her identity as a Chicana. Mrs. Smith is not part of her political involvement on campus to increase the number of Chicano students admitted or the number of Chicano faculty and administrators. Mrs. Smith's concern is about

Mrs. Smith—her culture, her beliefs, and her issues. Olivia recognizes that Mrs. Smith's interest in taking credit is largely fueled by her own children's failures and the same level of interest would be absent if Olivia were a failure or mediocre. The message is that she is a success *despite* her culture, family, and community. The immigrant is expected to rise above family and culture, not celebrate them. In pointing to the economic successes of immigrants as evidence of ample opportunity for hard-working individuals, attention is shifted away from the contributions racial ethnics make to creating American society because of their culture, family, and community. To script the narrative of Olivia's success in college as a consequence of the cultural capital acquired from the Smiths, places assimilation as the path to success and thus fitting within the master narrative. Such a narrative highlights individualism, ignoring not only Carmen's contributions but also the important political changes in higher education resulting from the civil rights movement, namely the collective struggle for affirmative action.

The emotional exchange between Olivia and her mother, as well as between Olivia and the Smiths, captures some of the pain and anger expressed in race relations in the United States today. As an immigrant parent, Carmen recognizes that the master narrative for her daughter's success means a rupture in their relationship and a loss of family and culture. Carmen tried to distinguish her work relationship to the Smiths and encouraged Olivia to seize opportunities and enter into the Smiths' family. Mr. Smith also encouraged Olivia to separate her relationship with Mrs. Smith from the relationship that Mrs. Smith has with Carmen. However, Olivia was unwilling to separate herself from her mother. The expectation of this separation between the immigrant mother and daughter relates to the expectation that first- and second-generation Mexican Americans will not identify with their parents, family, or community. Once they move "out of the barrio" they are expected to reject the political concerns of their community and not identify with the education, housing, employment, and health issues shaping the lives of Mexican immigrants and poor Chicanos. Instead, they are expected to embrace the political agenda of a monolingual, monocultural, middle-class American and to define issues and solutions from the position of privilege.

An individualistic approach to social mobility not only blames the victim but also reaffirms the master story of social mobility as the desired immigrant experience. It marks as failures all those who remain with their community. Thus, "out of the barrio" becomes the action taken by the "good" Latinos—those who do not wish to segregate themselves in Spanish-speaking communities, attend minority-dominated schools, frequent Hispanic businesses, belong to "ethnic" organizations, and participate in civil rights issues. These "good" Latinos assimilate and are willing to integrate society by living in predominately white communities and schools, speak only English, and participate in "nonethnic" politics. The "bad" Latinos are "in the barrio" because they choose to segregate themselves from mainstream America, campaign for "ethnic" issues and causes, maintain their language, culture, and ethnic identity, and vote for representation. Chavez recognized that Latinos are more likely to win elections when they constitute a majority of the eligible voters; however, she argues that "in order for this political strategy to work, Hispanics must remain in the barrio. It is a pyrrhic victory that can be won only at the expense of the ultimate social and economic integration of Hispanics in this society." The master narrative, even when presented in "brown-face," characterizes white domination as the mainstream and as American.

Communities of color have been divided by two narratives: the *one* who succeeds by leaving their culture of origin and assimilating into the mainstream (read white America), and the one who succeeds by retaining close ties to their culture and family of origin. Consequently, the General Powells and the Richard Rodriguezes in the world are praised for their ability to achieve in white America. Their sense of belonging and identity is gained as role models of assimilation and their ethnic racial roots become fossilized footprints left behind in order to make their passage to success. The script of the master narrative includes a mandate for sameness and frames difference as the obstacle to social mobility. Consequently, immigrants and their children dive into the melting pot of America in order to become members of the American family. However, many dive into the melting pot and remain disenfranchised from the democratic process. The master narrative ignores the realities of individual and institutional racism, the abundance or scarcity of economic opportunities available at various historical periods, and the overall social and political climate that immigrants and their children encounter. Furthermore, the master narrative denies the ways that immigrants use their culture, family, and community as resources to economic mobility, as spiritual inspiration, and as the basis of meaning in their daily lives. A counternarrative rejects ethnic difference as the source of economic, political, and social problems. Individual transformation prescribed in assimilation does not eliminate structural inequalities rooted in society. The painful and emotional discussion by Olivia serves as a microcosm of these larger issues in race relations in society today. The inability to address the ways that privilege is linked with oppression keeps the focus on getting "out of the barrio" and assimilation. In refusing to be "just like one of the family" Olivia rejected an assimilationist approach. Instead, she advocates for economic opportunity for her mother—a fair wage, social security, and other employment benefits. As Olivia proclaims, "The bottom line is that Mrs. Smith thinks that you are her servant." For racial ethnics is the United States, the question becomes, "Can we ever really become one of the family, or do we always remain the servant owing gratitude to white America?" The script of the master narrative is carefully constructed using paternalistic staging, casting immigrants in a subservient role.

NOTES

1. All the names are pseudonyms.
2. Quote appears on back cover of the book *Hunger of Memory*.

REFERENCES

Chavez, L. (1991). *Out of the barrio: Toward a new politics of Hispanic assimilation*. New York: Basic Books.

Coley, S. M. (1981). "And still I rise": An exploratory study of contemporary black private household workers. Ph.D. dissertation, Bryn Mawr College.

D'Souza, D. (1991). *Illiberal education: The politics of race and sex on campus*. New York: The Free Press.

Du Bois, W. E. B. (1903). *The souls of black folk*. New York: Bantam Books.

Feagin, J. R. & Vera, H. (1995). *White racism*. New York: Routledge.

Frankenberg, R. (1993). *White women, race matters: The social construction of whiteness*. Minneapolis: University of Minnesota Press.

Glenn, E. N. (1986). *Issei, Nisei, war bride: Three generations of Japanese American women in domestic service*. Philadelphia: Temple University Press.

Hondagneu-Sotelo, P. (1994). *Gendered transitions: Mexican experiences of immigration*. Berkeley and Los Angeles: University of California Press.

Ignatiev, N. (1995). *How the Irish become white*. New York: Routledge.

Katzman, David. (1981). *Seven days a week: Women and domestic service in industrializing America*. Chicago: University of Illinois Press.

McBride, T. (1976). *The domestic revolution: The modernization of household service in England and France, 1820–1920*. London: Croom Helm.

Mills, C. W. (1943). The professional ideology of social pathologists. *American Journal of Sociology, XLIX* (2), 165–80.

Omi, M. & Winant, H. (1987). *Racial formation in the United States: From the 1960s to the 1980s*. New York: Routledge and Kegan Paul.

Rodriguez, R. (1982). *Hunger of memory: The education of Richard Rodriguez*. New York: Bantam Books.

Rollins, J. (1985). *Between women: Domestics and their employers*. Philadelphia: Temple University Press.

Romero, M. (1992). *Maid in the U.S.A.* New York: Routledge.

Shorris, E. (1992). *Latinos: A biography of the people*. New York: W. W. Norton.

Skerry, P. (1993). *Mexican Americans: The ambivalent minority*. New York: The Free Press.

Sowell, T. (1983). *The economics and politics of race: An international perspective*. New York: Quill.

Stavans, I. (1995). *The Hispanic condition: Reflections on culture and identity in America*. New York: HarperCollins.

Steele, S. (1990). *The content of our character*. New York: St. Martin's Press.

Steinberg, S. (1981). *The ethnic myth*. Boston: Beacon Press.

Stiger, G. J. (1946). *Domestic servants in the United States, 1900–1940*. Occasional Paper No. 24. New York: National Bureau of Economic Research.

Winant, H. (1994). *Racial conditions, politics, theory, and comparisons*. Minneapolis: University of Minnesota Press.

Millie's[2] Story:
Motherhood, Heroin, and Methadone

Rivera: Chanelle was born addicted to dope.

Gypsy: Heroin.

Rivera: To heroin. Now how did you feel, Gypsy, when your baby was writhing in drug withdrawals?

Gypsy: Well, I felt bad, and . . .

Rivera: You felt bad, but you were still shooting up every day. You're still addicted. Your arms are like pincushions. How bad could you feel?

Gypsy: Well, I feel bad, but it's a drug that makes me keep using. You know, the addiction. And I want to stop for my baby. . . .

Rivera: How is it that after the baby was born addicted to drugs, you still managed to keep custody of the baby?

Gypsy: Well, it was—this was my first baby, and they gave me a chance to see how I'd do after I have the baby.

Rivera: But the baby's 11 months old and you're still addicted, right?

Gypsy: Well, I'm not using like I used to.

Rivera: Oh, Gypsy—please don't tell me that story. You're still hooking to get the money to buy drugs, right? [Gypsy nods]. . . . I had a bad dream yesterday. I was reading a terrible story about a child who was abused—a 4-year-old who was beaten to death by drug-addicted parents. And when I see this child, it breaks my heart, sweetheart. You know that? I can't—I can't believe that this baby's life wouldn't be better with somebody else as the mother. I hate to say that. I've never said that on the show to a mother of a baby before. But you are—you're hooking, you're using every day, the baby was born addicted to heroin. I mean, do you think it's best for the child to stay with Gypsy? (*Geraldo Rivera Show,* 19 April 1994).

*I*MAGES OF WOMEN DRUG ADDICTS on daytime talk shows as well as in the news help to create for the public an overarching narrative about the causes of and solutions to women's substance abuse. These stories often stem from a medical or therapeutic discourse thereby centering the location of and solution to our drug problem within the person and not the larger society. Where the medical model posits that drug addiction stems from a "metabolic disorder" and a genetic predisposition to drug use, the therapeutic model argues that women who use drugs have addictive personalities (including addictions to men who use drugs), antisocial personalities, and personal problems for which drugs provide an escape (Kirn, 1988). According to both these discourses and the popular views of addiction that stem from them, once using drugs, women can no longer control themselves (Maher, 1997). They become victims of the pharmacological nature of the drug whereby they will do anything for a hit including, for example, selling their own bodies. In countless talk shows and other forms of popular culture, drug-using women, especially women of color, are seen as highly sexualized or hypersexualized and prone to immorality. Highly dependent on their drugs, women substance users are portrayed as impulsive, desperate, selfish, dangerous, impure, and tainted.

Coupled with this narrative is one about junkie mothers. Motherhood, according to dominant social constructions, is natural, instinctive, primordial, and all encompassing (Glenn, 1994). Yet, the master story tells the public that for junkie mothers, the desperate pharmacological pull for drugs overpowers the biological urge of motherhood. As quoted above, women junkies are portrayed as unfit breeders and mothers, unable to think of others and provide nurturance.

In this chapter, we will present a counternarrative to the popularized images of drug-using women. It is part of a narrative of a poor, dark-complected, Puerto Rican woman, Millie, who at the age of 59 and after using heroin for years is now on methadone and is HIV positive. Born in Puerto Rico, Millie was brought to New York City when she was 11 by her mother who was estranged from her abusive husband. Millie has married or lived with five men since she was a teenager and had a total of six children with three of these men. Except for her last partner, all of them physically abused her. She has been raped numerous times, has sold drugs to support her habit and her children, and has been imprisoned. She also has had to endure discrimination and mistreatment because of her HIV-positive status.

Jennifer met Millie at a methadone treatment clinic where in the summer of 1994 she was conducting interviews with women who were former heroin users. It was only after about a month of observing Jennifer at the clinic that Millie offered "to write some things down." It is initially through Millie's written life story and later through extensive conversations with her during the past 4 years, that we learn a counterstory to the one so often told about women heroin users. Through her narrative, we learn that Millie has spent her life challenging the kinds of stories that society, the media, methadone clinics, and her own community would choose to tell about her. What Millie lets us know about her life does not fit within the monolithic picture that the public holds for heroin-using women. Millie does not frame her life exclusively within a psychological or individualistic discourse that claims that her own character weaknesses are to blame for her transgressions and failures to conform to traditional gender expectations. She acknowledges that she has done some terrible things in her life, but she wants others to know that she is also a person who embodies the assaults of living at the intersection of numerous forms of oppression and exploitation. Missing in the dominant stories told about women heroin users like Millie are struggles of poverty, racism, sexism, and women's amazing resilience, creativity, and agency that enables them to survive in the face of extreme adversity.

MILLIE'S TESTIMONIAL

When I left Puerto Rico [to New York City in 1951 at the age of 11] I felt very sad and lonely Because my Grandmother was always there for me. She had a lot of Grand and Great Grandchildren But I was her favorite. I even slept with her and she would make Special Food that she knew I like. I never disrespected her. I've hated when my father talk loud to her and he had a small house which he lived with his comon law wife and they used to fight a lot Because of my father drinking and whenever she leave him my Grandma would cook and wash his clothes and at dinner time she will Bring his food and he throw it Back at her and that really hurt me and make me very mad at him. But I couldn't do anything But just look at him dirty and tell him that he wasn't my father that my mother found me on a garbage can and he always threaten to hit me and I would run and run and stayed out till late at night that my Grandmother came out and bring me back into the house and he still sat outside his porch and I stick my tongue out to him. There were other times that I will see him fondling my Best Friend and I yelled at her to run and get up from his lap and tell him that I was goin' to tell on him and my Grandmother about his dirty doings. Well he really got mad and tell me that I was Goin' to Be like my mother Because I even looked like her. At this tender age of 6, or seven I knew enough to Let him know that what he was doin' was very corrupted. I never received any Love or Kind Word from my father. But I never hated him Because I have experienced pain loneliness hurt Deceived and any kindness came from my Grandma so. when I left P.R. I felt some kind of pain But also the Love that my Wonderful other mother gave me. But I had to Leave not Because I wanted But Because my mother was sending for us and we had to leave. the first night in New York was tears and pain missing my Grandmother and I guess my mother notice this I wanted to go back to the woman that gave me love. Later thru the coming months. I've noticed that things were not Good. I was goin' to Catholic School and my Brother too. My sister was goin' to [name] high and she Quit school to work at [name] Hospital. Well she was Making Good money but Spending a lot on herself. Not once she ever said take this quarter or the clothes she didn't want. Instead of looking my way she send them to P.R. to someone else. Well Between me and my sister there has never Been closeness. She has allways Depended on my mother and many times my mom has made it very easy for her with her kids and even when we were kids I had to do the work around the House and never had the pleasure like Other teen agers to go to a movie or park. I was never allowed to visit or Bring any Friends to the House. I have Been a loner thru all my Life. I grew up with much Disappointments and criticizm from my Own sister. Now my oldest Brother Being one year older than me is ok. and he show me that he loves me and help me if I need Help and always look for me. Only one time I came from school and my mom left instruction not to let me watch T.V. and Proceeds to Do the Dishes and Clean the House. I was about 12. Well I really got very upset Because I had no rights whatsoever in this House. I felt pushed around so I've, struck him in the head with a clock and when my mother came she hit me while my sister hold me and I pulled Back the Belt she was hitting me with. She murmured something of the trees striking Back the Leaves. this to me was Like Being Locked in Jail. When I hit 16 yrs. she took me Out of school and I went to my first Job as a nurse's aide at [name] Hospt. I've learned and was good at it Because I've, always like to Help Others. so my shift was from 3 P.M. to 11 P.M. Sometimes I never wanted to go home. to what? I gave her my pay and never saw any money. I never Bought me any clothes Because of my uniform being white. And I didn't Have any Social Life unless my mother's friend would come by and we all go to [name] Mt. by 6, or 5 cars allways a big bunch of families. My mother never sat down with me to talk about sex. This word was very dirty to me till one day I was cleaning one Hospital Bed and emptying trash & Drawers and I've found a condom close. I've put it in my bag and my mother always looked thru my things. Why? I don't know. Well she called on all my aunts and uncle and sister and they question? me about this condom. I said I don't know what this is. I put it in my bag. They all had their mouth Open in disbelief and they Kept Asking did I have Anything to tell my mother. I said no. How could I. She never talked about Sex or Condoms. I was a 16 yrs. old. Virgin with no knowledge of this. I really don't know. What they Said after that but since I've had met a guy where I worked he was 1 yr. older. By then I was 18 he was 19 and when I came out at 11 P.M. he would wait outside and Walk me Home. But I didn't know my mother was spying on me till I saw her one night Watching me and Him Walk Home. One day she told me to bring him home. This way

I wouldn't have to see him like she said around the corners. I did bring (his name) home. She took him to the kitchen and I've heard most of her questions and embarrassing me mostly. I couldn't believe it. Things like she doesn't even know how to take a bath or wash her underclothes yet less have a boyfriend. When he left he said to me I will never come to your house again. I was really furious with my mother because of what she's done. But I kept seeing him. We had plans for the future. Till one day his parents and mine were talking and we were out of the conversation, so I was goin' to be married whether I wanted or not. They did all the arrangement and took him and me to City Hall and we were married. The reception was Saturday in the meantime she never said a word and Friday I found out my dress, veil, cake, maids of Honor were part of me for that special day that was never special to me. A priest or Reverend arrived on Sat. 3 P.M. and we said our vows (not really). My husband got drunk that night and someone took us to a room that was rented for us. Seven days passed and our marriage was not consummated. Why? Because he brought me back home to my mother and said Mrs. [name] here's your daughter the same ways as the first day we've got married. I haven't touched her. This mean that if we're married and sleeping together and I haven't put a finger on her. I never did Before. She really didn't know where to put her face. I guess I felt very Proud of him and myself. She made the biggest mistake any mother could make with her daughter. I call it (lack of trust & communication.) This marriage never even had a chance to get up. We were too young. After a year or less I was pregnant with twins like me. Which I forgot she mistreated me. Why? Because his family was prejudiced and when I was 4 months he got in trouble. We went shoplifting and he got caught. I ended by myself like always and his mother threw me out because she said she couldn't support me and my belly of twins, so I need to go to this Lady House and iron and clean to support me and my babies inside. One night it was very hot and I was outside about 1 o'clock in the morning with my girlfriend. I couldn't sleep. His mother looked down and saw me and started to accused me of being unfaithful to her son and insulting me. I say this much who is goin' to look at me with this big belly and nothing to offer. My friend Lucia took me inside and told me to be quiet because this is what she is looking for. This way she will write her son bad things about you and he might believe her. I did went to bed and next morning at 8 A.M. she woke me up banging in the door. When I opened she told me that I will not be with him anymore and she was goin' to take his clothes back with her, so I defend myself by yelling back at her and cursing her. A slap came to my face and we fought. Even pregnant I fought back like a mad lion and messed up her face. She went upstairs. And I didn't know that she had her son one of the youngest. And about 2 P.M. I was standing in front of the building and he came to me very mad and told me the next time I fought with his mom he was goin' to fix me so I challenged him and went downstairs and changed clothes. Because pregnant or not I've always had a temper and this man was not goin' to threaten me. So I've stood in front of him arguing back and forth. And his sister-in-law told him not to fall for my arguing but he didn't listen and before I saw it coming he punched me hard in my face, knocked out on the floor. When I awoke I was on his mother's house bed. So I got up mad furious and went downstairs with a lot of pain. Like back ache, tooth ache and I was goin' crazy. Night come and when they found out I was doing bad the oldest son came by Sorry for what happened. That night I didn't sleep and in the morning I had birth pains. Being I didn't know where to go I've walked 7 blocks to my mother's house and on my way I had to stop because the pain was getting harder and no one in the street would stop to ask me can I take you somewhere. So I've kept on going. When I finally got to my mom's house I walked a lot of steps to this house. When I got inside I went straight to the bathroom thinking I had to go. But my mother took me downstairs and called the ambulance. I was really in Pain Back and Front because this pregnancy were *two* and it was my first. When the ambulance came they sat me on a big chair and put me in the amb. As soon as I lay inside my (male) cousin came with me to the hospt. and when the pain began stronger I've started pushing out and he got very nervous because the baby's head was showing and repeatedly the amb. att. kept telling me don't push. But I did. Finally we arrived at the hospt. and when we entered the elevator the first baby came out. It wasn't long I found myself in the second stage. The next baby was coming. So I pushed with everything I had in me and my two little girls were born. But what was to follow I couldn't never imagine. Because this wasn't Mother's Day for me. My first child was born with Black & Blue marks and a messed up a little arm. So they Baptized them as I was told they probably Wouldn't make it (yes) they were right. My first child died at about 3 o'clock the same day. But no one ever told me until late that night. I thought it was me that died I forgot that instant there was a god that he forgot me and I held on tight to the other twin. But life is not like you would wanted to be. I was waiting on my bed the following feeding time to feed my baby. I saw every baby been brought out to its mother to be fed and I happen to ask a nurse about mine which she reply your baby died this morning at 6 A.M. I said yes I know but there is another alive I had twins. She look like she said something very wrong and very unprofessional to fast too cold and then too hurt after the mistake too late. I was screaming and why me. This is all I wanted since I have lost everything else I was very much alone not my mother or anyone come by. Sometimes emptiness push you to degradation lower than you ever thought because of a word of love which we sometimes forget to say or show. Well I swore I will never be the same and I would pay back by hurting the people that put me there.

Millie describes the numerous traumas and horrors she experienced growing up poor, of color, and as a woman. Her story is not just a testimony of a private life, but is a story that is larger than her life. Putting herself on trial and serving as a witness in her own defense, the burden on Millie is to convince the "jury" (larger society) that her story is a legitimate testimonial because the assaults she has experienced have been inflicted upon her (Beverly, 1992). Millie uses her personal testimony politically to challenge the devastation of larger oppressions that profoundly affect her health and the well-being of her family and community. In contrast to individualistic psychological and medical models of addiction all too pervasive in master narratives, in talking about her "ills" such as her HIV-positive status, her heroin use, the loss of her children, as well as the deviant label others impose on her, Millie's story is a counterstory because she "shift[s] the site of onset [of her illnesses] from the body to the world—the social and cultural community within which [she] live[s]" (Folwell Stanford, 1994, p. 29). Millie's counterstory shows us that she is aware that her "diseases" are integrally connected to larger social ills such as sexism, racism, classism, and heterosexism and cannot simply and only be attributed to her own individual pathologies (Folwell Stanford, 1994, p. 29). Through her story, Millie tells us that she has had to "pay the price for and carry within [her] the symptoms of a sick world."

In her written testimony, Millie often expresses how she felt that the larger social ills of sexism, racism, and poverty meant that she was denied mothering and nurturance and denied the right to be a mother. Yet now Millie is aware of how her transgressions of traditional gender expectations, because of her heroin use and current dependence on methadone, threatens her ability to be seen as a good mother. It is her actions, rather than the actions of others, that now puts in question Millie's role as a mother. Millie, however, refuses to be totally inscribed by the master narratives concerning women and substance use by ironically adopting her motherhood and caring roles as primary in her life. In numerous conversations with Jenny, Millie argues that it is her purpose in life to care for others.

While it is true that Millie actively embraces the roles of mother and caregiver as an act of resistance to dominant stories, we also must recognize that she chooses these roles because society expects them of women. Millie wants to be seen as a good person and seeks redemption for past transgressions. Because the larger society, her own cultural group, and she herself equates being a good person with being a good mother and caregiver, it makes sense for her to want to reinscribe herself using these roles as primary themes in her life. Ironically, however, by reinscribing herself as a good mother and by seeking to be redeemed, Millie may be resisting the master narratives at work concerning women who use drugs, but is at the same time reproducing and becoming entrapped in master narratives concerning motherhood. Millie knows that as a drug addict and labeled deviant she is portrayed as selfish, irresponsible, hedonistic, and "unnatural." Therefore, to reinscribe herself as a good mother, she must show society how she has sacrificed herself for her children. She must also see herself as solely responsible for how they matured and demonstrate that she still possesses natural instincts toward motherhood.

THE PROCESS OF REINSCRIPTION: RESISTANCE AND REPRODUCTION OF MASTER NARRATIVES

Unwilling to fit herself into simplistic dichotomies that judge her as either a good or bad mother, Millie presents a much more complex picture of herself as a mother. She does acknowledge that when her children were young she was not always a good mother. Prominent in her story are examples of when she failed her children. Millie describes in writing, for example, her feelings about one of her babies who died at infancy from hepatitis that Millie contracted from needles.

> This time I used a dirty needle and I caught hepatitis and so does my baby inside. I went to visit my mother and a friend of hers notice my eyes being yellow and I was aching all over and messing up the sheets because my liver was damaged and my baby caught it. So I went in the hospital 7 months pregnant and they were scared because of my pregnancy. By the time, I've delivered my own baby they took her right away. My little girl was precious and so tiny and very sick with hepatitis and a very bad liver. She died the 3rd day and I was painfully hurt. Guilty, I did take some blame here.

Despite being acutely aware that she has not, at times, been a "model" mother, Millie knows that she has done and continues to do much for her children and grandchildren. Although inconsistently, Millie has been able to engage in meaningful activities and nurture her children's growth. In her story, Millie demonstrates that she has been able to delay gratification, put others first, and provide for her children even if it was through illicit activities or meant that she stayed in abusive relationships. Millie, for example, frames many of the assaults she endured at the hands of abusive men within the context of making sacrifices for her children. Contrary to the typical depictions of drug-using women as selfish, Millie describes how she martyred her own body and risked her personal well-being to benefit her children. Millie stayed with her second partner who was sexually and physically abusive because, as she describes, she "had nowhere to go and four kids." She further explains, "I didn't know what to do. The police would not help. When they came over, they said that there was nothing that they could do because he pays the rent and puts food on the table." Millie believed that her partner would not hurt their children, just her. At the time, Millie perceived that being a good mother and providing for her children meant enduring sexual and physical abuse.

After leaving her second husband, Millie became involved in another abusive relationship where she had another child—a result of being raped. By this time in her life, Millie describes herself as having a severe heroin habit. Her partner who was also addicted to heroin was undependable and could not provide for them. Millie had to find a way to support her family and her drug habit. With no job skills and only an 8th-grade education, Millie's choices were limited. Placing her four oldest children in foster care, Millie in desperation tried to survive "by sitting on a step holding her [fifth] child [a new born] begging for food and money. I would just sit there hugging my daughter wrapped in a blanket. Someone would come by and take her and feed her and clothe her. They were nice people and they said that she would be o.k. with them and that they would buy her pampers. I trusted them and let them take my daughter." Unable to make enough to survive and loathing herself for begging, Millie found work by dealing drugs. She said, "I needed to deal to survive. No one would help me with my children." Dealing drugs, however, is a complicated enterprise. While it allowed her to maintain her autonomy from men, not prostitute, get her children out of foster care, and make enough money to support her family, it also was an enterprise that allowed her to maintain her drug habit. In addition, although Millie perceived at the time that dealing heroin was the only way to attend to her family's needs, she does not calculate in her decision the devastating consequences of her actions. She is arrested fifteen days after delivering her daughter [fifth child] and is incarcerated while still bleeding from labor. To this day, Millie believes that her daughter has not forgiven her for being left in foster care during Millie's 2-year prison term. While Millie feels bad about what she did, she refuses to feel guilty because "I always provided for her even when I was in jail and there was nothing I could do about that. I am not going to let her make me feel like a bad mother. I have done a lot of bad things, but I have always been a good mother to my children."

Dealing drugs may not be considered "appropriate" economic activity for a mother as prescribed by the dominant and white middle-class constructions of motherhood, but for Millie, who grew up poor and with few opportunities, and felt the sole burden of caring for her children, it was one of the few ways she envisioned that she could support them. She could not imagine a legal job that with her skills would provide flexible hours and childcare for five children. Millie challenges those elements of the master narrative about motherhood that state that good mothers are only those who stay at home and, if they work, engage in legitimate and legal work. She is aware that dealing drugs is illegal, but she also knows that it allowed her to provide for her children and therefore refuses to totally "condemn" herself or be completely dismissed by others. Millie can both cherish her children and at the same time engage in activities that put her children in dangerous situations. Because Millie has provided for her children and has had to make sacrifices for them, she feels a right to assert and maintain her status as a mother. Although she tells us that she feels guilty that one of her sons was born addicted to methadone [a legal drug used as a substitute for heroin], Millie also recollects how assertive she had to be about her right to have a baby and to be a parent. In doing so, Millie challenges the master narrative about drug abusers as uncaring and liars. Millie writes in her testimonial:

> When I had my son, I was on methadone and he was born addicted. . . . I felt terrible about it. They had all these tubes in him, in his legs and arms and they couldn't get him to get off. They kept asking me if I did anything else. And I said no. One day a nurse came to ask me if I would give some urine because they wanted to test me. They didn't believe me that I hadn't used anything. She asked me to do that and I told her that they think I'm lying and she said well if you are then not only will you be in trouble but they will also take away your two children too. I was so angry when she told me that. I told her that if that urine came back dirty that I would go into that closet and light my two kids on fire with me. She was really shocked that I said that. I meant it too. No one was going to take my kids from me. When the test came back, she apologized to me for what she said.

Ironically, while Millie asserts her right to be a parent, the image of her burning herself and her children is in sharp contrast to traditional notions of mothers as protectors and caregivers.

Millie often feels that her motherhood status is challenged based on the stereotypes about people like her. Each time, Millie must intelligently and creatively fight numerous institutions and agencies for her right to be a mother and to have custody of her children, but in doing so, Millie also often demonstrates that she is only a "good enough" mother and like many other mothers has limitations. After suffering from a back-alley abortion, for example, Millie who was seriously hemorrhaging, had to go to the hospital. Sick, in pain, very poor, and alone, Millie struggled unsuccessfully to find alternative childcare arrangements. With no other choice, Millie felt forced to place her four children in foster care. After being discharged from the hospital she explains how she worked to get her children back. The public does not often see the arduous efforts many women like Millie must go through to keep their families together and survive. Typically, the dominant narratives tell us that because women drug users value drugs and men over their children and are out of control, they are incapable of acting thoughtfully and deliberately. Millie presents a counterstory to these assumptions. She writes:

> I needed to find an apartment for my kids and it wasn't going to be easy because I had to prove to myself and the court that I needed and love my children very much. . . . I had only them and they were put in different family houses. It was very hard to visit them the way they had the visits were—every other week see the 2 boys and the other week the 2 girls. I didn't have a car because I can't drive, no money because I wasn't working. But I always manage. The Lord saw to it that I find carfare to visit them. The day came when I was to bring them home and my social worker from Children court told me that she had to make a visit to my new apartment. Because in order to have my children back with me I needed a place furnished. Now all I needed was the bed blankets and when she came over that day she noticed that I didn't have them. That day I begged my social worker to please let my kids come home because I was so lonely without them. I needed my kids and they needed me also. My life was so empty and they kept me going. Finally she said o.k. Mrs. [last name] go on Monday to Court and bring them home. I've cried and cried and when Monday came I was there to bring my little children home.

Yet, Millie's story of self-sacrifice is not straightforward. While she has told us that she has worked hard to get her children back, Millie is not simply acting out of concern for her own children, as the master narrative would suggest that she should, but also out of concern for herself and her own loneliness. Through her comments, we learn the limitations Millie faces in trying to reinscribe herself as a good mother according to values that tell her she should place her needs second to those of her children.

Beyond assuming responsibility and caring for her children, Millie also takes pride in being a grandmother. As a grandmother to eight children, Millie has incorporated more people under her umbrella of care, sustenance, and nurturance. When her youngest son's girlfriend got pregnant and had a baby, Millie took care of her. Much to Millie's disappointment, however, her son's girlfriend rejected her and refused to acknowledge Millie as the grandmother after she and Millie's son, Darryl, broke up. While visiting the baby and her son's ex-girlfriend, Millie, angered by not being acknowledged as the grandmother, asserted her right to be recognized as the baby's grandmother based on the caring work and help she provided her daughter-in-law. She explains:

I wrote her [name] a letter I told her about how uncomfortable I felt over there and how I was the baby's grandmother and she didn't introduce me to anyone. No one wanted to know who I was. Her mother wasn't treating me right. I told her that she should remember that I was the one who took care of her. I was there for her and now look at what she has done. She shouldn't treat me that way after how much I have helped her. I want the baby to know who I am. I'm going to send her something every month so that she knows one day when she is older that [I] cared about her. I didn't abandon her.

One of Millie's granddaughters who is now 14 years old lives near her. Millie has assumed the role as her granddaughter's other mother since Millie's daughter is often away from home long hours working two jobs to support her family. Millie listens, advises, disciplines, at times feeds, and provides financial help to her granddaughter.

Millie's narrative also includes stories about how she has taken care of members of her extended family. Millie, for example, explains how she has cared for her sister when she has been sick, letting her stay with her and giving her sister her bed while she slept on the floor. Despite having very little money herself, Millie tries financially to help her elderly mother and has tried to make repairs on her mother's home and has bought her much needed gifts like an oven and stove. She has also made a commitment to her mother to care for her brother who has a drinking problem when her mother passes on. At the methadone clinic, Millie is always showing concern for people especially for those who are HIV positive. Millie describes how she helped one of the men at the clinic who was beginning to get sick by first talking to his counselor and then by calling her own doctor.

[My counselor] said that I needed to talk to his counselor. He does nothing. I told her that he is really sick and that he needs a doctor. I told her that he is dying and I don't want to see someone die. . . . I was in [my counselor's] office and I called Dr. S. [her HIV doctor] and said please, this is [Millie] and I was wondering if you could do me a favor. I have a friend here who is really sick and I was wondering if you could see him.

Although limited in her capacity to be an ideal mother and caregiver, Millie still asserts her status as mother and expands her caregiving position vis-à-vis her grandchildren, her extended family, adult children, and friends. In doing so, Millie reenvisions and reinscribes herself beyond the boundaries of the monolithic picture of women heroin users. Yet at the same time, in an effort to challenge dominant depictions of herself as a heroin user and a labeled deviant, evident throughout her story are ways in which Millie still lives within the gender constraints of the dominant culture and reproduces master narratives concerning motherhood. Many of the stories, above which are stories of sacrifice, help Millie in her efforts to reinscribe herself as a "good person," but they also entrap her in the dominant gender expectations she herself resisted earlier in her life. Millie cares for her sister and mother not only because she finds it rewarding but also because there are cultural expectations that she do this type of work. Staying with an abusive partner may have been a necessary strategy to ensure that her children were fed and had a place to live, but also the action shows how Millie, as a mother, felt a need to sacrifice her own well-being. Millie shares stories of the sacrifices that even now she has made in her effort to fulfill the sometimes unrealistic expectations that the master narrative prescribes for caregivers, mothers, and grandmothers. For example, because Millie believes that grandmothers are supposed to spoil their grandchildren and shower them with gifts to make them feel special, she will sometimes go into debt, juggle payments, and sometimes overpay for gifts in order to please her grandchildren. Millie explains one such instance:

> Well what I am going to do with this money [by selling brand-new pots and pans she mail ordered] is buy Marilyn [granddaughter] something really nice for her birthday and Christmas. I told her that I was going to get something for her, but I don't have no money right now. I thought that I would use the money from this to buy her something. And, then when this is due [the money for the pots and pans] because I don't have to pay for this for a few months, when this is due I will buy [mail order] something else and sell that and use the money for that to pay for this. You see? That way I'll always have money around. I need the money.

As a drug user and labeled deviant who has been portrayed as an irresponsible mother, to be exonerated for her past transgressions, Millie must also demonstrate that she can and does assume responsibility for how well her children have matured into adults. Millie clearly does this when she talks about her youngest son, Darryl, who still lives with her at times. In her narration about her life, Millie speaks a lot about her efforts to protect and care for him. She moved to Florida from New York hoping to find a better place to live for her son and encouraged him to pursue an education. Darryl, however, never completed high school and served a 2-year jail term for a minor misdemeanor charge that probably would have been dropped if he were white or came from a wealthy family. Millie feels responsible for Darryl and feels guilty that he has been getting into trouble. She believes he is not doing well because of all the domestic violence he witnessed while he was growing up and because she has babied him too much. Again, however, we see how Millie reinforces elements of dominant narratives that expect mothers, regardless of the "circumstances of her life," to be solely responsible for their children and that hold mothers entirely accountable for the persons their children become (Christian, 1994, p. 110).

Finally, Millie must also reinscribe herself as a good mother by demonstrating that she possesses "the 'natural' attributes expected of mothers" (Lewin, 1994, p. 334). For example, as part of her caring work and within the traditions of her Puerto Rican culture and Christian background, Millie often talks and writes about how she reads symbols, interprets dreams, and has visions that are part of the work she does as a caregiver. These allow Millie to care, protect, and provide for others when direct help and explicit words fail or seem useless. Now that Millie's children are all adults and some live far away, she says she can still help them by reading symbols, interpreting dreams, and invoking her ancestors. By doing so, Millie poetically weaves a web of connections between herself and those she loves in ways that transcend time and space. Millie, herself, describes how her body itself becomes a gauge for how her family is doing. Aware that intuition and anticipating the needs of others is important to caring work, Millie "reads" her body to figure out what is happening with her family. When there are extensive problems in her family, Millie describes that she often feels physically ill. She states: "I just don't feel right. I don't know what it is. Do you ever get that way that you just don't feel right? I feel like something is wrong inside of me. I don't know what it is, but I just have this feeling. Everything hurts. . . . There is something wrong and it is with my family. That is why I don't feel well."

While the intuitive and emotional work that Millie describes is important to her role as caregiver and mother, we must still raise the question of whether or not through these stories and by celebrating her strong intuitive sense, Millie is not also reproducing some elements of the master discourse concerning motherhood. For example, does Millie reproduce the idea that mothers should anticipate the needs of others and that motherhood instincts and bonds are so close, natural, and primordial that of course a mother would know when her children are in trouble even when they are not close by?

CONCLUSION

Despite her efforts to reinscribe herself as a good mother and seek redemption, Millie is never completely reformed. She still maintains the critical perspective her life experiences afforded her. For example, Millie recognizes that she stayed in abusive relationships for the sake of her children; she vows now that she will never again let another man hit her. Millie never has and still does not acquiesce completely to dominant gender, race, and class expectations, but rather in subtle and creative ways she continues to fight against, challenge, and critique the nearly daily assaults she experiences.

One might also characterize Millie's life story by arguing that, like the lesbian mothers Lewin (1994, p. 350) studied, Millie is a strategist who uses "the cultural resources offered by motherhood to achieve a particular set of goals." Yet this model and the notion of "strategy" seem to suggest a much more deliberate, well-planned-out method of resistance that has a particular goal in sight. The concept of strategy also seems to invalidate that resistance occurs at all. While the notion that Millie is a strategist might capture the creative and diverse ways Millie survives, it is more useful to look at her life through the tension of resistance and reproduction. By doing so, we gain a better understanding of Millie and many other women like her who face the complex and difficult task of carving out space for themselves within and against a very complicated web of master narratives and discourses. It is because of complicated and often competing discourses at work in our society that everyday forms of resistance and counterstories at times seem diffuse, uncertain, and tentative and sometimes reproduce, rather than challenge, master narratives. As ill-conceived and contradictory as everyday forms of resistance and counternarratives may seem to be, they keep the master narratives tenuous and the door open for possibilities and yet-unasked questions.

NOTES

1. Authors are listed in alphabetical order.

2. Millie has granted us permission to use her actual name but the names of her children and relatives have been changed to protect their anonymity.

REFERENCES

Beverly, J. (1992). The margin at the center: On testimonio. In S. Smith & J. Watson (Eds.), *De/Colonizing the subject* (pp. 91–114). Minneapolis: University of Minnesota Press.

Christian, B. (1994). An angle of seeing: Motherhood in Buchi Emecheta's *Joys of Motherhood* and Alice Walker's *Meridian*. In E. Nakano Glenn, G. Chang, & K. R. Forcey (Eds.), *Mothering, ideology, experience, and agency* (pp. 95–120). New York: Routledge.

Folwell Stanford, A. (1994). Mechanisms of disease: African-American women writers, social pathologies, and the limits of medicine. *NWSA Journal, 6* (1), 28–47.

Kirn, T. F. (1988). Methadone maintenance treatment remains controversial even after 23 years of experience. *Journal of American Medical Association, 260* (20), 2970–76.

Lewin, E. (1994). Negotiating lesbian motherhood: The dialectics of resistance and accommodation. In E. Nakano Glenn, G. Chang, & K. R. Forcey (Eds.), *Mothering, ideology, experience, and agency* (pp. 333–53). New York: Routledge.

Maher, L. (1997). *Sexed work.* New York: Clarendon Press.

Nakano Glenn, E. (1994). Social constructions of mothering: A thematic overview." In E. Nakano Glenn, G. Chang, & K. R. Forcey (Eds.,) *Mothering, ideology, experience, and agency* (pp. 1–29). New York: Routledge.

"How Would You Write about That?": Identity, Language, and Knowledge in the Narratives of Two Navajo Women

A little while ago I had something that was bothering me, something that was wrong. Finally, I talked to my grandfather about it—he stays over there (pointing with her chin to the rise behind her house). I went and told him about it and he listened to me. He told me that I would have to do some things to learn about why these things were happening to me. He told me to go home and sit down someplace where I was comfortable, to close my eyes and listen to what was wrong with me. So I came back here and at first I didn't do what he said. I didn't really understand—I thought, how will I have time to do this? And what is it that he means that I will know what is wrong with me? But finally I decided to do what he said.

I sat down in this chair. I sat here for a while and I had to empty my mind out of everything. Then, I don't know if I fell asleep or something, but I saw myself come right up out of my body like this— I could see myself and I flew way up and I could see myself here in the chair getting smaller and smaller until I was just little tiny, like an ant, way down below me. I was up in the clouds and I could see that I was traveling a long ways. I went into a cave and saw a beautiful woman there—she was dressed traditionally. She showed me another room and there was a baby in a cradle board—I realized that it was me.

I followed that little girl all through her childhood to one time when my sister and I were out herding the sheep and pretty soon we saw a big pile of tumbleweeds. And I had some matches in my pocket and I pulled them out and lit them on fire—just to see it burn. My sister and I watched it. When it was done burning, I saw a black charred thing like a stick in with the tumbleweeds—it was a snake that had been in there and burned.

Then I went to another place. I could see the snake going to a den where there were many other snakes—they were glad to see her. I flew back up into the sky and flew a long way. . . . I could see the earth below me and after a while I could see this little house way down below me. I started to come back closer and closer to the earth and pretty soon I could see myself in this chair, looked like I was asleep or something. And then I came back into my body. It was like I had been asleep and—Oh—I did not want to wake up! It felt so good to be way far away and I did not want to come back into my body. I stayed there—I was in my self but I was a long way away, like in a dream or something—for a long time, and then I began to come back.

I rested in my chair for a long time, thinking about what had happened. Then I decided to go and tell my grandfather about it and see what he said. So I went and told my grandfather about what had happened while I was meditating. He listened and then he said to me, "This is what has been wrong with you. This is what is wrong with you now and now we will know what to do to make you better." So my grandfather told me what I had to do. I went and did those things, and I have never had those problems since then.

    —Faye, age 73 (field notes recorded 5/12/93)

*F*AYE AND I[2] WERE SEATED IN THE LIVING ROOM of her home on the Navajo Nation, drinking tea made from herbs she had gathered. The wall behind the sofa where I was seated was covered with family pictures—of Faye and her husband on their wedding day, six of her seven daughters (one died in infancy), their husbands, and their children. I had come to Faye with a draft of a chapter in which I explored Navajo women's responses to generational changes, based on interviews with 31 Navajo women, including Faye and her daughter Ursula. In the chapter, women who were 30 years younger than Faye described their efforts to relearn or recreate an understanding of Navajo spiritual practices after having been raised in boarding schools some distance from their home communities on the Navajo Nation. In one of these excerpts, a woman spoke of her efforts to learn how to conduct a *kinaaldá*, or puberty ceremony, for her daughter by reading a book describing the ceremony. After reading this section, Faye looked at me and said, "There are some things that you can't learn from books." She went on to describe several examples from her own life and experiences, including the story presented above. She ended by asking me, "Now, how would you write about that?"

Faye's account described a process of meditation followed by consultation, through which she and her grandfather sought to understand or diagnose her condition. Within the context of this diagnostic relationship, two individuals who were knowledgeable about and experienced with healing practices drew upon shared systems of meaning to understand Faye's condition on the basis of the meditative experience she described. Her point in telling this story was that it was precisely these ways of understanding that could not be conveyed through text, but only created and recreated through interaction and shared experience. Faye's question—"How would you write about that?"—became the catalyst for this chapter. In it, I explore relationships among language, knowledge, and identity through an analysis of Faye's story and that of her daughter Ursula. In so doing, I examine the narrative of civilization, with its attendant themes of difference, otherness, and assimilation, as a framework against which Navajo women attempt to define themselves. Before turning to Faye's and Ursula's narratives, I turn briefly to the literature both to frame the historical and political context in which their narratives were constructed and to locate the themes developed here within a broader theoretical and empirical literature.

FRAMING THE MASTER NARRATIVE: CONSTRUCTING THE "OTHER"

Generations of Native Americans[3] in the United States and elsewhere have encountered the metanarrative[4] of progress, in which civility or civilization is juxtaposed against barbarism/nature (Cronan, 1983; Dunaway, 1996; Schulz, 1994a, 1998; Somers & Gibson, 1994). This racialized metanarrative, while varied at different historical moments, has been timeless in portraying American Indians as the antithesis of whiteness—uncivilized savages, pagans, less than human—in contrast to European Americans portrayed as civilized, Christian, and the epitome of humanness (Berkhofer, 1979; Cornell, 1988). This metanarrative supported warfare, genocide, and forced removal of American Indians beginning in the 1600s (Cornell, 1988; Drinnon, 1997; Takaki, 1993).

By the end of the nineteenth century, policymakers had articulated a multifaceted agenda grounded in this metanarrative, including the destruction of tribal languages and identities, the transfer of collectively held lands to private ownership, and the incorporation of tribal members into the labor force. Couched in the language of assimilation, and consistent with the myth of the American "melting pot," for American Indians, these policies meant the disappearance of distinct social and political identities. The physical genocide that American Indian groups had faced in earlier decades was replaced by policies and programs intended to eradicate distinct cultural or ethnic identities, as well as political rights within the United States.

Fundamental to the metanarrative of civilization and the inequalities that it supports has been the definition of differences between groups, defined by ethnicity, gender, nation, sexuality, social class, or other dimensions (Collins, 1990; Gans, 1992). The construction of identities that locate individuals in relation to others are one aspect of this process. Social constructionist perspectives emphasize the influence of social and historical factors in shaping both the process and the content or meanings of collective and self-identities. This framework emphasizes the symbolic nature of difference as it is constructed through interactions among individuals who are located within broader social, cultural, and historical contexts (Bourdieu, 1977; Calhoun, 1994; Nagel, 1996; Ortner, 1984, 1989; Sewell, 1989; Waters, 1990; Woodward, 1997). Boundaries between and within groups are constructed and reconstructed as group members interact and draw upon cultural tools or resources that symbolically define them as group members, distinct from others (Anderson, 1983; Barth, 1969; Nagel, 1996; Waters, 1990).

In addition to being a means for understanding the self, identities are political constructs used both to locate groups and individuals in relation to each other and to define the possibilities of group members (Collins, 1990; hooks, 1989). In this sense, identities become a lens through which to examine political and social relationships (Nagel, 1996; Schulz, 1998; Waters, 1990; Woodward, 1997). The extent to which identities can be freely chosen or created within these relationships is influenced by relative access to resources through which to claim or construct an identity. For example, Herbert Gans (1992) notes that many boundaries are, in his terms, "guarded," and cannot be crossed without permission—that is, one cannot claim such identities without permission or approval from a gatekeeper. Boundaries that are guarded or closed exist in order to protect or maintain inequalities "and to make sure that the less than equal cannot enter or can do so only by paying proper deference" (Gans, 1992, p. xiii). Thus, identities reflect and maintain social and political relationships between groups: They also have the potential to disrupt those relationships.

Efforts to incorporate American Indians into Western economic and social systems through assimilation, or the destruction of distinct group identities, were supported by Anglo definitions of American Indians as deficient. The language of assimilation ignored the powerful gatekeeping mechanisms that worked to exclude American Indians and other ethnic groups from being accepted as white, even as American Indians were encouraged to give up their tribal identities. Despite the imbalance of power/access to resources, Native Americans have negotiated, resisted, and contested pressures toward assimilation through organized, collective activities, including political mobilization and cultural revitalization (Dunaway, 1996; Gutierrez, 1991; Nagel, 1996).

Resistance has also occurred, although often less visible to outsiders, through day-to-day interactions, as individual actors seek to construct meaningful and coherent identities and lives in the midst of social and political processes and pressures. This invisibility is structured into the master narrative, in which Indian women are presented as either passive squaws, whose actions are guided by "natural" forces, rather than by knowledge or intellect, or as Pocahontas, whose agency is defined only in relation to Anglos (Green, 1990). The construction of knowledge in this metanarrative is also knowledge of a particular type—instrumental, objective knowledge that can be used to predict and harness the forces of humanity and nature toward the ends of a few (Beck & Walters, 1977).

Ontological narratives, or the stories that "actors use to make sense of . . . their lives" (Somers & Gibson, 1994, p. 61), help to define who we are, providing a framework for understanding our place and our actions in the world (Somers & Gibson, 1994; Taylor, 1989). Women's ontological narratives offer important insights into individual experiences and interpretations of social processes. In so doing, they both challenge the assumptions of the metanarrative and illuminate the ways that it has shaped action and self-understanding over time (Beck & Walters, 1977; Personal Narratives Group, 1989; Somers & Gibson, 1994). In this analysis[5] particular attention is given to interrelationships among language, knowledge, and identity as each surfaces throughout the narratives of two women, Faye and Ursula, both of whom identify themselves as Navajo. I argue that these themes reappear precisely because of their importance in resisting the master narrative of progress, assimilation, and civilization. While the analysis focuses on Navajo identity, throughout the narratives the speakers' identities as women, mothers, daughters, and granddaughters are also apparent, illustrating the intersections of multiple identities (Calhoun, 1994; Lemert, 1994; Woodward, 1997). These narrative accounts speak to the important role played by women's day-to-day actions in resisting assimilation or subordination to dominant social and cultural systems (Ward, 1993)—that is, in speaking and acting against the master narrative.

FAYE'S STORY

"Don't Ever Forget You're a Navajo": Constructing Identity.

Faye was born in 1918, in a *hogan*[6] located across the road from the modest ranch-style home where we sat in 1993 and talked about her life. During her birth, Faye's mother was assisted by her grandmother, who was knowledgeable in midwifery and the use of medicinal herbs. The second oldest of 12 children, Faye's early years were spent in the context of an extended family network that included her grandparents, her parents, 10 sisters, and 1 brother. During her childhood there were few schools on the Navajo Nation. Federal programs relocated Navajo children to boarding schools some distance from the reservation. The federal government at this time financed the Indian Boarding Schools on a per capita basis, providing an incentive for Indian agents to obtain children, often without the approval and sometimes without the knowledge of their parents. Many families, including Faye's, hid their children from the Indian agents to prevent them from being sent away to boarding schools. "There were two people that used to come around picking up children and forcibly taking them to Fort Defiance. A chubby fat Anglo man came out here in a horse and buggy and picked up children and forced them. We'd all hide somewhere—inside a barrel. We'd be sitting there while our parents talked to the chubby man." Eventually the family decided to enroll the older children in a boarding school not too far from their home. "My mother told me that my uncle and my aunt and my sisters were all going to school. I was 5 years old and I wanted to go. They used to take the students to Fort Defiance to boarding school. It was an army post and they turned it into a school. My mother said I started crying and wanted to stay" with her sister when they took the children to drop them off at the school. "My dad said it was OK, someday I'd make a good life for myself knowing two languages."

Faye described the strict rules and military orientation that she encountered at the school, typical of those of the period.

> The way they used to treat children when we went to school, it was just like the army—line us up. They'd blow the bugle, that means everybody gets dressed and go line up and start marching. If you didn't, you'd be given a good paddle. They got us up at 5:00 in the morning, even in the wintertime. It would be dark and everybody would be out marching around in the cold. One time I fainted out there and they took me to the hospital and the doctor told them I had pneumonia and I couldn't march any more so I got out of that. It was just like army life.

Despite these conditions, Faye loved school and went on to attend a boarding school in Santa Fe, New Mexico. In her sophomore year she left school to marry and subsequently completed her G.E.D. She continued her education as an adult, completing her bachelor's degree in education while raising 6 daughters.

Although Faye went away to boarding school at a young age, she continued to have close contact with her extended family. She spent summers at home and learned midwifery and herbal medicine from her mother and grandmother. She described her grandmother's lessons and advice about the knowledge that might be gained at school, saying:

> When I'd be herding sheep with my grandmother . . . she'd tell me certain things to go by. She'd say "You're a Navajo. When you go to that school you learn that language and listen for the good things there. Like me—I never went to school and you see these things here—this mother earth and the sunshine hits here and these plants—some are poison and some are herbs and medicines." And she used to tell me about the herbs and maybe several of them would be put together (to make medicines).

This account of lessons from her grandmother began with her explicit message reminding Faye of her Navajo identity. Having located Faye firmly within the group, her grandmother went on to use her knowledge of medicinal herbs to emphasize the potential risks as well as the potential benefits of Western values and beliefs. She noted the possibility for gleaning information and skills from the

Anglo culture that, when combined with Navajo knowledge and understandings, might be even more powerful, at the same time warning that some of the knowledge gained might be "poison." Both Faye's father's decision to allow her to go to school and her grandmother's advice emphasize that both cultures and languages have good things to offer, with the caveat that Faye must select carefully.

While recognizing the potential value of drawing on two cultures, Faye's narrative also emphasized the importance of maintaining a distinct Navajo identity. "That's what my grandpa used to tell me, 'You're a Navajo and don't ever forget it. So when you grow up to womanhood you can tell your grandchildren to live this way and they can have a good life. Whenever you're with your friends and they start to go a certain way, you can tell them don't ever forget you're a Navajo and go by these certain things." In addition to emphasizing the expectation that Navajo women will bear and rear children, this excerpt also conveys Faye's role in maintaining a sense of collective identity and links Navajo identity to a moral framework. Identity becomes a frame for acting in the world—for defining "a good life" (Taylor, 1989). As she recounts her grandparent's words, they claim Faye as Navajo and locate her in relation to past, present, and future generations of Navajo—distinct from outsiders/Anglos. Faye's narrative makes clear the expectation, conveyed through her grandparents' voices, that she will pass along this understanding of what it means to be Navajo to future generations. "My grandmother used to tell me when I was growing up—I herded sheep with her—she used to tell me a story. 'Someday you're going to grow up and have a family of your own. The first thing you have to think about is how you're going to help them have a good life'"—that is, a Navajo life.

"I Have to Teach My Grandchildren in the English Language": Language and Identity.

Faye was not alone in her attention to the task of conveying to later generations a sense of Navajo identity and history. As women spoke about what it meant to be Navajo, they noted the responsibility to convey to their children and grandchildren a sense of identity and an understanding of self in relation to the group (Schulz, 1994a, 1998), that is, to contribute to the cultural survival of the group. The challenges associated with this responsibility were linked with the profound economic and social transformations occurring during Faye's lifetime that interrupted the processes through which she and her grandmother had developed a sense of shared Navajo identity and history.

Among these were the challenges of language and shared meaning. While Faye was fluent in English and could converse with her grandchildren quite readily in that language, she struggled to convey ideas and concepts central to what it meant *to her* to be Navajo.

> In my own language I can know just about all the things that were taught by my parents and grandparents—the sun, the moon, the stars,

and everything. You're told how they were made in the Navajo language. My grandpa used to tell us we're a part of all that. We have water we drink, so we have these things, the minerals are part of us. The kids only know English. If these things could only be taught in the Navajo language. Some of them (children of her grandchildren's generation) don't understand Navajo at all. They don't really have an understanding of how, where they fit into the universe.

Faye's own understanding of herself as Navajo, conveyed by her grandfather, connected her not only to other Navajo but also to the earth, the minerals, the universe. Communicating this understanding to her grandchildren was complicated as she noted, "My grandkids are all English-speaking people." She went on, saying, "I can teach in the Navajo language. I teach my grandchildren. I usually have to teach them in English." In English, however, concepts that were central to Faye's identity as Navajo, including her understanding of herself within the context of the universe, were difficult to communicate.

To be part of a culture means to belong to roughly the same conceptual and linguistic universe. As children interact with adults on a day-to-day basis, they internalize codes or symbols that enable them to convey and interpret concepts and ideas communicated through speech, gesture, and visualization (Hall, 1997, p. 22). However, these codes, symbols, concepts, and ideas are not received as intact and static entities, but rather are constructed, molded, and modified through interaction and interpretation, modified in the face of changing social and historical conditions. Thus, while Faye sought to teach her children and grandchildren what it meant to be Navajo, she also struggled with Navajo identity as a fluid construct, the meaning of which was constantly created and recreated. This was compounded by the inability of her grandchildren to speak the Navajo language and her inability to communicate constructs essential to her own understanding of what it means to be Navajo to them in the English language.

The tension or challenge arises in attempting to convey a sense of shared history and common experience, while at the same time recognizing that future generations must forge the meanings of their own identities under social and political conditions that differ from those of preceding generations (Hall, 1997; Schulz, 1998). Identity is negotiated at this interface between history, memory, and contemporary circumstances. Faye attempts to convey to her grandchildren a sense of connection to the Navajo as a distinct group, not defined solely in relation to European Americans. At the same time, she recognizes that her own understanding of herself as Navajo was constructed out of experiences and social and political contexts that differed from those of younger generations (Schulz, 1998). The theme of subjective knowledge wove throughout Faye's narrative and crystallized in the story with which this chapter begins. Through that account, Faye emphasized herself as a source of knowledge. She and her grandfather both recognized her meditation/reflection as a valid—essential—means through which to understand the source of the problems she was experiencing. However, her experience both grew out of, and was interpreted or given meaning within, the context of the diagnostic relationship between herself and her grandfather, who was a healer.

Ursula's Story

"Our Opinion Was Important": Validating the Self as a Source of Knowledge.

This emphasis on maintaining trust in one's self as a source of knowledge was a central theme around which Ursula, the third of Faye's 7 daughters, organized her narrative. Born in 1947, Ursula attended school following World War II, during a period of renewed efforts to promote assimilation. These efforts included relocation programs that moved Native Americans from reservation communities to urban communities for employment, removal of tribal status for many groups, and, in general, an increased intolerance for distinct groups within the United States (Ourada, 1979).

Ursula described her experience attending a Catholic boarding school briefly in high school.

> I guess I was a very inquisitive person and I also was sort of like a natural-born skeptic or something because. . . . For example, when they would teach religion or something I would challenge them on certain issues. . . . And they would always say to me, well, these things you have to accept on faith alone, and they wouldn't give an explanation to things. . . . And many times, the response I get was well, (like) I wasn't challenging a manmade rule or something. It would be like, well, you're not being obedient. You're being bold and brassy and that's a sin you know—they didn't encourage assertiveness.

Ursula described the impact of these responses to her assertiveness, saying: "They kind of reinforced, you're a bad person rather than OK, you're speaking out. It's good that you're speaking out but let's take a look at all of the issues. And more and more messages I got like that, I had really bad feelings about myself."

The assaults to her sense of self occurred in the context of challenges to her beliefs in Navajo spirituality. "The experience I had was that at the time, the nuns would challenge some of my cultural beliefs. They would label it as paganism. Some of the more traditional cultural beliefs that I had. The more I learned about their religion, the more in my mind I saw in some areas where it really reinforced my traditional beliefs, I didn't see any difference. And I felt comfortable with doing both. But they would always try to stamp your traditional beliefs out." Reflecting her mother's and grandparent's philosophy that both Navajo and Anglo languages, beliefs, and spiritual practices had something to offer, that they were not dichotomous, but rather could come together in mutually enhancing ways, Ursula confronted a set of beliefs in boarding school that were incompatible with her integrative view. The "antipodal categories" of Christian/pagan, civilized/savage, intellect/nearly dumb (Cornell, 1988) imbedded within the master narrative of Nature/Civilization were very much in evidence in Ursula's account of her experience. Within the master narrative, Navajo spiritual practices—and by implication, those who practiced them—were considered pagan, devalued, and delegitimized.

In contrast to her experience in the boarding school, Ursula described her experience within her family as one of learning to trust herself as a source of knowledge. She described family meetings:

We called it the White Eagle Club, and my dad was president, of course, and we all elected officers now and then but my dad was always president. In there he used to encourage us to speak up, he'd teach us that it was important for our voice to be heard and our opinion was important. And if there was a family problem to be solved, everyone got in on the problem solving. Everybody. And when you got into your club meetings, the president recognized you to speak, you couldn't say no. "I don't know" was not acceptable, and "I have nothing on my mind, I have nothing to say" was not acceptable. So I guess you know that was good training for me as far as being in school. When I came home they encouraged that so it kind of balanced things out.

Her parents' emphasis on trusting herself as a source of knowledge included developing trust in her ability to "take the best from both worlds and make it work. . . . That, yes, conflicts would come up, but learning to recognize those differences and turning them into a positive thing."

"I Learned to Incorporate the Spirit of the Spiritual Meanings in Activities of Daily Living": Integrating Spirituality and Action

Like Faye, who described her father and grandfather as instrumental in the development of her identity, Ursula also described the important and active role played by her father. She noted that it was her father's decision that she would be the one child in the family to be immersed in Navajo spiritual and cultural practices. When her parents left the reservation during the summer months to do seasonal farm work, Ursula was left with her grandmother.

Now I look back and I thank my dad for forcing me to have that experience, because now I cherish those moments I had with my grandmother. She had a donkey and I used to sit behind her on the donkey and we'd go herd sheep. She taught me everything about rug weaving everywhere from taking the wool off the sheep, to carding it, to spinning it, and putting up the loom. Some of the songs that go along with putting up a rug loom. Songs that you sing while you're weaving. Some of the spiritual aspects, like you never put up a loom without saying a prayer, a chant. So from my grandmother I learned how to incorporate the spirit of the spiritual meanings in activities of daily living. 'Cause she didn't separate them out.

As an adult, Ursula continued to call upon those summers with her grandmother:

I think that particularly when I come up with a real difficult problem or a difficult emotion or something that I'm feeling [I call upon] some of the things my grandmother taught me. The main thing that she taught me was how to enjoy the moments. And just to be very attentive to every single moment and action. I guess that's what I learned from her. That those were just really important. And that if you lost your ability to concentrate on what you're doing, that's when you invited trouble and that's when you had accidents. And that's when she would say, "You lost your mind, you got to bring it back you know." Or else she'd say, "Your mind is wandering with your soul. Come back to your body. You got to pay attention here."

Ursula describes her grandmother's emphasis on focusing her attention on the activities she was engaged with, not allowing her mind to wander or to turn to self-reflection or meditation at inappropriate times. However, she also notes the ways that her mother and grandmother encouraged her to develop trust in her ability to solve problems or find solutions through self-reflection when appropriate, saying: "I'd always remember them saying 'Sleep on it.' Or 'Ask for an answer in your dreams.' What they were telling me was dream as an extension of your mind activity. You can learn to meditate in your dreams too, if you ask for it. Now, that comes naturally to me."

Both Faye and Ursula's narratives emphasized self-reflection, the importance of context, and responsibility to self and community for decisions made and actions taken. Meditation, songs, prayers, chants, and ritual actions (like never putting up a loom without saying a prayer) were all aspects of this knowledge. As an adult, Ursula's work as a professional nurse-midwife brought her into daily contact with Western notions of organizing time that sometimes conflicted with her ability to enact these lessons.

What I learned from my grandmother is every single action you do, you think about it ahead of time. It's sort of like, your actions are based on how you thought about it. Another way to say it I guess is you meditate the action. But when I get busy in the work world, rush, rush, rush, sometimes you just do things without careful thinking, or so and so wants it by such-and-such a time, and it's got to be done, just give it to them. That doesn't make you feel good because the quality of the work is—you know you didn't put your heart and soul into it a lot of the time.

"The Words I Speak Will Continue on for Generation upon Generation": Subjective and Collective Knowledge

Like Faye, Ursula spoke of the importance of subjective knowledge as well as the social nature of knowledge. This included recognizing one's self as part of a collective, with responsibility for making decisions based on "awareness of what is going on around you and what life holds in store for you" (Beck & Walters 1977, p. 63). Ursula emphasized her role in transmitting the knowledge and values of the Navajo to her children and grandchildren.

Some of my values, that goes back to my grandmother and then her mother. 'Cause my mom used to tell me stories about how her grandmother would teach her about womanhood and things like that. And I guess the concept they used to say is well "Someday I will journey out of my body, my body will return to the bosom of the earth, but the words I speak will continue on for generation upon generation upon generation." So they kind of instill in you that you have a responsibility to carry on the oral tradition.

Here the theme of individual responsibility for teaching future generations and for contributing to the collective memory of the group resurfaces. The knowledge to be conferred was not simply information, such as the history of the Navajo, although that was one important component (Schulz, 1994a, 1994b). However, the teaching stories also convey more abstract frameworks for ways of seeing and thinking about things. Repetition of the stories at increasing levels of abstraction offers the listener the opportunity to unravel imbedded meanings that emerge over time (Beck & Walters, 1977; Trudelle Schwartz, 1997).

Like Faye, Ursula described the challenges she experienced in teaching her children the values she had learned from her grandmother:

One of the challenges for me is teaching cultural values. Because when you acculturate into a new culture, called the dominant society, and the school system is teaching those values (those of the dominant society), some of the values you teach at home are really difficult to do. That's what I find with teaching my children. Just trying to instill in kids a respect for traditional values seems to be really difficult.

In contrast to her own experiences growing up, Ursula did not believe that the schools her children attended explicitly undermined or devalued Navajo language or spirituality.[7] However, she noted that the emphasis within the schools on objective ways of knowing interfered with her children's ability to trust themselves and their experiences as sources of knowledge. "I think still in school, people focus on what they call reality in terms of what they can see, hear, and measure. Everything is measurable. If something is not, then it doesn't exist. I see that in my children's behavior. They have a difficult time grasping, or internalizing, some of those values that have to do with the mind, the soul, and the spirit."

The rhythms of Ursula's adult life, and those of her children, are structured around the institutions of school and work, and she noted earlier her own challenges in incorporating spiritual practices into that routine. She described her children's reactions to efforts to teach them the meditative and self-reflective practices that she learned from her grandmother: "When I try to teach my children they look at me like . . . well, first of all they tell me, how do you do that. I try to tell them, but it's too exterior for them yet—it's not interior."

Ursula and her children interact with educational and labor systems that pattern their day-to-day practices in ways that make it difficult to maintain aspects of what it means to her to be Navajo and to convey those aspects to her children:

The work world is a lot different from the traditional world of telling time by the sun. You had a lot of tasks to do and as long as you got them done before the sun went down, that was the main thing. Nobody really cared whether you adhered to a particular schedule or what. But now we have to teach (our children) the value of appointments and keeping on time and things like that. Because that's what they need in order to survive in the work world.

The ideal articulated by both Faye and Ursula of integrating Navajo and Anglo worlds is challenged as Ursula prepares her children to participate in Western economic systems where time, demands, and expectations are externally monitored. These demands conflict with values she was taught by her grandmother—responsibility to the collective, the importance of meditating on actions, and learning to trust herself and her own judgment by reflecting and listening to herself.

Understanding clearly these constraints, Ursula actively sought opportunities for her children to be exposed to alternative sources of meaning. "The only time that they really can get it is when we have ceremonies. I'm real strict there. I herd them in. It happens so infrequently now that you have got to go in. So they do and I notice that then they begin to bring that in. The vibrations they can relate to it a lot better." Exposing her children not only to the abstract ideas but also to the experiences, sights, smells, sounds, and rhythms of ceremonial practices enabled them to absorb and internalize some of the meanings that, for Faye and Ursula, were so central to developing an understanding of themselves as Navajo. Ursula sought to ensure that her children had available to them the resources that would enable them to create their own understandings of a Navajo identity—that is, reflecting, but not replicating, Ursula's own understanding of her Navajo identity.

Conclusion/Discussion

Faye's question—"How would you write about that?"—became the point of departure and the underlying theme around which this chapter was organized. Drawing on the intersecting themes of language, identity, and knowledge in Faye and Ursula's narratives, this chapter begins to explore how it is that we know what we know, including how it is that we know who we are. The preceding pages examine intersections among subjective knowledge, identity, and language as social constructs, influenced by political and social relationships within and between groups. Knowledge and identity reflect these relationships and are constructed in ways that reinforce, resist, and disrupt them.

Social theorist Dona Richards (1980, cited in Collins, 1990, p. 69) suggests that Western thought requires objectification, a process she describes as the "separation of the 'knowing self' from the 'known object,'" and Collins (1990) explicitly links the objectification of subordinate groups to processes of domination. Throughout their narratives, Faye and Ursula resist both separation and objectification. They construct themselves as "knowing selves" and name the ways that the separation of the self distorts knowledge and disrupts an understanding of themselves as Navajo. They claim the ability to define their own reality, including framing their identities as Navajo and encouraging their children and grandchildren to understand themselves as knowing Navajo subjects. bell hooks (1989) elaborates the connections between identity and knowledge, noting that, "As subjects, people have the right to define their own reality, establish their own identities, name their history. As objects, one's reality is defined by others, one's identity created by others, one's history named only in ways that define one's relationships to those who are subject" (p. 42). In defining themselves as subjects, not objects, of knowledge, Faye and Ursula name and claim themselves and their histories, distinct from the history portrayed within the master narrative.

Self-definition is, inevitably, a social process. As Linda Hogan writes in her novel, *Solar Storms,* "I had been empty space, and now I was finding a language, a story, to shape myself by. I had been alone and now there were others" (1995, p. 94). Language and a "story" that locate and connect individuals to past and future generations help us to define ourselves and to understand who we are in relation to others. Attempts to destroy language and to deny the self or the collective as sources of knowledge are aspects of the process of domination that directly interfere with the construction of a sense of valued group identity. Faye and Ursula's narratives describe their own efforts, and those of their parents and grandparents, to maintain and convey to their children a sense of Navajo identity, language, and subjective knowledge. Their narratives should not be interpreted as simply "traditionalistic"—the voices of women who are mired in an unretrievable past, unable to face up to contemporary realities (Cohen, 1985). Both clearly recognized that their children and grandchildren live in a different time and encounter different challenges than they did in their own lives. Faye, speaking about her grandchildren, said, "Of course, they have their conflicts, too. I guess that's what my grandma meant when she said you have to think about how you're going to help that child have a good life." She used her own past as a resource, drawing on her memories and experiences to help her to understand how to help her grandchildren have a good life—to understand themselves as Navajo and to understand their place in the universe. For both Faye and Ursula that understanding was connected to language and to the self as a source of knowledge. At the same time that they sought to construct a meaningful and valued sense of self and to assist their children and grandchildren in doing the same, they struggled against the reification of what it means to be Navajo. Faye and Ursula recognized that their children and grandchildren would construct their own identities as Navajo, reflecting the social conditions they encountered in their own lives. Understanding the ways that these social conditions, including the ideologies embedded within the master narratives, might obscure an understanding of themselves and their history, Faye and Ursula sought to convey the history and experience as Navajo through their own understandings of what it meant to be Navajo. The challenge is to enable younger generations to assert themselves as knowing subjects who construct identities shaped, but not determined, by their histories.

NOTES

1. Each of the authors made important contributions to this chapter. The first author is responsible for the organization of the chapter and the analysis that links the themes within the interviews to the sociological literature on identity. The second and third authors contributed their stories and their analyses of their experiences through their oral narratives. All three authors discussed the contents and presentation of ideas.

2. Unless otherwise indicated, use of the first person ("I") in the text refers to the first author, Amy Schulz.

3. Political and symbolic meanings are associated with the terms used to refer to those who lived in North America prior to the arrival of Europeans. These include *Native American, American Indian, First Nation, Indian, Native,* or *Indigenous*. There is disagreement regarding the appropriate term to use, or whether it is appropriate to use any one term to refer to the many groups that are incorporated within this broader conceptual category. Most of the women interviewed for the study from which these narratives were drawn used the term *Indian,* although as described elsewhere (Schulz, 1998) many also distanced themselves from the meanings that are associated with this term. Recognizing the politics and disagreements surrounding this issue, I use the terms *American Indian, Indian,* and *Native American* interchangeably to refer collectively to the descendants of those who lived in North America prior to the arrival of Europeans. Similarly, the language used to refer to European Americans is complex and carries with it both political and symbolic meanings. In sections of this paper where I draw on primary and secondary historical documents to examine U.S. policies and ideologies, I use the terms *European colonists, European Americans,* and *white* interchangeably to reflect both the geographic origin and the Western belief systems that shaped these policies. In general, when using the narratives, I use the terms most often used by the Navajo women to refer to whites, *Anglo* and *biela'gáana.*

4. I use the terms *metanarrative* and *master narrative* interchangeably to refer to dominant narratives that provide an overarching framework for interpreting social relationships. The socially constructed nature of metanarratives and the political relationships imbedded within them are obscured, while alternate narratives tend to be repressed or delegitimized.

5. See Schulz (1994a, 1998) for discussions of the methodology, sample, and analysis process for the study from which this chapter was drawn.

6. A *hogan* (or *hooghan*) is a traditional Navajo dwelling.

7. Not all women I interviewed on the Navajo Nation shared this perspective. Others felt that, although the schools no longer explicitly promoted assimilation, children continued to be exposed to the racialized ideologies that constructed Indians as deficient through their day-to-day interactions in the schools, media, and experiences off the reservation (Schulz, 1994a).

References

Anderson, B. (1983). *Imagined communities: Reflections on the origins and spread of nationalism.* London: Verso Press.

Barth, F. (1969). *Ethnic groups and boundaries: The social organization of culture difference.* Boston: Little, Brown.

Beck, P. V. & Walters, A. L. (1977). *The sacred: Ways of knowledge, sources of life.* Tsaile, AZ: Navajo Community College Press.

Berkhofer, R. F. (1979). *The white man's Indian: Images of the American Indian from Columbus to the present.* Norman: University of Oklahoma Press.

Bourdieu, P. (1977). *Outline of a theory of practice.* Cambridge: Cambridge University Press.

Calhoun, C. (1994). Social theory and the politics of identity. In C. Calhoun (Ed.), *Social theory and the politics of identity* (pp. 9–36). Cambridge, MA: Blackwell Publishers.

Cohen, A. P. (1985). *The symbolic construction of community.* London: Routledge.

Collins, P. H. (1990). *Black feminist thought: Knowledge, consciousness, and the politics of empowerment.* Boston: Unwin Hyman.

Cornell, S. (1988). *Return of the native: American Indian political resurgence.* New York: Oxford University Press.

Cronan, W. (1983). *Changes in the land: Indians, colonists, and the ecology of New England.* New York: Hill and Wang.

Drinnon, R. (1997). *Facing West: The metaphysics of Indian-hating and empire-building.* Norman: University of Oklahoma Press.

Dunaway, W. A. (1996). Incorporation as an interactive process: Cherokee resistance to expansion of the capitalist world system. *Sociological Inquiry, 44* (4), 455–70.

Gans, H. (1992). Preface. In L. Fournier & M. Fournier (Eds.), *Cultivating differences: Symbolic boundaries and the making of inequality* (pp. vii–xv). Chicago: University of Chicago Press.

Green, R. (1990). The Pocahontas perplex: The image of Indian women in American culture. In E. C. DuBois & V. L. Ruiz (Eds.), *Unequal sisters: A multicultural reader in U.S. women's history* (pp. 15–21). New York: Routledge.

Gutierrez, R. A. (1991). *When Jesus came, the corn mothers went away.* Stanford: Stanford University Press.

Hall, S. (1997). The work of representation. In S. Hall (Ed.), *Representation: Cultural representations and signifying practices* (pp. 15–75). London: Sage.

Hogan, L. (1995). *Solar storms.* New York: Simon & Schuster.

hooks, b. (1989). *Talking back: Thinking feminist, thinking black.* Boston: South End Press.

Lemert, C. (1994). Dark thoughts about the self. In C. Calhoun (Ed.), *Social theory and the politics of identity,* (pp. 100–30). Cambridge, MA: Blackwell Publishers.

Nagel, J. (1996). *American Indian ethnic renewal: Red power and the resurgence of identity and power.* New York: Oxford University Press.

Ortner, S. (1984). Theory in anthropology since the sixties. *Comparative Studies of Society and History, 26,* 126–66.

———(1989). *High religion: A cultural and political history of Sherpa Buddhism.* New Jersey: Princeton University Press.

Ourada, P. K. (1979). Dillon Seymour Meyer. In R. M. Kvasnicka & H. Viola (Eds.), *The commissioners of Indian affairs, 1824–1977* (pp. 204–19). Lincoln, NB: Lincoln University Press.

Personal Narratives Group (Ed.). (1989). Conditions not of her own making. In *Interpreting women's lives: Feminist theory and personal narratives* (pp. 19–23). Bloomington: Indiana University Press.

Richards, D. (1980). European mythology. In M. K. Asante & A. Sa. Vandi (Eds.), *Contemporary black thought* (pp. 59–79). Beverly Hills, CA: Sage.

Schulz, A. (1994a). "I raised my children to speak Navajo . . . . My grandkids are all English speaking people": Identity, resistance and transformation among Navajo women. Unpublished dissertation, University of Michigan. Ann Arbor: University Microfilms.

———(1994b). "I didn't want a life like that": Constructing a life between cultures. In C.

E. Franz & A. J. Stewart (Eds.), *Women creating lives: Identities, resilience, and resistance* (pp. 127–40). Boulder, CO: Westview Press.

_____(1998). Navajo women and the politics of identity. *Social Problems, 45* (3), 336–55.

Sewell, Jr., W. (1989). Towards a theory of structure: Duality, agency and transformation. CSST Working Paper #29, the University of Michigan, Ann Arbor.

Somers, M. R. & Gibson, G. D. (1994). Reclaiming the epistemological "other": Narrative and the social constitution of identity. In C. Calhoun (Ed.), *Social theory and the politics of identity* (pp. 37–99). Cambridge, MA: Blackwell Publishers.

Takaki, R. (1993). *A different mirror: A history of multicultural America.* Boston: Little, Brown.

Taylor, C. (1989). *Sources of the self: The making of modern identity.* Cambridge: Harvard University Press.

Trudelle Schwartz, M. (1997). *Molded in the image of Changing Woman: Navajo views on the human body and personhood.* Tucson: University of Arizona Press.

Ward, K. B. (1993). Reconceptualizing world systems theory to include women. In P. England (Ed.), *Theory on gender/feminism on theory*. New York: Aldine de Gruyter.

Waters, M. C. (1990). *Ethnic options: Choosing identities in America.* Berkeley and Los Angeles: University of California Press.

Woodward, K. (1997). *Identity and difference.* London: Sage, and The Open University.

Voicing Complexity

"I've Got to Try to Make a Difference":
A White Woman in the Civil Rights Movement[1]

*W*E DON'T KNOW MANY STORIES about women as political activists. The ones we do know are mostly about women's pursuit of their own political rights. The few stories we've heard about the activism of white women in the civil rights movement have been about women who started there, became disillusioned with their role on the sidelines in that movement, and created the "second wave" of the women's movement (see e.g., Evans, 1979). In that story, white women's activism in the civil rights movement is really the starting point for a new phase of the women's movement.

But what if we ask how and why white women got into the civil rights movement in the first place? And what of women who made antiracist activism their main commitment? These white women, like their male counterparts in the movement, were engaged in a political struggle not to secure their own rights, but rather to end a system of racial oppression that apparently benefited them. Unlike their male counterparts, though, the women in the civil rights movement were taking political actions that were outside the bounds of traditional gender roles. What is the story behind those facts? How and why did some white women get there? It is this story—of white women's involvement in civil rights activism—that we *don't* know very well (see Barnard, 1990; Colby & Damon, 1992; Daloz et al., 1996; Stalvey, 1970; Tatum & Knaplund, 1996, for exceptions).

Because I was interested in that story, I interviewed my friend's stepmother, Noma Jensen Genné, who had been part of the national staff of the National Association for the Advancement of Colored People (NAACP) from 1943–47. In this essay, I will examine how our ideas about women's lives make it difficult to hear some parts of her story. I will argue that familiar narratives about women's lives get in the way of less familiar, equally important, ones, leaving us "deprived of the narratives . . . by which [women] might assume power over . . . their own lives" (Heilbrun, 1988, p. 17). I will begin by recounting Noma's story, as she told it to me.

NOMA JENSEN GENNÉ'S STORY

At our first meeting, Noma Genné began with the same question I had, in telling me her story. She was aware of other people's curiosity about how she ended up on the NAACP national staff: "There have been—oh, I can't tell you the number of times—when people heard that I was the only white person on the national staff of the NAACP would ask, 'Why did you take the job?' And 'How did you get the job?' And I've said, 'Well, I think I was in the right place at the right time,' but that is too simplistic an answer because there are a lot of reasons for it." In explaining how she ended up in "the right place at the right time," Noma told me that she had little direct experience with people of color in her childhood and adolescence in upstate New York (Saratoga Springs), during the 1920s and 30s: "When I was growing up in school there were only white people. The only time we had black people—colored people, Negroes—was in the summer time when they came to work at the race track or the restaurants there." Despite the absence of black people in her world, Noma was exposed to her father's race prejudice. Her father expressed contempt for "Negroes" as for many groups, approving heartily only of Scandinavians (his background was Danish on both sides)—and even then, not Swedes.

In the context of this life experience, Noma explained that, a few months into her first year in college, "I started talking with a young black woman who was also in teacher's college. The reason why we even started talking was because we were both enamored with one of our professors." Through her friendship with Julia and the incidents they experienced together, Noma feels that she developed an understanding of racism.

But how—with her limited exposure to black people, and her extensive exposure to racist attitudes—did Noma form this friendship? In her own mind, it was simple: Julia was an attractive, intelligent person, and they shared an affinity for their English teacher. Noma also pointed out, "I was fortunate in the fact that my mother was not race prejudiced . . . she felt that so many of the things that my father said were just bad, about people." Somehow, then, Noma warded off her father's attitudes: "When I would hear my father rail forth . . . I would just close my ears and not listen."

A great deal of Noma's account of her early family life involved her own usually quiet rebellion against her father, and her mother's usually tacit support. One critical conflict took place around religion. Noma's mother was French Canadian and had been raised Lutheran, but the family was not churchgoing. Noma grew interested in attending church because of her close relationship with a churchgoing neighbor couple who had lost their son and taken an interest in Noma and her brother. This couple offered to take the two children to their Baptist church with them. Noma's mother offered no objection, and the social life and activities associated with the church opened up worlds for Noma that were both fun and filled with meaning for her. When she reached her teens, she wanted to join the church. Her father refused to allow it; Noma eventually defied him and moved out of the house for a period while he cooled off.

This open conflict with her father about religion was, in Noma's view, an aberration. Generally Noma felt that, like her mother, she avoided confrontations with her father. "I've always been the kind of person that gets very upset when people have these violent confrontations. I never wanted to argue in any kind of heated discussion. And I always knew [with my father] it would be heated."

Interestingly, Noma's father strongly supported Noma's education, including her aspiration for college: "In my high school, I fortunately was an honor student. In my senior year I won the home economics prize. So when my father heard that, he thought I would be going into home economics, and I said, well, I think I want to go to teacher's college, and I think I want to teach. That was okay with him." In retrospect, though, the important thing about college for Noma was not so much the coursework, or the preparation for teaching, but her friendship with Julia. In her mind, that relationship was profoundly formative of her commitment to antiracist activism. The pivotal experiences involved personal exposure to racist acts. She explained:

> I lived about four miles from Temple University and so, with the carfare and everything—it was the Depression—I didn't have the money for carfare going back and forth. For lunch I had to eat there somewhere and Julia did too. Julia must have been pretty confident of the fact that I would not be rambunctious when something happened in a restaurant, because I'm sure she knew that something was going to happen, and I didn't.

In Noma's view, then, Julia was both experienced with racism, and experienced at sizing up whites; she had sized Noma up as a white person who could benefit from these experiences and would not make a bad situation worse.

> The first experience I remember is they just refused to serve us. We sat there and we sat there! We finally gave up and walked out. But it was awfully hard for me to concede to it. She was not only a lovely person in every way, but she was beautiful. . . . How could anybody be disrespectful and unkind to somebody that just looked so good? If she had been a black person that had been unkempt, I probably would have understood why we were not served.

Noma expresses her sense of the injustice of the failure to be served as having been aroused not so much by the generic injustice involved, but by the highly specific injustice of failing to serve this particular, attractive, tidy, person.

Bound up in this thinking is both an intuitive tendency to take people one at a time and a search for some reasonable justification for disrespectful behavior (unkemptness). This combined capacity for valuing individuals, for outrage at injustice, and for serious consideration of the perspective of others is present in Noma's responses to many subsequent situations.

Noma's education was only beginning, with this incident. "The next time we went—Julia waited a while, for I guess she didn't want to expose me to this too quickly—the second time we went to another restaurant. And the food was so unpalatable that we couldn't eat it. So here on the little money that both of us had, you know, we had to spend it—but that was it." Soon after these experiences, Noma learned about a group of theological students who were involved with an "interracial fellowship house."

> A woman who was well-to-do had a large house and was interested in doing something about bringing about better relationships between colored and white people. . . . She said, "I've got this large home, I'm all alone, and I'd love having you here." She said, "I'm not a good cook, but I've got money for the food, so you come and if there isn't food made, you just help yourself, and make the food and stay and talk." And that's what we did.

About 20 young people—black and white, male and female—"could talk freely and eat together" and that group included Noma and Julia. Throughout those college years, then, Noma felt that "being a close friend of Julia gave me the opportunity to sound off and talk to her and to try to get some meaning out of all of this that was happening. Julia certainly had a much better understanding of it than I had, because she had been living it. She had been living it and I hadn't." For Noma, then, this friendship provided her with an extended education that allowed her to develop an understanding adequate to support a personal commitment to antiracist activism.

When she graduated from Temple in 1940, she took a job with the Cleveland Baptist Association. "My principal job was to work there primarily with young people, both Negro and white. When I took the job I had great aspirations for what I would be able to do. [But] I had a very, very difficult time." Noma's main task was to direct a children's camp. In her first year, she was extremely distressed that the camp turned out to be all white: "I went ahead with the camp, thinking there would be black children, as well as counselors at the camp. Not a black person anywhere." She spoke to her supervisor, who explained that the Baptist churches there were deeply segregated, and that although they occasionally exchanged ministers for a Sunday, the black and white churches were not used to joining together. After reflecting on this, Noma decided that she would make her priority recruiting black children for the camp the next summer. Her supervisor approved, and she was "on a cloud—I thought, boy, this is my chance." However, "I worked my tail off trying to get a black child to come to that camp, and the only black child I got was the daughter of one of my personal friends."

Noma expressed her discouragement not only to her supervisor but also to her minister, who was the only white member on the board of the Cleveland NAACP. Recognizing a common commitment, he invited her to join him in the NAACP. Soon thereafter, Shirley Graham, from the national NAACP office, visited Cleveland. Her minister asked Graham if there were openings on the national staff and indicated that "Noma is really wasting her time and she is wasting her talents by being here. I think she could do a good job within the NAACP."

Graham recounts this incident in her memoir of her husband, W. E. B. Du Bois (Du Bois, 1971). In that account, she describes Noma:

> Like so many first-generation Americans [both of her parents were immigrants], she was deeply patriotic and highly idealistic about all things American save one thing—race prejudice. After college graduation she became a social worker in Cleveland, where her convictions and ideals regarding work in Negro communities frequently clashed with the policies of her employers. When, after one of our meetings in Cleveland, she came to speak to me, I found her unhappy and frustrated. . . . When I returned to New York, I talked to Walter White about her. After some correspondence she came to New York and applied in person for a job on the staff. Her natural charm and utter sincerity, added to her qualifications won ready acceptance. (p. 55)

At the national office, Noma was asked by Thurgood Marshall and Roy Wilkins to initiate a new position: educational field secretary.

> I think the primary reason why Thurgood was so interested in having me do this was because he was already involved in some lawsuits in schools, and he made it very plain in talking to me. He said, "Noma, if we could do something in the schools, there would be a lot of lawsuits that we wouldn't have to go on with."
>
> But I was given the prerogative—a great responsibility—of devising the program. . . . And fortunately I had the good sense, I think, to know that I'd have to leave "race relations" out of it. That was such a trigger word, as it still is in some places today. So fortunately I hit upon the whole concept of "intercultural education". . . . I had to deal with mostly superintendents of schools, and of course they were all white: superintendents of schools, boards of education, community groups like the YWCA that were interested in doing things.

Noma searched for models for a program and found one in Springfield, Massachusetts. She asked for permission to visit Springfield and study the plan in action. She was enthusiastic about what she found. In March 1944, Noma described the key elements of the Springfield plan in an article for *The Crisis:* "It is a program of education in tolerance and practical democracy. The four basic principles of the program are that (1) education in tolerance is not a job for the schools alone. . . . (2) that there must be a sympathetic study of the backgrounds of minority groups; (3) a frank discussion of prejudices; and (4) a diffusion of the program throughout the entire school system." Introduced in the Springfield schools in 1939, this curriculum seemed to Noma to be enormously successful: "Here was not an 'experiment,' but a vital, working plan that was revolutionizing a New England city" (see Chatto & Halligan, 1945; Fine, 1944; Smith, 1944; Wise, 1945, for details of the Springfield plan).

When she returned from Springfield, Noma recommended that the Springfield plan serve as a model for other schools in the North. She was enthusiastic about the fact that the program integrated attention to race, immigration, nationality, and religion and tied them all together with a focus on democratic values and process. Together with Roy Wilkins, she set up an itinerary and set off to encourage cities, school systems, and individual teachers to implement this new program.

> There was no question about it that this whole idea of intercultural education really took off, and I had four really wonderful, wonderful years. I only traveled north of the Mason-Dixon Line, because the schools in the south were totally segregated, but it was such a rewarding experience for me. I worked harder in those four years than I ever worked before in my life, or ever worked since. I was working 14–16 hour days sometimes, and I traveled a lot, and I knew I was being watched.

Noma's work with the NAACP ended when she married Joe Genné in 1947. She met him when she was sent to Gary, Indiana, 2 years earlier, to investigate a strike by white students protesting the presence of black students in their school; Joe had been sent from Chicago to work with her. The situation in Gary was dangerous and frightening.

> Walter White and the Board of Directors sent me there to investigate what was going on, because it was in the New York papers, about the strike. . . . The white students were on strike . . . picketing. . . . Joe and I both were very fearful that there was going to be some violence, and . . . we found out . . . that I was being followed. And so they said I had to get out of there. We went on the night train to Chicago. Joe went

with me to the place where I stayed cause he said, "You can't go by your-self." So we went in a taxi to where I had been staying, we got on a train, and then we had to call Walter White. And I was so afraid some-one was listening in on that conversation with Walter White. I was being very careful, but I had, you know, I had to tell him, "We did gain evi-dence." So he said, "You need to go to Washington."

Noma and Joe had uncovered evidence that American Nazis were involved in fomenting the strike. On their long train ride to Washington, Noma discovered in Joe a true soul mate; he understood her sense of isolation from white friends and relatives. As she put it, "I think most of my friends were nonplussed about [my work]. I mean, they didn't know what to make of it, and so when we'd get together we'd talk about other things, we never talked about my job." With Joe, everything was different:

He seemed to share the feelings that I had about wanting terribly to be able to know and talk with someone who knew what you were talking about, and you didn't have to go into long explanations because he had experienced these things. He had the same kind of thing I had about people not talking to him, not understanding what he was doing, that I had. He had experience with people just like I had, where people would just close up and talk about everything else but what you were doing.

When Noma left the NAACP job to marry Joe and move to Chicago, she planned and delivered lectures on "Racism" to returned black and white service-men at Roosevelt College. However, in December of 1952, Joe died suddenly, not long after the birth of their daughter, Maria, and Noma's path took some unex-pected turns. She moved to Long Island, where Joe's sister lived, and took a job in religious education. When Maria was about 9 in 1960, Noma decided "We've got to leave this WASP-ish town because this isn't the kind of environment—Joe would never do this, bring up a child in an environment like that. I thought, I've just got to get out of here."

So Noma and her 9-year-old daughter moved back to Hyde Park in Chicago, and Noma looked for a job that would support them. She accepted a position with the Chicago YWCA and became director of the integrated USO Program (serving black and white servicepeople, with a fully integrated staff); she held this position for 13 years. In this job, Noma felt that "the experience that I had in the field of race relations made it better—made me much more capable than I would have been otherwise."

Now retired, when she reflects on her years at the NAACP it is clear that Noma is proud of what she accomplished. Roy Wilkins wrote to her that "You've rendered intelligent and devoted service." She also recalls that when she said good-bye to Thurgood Marshall, he said, "It's been good working with you, Noma—I'm awful glad you saved us a lot of money." She knew he appreciated the fact that she had "really been successful in a number of instances getting boards of education and community people together and working on this whole business of integration." Generally, though, Noma dwells on the privilege it was to encounter three people in the course of her work at the NAACP: Thurgood Marshall ("when he entered a room he soon became the center of attention") W. E. B. Du Bois ("I was so awed by him! He was so brilliant! I was thrilled to have the opportunity to be near him, observing his mannerisms and hearing him hold forth on pertinent subjects"); and Eleanor Roosevelt ("I covet the memory that I have of hearing her speak many times and being in her presence").

At the end of one of our interviews, Noma and I talked about race relations today—about her discouragement over continuing racism, about the progress that has been made, and about the progressive work her daughter and step-daughter are doing. She recalled a visit with Julia many years after those incidents when they were both at Temple. "She came to visit me in Saratoga during the racing season. . . . And we went to the races together and she wanted to take me out to dinner somewhere, and we went to one of the really nice restaurants, and I . . . I mean there are such extremes! In our early relationship we were refused service, and then to be able to go to a top-notch restaurant in Saratoga . . . how do you put that together?" At this point in her life, Noma is grateful for the progress that's been made and for the experiences she had working in the movement: "There is so much that is still to be done. . . . I'm so thankful that my mind has stayed so clear because I have all these vivid memories of all this that has happened. What it is doing is greatly enriching my life because . . . I see this pattern that has evolved."

UNCOVERING STORIES

Noma's story is not familiar, yet part of its power is the fact that embedded in it are some stories that *are* familiar. These familiar plots may help conceal some unfamiliar features not only of this story but also other women's stories. Carolyn Heilbrun (1988), a theorist of women's biography, has suggested that the plots used to describe women's lives are different from those used to narrate men's; they take place on a smaller scale and are shorter, often ending with marriage. These "plots" are used, then, not only by writers of fiction and biography but also by women ourselves, to understand our own lives. She suggests that these familiar, or conventional, narratives may crowd out less familiar, more unconventional understandings not only of other women's lives but of also our own.

Noma's story includes some of the plots that are familiar in tales of women's lives: the "friendship of two women" plot, and the "tragic romance" plot. We will see that in Noma's life these plots were certainly not conventional in their details, but the very familiarity of the plots tends to drain the political and social meaning from Noma's story and to overshadow the "quest" and "adventure" plots (usually reserved for men), that are also there! Noma's friendships with two black women (Julia and Shirley Graham) and her love relationship with Joe Genné were deeply meaningful and important aspects of her story. These relationship stories tend to overwhelm the narrative, suppressing other stories we need to know: stories of Noma's self-education, her agency in her own life, her courage, and her political commitment.

The (Interracial) Friendship Plot

Noma explains how she came to understand something about racism by discussing her friendship with Julia; this is not merely a friendship of two women, then—a relationship of intimacy founded on similarity. It is partly that (recall their shared crush on their teacher); it is also—like formative friendships of many whites who become involved with antiracist activism—a relationship founded on recognizing and examining their racial differences (see also Stalvey, 1970).

Noma attributes to Julia a kind of mentor role and points out that the racist incidents that she witnessed really happened to Julia: "I was thinking about what they were doing to her because I knew that it wouldn't have happened to me but it was happening to her." In my first conversations with Noma, she emphasized the power of these experiences and Julia's capacity to teach her about racism. In these accounts, Noma seemed to be the object of overwhelming events and careful tutelage. In our third interview, I mentioned to Noma that "It's interesting that you feel you avoid conflict temperamentally, but you chose to take on race relations as a topic." She responded: "I have really very strong feelings about the equality of people and their *right* to equality [emphasis hers]. And, then as I say, the experiences that I had with Julia, that was all greatly—that feeling was greatly accentuated. I thought, well, *I've got to try. I don't know what I can do, but I've got to try to make a difference, because I felt so strongly about it* [emphasis mine]." In this response, Noma makes clear that her own reaction was critical, and it was her reaction of *commitment* that actually moved the story—and events—along.

A second important interracial friendship of Noma's was with Shirley Graham, the NAACP staffer who first encouraged her application to work there. When Noma came to New York:

> I knew I had to find a place to live and Shirley said she needed to find a place to live, too. . . . I found out about this apartment in the paper, the Julliard Apartments, at 122nd St. and Broadway, and I rented it. I think the doorman—I thought he was going to have a heart attack when he

saw Shirley. But he accepted it. He looked at me as if I were dirt you know, pulling something like that off, getting a black person into that building. . . . We had many black persons as well as white persons there in our apartment . . . we warned them all about the doorman.

When I indicated that she had a lot of will and a lot of courage to take on this situation, Noma agreed she had will but not courage; she connected her experience to those with Julia: "As long as I live, I can still get upset when I think about how awful it was to see this friend of mine treated that way." The heart of the story for Noma, then, is the pain suffered by her friends and her love for them. The pain and the love are real and important elements of the story, but so, I would argue, are Noma's courage and her commitment to act not only on behalf of her friends but also on behalf of people she didn't know.

There is more to notice about the *form* of Noma's love of her friends. She had no condescension or sense of superiority in her affection. She speaks and writes with great respect, admiration, and warmth not only about Shirley and Julia but also about her colleagues and employers at NAACP. At the same time, Noma was far from "color-blind." She mentioned that while she worked for the organization, "I must admit that I went to more social gatherings than at any other time in my life—I was always invited and I was usually the only white person."

Despite her emphasis on her inclusion, and her admiration of many of the people she worked with, Noma does not romanticize her relationships with her colleagues. She has a practical, down-to-earth sense of how she was seen. For example, I asked her whether or not there were black staff members who didn't like her being there, who opposed having a white person on staff. She replied, "I think probably there were some but it was so negligible that I never felt it. I think that they recognized that I was doing a job they couldn't do. If I had taken one of their jobs, I think it would have been a whole different kettle of fish." Obviously Noma was comfortable with her role as a white person at NAACP. When she was first interviewed, Noma reported, "Walter White interviewed me and . . . he was very blond and blue eyed, fair skinned. And I had been of course [working at] the camp for 2 months. I was really brown, and of course my hair was brown then rather than the grayish stuff it is now, so after he had talked with me for awhile he said, 'Noma, you're not going to have any trouble. A lot of people are going to think you're colored.'"

Moreover, she pointed out, "Thurgood Marshall and Roy Wilkins . . . talked with me at length. I think they sensed that I felt comfortable with them. It would have been stupid for them to hire me [otherwise], because I had to work with black people. . . . But they knew I was doing something they couldn't do. They used to tease me about it. They'd say, 'Did they expect you to be white?' And I said, 'Half the time, they didn't.'"

She describes her first trip:

I went by train from New York to Minneapolis and when I got off the train there were a half dozen people, both colored and white. I could see that they were a little bit upset about something but I didn't know why. But one black woman with a beautiful warm smile [someone who later became a close friend] came up to me and said, "Miss Jensen, we don't have a big home but my husband and I would like you to stay with us while you are here." And I said, "Oh, how kind of you." She told me after what had happened. They had made a reservation for me in a black hotel thinking that I was black, and when they saw I wasn't they got very upset.

In addition to the importance of her own active commitment and pursuit of knowledge about race and racism, and her capacity for comfortable, genuine peer relations with black colleagues and friends, Noma's self-awareness about her own race is striking. She was apparently quite aware of her race privilege and comfortable talking openly about her own "whiteness." In fact, at our first interview, she started by showing me photographs of her as a young woman and pointed out that her granddaughter had recently commented, "Grandma, you were once good looking." She had answered, "Well, honey, fortunately I was, because *I was exhibit A, the only white person,* so the photographers went crazy [emphasis mine]." She went on to point out: "I was in these various places, and . . . there were so many—where black and white people were just not together in 1943. And to have a white woman come and speak at one of the big rallies in the black church . . . I thought well, I'm sure that is why they are taking pictures."

Noma's feelings about her whiteness were not simple. She was grieved by the actions of white racists. In fact she said:

The only people that I think I really feared—and I can't say that it was an intense fear because of the protection I got—but these radical white people that would come and with their snarly voice say "nigger-lover," "commie," and stuff. They would look at me and I know—I'm sure I shuddered many times because of them. But at the same time I was very aware that there were black people there that were going to protect me, and a number of times they would circle around me so that nobody could get close to me.

Noma also felt alienated from white friends and relatives who were uninterested in her work and mystified by her politics (a common pattern for whites who become active in antiracist activism; see Barnard, 1985; Tatum & Knaplund, 1996). It was this alienation that was so thoroughly addressed by her romance with Joe Genné.

The Tragic Romance Plot

Noma's relationship with Joe Genné is the stuff of movies: the exciting encounter with him in the context of the dangerous Gary school strike; the night train to Washington, the long night of intimate conversation; finally, perfect understanding with a white person who shared the same politics, the same commitment. Noma's love and admiration for Joe are visible in her intensity and delight when she talks of him even now. She saw him as brilliant, an avid reader, and as deeply committed to civil rights as she was ("We basically felt so strongly about the fact that all men were created equal . . . that motivated a lot of what he did, just like it motivated a lot of what I did, although his was an avocation all the time"). This story is the most familiar of all: the story of true love overcoming obstacles—ending with marriage and a safely domestic life for the woman, who therefore serves as muse and support to a gifted man. Noma and Joe's love story can be fit to that mold, but there is much more to it than that.

Heilbrun outlines the normal marriage plot:

> For a short time, during courtship, the illusion is maintained that women, by withholding themselves, are central. Women are allowed this brief period in the limelight—and it is the part of their lives most constantly and vividly enacted in a myriad of representations—to encourage the acceptance of a lifetime of marginality. And courtship itself is, as often as not, an illusion: that is, the woman must entrap the man to ensure herself a center for her life.

There are some ways in which Noma's story, as she tells it, fits this account. As soon as Joe Genné enters the narrative, he dominates it; and either their marriage, or his death, seems to end it.

Nevertheless, Noma's story departs from this plot in several important respects. First, in the narrative of her life, Noma accords central roles both to her friendship with Julia and to her experience working on the national staff at the NAACP. Though meeting and marrying Joe did seem like "endings" to Noma's story, her life *before* meeting him is represented as rich and full. Thus, it is not his courtship of her that makes Noma central in the narrative.

Second, though the narrative does seem to end with Noma's marriage, or Joe's death (endings Heilbrun says are the only ones conventionally allowed to women; see e.g., p. 121), in fact there is great continuity in Noma's lifelong pursuit of a career in which she could make a contribution to improved race relations. Noma was employed for all but 3 years when Maria was a baby: "I talked this over with my husband. I wanted very much to be able to be home until it was time for Maria to enter school, and then, I was going back to work, because I knew that I wasn't really the typical housewife. And he felt so strongly about women having the same opportunities as men that he was all for it."

Noma's early return to paid employment was precipitated by Joe Genné's death, but it is clear that she fully intended to return a few years later in any case. While Noma stressed Joe's role in supporting her nontraditional self-definition, she also pointed to the importance of her own long independence in shaping it. "Most of my friends ended up getting married very shortly after college, and I think the main reason was they didn't know what jobs they could do. . . . I thought I really had privileges that were rare. I was very conscious of it." It is clear that Joe was a strong supporter of Noma's work, her independence, and of women's rights more generally. It is equally important that Noma *avoided* marriage to other men who might not have been.

When Noma moved to Long Island with Maria after Joe died, she needed to find a job. In her account of that period, we can see both Noma's tendency to represent events as happening to her and her recognition of the role of her own qualifications: "Joe's sister was a member of a Presbyterian church. . . . They were looking for a director of the religious education program, and this was the background that I had had—the courses that I had taken at the Baptist Institute, a college degree, and everything. They said, 'You want the job, you have it.' But it was a blessing." Carol Tomlinson-Keasey (1994) has pointed to the way in which chance and circumstance—what she calls "serendipity"—plays an important role in the course of women's lives. Noma does point to serendipity—here and in her account of returning to Chicago—but she also provides evidence of her own agency (her background, her qualifications), if we are alert to it. Tomlinson-Keasey suggests that Bateson's notion of "improvisation" (Bateson, 1989)—making something out of circumstances—may actually capture women's lives best; certainly it seems a more adequate description of Noma's life.

IMPROVISATION: AGENCY IN WOMEN'S LIFE NARRATIVES

Improvisation inevitably takes place in the context of constraint. It is important, though, not to be misled by the appearance of constraint to a false assumption of passivity or helplessness (see Stewart, 1994; Grossman & Stewart, 1990). Tomlinson-Keasey (1994) points to the important role of discontinuity in the narratives of women's lives and suggests that this discontinuity is the result of women's vulnerability to pressures from the lives of others. While this is no doubt partly true (Noma moved to Chicago and left the NAACP to marry Joe; Joe died and she moved to Long Island), it is also true that some discontinuities in Noma's narrative are driven substantially by her own decisions and frustrations. This may not always be evident, because Noma often emphasizes the role of others. For example, she explained that Shirley Graham came to visit Cleveland, and Noma's mentor asked her if there were openings for Noma in the NAACP: "And he said, 'I think she could do a good job within the NAACP.' So she went back to New York and talked with Walter White, and was hired by him about 2 weeks later."

In this narrative, it seems that Noma was "rescued" by these good people's actions. However, in describing the period leading up to this event, Noma said, "When the camp [that she had only been able to recruit one black child for] was over, I knew that I had to leave, that I needed to be thinking seriously about going, taking another job." She said she told her mentor, "'I'm just wasting my time, I'm wasting your time too.' I had a lot of energy and I wanted to change the world." Moreover, Shirley Graham's account of her visit to Cleveland describes Noma as "unhappy and frustrated," not according to her mentor's report, but "when she came to speak to me." In short, Noma had, by her own account, made up her mind to leave and, by Graham's account, was actively communicating her desire to find more satisfying work. Thus, the apparent discontinuity and serendipity in Noma's account, while partially accurate, may conceal the continuity in her active search for a way meaningfully to contribute to improved race relations.

When Noma made the decision to move back to Chicago, she did emphasize her own decisive feelings ("I felt we've got to leave this WASP-ish town"), but she also accorded some agency to her dead husband: "I kept thinking about her father, about my husband. I thought, Joe would never do this, bringing up a child in an environment like that."

In telling the story of her life, then, Noma draws on the conventional plots and themes available for understanding women's lives—themes emphasizing relationships, contingency, chance, and the impact of others' actions—but her story goes well beyond them too.

UNFAMILIAR THEMES: NEW PLOTS FOR WOMEN'S LIVES

Among the themes that cry out for recognition are Noma's commitment to a meaningful role in the workforce and to the pursuit of social justice and social change. In addition, though she attributes little importance to them, Noma offered accounts of her negotiation of the race and gender politics and pressures that were part of her experience. We have seen that Noma regularly encountered white and black people who were surprised that she was white. Some of her experiences were amusing (like the train station scene quoted earlier), while others were painful. When she went to Cleveland she found that the people she was working with "weren't used to being with a white person who was concerned about race prejudice; they'd just sit there when I tried to get into conversations." Equally, she was pained to discover that her white friends and relatives were not interested in her work. It is important to understand the power of Noma's relationship with Joe Genné in confirming and supporting her work and her commitments, but it is equally important to learn from Noma's story about how she herself understood, and lived with, the complexities and difficulties in her situation. It is clear that her capacity to form strong, loving interracial friendships was an important resource, but so were her capacities to see the humor in many situations, to trust that caring black friends and colleagues would protect her, to operate without the support of white friends or family, and to find the courage to face danger and risk.

Finally, there is much to learn about how women like Noma, who played roles in the public sphere before the advent of the "second-wave" women's movement, found the strength for the work they did. We have seen that, without a formal "feminist" consciousness, Noma understood herself to have a role in the world of work and politics whether she was a young, unmarried woman; a wife and mother; or a single mother in the 1950s and 60s. To some degree, she saw herself as "exceptional," not so much in her talent or skill (though she was talented and skillful!), but in her opportunities:

> I'm sure I was conscious of the fact that I was very privileged, that I was getting recognition as a woman. . . . I never took it for granted, I'm sure of that. I thought I really had privileges that were rare. I was very conscious of it. I think too I can honestly say that it also instigated me to say and to think and to do . . . the very best, because I was in a situation that was being watched by a lot of people—whether or not I was capable as a woman of doing it.

In the diary she kept in 1945, Noma recorded some of the less pleasant aspects of being a woman in her line of work. On March 6, she wrote of her night in a railroad sleeping car: "I had the ghastly experience of having a man try to climb up into my berth last night. He tried it twice. When I threatened to scream, he climbed down. I slept very little for fear that he would do something to me while I slept."

When she told me this story more than 40 years later, Noma explained that as a result of that experience she was not afraid to travel on a train at night, since she just "always insisted on a lower berth." When I asked how a lower berth could possibly be safer, she laughed and shook her head, saying that many others in her life had reacted to her thinking with similar doubt.

Noma's reliance on humor, modesty, and common sense in coping with many situations did not preclude a certain toughness when appropriate. On March 18 she noted in her diary, "I spoke this afternoon at a meeting of the Minneapolis Branch of the NAACP. Mr. Jones ignored me when I came in and introduced me in a rude way, so I reciprocated and rudely ignored him!"

On many occasions, Noma recorded distress about what she saw in the schools she visited. For example, on February 20, she met with a principal who had a "persecution complex" about "the fact that he is white." And on February 21, "I found much to my dismay all of the white children sitting on one side of the room and the colored children on the other." Equally often, though, Noma drew strength from positive evidence that "intercultural education" was working. On February 9 she wrote, "While in Trenton I was taken to Parker School where I saw a beautiful new building and a fine demonstration of interracial unity." On March 7 (the day after the man tried to climb into her berth on the train) she commented that one Chicago teacher "was doing a fine job with [a curriculum on] Races of Mankind."

Noma also drew strength from evidence of her own personal success. For example, on April 4, she wrote, "I had another job offered to me today. . . . If it were not a field job I might consider it. Anyway, it is nice to know that I am gaining recognition for my work outside of the NAACP."

Finally, despite the indifference and rejection of many whites who were close to her, Noma drew strength from her awareness of the work of at least one other white woman. Eleanor Roosevelt was one of Noma's three "heroes." Noma mentioned that although she heard her give many speeches, and Mrs. Roosevelt attended most of the board meetings of the national NAACP, "We never had the chance to talk." Nevertheless, Noma said, "I really felt the way she would look at me that she was glad to see a white woman doing this." This modest fantasy— this sense of a race- and gender-based tie—is a poignant expression of one of the reasons we need to know Noma's story: because it is important, when the work is hard, to feel that it matters who is doing it.

It is surely important that we be able to draw strength and knowledge from the stories of women like Noma Jensen Genné. And we need to know *all* of the facets of the story of Noma Jensen Genné—not just the story of her relationships. We need to hear that she was not born to her politics or values, but rather developed them in a long process of self-education that included making the most of ties with the neighbors who took her to church, the smart, beautiful, young black woman in her class, and the many civil rights activists she encountered. We need to hear not only about the fairy-tale marriage to her soul mate but also about the lifelong commitment to equal justice that they shared and that she continued to enact long after his death. Finally, and perhaps most of all, we need to hear the details—about how she reacted to what happened to her and how she found the strength to stay the course. The most important "story" of this white woman's commitment to racial justice—at least the one with the greatest promise of helping others to make and keep similar commitments—lies not in the larger, obscuring "plots," but in the particular moments when her convictions were forged, her courage tested, and her commitment found.

NOTE

1. I am grateful most of all to Noma Genné for her great generosity in sharing her life with me. I am also indebted to her daughters; both Beth Genné (who introduced us) and Maria Genné shared their knowledge and experience of Noma and her life with me. I am

also grateful to Rosario Ceballo, who offered support, insight, and challenges to my thinking throughout the process of interviewing Noma and writing this chapter; and to Julie Stubbs, who enthusiastically researched the Springfield plan.

REFERENCES

Barnard, H. F. (Ed.) (1990). *Outside the magic circle: The autobiography of Virginia Foster Durr.* Tuscaloosa: University of Alabama Press.

Bateson, M. C. (1989). *Composing a life.* New York: Plume.

Chatto, C. I., & Halligan, A. L. (1945). *The story of the Springfield plan.* New York: Barnes & Noble.

Colby, A., & Damon, W. (1992). *Some do care: Contemporary lives of moral commitment.* New York: The Free Press.

Daloz, L. A. P., Keen, C. H., Keen, J. P., & Parks, S. D. (1996). *Common fire: Lives of commitment in a complex world.* Boston: Beacon Press.

Evans, S. (1979). *Personal politics.* New York: Alfred A. Knopf.

Du Bois, S. G. (1971). *His day is marching on: A memoir of W. E. B. Du Bois.* Philadelphia and New York: J. B. Lippincott.

Fine, B. (1944). The Springfield plan: For education against intolerance and prejudice. *The Menorah Journal, 32* (2), 161–80.

Grossman, H. Y., & Stewart, A. J. (1990). Women's experience of power over others: Case studies of psychotherapists and professors. In H. Y. Grossman & N. L. Chester (Eds.), *The experience and meaning of work for women* (pp. 11–34). Hillsdale, N.J.: Erlbaum.

Heilbrun, C. (1988). *Writing a woman's life.* New York: W. W. Norton.

Jensen, N. (1944). The Springfield plan. *The Crisis,* (March), 79 ff.

Smith, H. H. (1944). Your town could do it too. *Woman's Home Companion* (June), 30 ff.

Stalvey, L. M. (1970). *The education of a WASP.* New York: William Morrow.

Stewart, A. J. (1994). Toward a feminist strategy for studying women's Lives. In C. E. Franz & A. J. Stewart (Eds.), *Women creating lives* (pp. 11–36). Boulder, CO: Westview.

Tatum, B. D., & Knaplund, E. G. (1996). *Outside the circle? The relational implications for white women working against racism.* Stone Center Work in Progress, #78. Wellesley College, Massachusetts.

Wise, J. W. (1945). *The Springfield plan.* New York: Viking Press.

Tomlinson-Keasey, C. (1994). My dirty little secret: Women as clandestine intellectuals. In C. E. Franz & A. J. Stewart (Eds.), *Women creating lives* (pp. 227–45). Boulder, CO: Westview.

A Continuing Commitment to Social Change:
Portraits of Activism throughout Adulthood

"If you sold your soul in the 80s, here's your chance to buy it back."

*T*HAT IS THE ADVERTISING SLOGAN for the recently re-released Volkswagon Bug, icon of the idealistic late 1960s and early 70s. The ad captures in 15 short words the "master narrative" about young adults of the 1960s—they were all "sell outs" to corporate America. Ironically, if not cruelly, corporate America is now appealing to that very idealism stifled by the pressures of "growing up"—and of social-class maintenance or upward mobility. "Selling one's soul" is represented as something that individuals are to be somehow blamed for, as if it were independent of the structural, political, and economic changes toward conservatism in the United States that followed the major efforts toward more radical social change during the 1960s and early 1970s. This master narrative also ignores the real challenges that accompany adult responsibilities such as parenthood that many people—particularly women—face without adequate support. This chapter will provide two stories that are outside of this dominant narrative. They are the stories of white women who were activists as young adults in the 1960s and who sustained an active commitment to social change through midlife.

In 1983, another cultural representation of the dominant narrative about 1960s activists appeared with the release of the popular film *The Big Chill*. The movie portrayed a group of old friends, gathered for the funeral of their fellow University of Michigan graduate who had committed suicide. The group had gone to the university during the late 1960s or early 70s, a time of tremendous student activism against the war in Vietnam and for civil rights and women's liberation. Two of the men referred to themselves as having been "revolutionaries" during the time, now one was a famous TV actor, the other a successful small-business owner whose company was about to get bought out by a large corporation. They mused, "Who'd have ever thought the two of us would be making so much bread?" During one of the group's evenings together after the funeral, the conversation turned to their earlier idealism and goals for changing the world. One of the women, clearly concerned with what seemed to her to be a critical disjuncture between their lives then and at this untimely reunion, said, "I hate to think [our commitment] was all just fashion." While one of the men tried to remind the group that they had "accomplished things," another woman summed up her own discomfort with the phrase, "Sometimes I just take that time and pretend it wasn't real, just so I can live with how I am now."

The Big Chill depicted a popular cultural myth about 1960s-era activists, particularly white, liberal, male students who were active in the New Left (exemplified by Students for a Democratic Society and grounded in leftist intellectual ideas from earlier in the century): that they grew up, lost their idealism, and "sold out to corporate America." One of the women interviewed for this chapter said that the idea that 1960s activists had "sold out" did not resonate with her. However, she added, "I think there is tremendous pressure in this culture to buckle in and be a capitalist, and if people have done that it's too bad, but it's not like they did it without tremendous pressure on them." Perhaps some clues to the "selling out" narrative lie in the popular definitions of activists as white, liberal, male university students. While they were certainly not the only people to be politically active during the 1960s, nor were the kinds of activism they engaged in the only kinds of activism, it is in many ways their activities that garnered the most attention, their political insurrection at the time the most threatening to the status quo, and (perhaps because of this) they who were the most pressured to "become capitalists."

Historian Alice Echols (1992), in an essay on "remapping" the 1960s to include an analysis of gender stated, "Books by white male New Leftists . . . stand as representative of 'the sixties.' Their experiences are presented as universal, as defining the decade" (p. 12). Motivated by this skewed representation, journalist Margot Adler (1997) wrote a memoir of her own experiences during the 1960s, noting that "by position and gender I was never part of the dominant story" (p. x). Adler characterized the "classic" accounts of the 1960s as follows:

> Over the years various autobiographical accounts have appeared, usually by men of a certain fame. They are usually sad and occasionally embarrassing; heavy on sex and drugs, with politics kept to a minimum; told with the supposed voice of experience and an odd absence of doubt, as if their authors once were lost but now truly know where they are going. But if these writers were painters you would say that their present canvases are much smaller now. And if they were starship captains you would say they had given up the search for new worlds. (p. ix)

Gender, class, and race all shape how "the sixties" have been memorialized and depicted in the media and in many areas of academia—as a decade of radical activity in the form of marches and demonstrations on the part of white, middle-class, male students for free speech, civil rights, and against the Vietnam War. The decade also saw extensive participation by many others, however, in the civil rights movement, El Movimento (the Chicano liberation movement), and the "second wave" of the women's movement, for example (see e.g., Echols, 1992; Hurtado, 1996, for critical analyses of dominant representations of the sixties; see also Burns, 1990).

In many of these movements with the exception of the women's movement, women's presence was often devalued, and women were relegated to behind-the-scenes, support positions (see e.g., Cole, 1994; Evans, 1979; Thorne, 1975). Both of the women interviewed for this chapter recalled that aspect of their participation in the antiwar movement. One said, "What I remember about [Resistance, the antidraft organization], especially in regards to being a woman, was that we were very much support only." The other said:

> At the time, in the 1960s, I think the men were still the dominant group doing this. At that time there was more of a sense of "they're sort of our helpers, sort of a tag-a-long." It was noticeable. [They] expected the women to take care of the food. I think some of those stereotypic 1950s roles still carried into that time, and I think that influenced the women who were involved in those activities to separate themselves out and come together in women's groups, and say, "Well hey, look at the way these guys are treating us, we're not just here to be their handmaidens, or cook their meals while they're off doing something else."

Indeed, Evans (1979) provided compelling evidence that it was the experiences of sexism in the civil rights movement and in the New Left that raised women's consciousnesses about gender and compelled the beginnings of the second wave of the U.S. women's movement. In addition, for many women these experiences may have been the beginning, or a continuation, of a lifelong project of political and social change that shaped their adult careers and commitments in critical ways.

There is, no doubt, much more work to be done, and much has already begun, to provide a more complete representation of the activities and lives of those who took part in shaping U.S. history during one of the most famous, and infamous, decades of the century. In addition to broadening the picture of who was a "typical 1960s activist," it is also important to interrupt the dominant "selling out" narrative, which at once obscures and belittles the important work toward social transformation many were committed to then and continue to be committed to today.

In fact, the considerable literature on the later adult lives of (usually white and liberal) 1960s activists belies the popular conception of "selling out to corporate America." For example, many studies have shown that former activists' political attitudes and behaviors remained consistent throughout adulthood. Former student activists tend to be more politically liberal and to maintain a higher level of political involvement compared to others in their cohort (see, e.g., Cole, Zucker, & Ostrove, 1998; Fendrich, 1974; Fendrich & Tarleau, 1973; Fendrich & Turner, 1989; Hoge & Ankney, 1982; Jennings, 1987; Marwell, Aiken, & Demerath, 1987; Nassi, 1981; Sherkat & Blocker, 1997). In a recent study of "run-of-the-mill" antiwar activists from the 1960s, Sherkat and Blocker (1997) found that former protesters were also more likely to have "new class" occupations—positions concerned with producing knowledge or helping others outside of the private sector such as lawyer, artist, performing artist, social worker, teacher, social scientist, journalist, academic, writer, clergy, or librarian.

For the remainder of this chapter, I will present the stories of two white women who were participants in social change movements of the 1960s. After the 1960s ended, their commitment to social justice remained strong, even as it evolved over time as their personal lives, and the world, changed.

A Continuing Commitment to Change: Two Women's Stories

In the fall of 1997, I interviewed two women who were part of a unique sample of women who had graduated from the University of Michigan in the late 1960s and early 1970s. The sample was made up of women who were known to have been politically active in Ann Arbor, Michigan, during their student years. In 1991, in conjunction with the fourth wave of the Women's Life Paths Study of women graduates from the University of Michigan Class of 1967 (see, e.g., Tangri & Jenkins, 1986), Elizabeth Cole and I collected a sample of student activists. We used a variety of archival and referral sources[1] to gather names of women who were known to have been politically active while at the University of Michigan (see Cole, Zucker, & Ostrove, 1998, for a more extensive description of the sample).

The two women I interviewed for this project were among the 39 women who participated in the 1992 questionnaire study. They were chosen because they lived in a geographical area that was accessible to me at the time I was conducting the interviews, and because their questionnaires reflected that they had maintained a commitment to political or social change activities through midlife (as had many in the sample, see Cole, Zucker, & Ostrove, 1998). Sara Wright's[2] story is somewhat unique in that she was not a "traditional" student activist—she grew up working class and by the mid-1960s she had been married and was the mother of two young girls. She still participated in much of what is considered to be primarily "young, middle-class student" protest activity in Ann Arbor during the late 1960s and early 70s. Paula Adams grew up in a middle-class family and fits the more traditional profile of a student activist. Her activism became her full-time career when she was in her 30s. She describes this as one contributing factor in a major change in her health and life activities—but not her politics—at midlife.

SARA WRIGHT: "I WANTED TO BE INVOLVED WITH THE WORLD AROUND ME"

Sara Wright came to Ann Arbor in the early 1960s, married and a mother of one young girl. Her story demonstrates how motherhood critically shapes both the content and expression of activism (see Pardo, 1990, for further discussion and for critical analyses with respect to class, race, and gender that importantly expand definitions of what constitutes activism). Sara Wright had left a community college in her hometown to follow her husband, who wanted to transfer from the same community college to the University of Michigan: "[W]e came to Ann Arbor because he wanted to. . . . this was the 50s mentality, [and] he wanted to finish college. It was sort of like, well yeah, of course the husband needs to do that, and the wife follows and helps out. So [that was] the set up . . . he would go to school and I would get a job, which we did." Sara worked as a waitress and a short-order cook and took the afternoon shift so she could be home while her husband was in class, then he could come home and take care of their baby daughter while she worked. Their marriage did not last, and the related conflicts led Sara to a series of events and revelations that were among the galvanizing forces for her subsequent political activism. As she described their first years together, "As I got out and was working more, I got dissatisfied with his lack of involvement and support and equal roles and stuff. He was also getting tired of the responsibilities." By this time they had a second daughter, and their older daughter had been diagnosed with developmental disabilities, which "made things more stressful."

On leaving her husband, Sara was left with about $10 in her pocket, no home, no phone, no car, and two daughters to support. She lived with her parents temporarily, but her goal was to move closer to where she had friends and connections for special education for her daughter. She received emergency welfare, but finding an apartment as a single mother under those circumstances proved difficult. She finally got a job and an apartment within walking distance of each other. These were experiences, she said, that were a big influence on her "wanting to have things change" and getting involved politically.

At this time, she recalls, Sara was beginning to get involved in antiwar activity and became friends with a woman who was an important influence on her political involvement. Together they joined the Women's International League for Peace and Freedom and Students for a Democratic Society (SDS), which Sara and her friend dropped out of when the organization began advocating more violent activities. She attended an antiwar demonstration in New York City with her then 5-year-old daughter and got involved in the grape boycott as well. I asked her to elaborate on both the personal and broader political experiences that motivated her commitment at that particular time. She said:

> [H]aving experienced . . . sitting in a waiting room at the DSS [Department of Social Services] and feeling like there needed to be more social justice in the world, and getting interested in that, and that tying in with social justice to African Americans and civil rights, and social justice to civilians in Vietnam, and the women and the children. And then there were local . . . politics that I was involved in, trying to get a more liberal mayor, a new third party, [I] got involved in leafletting for that. It really kind of all tied together in that sense.

She went on to characterize other potential influences on her political activity, namely, those from her childhood:

> I suppose there could have been a little bit of influence of my family of origin background. I sort of have some memories of my father talking a lot about Gandhi, and having *LIFE* magazines with his picture. Even though I grew up in a real conservative, Protestant culture, it so happened that my father was real liberal. In fact, he got kicked out of his preaching job because he was too liberal. [He] was a big FDR supporter in the 30s and 40s. So I had some of that influence way back then. My oldest brother worked on the Henry Wallace campaign, people thought Wallace was communist. I remember the McCarthy era, I was in early high school, I remember talking to my older brothers, we were really incensed about all of that stuff. So some of the seeds were planted back then!

By the late 1960s, then, the combination of childhood influences, recent experiences that made her personally and acutely aware of the need for social change, and a community of like-minded friends saw Sara involved in a number of different local, national, and international political activities. All of these also led to her engagement with the nascent women's movement, which she describes as having been a "great support system, really validating some of my thoughts and beliefs about women's role in the world that was down under . . . it was very supportive and influential." Importantly, her family commitments also influenced her political activities: "Being a mother at the time affected the amount of time I could spend on political involvement. [I always] made sure we had dinner together and dinner on the table, [I] didn't want things to be catch as catch can."

At about this same time, Sara needed more financial security and found work as an assistant at a research institute at the university, all along planning to return to school to finish her undergraduate degree in psychology or social work. Work gave her important contacts with people in those fields and also solidified her commitment to "real" social service. The following quotation exemplifies Sara's desire to have all aspects of her life be consistent with her social and political values: "After a bit I was starting to get a bit disturbed about all of the hundreds of thousands of [grant] dollars . . . that were going into all these research projects when some of that should go into service to the poor! And I got a bit disenchanted with all of that, so I was looking to leave that work and go into social work."

In her 30s Sara did become a social worker, through a special program for "returning students" that did not require her to have a bachelor's degree. Always committed to making the world a more just place for all people, her activist concerns turned to social service as a form of effecting social change. Her personal, political, and professional activities centered, and continue to center, on families and people with disabilities. She describes the influence of her daughter's disability on her social change work: "Another influence related to social justice issues and my moving into social work was the fact that [my daughter] has developmental disabilities. . . . So, trying to get services for her and connecting with mental health services and rehab services was huge influence on all of these things that I ended up working on and working toward." In the 1980s, with some other parents of developmentally disabled children, Sara started an organization to provide independent living apartments to adults with developmental disabilities. The organization is still strong, and Sara has been president and/or on the board of directors since its inception.

> Currently, I'm on community coalition groups trying to get money for services to certain target populations. . . . I started [programs at my agency] for support to single moms, children, the elderly. [I'm a] member of the Children's Defense Fund. Where I work we organized some of the single moms in our healthy families program to go to the Children's Defense Fund's march in Washington. But that all continues to evolve. . . . I [recently] hired a woman who is very interested in social justice issues, working with Call to Action group, a socially oriented Catholic group. She's going to be doing direct work in the churches, teaching social justice and organizing people to get more involved in their communities, doing volunteer work, picketing, etc. So those are all things that I'm still involved with.

As her career grew and evolved into what it is today, Sara also built family relationships that were consistent with her social ideals. When she was in her 30s, Sara married a man who was also a social worker. It seemed that Sara was in the rather interesting position of having had a "pre-women's movement" marriage and a "post– [or during–] women's movement" marriage. I asked her to talk about the influence of the women's movement on her second marriage:

[Before my second marriage I was] living in communal household—it wasn't like [my] previous, nuclear family set up! We all had responsibility, had weekly house meetings, a board with chores, children had things they had to do—not a hierarchical structure at all. All the adults had jobs outside of the home, [and the] men did equal amount of chores, cooking, childcare. That's how it started, and that's what my [now] husband saw from the beginning. I had this bumper sticker on my car when we first met, "Run for office not for coffee." So he always says "I went into this with my eyes open!" So he came into the household and joined the group. Then when we bought our own house, we continued that same role division in our own family, the two of us worked full time, [my daughter] had a part-time job and contributed some of her expenses. We had a rotating chore list.

Throughout her life, Sara describes herself as having been on a "spiritual journey" and is inspired and sustained by the idea of Jesus "preaching a social gospel, not one of 'I'm dying to save you.'" In general, she exemplifies living a life in accordance with her ideals and remained committed to social justice well after the public and ubiquitous movements for social change had waned. As she describes it, coming home to watch TV "wasn't my interest in how I wanted to spend my limited time being alive. I wanted to be involved with the world around me, the community. . . . I wanted to be part of it." She summarizes her life in her adopted hometown and the social and political commitments she forged there as follows:

My attitude is that I feel like I was fortunate to be here at that time in general, and at that time in my life when I was a single parent with no money. I feel like, well, this town's been good to me since, and I've been good to it because I've contributed a lot. It's been a good fit. . . . I'm still an "antidogma" person, still questioning whether it's about politics, social policies, social work methods, the way history is written, or religion. Also, I recognize the need for personal meditation time, whether it's playing Bach on the piano, reading, or looking at the trees in my backyard. This replenishes the spirit.

PAULA ADAMS: "STANDING FOR WHAT I BELIEVE IN"

Paula Adams came to Ann Arbor as a transfer student during her junior year of college. The University of Michigan, in contrast to her previous school which was disappointingly inactive politically, fulfilled Paula's desire for active involvement in political work that she had begun quite early in her life. She describes her earliest political action:

When I think of political activism, I think all the way back to my parents and growing up with a real strong ethical, not religious, but humanist, ethical thing, treating people well. And I don't know where I got this, but this thing of speaking truth, being honest, standing for what you believe in. I think second grade was the first time I can remember what I considered taking a political action, which was refusing to pledge allegiance to the flag. My parents didn't even know I was doing it. I stood, but I didn't say anything. I did not believe in God, so I wasn't going to say something I didn't believe in. And I remember feeling different, but, and this is a little embarrassing, I also remember feeling superior, like I was not falling for what everyone else was falling for.

This sense of self-righteousness undergirded a lot of Paula's early political work, much of which she describes as "very heady, very righteous." Her long-time commitment to activism eventually necessitated a shift in this attitude. In the meantime, though, her political work mostly centered around the Human Rights Party and the antiwar movement, both of which contributed to an important sense of efficacy:

What I got the most out of early political work was that I found a way to be very public and supported in not just falling for the mainstream thing, which I'd started as a little kid. Here was a whole bunch of people accusing people, you know, if you're not part of the solution you're part of the problem kind of thing, it was very black and white. It was very righteous. We knew we were right. And some people risked, and lost, their lives, and went to jail, and did a lot of things, and I never did any of those things. But we were standing up, and we were saying, "This is what we believe." It was very heady, there was a righteousness about it. You had other people. Also, you didn't have to settle for the things most people settle for. You could change things, and we did. Things did not have to be the status quo. That was very powerful, and encouraging. That part of it I've never, I still, if I come across something that I don't feel is right, I immediately have the reaction "I can do something about this," and often do. [JMO: Do you attribute this to having been a part of movement that succeeded?] It's hard for me to know if it really succeeded. It's clear that the same problems are still here. We stopped one thing, one horrible thing [the war], but the reasons for it, the underlying disease, is still here. It's kind of bittersweet.

The sense of power and efficacy is echoed in Adler's (1997) memoir, recalling the free speech movement in Berkeley, California, the civil rights movement, and the antiwar movement: "We believed that anything was possible and that everything was open to reexamination. That ecstatic sense of possibility, a feeling that is so hard to come by today, was borne out by reality; sweeping changes were happening every day, brought about by concerted human action" (pp. x–xi).

Paula brought her determination to set things right and her sense of efficacy with her when she moved away from Michigan in her late 20s, after getting married. While her marriage did not last very long, she remained in her new home and began a new stage in her activist career. Paula described these stages in a way that demonstrates the importance of women sustaining their political involvement and "coming into their own" *after* young adulthood: "In my 20s I was a 'rank and file' follower—partly because of the sexism in the groups and also my internalized sexism—I did not feel empowered to take on leadership."

When she was in her early 30s, Paula was working in early childhood education and also continued to be very active in the peace movement. "I became more and more active and confident. I continued to march and demonstrate and vigil against new and old weapons systems, government actions, etc." She and a friend started a local chapter of the Women's International League for Peace and Freedom, and a different friend and she started a local chapter of Parenting for Peace and Justice and Educators for Social Responsibility. When she was in her late 30s, she decided to become a full-time activist and started a new organization designed to teach children about peace issues:

In my later 30s I had some insights that came from analyzing my frustration at the constant *reacting* our peace groups were doing to government *actions*. It seemed like we were letting our agenda be set by them. I think that wanting to set my own agenda and feel more power over my own life came a good deal from the growth I had made in the women's movement. I decided that the weapons systems, violence, wars, etc. were symptoms of a deeper illness. The deeper illness was the view we had as a nation of what we deserved in terms of the raw materials of the world to feed our economic system; our racism, sexism, earth exploitation, etc. These symptoms were potentially fatal, of course (nuclear weapons, etc.), but I wanted to work on the underlying illness. And I thought about where people develop their attitudes about these things. . . . School, home, church—organized systems. So I quit my job and decided I would use my skills to work in those institutions on those particular things.

As she began this project and created materials for schools and began after-school peace groups for children, she describes herself as "still very, very righteous." A courageous friend, and one who played a critical role in many ways in helping to sustain Paula's political life, assisted her to the realization that she had to shed her self-righteous attitude in order to be more politically effective.

Here, in describing the role of her friend, she also highlights the ways in which class shaped her opportunities for activism:

> This righteousness really bothered him. He said, "You know, you are priv-ileged to do this work. You are doing it because your parents are willing to support you, because people are giving you donations, it's a privi-lege! You are separating yourself from other people the way you present yourself, people can't even *begin* to think they can do anything like what you're doing." And it was really a lot of soul searching, and within a cou-ple of years I think I really started making some good progress on feel-ing I'm "better"—because I'm a full-time peaceworker. I realized it was really undermining my efforts to communicate with people.

Paula worked hard to shift this attitude. She did a lot of work on conflict resolu-tion and mediation and learned how to listen and how to try to identify with people who wanted different things from what she thought were important. This also introduced her to conflict resolution trainers and peace activist colleagues who were role models and critical sources of sustenance and motivation when she got discouraged. She told me an important story about what she learned when she was doing a "home meeting" about nuclear weapons, at which there was a woman in attendance with a baby on her lap:

> [This incident] helped me realize that if we are going to make basic changes, we are going to have to be able to understand why people be-lieve what they do, why do they need the weapons. . . . [At this meet-ing] I said, "You know, that baby sitting on your lap is one of the most important reasons that I would think you would have to be concerned about nuclear weapons." And she just got furious, she said, "This baby is my reason for *wanting* nuclear weapons, all those people want what we have—I want my baby to have more than I did—we have to keep them from taking what we have." I never would have understood that point of view, it was incredible to hear that. I never understood how scared peo-ple are, [how they're] saying "Those people would never be as good to us as we are to them. . . ." It wasn't until I stopped talking and started listening that I learned that.

I was curious about whether Paula attributed this change to becoming older. She said she did not think it would have happened if she had not had that friend who was willing to be so honest with her. She noted, "I know people at my age who are just as righteous as they ever were!"

The funding for Paula's peace project lasted for about 5 years, then she had to return to teaching in order to earn money. Eventually, Paula moved away. However, her peace project—and her colleagues who stayed with it—continued to have an important influence in the schools.

By the time Paula was contacted in 1992 to participate in the study of former student activists, she had become quite ill with a disabling chronic illness. She describes her process of development as an activist as it relates to her having become sick:

> The general pattern is like, being the "go-fer" and the support system and the groupie, then moving toward taking responsibility, and in that process I took the whole world on my shoulders. I spent maybe 10 years just weighed down, it's a huge responsibility to decide you're going to change the world. There's just too much to do, even though I had it somewhat narrowed within that. And there were several other life things that happened, but through getting sick, the illness that I have is basically the workaholic illness. The person who just does it all, who finds a way to do it all, who stays up all night or whatever, because it's all my responsibility. I have to do it, and no one else can do it quite as well! And if I don't do it, it's not going to get done. Those are the things that run through your head, but you cannot sustain that.

When Paula and I met in 1997, she was back to working part-time with an environmental organization. This was work that she chose "because it had value to me. I wanted a career that would be [fulfilling] spiritually and politically and intellectually, and that I could handle physically." While her political activities have lessened considerably, she is still more active than many people—she attends every township meeting where she lives and does environmental work on land preservation at the county level, and does a lot of letter writing. For her, though, it is all "just less than the image I have of myself, fighting injustice at every minute." Paula retains a very big picture of the world and of the importance of peace and justice and has refocused her activism toward environmental issues. Because of the physical toll that her work has taken, and because of other factors that precipitated her getting sick, she thinks differently now about how to use her time and how to spend her energy, and likens the process to aging. Underlying this comment is a similar sentiment to that of Sara Wright, who also wanted to think well about how she spent her "limited time being alive." As Paula Adams said:

> I think that eventually you do realize that there's a limit to the number of years. . . . It translates immediately to there's a limit to the number of hours in the day. Because if there's a limit to the number of years,

then okay, how are you going to spend your time?. . . This day, are you going to live it in the same balance of what your values are, so that when you run out of time, you will feel good about how you've spent it?

Conclusions

This chapter examined the lives of two white women who were politically active in the late 1960s and early 70s and who remained politically and actively committed to social change throughout their adulthoods. Along quite different paths, and motivated by different personal, local, and global concerns, both Sara Wright and Paula Adams built their lives according to their ideals. They did not "sell their souls" in the 1980s, nor do either of them subscribe to that "master narrative" of the fate of the women and men of that politically active generation of young adults in the United States. When I asked Paula what she thought about activists from the 1960s having "sold out," she admitted that maybe there were people who were active at the time because they "just got caught up in things" and then stopped, but

> I think that many people have retained. What's different now is it's less dramatic. . . . What people are doing now has to do with more systemic changes, so you don't see it as much. I mean, they're working for non-profits, there's thousands of people doing all kinds of neat things. People are running for office. Probably some of them even joined corporations thinking they could do well. And some of them probably have made changes, and a certain percentage probably left it all behind. There are so many ways to do things.

Both Sara and Paula credited their own involvement in the women's movement with empowering them to change their own lives and more actively work toward the world they envisioned. For Paula, the women's movement also helped her realize that she has to take care of herself in order to be an effective activist. For both women, spiritual and moral convictions about how the world should be have sustained them, as have the personal experiences, needs and support of their family members, and relationships with others who have similar values. For Sara, her husband plays an important role in this regard; for Paula, the friend who "called her" on her righteousness, as well as other political colleagues and members of a women's spirituality community she is part of, have been important sources of sustenance.

This chapter also illuminates the ways in which gender and class shape both the time commitment and the content of activism, both during the 1960s and after. For both women, concerns for the next generation—either their own children, in the case of Sara, or other children, in the case of Paula—were central to the issues (disability rights, education, nuclear disarmament) they were committed to beyond their young adulthoods. We also saw, in the case of Sara, how being a mother had implications for the amount of time she spent in political activity, as her commitment to her family sometimes took precedence over attendance at evening meetings. With respect to class, Sara's own experience of class-based discrimination was the catalyst for some of her social change activity. Paula's class privilege shaped both her opportunity to be a full-time activist and the attitudes that underlay, and sometimes hindered, her work.

Making these women's stories more public provides only one set of counternarratives to the dominant narrative of the fate of 1960s activists. The lives of those who resisted giving up their political and social visions when "the sixties" were over represent one important "untold story" about the legacy of the social change movements of the 1960s and 70s. We need more information about the "post-1960s" lives of many different women, and men, to understand the differences and similarities in their experiences with respect to gender, race, and class. The stories told here also provide a critical antidote to the myth that "growing up" means giving up big dreams and large visions for the world, which young men and women of all generations, not just those who were young adults in the 1960s, are pressured to do.

NOTES

1. Archival and referral sources included collections of the student newspaper, the *Michigan Daily*; a list from a 1987 reunion of 1960s activists; a collection of papers by Bret Enyon catalogued at the University of Michigan's Bentley Library relating to Enyon's "interest in the radical causes and issues of the 1960s and 1970s"; and interviews with women who were currently working at the university and who were politically active students in the late 1960s.

2. The names used in this chapter are pseudonyms.

3. Acknowledgments: Many thanks to the two women who contributed the stories of their political and personal lives to this chapter, and who read and provided helpful corrections and clarifications to the chapter itself. Thanks also to Mary Romero, Abby Stewart, and all of the other chapter authors for inspiration, stimulating conversation, and very useful feedback; to Elizabeth Cole for collecting the sample of activists in the first place and being so supportive of this project; and to Alyssa Zucker for her generous assistance with revisions.

REFERENCES

Adler, M. (1997). *Heretic's heart: A journey through spirit and revolution*. Boston: Beacon.

Burns, S. (1990). *Social movements of the 1960s: Searching for democracy*. Boston: Twayne Publishers.

Cole, E. R. (1994). A struggle that continues: Black women community and resistance. In C. Franz & A. J. Stewart (Eds.), *Women creating lives: Identities, resilience, and resistance* (pp. 309–24). Boulder, CO: Westview.

Cole, E. R., Zucker, A. N., & Ostrove, J. M. (1998). Political participation and feminist consciousness among women activists of the 1960s. *Political Psychology, 19*, 349–71.

Echols, A. (1992). "We gotta get out of this place": Notes toward a remapping of the sixties. *Socialist Review, 22*, 9–33.

Evans, S. (1979). *Personal politics,* New York: Alfred A. Knopf.

Fendrich, J. M. (1974). Activists ten years later: A test of generational unit continuity. *Journal of Social Issues, 30*, 95–118.

Fendrich, J. M., & Tarleau, A. (1973). Marching to a different drummer: Occupational and political correlates of former student activists. *Social Forces, 52*, 245–53.

_____(1989). The transition from student to adult politics. *Social Forces, 67*, 1049–57.

Hoge, D. R., & Ankney, T. L. (1982). Occupations and attitudes of former student activists ten years later. *Journal of Youth and Adolescence, 11*, 355–71.

Hurtado, A. (1996). *The color of privilege: Three blasphemies on race and feminism.* Ann Arbor: University of Michigan Press.

Jennings, M. K. (1987). Residues of a movement: The aging of the American protest generation. *American Political Science Review, 81*, 365–82.

Marwell, G., Aiken, M., & Demerath, A. J. (1987). The persistence of political attitudes among 1960s civil rights activists." *Public Opinion Quarterly, 51*, 359–75.

Nassi, A. J. (1981). Survivors of the 1960s: Comparative psychosocial and political development of former Berkeley student activists. *American Psychologist, 36*, 753–61.

Pardo, M. (1990). Mexican American women grassroots community activists: "Mothers of East Los Angeles." *Frontiers, 11*, 1–7.

Sherkat, D. E., & Blocker, T. J. (1997). Explaining the political and personal consequences of protest. *Social Forces, 75*, 1049–76.

Tangri, S. S., & Jenkins, S. R. (1986). Stability and change in role innovation and life plans. *Sex Roles, 14*, 647–62.

Thorne, B. (1975). Women in the draft resistance movement: A case study of sex roles and social movements. *Sex Roles, 1*, 179–95.

"In My Heart I Will Always Be Hmong":
One Hmong American Woman's Pioneering Journey toward Activism[1]

"WHAT DO YOU KNOW ABOUT ASIANS?" a young Chinese American woman asks a young white man of Italian descent. He replies: "I'm going to be honest with you. I completely believed the stereotype. Asian people are hard workers, they're really quiet, they get good grades because they have tons of pressure from their families to get good grades. . . . Asians are quiet so people can't have a problem with them" (Reid, 1995). This exchange between two college students succinctly captures the master narrative about Asian Americans—the "model minority," quiet, hardworking, and passive enough that they do not threaten the status quo. While the young woman did not specifically refer to women in her question, the quiet, passive depiction of Asian American women has been a component of this pervasive stereotype. Illustrating this point in her classic essay, "Invisibility Is an Unnatural Disaster: Reflections of an Asian American Woman," Mitsuye Yamada (1981) recounts her experiences teaching the Asian segment of an ethnic American literature course, discovering that her white students were offended by the angry tone of the Asian American writers. Yamada was puzzled by this response, since her students had not been offended by the writings of African American, Chicano, or Native American authors. One student explained, "*Their* anger made *me* angry because I didn't even know the Asian Americans felt oppressed. I didn't expect their anger" (p. 35).

The myth of the passive model minority obscures the reality of racism in the lives of Asian Americans and also obscures the diversity of experience within the Asian American community. Very diverse ethnic groups from the continent of Asia and the Pacific Islands have been subsumed by the racial discourse of U.S. society into one presumably homogeneous group. As seen in the opening exchange, the young woman does not ask her companion what he knows about Chinese Americans, but rather what he knows about the constructed racial category that has been imposed upon her by U.S. society.

In fact, what is often described as the Asian American community in the United States consists of more than 10 million people and is made up of 43 ethnic groups, including 28 from the Asian continent and 15 from the Pacific Islands (Yang, 1998). While each national group has its own unique immigration history shaping its experience in the United States, these narratives are not generally known.

One group that has been particularly disadvantaged by the homogenizing myth of the "model minority" is Southeast Asians (Vietnamese, Cambodians, Lao, Hmong, and Mien people). They comprise 13.6 percent of the Asian Pacific American population, a large percentage of whom are foreign born (Yang, 1998). Between the end of the Vietnam War and 1997, 1.5 million refugees from Vietnam, Cambodia, and Laos emigrated here—marking the largest refugee population to be admitted to the United States. Many from the Southeast Asian community have had little or no education and live in more impoverished conditions than other Asian Americans (Yang, 1998). While the model-minority myth conjures images of talented math and science students supported by upwardly mobile parents, this picture falsely assumes that Southeast Asian refugees have also attained the same kind of success.

In reality, many Southeast Asians struggle to survive in this fast-paced and technologically advanced society. A vast majority of Southeast Asian refugees worked in agriculture in their homelands, and it has been hard for them to find similar work in the United States. Many live in large cities and must rely on blue-collar and service jobs to support their families.

The model-minority myth has not only disguised the economic and social hardships that Southeast Asians have encountered but also fails to recognize the educational struggles of refugee children. The high school completion rates are approximately 35 percent for Cambodians, 36 percent for Laotians, and 58 percent for Vietnamese, well below the overall average of 82 percent for Asian Americans as a group. Because of the widespread attitude that Asians are academically successful, many schools do not monitor or even record the dropout rates among Asian Americans. Consequently, some school districts do not realize, for example, that many Southeast Asian parents are not educated or that as many as half of the female Hmong students in their schools drop out before graduation (Walker-Moffat, 1995, p. 22).

Our presentation of Mai's story is an effort to interrupt the obscuring effect of these intertwined master narratives, the passive model minority and the homogeneity of the Asian American community. Through the presentation of Mai's story, the story of a Hmong woman, we hope to make visible the unique experiences of young Hmong women coming of age in the United States. Their largely untold stories are often narratives of family trauma, cultural conflict, racism, and success—narratives of the struggle to both affirm and transform their place as Hmong American women both in and out of the Hmong community.

As authors, the perspectives we bring to this discussion are those of women who have also considered the issues of identity and duality personally and professionally. ThaoMee is a college-educated Hmong woman who immigrated to America when she was 3. She has firsthand experience with the questions to be raised here. As an activist and advocate for the Hmong community, she sought out other Hmong women activists whose lives might be a model for her own. Beverly is an African American woman whose interest in cultural conflict and questions of identity have their roots in her own experience growing up as one of few black women in a predominantly white community. We believe our differing histories yet common identity as women of color in the United States provide a useful lens with which to consider these issues.

WHO ARE THE HMONG?

"We came to the U.S. in 1976, so we were the first wave [of Hmong immigrants]. Like many other Hmong families, my family had to leave because of the war. My father was a soldier, and if he didn't leave he would be persecuted. . . . We left in 1975 and stayed a year in refugee camps." These few sentences, uttered at the beginning of Mai's interview, very succinctly capture the limit of what most non-Hmong know about the Hmong journey to America. Though in many ways the Hmong story is a narrative of war and its aftermath, the complexity of crossing cultural as well as political borders is an important dimension of the less well-known Hmong experience in the United States. Because this historical and socio-logical context is so important in understanding Mai's narrative, we want briefly to set that context here.

Hmong, which means "free," is the name of a people who originally lived in the southwestern mountains of China. However, when the Qing dynasty assumed power in 1644, the Hmong suffered economic, social, and political oppression by the new rulers. To maintain their sense of autonomy, many migrated to Vietnam, Laos, Thailand, and Burma (Chan, 1994). Most of the Hmong in the United States today have their origins in Laos.

In Laos, the Hmong lived in relative isolation and peace as farmers using slash-and-burn agriculture to cultivate the land. They lived in the highest northeastern mountains of Laos in order to have the freedom to live according to their own cultural traditions, unimpeded by the cultural ways of the Lao. Low-land Lao, the majority in Laos, referred to the Hmong as Meo, meaning "savage," because they considered the Hmong to be primitive and dirty (Chan, 1994). The Hmong, however, were a proud people who kept to themselves unless their independence was threatened.

When the Vietnam War started and Laos was under threat of becoming a communist country, the Hmong people's lives were changed forever. The U.S. government sought the Hmong people's help in the "Secret War in Laos" (Chan, 1994). Recruited and trained by the CIA, Hmong men fought against the communists in Laos, hoping to protect their freedom. The Hmong blocked the Ho Chi

Minh Trail from Hanoi to Saigon. Additionally, they rescued downed American pilots. In exchange for their support, the United States promised to protect the Hmong regardless of the outcome of the war. It is estimated that at least one-third of the Hmong population perished during the war, yet after the signing of the Paris Peace Accords in 1973, the American government left the Hmong defenseless in Laos.

Although the Vietnam War officially ended in 1973, the genocide of the Hmong did not begin until the communist Pathet Lao government obtained control of Laos in 1975. Due to the Hmong people's opposition to communism and their affiliation with the United States, the Pathet Lao imprisoned thousands of Hmong in "reeducation" camps. Fleeing for their lives, more than 40,000 Hmong, Mai's family among them, escaped Laos on foot and made their way across the deadly Mekong River in order to reach refugee camps in Thailand. In an effort to honor its obligation to the Hmong people, the U.S. government worked to resettle many of these refugees in the United States.

Today there are more than 200,000 Hmong refugees living in the United States. The largest populations of Hmong reside in St. Paul, Minnesota, and in California's San Joaquin Valley. Although the Hmong have lived in the United States since the late 1970s, their acculturation into the dominant society has been difficult because of their strong cultural ties. As nomads, their traditions and cultural values have been the primary source of an "identity." Yet these traditions and values have isolated them from the dominant culture, stunting their progress and adjustment process in American society. In the *Los Angles Times,* Mark Arax (1996) wrote that "sociologists regard the Hmong as the most disadvantaged immigrant group ever to land in America." In fact, Ronald Takaki (1989), author of *Strangers from a Different Shore,* stated that "most Hmong are barely surviving." The problems the Hmong face stem both from the abrupt move from their homeland to this country as well as the dramatic differences between American society and Hmong society.

CULTURAL CONFLICT AND GENDER ROLES

Whereas American society focuses on independence, individualism, and the self, the Hmong, like many Asian ethnic groups, emphasize interdependence, collectiveness, and community. In contrast to the mainstream American model of the nuclear family, which launches its children for a life of independent living, often at great distances from their parents, the primary social unit of the Hmong is the extended family, which holds its children close. Characterized by a rigid system of hierarchical roles based on age, birth position, and gender, the obligations, responsibilities, and privileges of each role within this extended family are clearly delineated according to a vertical structure. As Huang (1994) writes, "The boundary around the family is explicit and inflexible. While members of the family may leave the family and kinship group for specific purposes, they are expected to return to this innermost family circle" (p. 49).

In this patriarchal and patrilineal society, the gender roles of men and women are especially rigid (Meredith & Rowe, 1986). Traditionally, the man maintains strict control of the entire household and makes all decisions. While he has the freedom to do as he pleases within reason, the Hmong woman usually has very few rights and is confined to the home. Her responsibilities revolve around her family and the maintenance of the house. Her chores include child rearing, cooking, cleaning, and taking care of the in-laws. Women are taught to be quiet, submissive, and obedient, especially to the men in their lives.

While sexism persists in the United States, the equality of men and women is articulated as a cultural value. Young women, like young men, are expected to leave home and pursue educational and employment opportunities, in addition to creating families. This notion of women being equal to men is foreign to the Hmong community and has disrupted an important aspect of Hmong culture—strict gender roles, especially for women.

With these basic Hmong values coming into direct conflict with U.S. culture, the acculturation process for the Hmong has been very difficult, especially for the elders. A huge generation gap has emerged between parents who have grown up only knowing the Hmong way of life and their children who are coming of age within the U.S. context (Trueba, 1990). In the United States Hmong children are socialized in school to become "American." They are taught values that directly contradict their traditional beliefs. In school, they are expected to be active participants in the classroom. Individualism and independence is highly encouraged and even expected. At home, these values are especially condemned for girls. The traditional values of being quiet, submissive, and obedient are still required to be considered a "good" Hmong daughter. Those who stray from this definition are labeled "bad" or "disobedient," even when their behavior is otherwise quite appropriate. As a result, many Hmong adolescent girls become confused by the conflicting expectations of their different environments and elders (parents versus teachers). This tension has created much hardship for first-generation Hmong refugee adolescent girls growing up in traditional Hmong households. How can they be Hmong in America?

BEING HMONG AND AMERICAN: THE CHALLENGE OF BICULTURALISM

The challenge of negotiating two cultures is a common immigrant experience, further complicated for immigrants of color by the racism embedded in U.S. society. Because one remains visibly identifiable as "other" even after one's native language has been lost and traditional dress has been abandoned, it has not been possible for communities of color to completely assimilate into mainstream society. Comments such as "Where did you learn how to speak English so well?" are commonly experienced by those with Asian facial features even when their families have lived here for several generations (Kitano, 1997). The impossibility of full assimilation is highlighted by a Vietnamese high school student who says:

> People ask me, "Why can't you be both Vietnamese and American?" It just doesn't work, because you run into too many contradictions. After a while you realize you can't be both, because you start crossing yourself and contradicting yourself and then it's like math, when two things contradict each other they cancel each other out and then you are nothing. You are stuck as nothing if you try to be both. So I chose to be Vietnamese. I'm not sure I really could have been American anyway. (Olsen, 1997, p. 54)

As this student observes, while assimilation into whiteness has been a route to Americanization for many European immigrants, this option is not available for everyone. For Southeast Asians, as with other groups of color, the barrier of racism has encouraged a dual consciousness, or what Kitano calls a "hyphenated identity." Antonia Darder, author of *Culture and Power in the Classroom* (1991), describes such a hyphenated or "bicultural" identity among communities of color as a form of resistance, "a mechanism of survival that constitutes forms of adaptive alternatives in the face of hegemonic control and institutional oppression" (p. 49). A bicultural identity allows people of color to create their own cultural reality by accepting or rejecting different aspects of each culture. But a bicultural identity is not easily achieved.

For some the attempt to bridge two worlds may result in alienation from both. Having rejected the traditional ways of the family, yet unable to find full acceptance in the dominant culture, a young person may often experience marginalization. Relying on their equally marginalized peers for a sense of community, these alienated adolescents may be at particular risk for gang membership.

In fact, the clash of Hmong and American values, coupled with issues of racial discrimination and prejudice, has been extremely problematic for Hmong adolescent girls. It is difficult to straddle two worlds when they are so very far apart. The strain of the effort and the isolation that comes along with not fully identifying with one cultural group has been quite painful for many of these adolescents. Many Southeast Asian girls in general, and Hmong girls in particular, turn to gangs for a sense of community or participate in self-destructive activities such as prostitution and using drugs; some are driven to suicide (Thao, 1997).

Yet this is not the only story. In an effort to tell a different tale, we present here the narrative of a Hmong woman who is finding a way to negotiate the cultural conflict and assert her identities as Hmong *and* American through her role as an activist. In the process she raises new questions still to be explored. One of seven Hmong American women interviewed for this study, we have selected Mai's narrative to highlight here because her story vividly embodies many of the complex dimensions of a Hmong woman refugee's life.

COMING TO AMERICA

Mai is a 29-year-old, single Hmong American woman. At the age of 7, she fled her war-torn country of Laos in search of safety. Her family escaped to the refugee camps in Thailand and resided there for a year until they were relocated to the United States. They were one of the first Hmong families to arrive in her community. Mai was one of the first adolescent Hmong refugee girls to grow up in the United States. Her story speaks to issues of racism, sexism, education, activism, community work, and cultural negotiation in both complex and illuminating ways.

The move from the refugee camp in Thailand to the United States was an abrupt one with little advance notice. From the perspective of a 7-year-old, it was the emotion that was most memorable. "My mom was crying and everyone was crying. She was hanging out the window of the bus crying and I was crying. I didn't know why but I just felt so sad. All these people were reaching out, touching each other . . . they are all saying, 'Oh we are never going to see each other again.'" The visual images of her homeland were also impressed on Mai's memory. "I remember looking out the window and saw green rice paddies and beautiful farm houses. And it was in me forever and ever. And that is why I always wanted to go back to see this."

The abruptness of their departure also took their U.S. sponsors by surprise. "No one was at the airport to pick us up." Eventually someone did come, a representative of a Catholic charity that sponsored Mai's family. To Mai the appearance of their sponsor was startling. "He was a very tall, blonde, hairy man . . . we had never seen a foreigner before and he was so strange." Their housing was not yet ready, so they were taken to an empty college dormitory in the Midwestern city that would be their new home.

When asked to reflect on her family's journey to the United States, Mai explained, "I think my life has always been very difficult and adjusting has always been difficult because I was thoroughly identifying as a stranger. I always felt strange in this land. Ever since I came to this country, I always felt out of place. . . . Even as a child, I was very sad, very lonely, and very unknowledgeable."

THE LONELINESS OF SILENCE

"For the longest time in my life, I thought I was just dreaming this stuff. I didn't really think it existed because my family didn't talk about it." Meaningful experience demands expression. Yet for Mai, the trauma of being torn from the familiar sights and sounds of her homeland was not a subject of family discussion. Vivid memories of beautiful landscapes and sweet smells of Southeast Asia lingered in her mind like a powerful dream. Though only 7 when she left Laos, her connection to her homeland was strong, and the pain of separation was real. Still, Mai quickly adapted to American culture, learning English and experiencing racism. "They threw eggs at our house. They made prank calls. I mean they did everything."

Perhaps what made this period most painful for her was her sense of isolation. Not American enough for her white peers and too American for her more recently immigrated Hmong classmates, she felt like an "oddball" wherever she went. And there was no one to talk to about it.

> I was one of a few Asian students in my school for a very long time. And then when there were more and more Hmong refugees coming in, there were more Hmong students. But during that time, my English was getting better and their English was still different from mine . . . they were in ESL and I was never in ESL. So my classmates distinguished the difference between [my cousins] and me. Even though they discriminated against me, it was a different kind of discrimination that they had against my cousins. It confused the hell out of me because I thought if they hate me why do they hate my cousins even more? Why do they make fun of them even more? I knew they made fun of me and that made me sad already. But when they made fun of my cousins, that made me even sadder. Why didn't they feel bad? Shouldn't they want to help my relatives? And so race issues and racism really affected me a lot. I was very angry. I would have been a leader of a gang because I was so angry at the world. Internally I was rebellious.

In her essay, "Connections, Disconnections, and Violations," Jean Baker Miller (1988) describes what happens when a woman is unable to voice her experiences to an empathic listener. Faced with those who are indifferent (or perhaps hostile) to who she is and what she has to say, she feels the threat of "condemned isolation" and may look for ways to become more palatable to those around her, but this is not easily accomplished. Too often it requires that an individual distort her own experience, herself, in complicated and painful ways. As Miller (1988) writes, "In order to twist herself into a person acceptable in 'unaccepting' relationships, she will have to move away from and redefine a large part of her experience—those parts of experience that she has determined are not allowed" (p. 8).

In Mai's case, so much of her experience was not allowed. When she tried to make connections with those she saw as most like her—other Hmong people—they made fun of how she looked and how she talked. A dark, skinny bilingual girl with braces, Mai had a stronger grasp of the U.S. culture than her Hmong peers. She spoke better English and her mannerisms were very similar to her white peers, but at the same time she also had a strong grasp of her Hmong identity as well. She could speak Hmong fluently and was able to communicate with her new refugee classmates. However, within the Hmong community she was disrupting the traditional norms of a Hmong girl—no longer staying home, cooking, cleaning, sewing. Her mannerisms, behavior, and attitude challenged everything a typical Hmong girl was supposed to be, and she became known as a "devious," "promiscuous," and "disrespectful" daughter.

> I was seen as very Americanized because I was always wearing shorts and people thought that was very inappropriate. . . . I also had a bad reputation for going out late at night with just girls. I mean I wasn't even dating. The Hmong community thought it was a very inappropriate thing for a normal Hmong girl to do. But I was just doing things that a normal [American] teenager was doing.

Though she "totally embraced" the Hmong community, the community was rejecting of her. Too Hmong for the Americans, and too American for the Hmong, Mai retreated into silence, unable to articulate the pain of the condemned isolation she felt. "I didn't know how to verbalize it so I withdrew and became very quiet. . . . They thought I was mute. I was internalizing everything." The loneliness of her silence was excruciating. Her high school years were marked by suicidal thoughts and a sense of invisibility. "I was very, very suicidal in high school. . . . I was worried about the world, about my family, about myself. I felt really helpless. I didn't know what to do to help myself. In high school, I was very out of it. Even though there wasn't any direct racism, I could still feel it. I guess I was just very sensitive in that way."

Counter to the model-minority myth, Mai struggled academically. She did not see herself reflected in the curriculum, which made her feel even more marginalized in her community.

> I knew I could do better in school. I just had so many questions and just never felt comfortable. I mean now I understand . . . you never had Asian American studies and I always thought, "Why aren't we in the book?" I just never verbalized anything. . . . I just always felt uneasy. I would wonder why we would study the Renaissance. . . . What the hell does the Renaissance have to do with my life? I mean, every year I always studied the Industrial Revolution and I just didn't understand because it had no sense or relevance in my own life, you know. And when we studied world history we never got to Laos and I just felt really bad about it. So I just had a very difficult time.

Not only was school difficult but also the gender norms of the Hmong community were increasingly in conflict with American expectations.

> At that time during the 80s, Hmong girls were taught to be very interested in family and [during high school] already started thinking about starting their family. Although I enjoyed their company very much, their conversations always ended in, "Oh, so who are you going to marry?" My conversation with my white friends and other people were always [about college]. It was so different and even back then I realized that. I questioned myself about why those conversations were going like that. I kept thinking something is wrong because my interests and conversations were so different.
>
> At the same time, I was going through this thing, this survivor's guilt. I was thinking, "No matter what, I have to do something to contribute back to my community and those refugees that are still left behind." Even at a young age, I was aware that there were refugees still back there because my relatives were still there. So . . . I had this schizophrenic life, where I was like "Yeah, I am going to college" with my white and Vietnamese friends but with my Hmong friends, I was like "Yeah, yeah, let's see what guys come visit us."

A bicultural identity is one that incorporates selected aspects of both the home culture and the dominant culture (Phinney, Lochner, & Murphy, 1990). Biculturalism is sometimes seen as an effective strategy for members of marginalized groups because it integrates both cultures and does not require abandoning one for the other. However, in Mai's case, the Hmong cultural choice to marry at an early age and the white middle-class American expectation to go to college seemed mutually exclusive. And the goal of helping other Hmong refugees seemed alien to both the traditional gender roles of the Hmong community and the individualism of mainstream Americans. Mai recognized these contradictions in her life, but she couldn't articulate them and didn't know how to resolve them.

Finding Her Active Voice

At the end of her high school years, Mai reconnected with an old friend, a young woman whose refugee experience mirrored and validated her own. With See, Mai was able to voice both her passion and frustration as she sought to find her place as a Hmong woman in America. She recalls, "See understood what I was feeling . . . that I cared deeply for Hmong people but I just didn't know how to help the Hmong community. She was the only person I could share this with and this had been my vision for hundreds of years even before I was alive. I was born to do this."

Mai's journey eventually led to college, an uncommon path for Hmong women (Lee, 1997). But it was in college that Mai learned to name her experience, and in the process discovered that she could change it:

> I met professors who were activists. . . . After I saw my professor get arrested, I was joyful because he was protesting . . . and I was really inspired by that . . . and then learning about race issues in this country. And all that made sense to me. . . . Now there are words for how I was feeling. It's racism, it's socialism, it's you know democratic issues, gender issues . . . and there were labels for things that I was feeling. Before I was just feeling things and I didn't have any words to describe it.

Mai began to immerse herself in an exploration of these social issues through relationships with other people of color. "I started to join Asian clubs and Black Alliance clubs and Mexican American clubs even though I wasn't even Mexican or Black." Her immersion experience and the redefinition of self that accompanied it parallels descriptions of the racial/ethnic identity development process commonly experienced by adolescents of color (Tatum, 1997). No longer willing to be invisible, Mai began to speak up. "My classmates didn't know about refugees or the Hmong . . . because when they talk about Asian Americans they never talk about me . . . they just talk about Japanese and Chinese. So being a loudmouth, I became the spokesperson on these issues." In speaking up, Mai simultaneously challenged the intertwined master narratives of the passive model minority and the homogeneity of the Asian American community.

Though Mai now fully embraces her identity as a "loudmouth" activist, it stands in sharp contrast to the silenced student she was in high school. In high school she was unable to see the structures that were so powerfully shaping her experience. However, once she could name her oppression, she felt liberated. By voicing her experiences and becoming an advocate for the Hmong community, she was able to claim her bicultural identity in an affirming way.

Mai's activism took several forms. One of the first two Hmong women to attend her college, she established the first Hmong organization there and organized a tutoring program to raise the educational achievement of Hmong adolescents. The success of her tutoring program convinced her that she could make a difference. Mai was inspired to look for more ways to act in her community on a local, national, and international level.

> [I received a] newsletter that they were going to have an international conference on asylum seekers, so I thought, this is my chance to work in D.C. and make a difference. So I called up [a Southeast Asian advocacy group] and asked if I could do an internship. They said that they had never done student internships and I said, "Why don't you start one?"

and they did and I was the first intern. They were surprised that a Hmong woman would call them because, you know, in the 80s, I think Hmong women were still seen as very passive and [there I was] this young stupid girl calling who knows nothing but I had a lot of passion.

Mai's activism clearly strengthened her connection to the Hmong community but it also again challenged gender expectations of what a "good" Hmong girl should be. "Of course my parents were like don't go, don't go. . . . I went with or without their consent and I said, 'Mom, later on it will help me a lot . . . trust me please.' She said, 'Don't do this, you're giving us a bad name, you're not being a good daughter,' and all this shit. And I said, 'Mom, I just know in my heart that it is going to help me' . . . and it did!"

While in Washington, Mai learned about a language institute where she could improve her spoken fluency in Hmong and learn how to read and write it. Again she went without her parent's consent.

My mom said "Oh no . . . you just got back from D.C. and you know what everyone thinks of you now. Don't go!" And I said, "Mom, I have to go and learn Hmong if I want to be successful at anything." So I went to Hawaii without their consent again. . . . I said, "Mom, this is going to help me." I lived there for a summer and learned Hmong and am fluent. And all these things they helped me a lot. They opened many doors for me. It helped me in so many ways because when I need to remember anything Hmong, I just write it down.

Clearly Mai's immersion in Hmong culture and advocacy was empowering for her. In many ways her activism was a brilliant solution to her bicultural dilemma. During her college years and now in her career, Mai has been able to use her understanding of the American culture and her command of the English language to articulate the concerns of the Hmong community to the non-Hmong world. In doing so, she maintains strong ties to the Hmong community. To those who would say that she is no longer "Hmong enough," she can point to her knowledge of Hmong folklore and her openly political stance against the oppression experienced by Hmong people as evidence of her allegiance to and pride in her ethnic identity. This emissary strategy has been documented among other ethnic groups whose members are viewed as operating outside peer-group norms. For example, some academically successful black students who are teased by their peers for "acting white" are able to deflect such criticism by connecting their own achievements to the advancement of their racial group (Zweigenhaft & Domhoff, 1991). Though this strategy can be very effective, as it seems to be in Mai's case, for Hmong women it still leads to relatively uncharted territory. Her activist stance disrupts the master narrative of the generically pas-

sive Asian woman as well as challenging gender norms within her own community. As her narrative unfolds, Mai continues to use her activism to bridge both
cultures on a personal and professional level. But as a pioneer she is on a difficult path.

MORE THAN ONE WAY TO BE A HMONG WOMAN?

A great challenge in Mai's life has been to create a place for herself both within
and outside the Hmong community. By creating this place for herself without
choosing between either of her cultures, Mai has embraced some attributes,
such as assertiveness and independence, that are viewed negatively within traditional Hmong culture, especially when possessed by women. These characteris-
tics have compromised her legitimacy as a "real" Hmong woman in her
community. Still single, childless, and living on her own at 29, she has not
achieved "adult" status in the eyes of most Hmong. She has not based her identity as a woman on a man. In essence, Mai is challenging the cultural norms
for Hmong women, thereby threatening the basic notions of what it means to
be a Hmong woman. Can Mai still be Hmong if she does not abide by these cultural norms? Clearly she struggles with this question. "That is always at the back
of my mind because people want me to do these things. Do I want to get married? . . . So that question of 'What am I here for?' is once again on my mind at
midnight when I can't get to sleep."

Though Mai asks herself these questions in the solitude of her bedroom at
midnight, she is not alone. She is one of a cohort of Hmong women who are redefining Hmong culture. Researcher Stacy J. Lee (1997) studied a pioneering
group of Hmong women who like Mai pursued higher education. Lee argues that
the question of cultural authenticity, with which Mai and her counterparts struggle, falsely assumes that culture is static. Lee (1998) writes, "Researchers who
equate culture with ethnicity overlook the possibility that individuals can desire
to transform their cultures and still have pride in their ethnicities" (p.10). In the
Hmong community in the United States, Hmong women like Mai are doing just
that. Evidence of that emerging cultural shift can be seen in Mai's description of
her mother's new sense of pride and understanding in what she is trying to
accomplish.

> When we organized a women's organization in the city, we had a lot of
> opposition. And people said, "Oh, it is going to divide the community."
> One man in particular opposed it. So I used my connections in D.C. and
> it happened. So I said, "Mom, see it is helping us out." For the first time
> my mom was very proud of me because I could help the community
> with their problem, using the experiences I had from [things] that they
> had forbidden me to do but that I went ahead and did. Ever since then,

she really trusted me. Now I want to work in D.C. or go to Thailand and she says go, go, go!!! Back then she forbade me to do anything but now she actually pushes me to. And she is very supportive. . . . She used to be so worried about what people would say about me, but now, now she is very, very supportive. And I feel great! If I haven't done anything else in this life, I am just really happy that my mom really understands where I am coming from.

Even though Mai has become a successful career woman and activist in a way that conflicts with all the traditional expectations of Hmong women, Mai is still very much Hmong. She preserves her ethnic identity through language and uses her bilingualism to advocate for the Hmong community. Her professional work revolves around improving the lives of the Hmong, especially Hmong women. On a personal level, Mai still eats rice, chili peppers, and Hmong vegetables. She dates Hmong men and attends Hmong parties, religious rituals, and events. She takes pride in her knowledge of Hmong folk songs, knowledge that few young Hmong Americans can claim. All these things make her Hmong, but she also acknowledges that at the same time she is very much American. She does not fail to recognize this aspect of her identity, but she wants to confirm that "In my heart, I will always be Hmong," even as she seeks to change the definition of what it means to be a Hmong woman.

Mai's bicultural narrative is extremely important to understanding the growing number of Southeast Asian adolescent refugee girls in the United States. Even though Mai is specifically Hmong and each Southeast Asian community is very distinct, they are now connected through their experiences here as Southeast Asian refugees living in America. Mai's narrative offers a solution to a dilemma shared by other Southeast Asian adolescent refugee girls. The unbearable silence imposed on her by both the racist master narrative of mainstream American culture and the sexist master narrative of the Hmong community was interrupted when she was able to claim her activist voice. The homogenizing "myth of the model minority" did not leave room for the uniqueness of her Hmong experience or the expression of her pain caused by the overt and covert racism around her. However, gaining the language to name her experience for herself, as she did in college, was an important step toward finding the path to change it. Clearly, speaking up in this way is outside the patriarchal gender norms for a young Hmong woman, and her struggle to resist those norms has not been an easy one, sometimes resulting in criticism from both friends and family. Yet her ability to remain grounded in her cultural heritage, through her continued affirmation of her Hmong identity, allows her to be one of the pioneers in her community helping to change those norms. She has not renounced her Hmong identity but is inventing a new way to be a Hmong woman in the United States.

Hopefully, this narrative of a Hmong woman carving a new place for herself and her community in the United States has made more visible the experiences of young Hmong women coming of age in the United States and offers light on the path for other Hmong women. Mai's story is ultimately one of hope for all young women who feel themselves alone on the edge of cultural transformation.

NOTES

1. ThaoMee would like to dedicate this chapter to her mother who is her source of inspiration and courage. "Thank you for always believing in me!"

REFERENCES

Arax, M. (1996). Reunions end 20 year trek for the Hmong. *Los Angeles Times* (Nov. 28), p. A1, 31.

Chan, S. (Ed.). (1994). *Hmong means free.* Philadelphia: Temple University Press.

Darder, A. (1991). *Culture and power in the classroom: A critical foundation for bicultural education.* New York: Bergin and Garvey.

Huang, L. N. (1994). An integrative view of identity formation: A model for Asian Americans. In E. P. Salett & D. R. Koslow (Eds.), *Race, ethnicity and self: Identity in multicultural perspective* (pp. 42–59). Washington, D.C.: National Multicultural Institute.

Kitano, H. (1997). A hyphenated identity. In B. Thompson & S. Tyagi (Eds.), *Names we call home: Autobiography on racial identity* (pp. 111–18). New York: Routledge.

Lee, S. J. (1997). The road to college: Hmong American women's pursuit of higher education. *Harvard Educational Review, 67,* 803–27.

_____(1998). "Are You Chinese, or What?": Ethnic and racial identity among Asian Americans. Paper presented at the American Educational Research Association Meeting, San Diego, CA, April 13.

Meredith, W. H., & Rowe, G. P. (1986). Changes in Hmong refugee marital attitudes in America. In G. L Hendricks, B. T. Downing, & A. S. Deinard (Eds.), *The Hmong in Transition* (pp. 121–34). Staten Island: Center for Migration Studies of New York, Inc.; The Southeast Asian Refugee Studies of the University of Minnesota.

Miller, J. B. (1988). Connections, disconnections, and violations. Work in Progress, No. 33. Wellesley, MA: Stone Center Working Paper Series.

Olsen, L. (1997). *Made in America: Immigrant students in our public schools.* New York: New Press.

Phinney, J. S., Lochner, B. T., & Murphy, R. (1990). Ethnic identity development and psychological adjustment in adolescence. In A. R. Stiffman & L. E. Davis (Eds.), *Ethnic issues in adolescent health* (pp. 53–72). Newbury Park, CA: Sage.

Reid, M. (Producer/Director). (1995). *Skin deep: College students confront racism.* San Francisco: Resolution/California Newsreel.

Takaki, R. T. (1989). *Strangers from a different shore: A history of Asian Americans.* Boston: Little, Brown.

Tatum, B. D. (1997). *"Why are all the black kids sitting together in the cafeteria?" and other conversations about race.* New York: Basic Books.

Thao, T. (1997). Personal Interview by ThaoMee Xiong with True Thao, MSW.

Trueba, H. T. (1990). *Cultural conflict and adaptation: The case of Hmong children in American society.* New York: Falmer Press.

Walker-Moffat, W. (1995). *The other side of the Asian American success story.* San Francisco: Jossey-Bass.

Yamada, M. (1981). Invisibility is an unnatural disaster: Reflections of an Asian American woman. In C. Moraga & G. Anzaldua (Eds.), *This bridge called my back: Writings by radical women of color* (pp. 35–40). New York: Kitchen Table Press.

Yang, K. (1998). Personal interview by ThaoMee Xiong with Ms. Yang, Executive Director of the Southeast Asian Resource Action Center (SEARAC).

Zweigenhaft, R. & Domhoff, G. W. (1991). *Blacks in the white establishment?: A study of race and class in America.* New Haven: Yale University Press.

Inventing a Labor of Love:
Scholarship as a Woman's Work

*W*OMEN HAVE, HISTORICALLY, BEEN UNDERREPRESENTED in the professoriate. They were therefore excluded from the social construction of academic knowledge in the university, the social institution charged with the production and transmission of such knowledge through research and teaching. Even now, more than twice as many men as women occupy full-time faculty positions (U.S. Dept. of Education, 1990); only 15 percent of full professors nationally are women (Fox, 1995, p. 231).

These statistics raise the daunting questions of how women who have had so little part historically in creating the academic enterprise join it, how they advance in academic careers (if, in fact, they do), and how they position themselves to contribute freely and in meaningful ways to research and teaching, as well as to the preparation of future researchers and teachers. How do women construct themselves as scholars and professors in advanced career, and how do they position themselves to contribute authentically to audiences whose previous visions of scholars and professors included only male faces? How do these women resist and transcend their own peers' and students' expectations that they should act like men? My purpose in this chapter is to consider the case of Rachel Teller, an academic scientist, who at early midcareer is, I believe, crafting her academic labors in ways that are meaningful to her students, her colleagues, and, importantly, herself.[2]

A MASTER NARRATIVE, COUNTERNARRATIVE, AND REVISED NARRATIVE OF ACADEMIC WORK

Before proceeding with Rachel Teller's accounts of her self-construction as a professor and scholar, I will present briefly one of the master narratives *against which* Rachel and others like her may write themselves. I present this master narrative through the eyes of another woman, author and social scientist Susan Krieger, who, early in her career, resisted her own (and her students') well-socialized expectations of what being a professor means. This is the master narrative with which Krieger struggled:

In the back of my mind is a college professor in a long, gray overcoat. I found him as an undergraduate and he has not yet left me. He, and he is a he, walks into a classroom and mumbles a few words into the collar of his coat and in the general direction of waiting students. Whether the students can make out all his words is unimportant. It is their responsibility to fill in what they have missed or to go with what they have heard. The professor does not stay long in the classroom. Sometimes he says only one sentence. . . .

I imagine that my professor wears an overcoat because he is teaching at a campus in New England. It is winter and snowing outside. He, or the room that he enters and stays in briefly, is cold. Yet his clothing is not only a result of the temperature. The professor wishes to hide and finds the protection of his overcoat comforting. He is largely unaware that his coat keeps others from knowing him, or from thinking that they know him because they see him. What matters to him is nothing personal, but, rather, what the students make of what he puts before them. (1991, p. 135–36)

Though presented in caricature, this image embodies Krieger's interpretations of her students' and colleagues' expectations of her.[3] She conducts research, writes, teaches, and otherwise constructs herself against this image. But what specifically does Krieger strive to write against? What messages does the professor in the long gray overcoat project to Krieger—and possibly to other women—about what it means to be a professor? I suggest the following:

- professors engage in solitude with their studies, even teaching from protective distances;
- the emotional "comfort" professors derive from their work comes, in good part, from the distances—or "protections"—of professorial (professional) overcoats, maybe more than from the knowledge that lies, protected, inside;
- professors contain their academic knowledge—or perhaps, their knowledge contains them, thwarting human connection;
- well-cloaked professors, though speaking (curtly) of their disciplines and topics of study, have little to say in public about what these mean to them personally; professors can never take off their coats;
- once they assume their protective garb, professors don't change through their lives.

Though carrying out his teaching duties, the cloaked professor says little to his students about what the content of his teaching—and of his own study—

means to him, how he came to pursue it, and how he lives with it now. He simply pours that content out (for Krieger, carelessly), assuming that students will contain it, and that perhaps through time (and graduate study) some may, like him, become contained by it. Those students who "succeed" will become professors just like him.

Moreover, this cloaked professor projects a number of dualisms: Through the overcoat, he signals that who he is as a professor and scholar is different from who he is as a person, a side of him he does not wish to reveal. He emphasizes research over relationship, scholarship over social interaction, thought over emotion, his own understandings over those of his students. He favors the conduct of research (which he disassociates from relationship and emotion) over the more relational and emotional work of teaching (which he disassociates from research and from scholarship generally). In fact, he may define research and scholarship through what he *believes they are not*—namely, relational and teaching oriented. He keeps to himself and his study, and he seems above feeling. Not least, as Krieger says, he is definitely a *he*. Judging from Krieger's responses to him, he is especially distant from his women students, and therefore, unlikely to inspire them to intellectual pursuit (except, perhaps, in resistance).

But given the cloaked professor's commitments to one side of his dualisms, is it enough simply to argue for what lies on the other side? Some scholars, in attempts to enlarge intellectual endeavor, and to balance the effects of nonrelational and nonemotive professors on students' learning, seem to believe so. For example, rather than focusing on research, they emphasize teaching and other forms of relational endeavor (thereby casting teaching more as relational than substantive). Within the professoriate, they fashion themselves as teachers and community builders, in contrast to researchers and scholars, thereby dividing the professoriate into two distant camps. The emerging image of the professor as relational and as building community, within the university and beyond, stands, in a sense, as a logical counternarrative to the master narrative that Krieger describes. And it is one to which some educators, sincerely concerned with women's educational needs, have gravitated, claiming its improved fit with women's lives (for example, see discussions of teaching in Belenky et al., 1986).

But is this enough? In presenting the story of Rachel Teller, I propose yet another narrative—one that blurs the division (and "di-vision") reified by both the cloaked professor (emphasizing mostly research to the exclusion of relationship) and the relational professor (emphasizing interaction and connection, usually through teaching, while downplaying research). Rachel Teller invoked an altogether different vision of the university professor—as encompassing research *and* relationship, scholarship *and* social interaction, subject *and* subjective meanings. Working against the norm, Rachel conducts her research in relational ways, and she relies on her relational work with students, including her teaching, to enact her research. In this chapter I present Rachel's revision in the hope that it will become accessible to others who, like Krieger, desire greater authenticity in their scholarly and professorial labors.

Rachel's image, then, reaches beyond current disputes over what it means to be a professor and scholar in the postmodern American university. If, to date, we know but little about her narrative, it is because scholars working in a diverse array of fields and disciplines are just now inventing it as revised professional practice that they, like Rachel, enact in their labs and classrooms.[4] I hope this chapter helps give voice to their enactments.

RACHEL TELLER'S RECONSTRUCTIONS OF THE PREVAILING NARRATIVES OF SCHOLARLY WORK

In constructing herself as a scholar, Rachel disrupts the cloaked professor image while deepening (and substantiating) the image of the relational professor. She does this in three ways: by articulating the personal meanings of her scholarship and its relational foundations; by enacting scholarship as a complex relational labor; and by attending to relational changes in her scholarship and her life, and thereby to personal and intellectual changes in herself.

Articulating the Personal Meaning of Her Scholarship and Its Relational Foundations

Often in public discourses about what it means to be an academic, professors distinguish between work and home, scholarship and family affairs, professional responsibility and personal commitment. Rachel adds little to such discourses of "di-vision;" in her life, the personal exists alongside the professional. Her professional work holds deep personal meaning for her, and she defines herself personally through this work.

"My professional life and my personal life are totally intermixed," she explained. "I have a very full life that's not in my laboratory or around my office. [My husband and I] have our children—we like to travel . . . soccer, I take the kids figure skating. . . . I'm a real fanatic about that. We like to be outdoors as much as possible. We garden. But when I think about, 'Who am I, or what do I do?' I really think of myself as a scientist, a research scientist," she said. "I'm very passionate about my work and I, I love it."

"I do love to do this kind of work," she continued. "So it's not like I imagine myself, if given the opportunity, what would I, you know, say, 'Okay, I'm going to stay home because I have very young children, and this would be a chance to kind of be a great mom,' and that sort of thing. I think I already am a great mom, and I don't know, I don't know—it's pretty wound up for me [the two—the personal and professional]."

In speaking personally about her intellectual and professional work, Rachel portrayed herself as in close relationship with that work—a relationship she nurtured from girlhood through midcareer. "I have a real love of the natural world," she said, "and I . . . feel real fortunate that I get to do that, get to have a job where I really just get to pursue something that I love to do."

But Rachel's self-portrayal as *in relationship* did not stop at her relationship with the scientific questions and issues she pursued; it extended to her students and colleagues—to groups of people connected to her and to each other through their interrelated scientific interests and commitments. She explained how this web of connections had come together for her:

[When I first joined this faculty, as a junior professor,] I had this, sort of, array of things that I was interested in, in graduate school. . . . So . . . although my interest was multifaceted, I was focusing more on one part when I arrived. . . . But after I arrived . . . I tried to work on other parts of it, and sort of, develop some of those other ideas. I still do work on [that earlier facet] . . . or some of my students [do]. . . . So, it's not like I have abandoned those areas, it's just, it's always been my goal—it's too big a goal for, you know, to have going simultaneously, I think, for one person. . . . [And] now that I have a lab group and multiple people working on things— . . . I think it's probably true for most people—I feel like I'll probably have more things that interest me, and more ideas in my lifetime, than I will ever get to finish, or even start on, let alone finish. So . . . having graduate students and post docs who are working on topics that are related to the things I'm interested in—I get a very vicarious sort of thrill from, you know, watching them analyze their data, and sort of, cheering them.

Rachel spoke at length about how she balanced the individual yet interrelated interests of the members of her lab group:

I have never told any of my graduate students what to work on, you know. I don't assign them projects but . . . I know that I directly influence what they work on. And so, although some of the time they work on things that are of interest to me, or something that I would have done myself if I had been able to clone myself up, their . . . choosing to develop an area that I think is interesting—is really, really satisfying for me. And because we read together, and discuss papers, and, you know, figure out how to analyze their data—or whatever steps in the process they're in—it's very educational for me. I feel like I'm a part of their—[a] really positive part of being a professor is being able to be around people who love to think about problems and try and figure them out.

Rachel saw herself as committed to an area of study composed of multiple overlapping problems and issues, expressing themselves at different times (and places) in her life, often through the work of her students, each of whom created one or more "facets" of the "multifaceted" area as her or his own. Thus each of her students might add in substantive ways to their shared area of study. In brief, Rachel's relationship to her own research reflected similar relationships to research among her students, each of whom used the content of their studies to relate to Rachel and to each other.

Although Rachel's lab group was a prominent part of her work life at Cameron University, another group that she had helped create held special import for her, for it too was a context within which she situated and realized her deepening (and expanding) work in science. This second group crossed Cameron's administrative boundaries, enabling Rachel to reach beyond a university structure that separated her from colleagues in other departments with interests akin to her own. "It collects [people with my interests] out of all these [departments], and unites them. . . . And it's a way to link people who are thinking about the same things on campus," she said.

Unlike Krieger's image of a professor who holds himself apart from his own academic knowledge and from his students, Rachel portrays herself as personally related to her knowledge, and to her students and colleagues through that knowledge. Her narrative also suggests that scholars may remain emotionally attached to inquiry even as the content or focus of their studies changes through time. As she said, "I chose to become a professor because it is a career which, in the perfect world, allows you to pursue ideas—in which you exist in an environment where other people are interested in ideas—that's very creative, that's very challenging."

In sum, Rachel expresses her scholarship and professional efforts within a metaphor of relation, thereby creating a rhetoric for articulating the personal meaning of her work in ways that blur traditional personal/professional divisions. Moreover, within Rachel's narrative, relationship as metaphor refers to her connections, not only to persons (alone or in groups) but also to the *subject matter—the scientific knowledge*—she constructs. Though current writings on relationship as a theme in women's development emphasizes women's connections to *persons* (see, for example, Belenky et al., 1986; Gilligan, 1982), Rachel's narrative suggests that relationship may also include women's connections to *knowledge*—in this case, academic knowledge. Rachel's narrative also suggests that relationship may assume the power of metaphor in a woman's professional thought and talk.

Enacting Scholarship as a Complex Relational Labor

Relationships that work require thought and effort. Given Rachel's relatedness to the particular scientific questions she pursues—and to persons whose scientific pursuits are bound up with her own—we may surmise that much of her work life is dedicated to relational labor. As Rachel's continuing narrative shows, this relational labor entails more than *building and making* (for example, building a lab group and contributing to the making of a colleague group). It also entails *caring for* and *defending* relationships previously created and, at times, *revising* and *ending* them.

From commentary on my interview with Rachel:

> In our first yearly interview, Rachel Teller spoke at length, and with much excitement, about the natural world she loved, about the personal meaning of being a scientist, about her wonderful lab group and colleague group, about how much fun research could be. I could tell, from the instant she walked into the room a year later that this time, she would be more subdued. But not until later did I appreciate signals she gave off. The crucial events in her life, and how she was making sense of them, did not surface until halfway through our talk that day, well after she had taught me a bit about her efforts to "synthesize" problems spanning diverse domains of knowledge and how her lab group had helped her in this.
>
> *As I heard it, this is what she had come to understand:* that in light of Cameron University's most recent wave of financial stress, her academic department was at risk—and so too were lab and colleague groups she had created to hold and support the scientific endeavors which, she said, were so expressive of who she was.
>
> In brief, her relationship to her research—and her relationships to students and colleagues mediated by their joint research interests—were now seriously at risk.
>
> *And this is what I then thought:* that given how closely tied *she* was to her studies in science, and to those who studied with her, that in a sense, she too was at risk—or at least felt that she was.

This is what she saw happening:

> Because of the general lack of support of my involvement in the program, and because of [one of the departments for which I teach] telling me, "Why are you teaching that? A course [on that topic, my area of expertise] doesn't have anything to do with [the knowledge represented by this department]"—and saying things like that—I, I just figured this out about a week ago that I sort of feel like I've been circling my wagons smaller and smaller. . . . When you're under siege, you know, you circle the wagons. . . . I realized that there was so much animosity on campus toward people in my area, and toward some of the programs that were being developed, that I decided to put my energy more into the local

scene . . . there was . . . a lot of energy [we put] into . . . solidifying ourselves . . . at the department level and [at the level of the] lab group. . . . Some things are eroding, you know . . . [and] I mean, it's very emotionally charged all the time.

In realizing what she was up against, and what she therefore stood to lose, Rachel tightened her hold on the relationships she held most dear, fearing their loss. But as she reflected further on what was happening at Cameron, and on her instinctive protective actions, she began to let go—first of the interdepartmental colleague group that she left to senior colleagues to defend, then of Cameron itself, and finally, and hardest of all, of her lab group.

In early midcareer, shortly after earning tenure (perhaps the major achievement of a professorial career) Rachel came face to face, not with job loss (her tenure protected her job), but ironically, with loss of her *work*, including the two groups so central to her own and her students' pursuits of the questions and issues—the science—they loved. She thus came face to face with the potential loss of that science itself. Her relationships with her area of study in science and with her students and colleagues—all of which she had forged with care earlier in her career—were now under fire, and because these were tied (relationally) to who *she* was, so was she. She "circled her wagons," she resisted attacks on her department and lab group, she thought deeply about protective strategies. Yet in the end, given the foresight that things simply would not get better, and given an unexpected opportunity to leave Cameron for a safer, more supportive environment at another university, Rachel gave up her efforts at Cameron.

Was she happy? Did she see the move to a new, more supportive university as an improvement? A relief? Yes, but she also was aware of what she was leaving, and it tore at her. As she reviewed her relationships at Cameron, she realized, with the clarity that often illuminates endings, what she had learned, what she had come to love, and what now she had to let go. Facing the closing of her lab group, she said:

I value [in this work] the time, the luxury that this kind of job affords for conducting scholarly activity. And having the time to think about areas and issues in [my field] that are, at one level, very fundamental to . . . processes in [science], and are very difficult to understand. And I value that being an academic means I get to work on these kinds of problems. And I value being in a community of people that does the same kinds of things—that like to think for a living, and, and get really excited about ideas. . . . But the satisfaction also comes from the group interaction, the discussion of ideas with my students, or post docs, or colleagues, where the idea itself becomes something that's an emergent property of the people.

To Rachel, relational academic labor entailed the creation, care, support, protection, and, at times, ending and rebuilding of her relationships to her area of scientific study and to the persons who created it with her. Early in her career at Cameron, Rachel and her students constructed a lab group, and she and her colleagues constructed an interdepartmental colleague group; through the years, she fostered the development of these groups. Later, during crisis, she stepped up to protect her department and lab group. Later still, she decided to leave Cameron for new relational opportunities, purposefully disconnecting from some relationships for the sake of other improved relationships (Brown & Gilligan, 1992). In this last relational act, she cleared spaces in which to rebuild meaningful (though no doubt revised) forms of scholarly relationship in her life and career. Viewed in light of Rachel's narrative, a sequence of relational activities may constitute a woman's academic life.

Attending to Relational Change and thereby to Personal and Intellectual Change

Unlike the cloaked and unchanging professor Susan Krieger remembers, Rachel changes over time, as do her relationships. The relational developments in her life may, in fact, account for the changes in her.

Rachel developed her relationship to her area of scientific study through her graduate career, and this commitment bloomed and evolved through her pre-tenure years at Cameron. It was in full force in her early midcareer as she made the decision to leave Cameron for a new job. Settled in her new university, she reshaped her studies by asking new questions that her new location invited and that might give her a fresh look at the scientific issues that mattered so much to her. She saw this change more as a movement from facet to facet of her complex interests than as a drastic reformulation. Her relationships to her Cameron-based lab and colleague groups materialized during her early years there, but she had to sharply curtail these as she moved on to her new university. As she settled into her new site, she began to reconstruct lab and colleague groups, but in revised form, reflecting the unique affordances and constraints of her new environment and reflecting also what she had learned about working with students and colleagues through the years.

Rachel's relationship to her husband and children also were transformed by the move to a different university. Living now in a new city and new neighborhood, Rachel spoke of her efforts to resituate them all. "One of the reasons that we moved . . . was that we wanted to [be in a place that was] more conducive to being human," she said. "We have tried, very hard, this year to connect our kids up in ways that they feel excited, and I feel like I really spent last year taking care of my family. . . . We've really, I think, worked very hard in, in making life happy for them . . . [and] I've finally started to do something for me [as well]." Thus Rachel took as much initiative in developing her family relationships as she did her work relationships.

Beyond reconstructing and extending her research agenda and work and family relationships, Rachel began to attend to other, heretofore ignored, aspects of her professional life. First, she saw (and seized) opportunities to develop her teaching relationships. At Cameron, logistical constraints such as large undergraduate class sizes encouraged her to lecture, a teaching mode where, in her view, "people are far away"—where "they're so disconnected from it [the subject matter of the class] . . . that they're not making connections," while she, as teacher, fully realizing the problem, was "trying to think of ways to change the way I teach . . . trying to figure that out—how to engage it." Now in her new university, she did more than simply ponder this problem. Rather, she worked actively at teaching her undergraduate students "to think like scientists." The resources in her new site allowed her to work out new ways to relate to her students and to relate to herself as teacher.

Second, she saw that at this stage of her career, she might grow more fully into her disciplinary community. "I feel like I'm close [to my field], and I'm getting closer," she said. "I think that . . . the work that I'm doing now . . . will be . . . really . . . of value and of interest to lots of people. So, I think . . . that's what . . . makes you feel close. Or not close. . . . I think that some of [my] projects . . . will be very interesting to people . . . so I'm pretty excited about [that]."

And finally, for the first time in her career, she glimpsed the possibility of forging a meaningful relationship with her university and with communities beyond it. "Since I've moved [here], I can see that the involvement in the university-level processes is also of interest to me," she said. But she hesitated. "I'm not exactly sure . . . where I want to put my energy. As I get older, I know that I'm finite, and I can only put my energy in so many places." Despite this concern, she persisted in contemplating the value of such work. "I think . . . that's also part of [it] . . . —to make sure that the scholarly climate, and the quality of education is high, or is the best that it can be, is something that is also a role of a professor. And, and I think that we also need to communicate, not just with other professors, but with . . . the broader community. So people understand what it . . . is that we do here . . . who we are."

In sum, I saw Rachel in early midcareer as enmeshed in her science in increasingly complex ways—through multiplying relationships, all anchored in the scientific knowledge she had constructed (and reconstructed) attentively throughout her career, all the while reconstructing herself. Rachel's continuous self-constructions seemed always moored in her scientific passions and commitments—and in her relationships with persons, groups, and communities who shared them. My guess is that in standing true to the *personal meanings* of her scholarship—including the diverse relationships (to scientific knowledge, persons, communities) that expressed those meanings, and the relational metaphor that framed them—she remained true to herself, as did her scholarly work.

"So . . . it was that," she said, the last time we spoke, "having . . . everything stripped down to the bare bones, building it back up." For Rachel, the disconnection from her relationships at Cameron was hard, and it no doubt felt to her like "a stripping down to the bare bones," a giving up of all she had previously and so passionately created. But rather than viewing the break as a series of losses, she turned it into an amazing adventure—an opportunity to recreate herself through new and emerging relationships imbued with meaning.

"It's been very exciting," she said several times through our last talk. "When I am not totally exhausted," she added, now with clear laughter in her voice, "I feel really excited."

REFLECTIONS ON AN ACADEMIC WOMAN

I close with three reflections on Rachel:

First, Rachel creates herself professionally and intellectually through a relational metaphor which, in all likelihood, she draws from her life's learning as a woman attuned to her connections to others (Gilligan, 1982). In transferring her relational knowledge and way of knowing from her personal experiences to her professional work (including her science), she renders her professional work as personal. Moreover, as she draws on a relational metaphor to create her science and her professional self, she engages in truly *creative* acts. This is largely because in the past, most aspiring scholars (males) created themselves and their work exclusively from the imagery of men's lives (their teachers, also males), thereby excluding women's relational images. In asserting her personal knowledge about relationship in her professional work, Rachel recreates a corner of her profession, and possibly a corner of her scientific field.

Second, although Rachel's narrative indicates that she acts from personal commitment to her relational metaphor, in doing so, she also acts from courage. She sets aside the certainties and comforts of academic convention (symbolized by the cloaked professor) to speak, as Gilligan says, in "a different voice" that some of her colleagues and students may need to learn *to hear in a different way*—an experience that she, as teacher, may need to support.

Finally, though stemming from her talent, knowledge, commitment, and courage, Rachel's actions also stem from flashes of good luck and opportunity (for example, her new job) and the flexibility and freedom to respond to them, options not readily available to all women. Yet she does not hesitate to make the most of these gifts of good fortune when they come her way.

NOTES

1. Acknowledgments: The research on which this chapter is based was supported by grants from the College of Education Institute for Research and the All University Re-

search Initiation Grant Program at Michigan State University. I wish to acknowledge the helpful advice of Estela Bensimon, Aída Hurtado, Adrianna Kezar, Aaron Pallas, Mary Romero, and Abby Stewart. My very special thanks to "Rachel Teller."

2. Rachel was one of 38 professors I interviewed annually in a 3-year study of learning and identity development after tenure. Though representing diverse fields and disciplines, all worked at the same large public research/landgrant university. Twenty of the 38 worked in the sciences. To preserve confidentiality, I refer to all persons and places by pseudonyms, blur the exact years of the study, and mask or erase other identifiers. I do not reveal study participants' specific disciplines or areas of study since doing so might identify them. Thus, I refer to Rachel in only the most general of disciplinary terms (as a scientist) and without reference to her specific field or to the research issues and questions she addresses.

3. Krieger's image, though presented as unique, personal experience, echoes the concerns of numerous feminist scholars (see, for example, Acker & Feuerverger, 1996; Maher & Tetreault, 1994; Martin, 1982).

4. See writings by teacher-researchers examining, reflexively, their own and their students' learning of the subject matters they teach (described in Neumann, Pallas, & Peterson, in press). See also Keller (1985), Behar and Gordon (1995), and Csikszentmihalyi (1996).

REFERENCES

Acker, S., & Feuerverger, G. (1996). Doing good and feeling bad: The work of women university teachers. *Cambridge Journal of Education*, *26* (3), 401–22.

Behar, R., & Gordon, D. A. (Eds.) (1995). *Women writing culture*. Berkeley and Los Angeles: University of California Press.

Belenky, M. F., Clinchy, B. M., Goldberger, N. R., & Tarule, J. M. (1986). *Women's ways of knowing: The development of self, body, and mind*. New York: Basic Books.

Brown, L. M., & Gilligan, C. (1992). *Meeting at the crossroads: Women's psychology and girls' development*. New York: Ballantine.

Csikszentmihalyi, M. (1996). *Creativity: Flow and the psychology of discovery and invention*. New York: HarperCollins.

Fox, M. F. (1995). Women and higher education: Gender differences in the status of students and scholars. In J. Freeman (Ed.), *Women: A feminist perspective* (5th ed.) (pp. 220–37). Mountain View, CA: Mayfield.

Gilligan, C. (1982). *In a different voice: Psychological theory and women's development*. Cambridge: Harvard University Press.

Keller, E. F. (1985). *Reflections on gender and science*. New Haven: Yale University Press.

Krieger, S. (1991). *Social science and the self: Personal essays on an art form*. New Brunswick, N.J.: Rutgers University Press.

Maher, F., & Tetreault, M. K. T. (1994). *The feminist classroom*. New York: Basic Books.

Martin, J. R. (1982). Excluding women from the educational realm. *Harvard Educational Review*, *52* (2), 133–48.

Neumann, A., Pallas, A. M., & Peterson, P. L. (In press). Preparing education practitioners to practice education research. In E. C. Lagemann & L. S. Shulman (Eds.), *Issues in ed-*

ucation research: Problems and possibilities. Commission for Improving Educational Research, National Academy of Education. San Francisco: Jossey-Bass.

U. S. Department of Education. (1990). Distribution of full-time faculty members by age and discipline at four-year institutions, 1987. Table reprinted in *The Chronicle of Higher Education Almanac* (September 5), 22.

Berta's Story:
Journey from Sweatshop to Showroom

En la costura . . . se ve tanta injusticia. . . . yo veo personas que estan cosiendo y tienen la "stroller" a un lado con ellas. Yo lo he vivido. He llegado a los talleres y yo siento que el aire me falta; no tienen ventilación. Esa pelusa que suelta la "overlock" la esta inhalando la gente . . . un bebé de siete meses esta respirando esa pelusa todo el santo día, que bárbaros!

(In the garment industry . . . we see so much injustice . . . . I see people sewing next to a stroller. I have lived this. I have arrived to the shops and I feel I need air; there is no ventilation. The lint coming out of the "overlock"[1] is inhaled by people . . . a seven-month-old baby is breathing that lint all day long, how dare they!)

$\mathcal{F}$OR 15 YEARS BERTA,[2] A LATINA IMMIGRANT, has negotiated multiple locations in her work life. In the process, she has crafted several identities, some in response to the realities of life in the United States and others in resistance to these limitations. When Berta discusses her occupational life, we learn how she travels among a variety of work sites in Los Angeles' garment industry. These working localities extend throughout the process of production; she advances from sweatshops to showrooms in the apparel industry. In fact, her job as "quality control"[3] person gives her a level of access and mobility that few workers ever attain. Moreover she constantly negotiates racial, gender, immigrant, and social-class structures that impact her day-to-day life.

Berta's story relates the complexity of life in the garment industry that is typically erased by master narratives' concern with the "global apparel industry." In studies of the global apparel industry researchers insist that economic dislocation alone forces poor people to migrate to centers of production. Once Latina immigrants arrive in Los Angeles, sweatshops offer them their first job opportunity. Because Latinas arrive with few skills and little education, they are trapped in these badly paid occupations.[4] In this process, a particular image of Latina garment workers is constructed. Within "globality discourse" the focus is on clothing production in developing countries, not within the United States. An example is the apparel *maquiladora* industry in the Mexican border region (Carrillo, 1994; Fernandez-Kelly, 1983; Tiano, 1987). Most research on sweatshop conditions in the United States is either historical (Furio, 1979; Glenn, 1983) or focuses on the macrolevel. Few studies investigate the lives of present-day women who labor at the sewing machine (Fernandez-Kelly & Garcia, 1985; Lamphere, 1987; Waldinger, 1986). Moreover, statistical surveys often miss undocumented workers. In contrast, Berta's story offers a local account to counter the emphasis on macrostudies in master narratives. Globality discourses construct Latina garment workers as "unskilled" laborers who remain at one site and task throughout their career.

Scholars have not quantified the way in which Latinas simultaneously participate in several jobs in the labor market. Latinas are either considered to work at a shop or at home, when many of them work at both sites at the same time. Latinas are treated as a homogeneous group providing "cheap labor." However, Berta is a highly skilled worker who does multiple jobs in order to survive. She challenges globality discourse. Like many Latinas and garment workers she can design a garment from beginning to end and then use the various tools efficiently to produce apparel. As Berta demonstrates, Latina garment workers are not unskilled workers with limited mobility. Rather many women are highly skilled, with work lives that pass through multiple working sites and stages. We can use the globality discourse as a starting point in understanding these women's experience. Thus, Berta traveled to the United States because of the lack of job opportunities for her and her husband in Mexico. This step can be explained in terms of processes of capitalist production at the global level. Once Berta migrated to Los Angeles, though, her negotiation of gender, race, age, social class, and immigrant status could not be reduced to capitalist functions (Cvetkovich & Kellner, 1997, p. 2).

By beginning with Berta's standpoint[5] we can comprehend the global apparel industry as she experiences it in her everyday life. Cvetkovich and Kellner (1997) would define Berta's story as "translocal."

The notion of the translocal speaks to the challenge of providing an analysis of a global system of social relations without overgeneralizing or establishing hierarchies in which some sites are more global or more important than others. . . . Translocal analysis finds its object not just in national political struggles or economic relations but in individual experiences . . . in the spaces of everyday life. (pp. 24–25)

In other words, instead of attempting to understand Berta's life experience through globality discourse, we will examine global social relations through Berta's individual life experiences. In the global apparel industry master narrative, women stand divested of any agency. According to the master narrative, Latinas are powerless automatons of the system of production, incapable of understanding or overcoming their own exploitation; Berta's translocal story overturns this simplistic vision. In contrast, we see Berta making choices, albeit limited by gender/racial hierarchies and structural factors, crafting her own identity. I would like us to know this Berta who constructs herself through her agency.

A quick reading of Berta's life might seem to uphold the Horatio Alger myth: if you just put your mind (and back) to it, then you can succeed. In fact Berta's story is the exact opposite. Despite all her work, Berta has not achieved any radical class transformation. Like many garment workers before her, she has merely negotiated a system that has allowed her to survive. Some workers have been less or more successful in their negotiations of their survival. What Berta's story allows us to see is how one woman trying to make a living moved within the garment industry over a 15-year period. That she ends up an artisan and not a designer, underscores her inability to overcome her location in the U.S. labor structure.

BERTA'S STORY: A COUNTERNARRATIVE

Following Berta through her own life and her everyday world (Smith, 1987), we learn about the different layers of her travels and border crossings. As Berta moves among three sites, shifting her identities, she struggles with both imposed constructions and her endeavor of self-affirmation. Berta physically travels from Mexico to the United States, but she continuously reenacts migration after her arrival. She moves between Latino communities and the outside majority neighborhoods in Los Angeles. Berta also crosses borders between occupations in the garment industry. She is not only a sewing-machine operator but also a supervisor and sample maker. As she succeeds in her mobility, Berta designs and sews original gowns of her own creation. Berta's creations provide her with self-affirmation as an artisan.

The first border Berta crossed was the U.S.–Mexico border that divides two cultural and regional spaces. Berta was born in Mexico City in the 1950s and raised in a working-class family of six children. Her father was a shopkeeper and her mother a housewife; they provided for their kids as best they could. She was the youngest, and was able to follow her brothers and sisters through the Mexican education system. Both mother and father instilled in her a strong discipline of hard work and a thirst for education. Her parents' dream was to see Berta graduate from college. But she had her own plans. By the time she graduated from high school she eloped with her boyfriend José and got pregnant. Her family was disappointed. The young couple worked hard to save some money to go to *el norte*. Many of their family and friends were already in Los Angeles. The work prospects in Mexico City, for a couple like them, were not good, because the economy in Mexico in the late 1970s looked bleak. They figured the best thing they could do was take their 11-month-old baby and go to the United States. Berta has a difficult time remembering their migration and does not like to talk about it. The master narrative emphasizes economic factors alone as the main reason for individual's migration. Agency is absent in these accounts of "push" and "pull" factors explaining the migration of masses of people. Yet individuals like Berta and her husband must make personal decisions to make the trek (Hondagneu-Sotelo, 1994).

As an undocumented immigrant coming from an urban setting, Berta engaged a city that provided her with a Latino community network necessary for survival while simultaneously limiting her mobility and work options: Border crossings got enacted on a daily basis in segregated Los Angeles. Berta had to learn a new language and culture to survive in her new environment. This entailed fresh tactics to maneuver around racial and ethnic obstacles. Moreover, she learned how to negotiate new gender and class constructions different from the ones she had previously experienced in Mexico. Employers' racial constructions of Latinos(as) intersected with their views of gender. Berta's worth from her employer's perspective typically defined her as part of a uniform mass of cheap and expendable labor. Berta found that sweatshops abounded, and Latinas were always welcomed as new hires. Meanwhile her husband José found employment in construction. The couple could now move into their own apartment, make arrangements for childcare with relatives, and Berta could start her career in the garment industry.

During this period, Berta crossed occupational borders, seeking better wages. She combined sweatshop work with work at home, and homework with paid domestic work. She gained skills, and first opened her own contract shop, later became a quality-control middle person. She began her work history doing multiple jobs; yet once she became a "success," she continued working at several jobs to make ends meet. She never gave up the struggle of giving her children the possibility of a better life and dreamt of a better future for them. However, she remained trapped by the ever-present obstacles.

As Berta moved within these localities, she formulated different forms of resistance. The master narrative would not recognize her resistance, since Berta did not organize or participate in labor organizations. In fact, given the ways in which Berta tried to subvert exploitation, master narratives would define her as a passive victim. Under closer examination, we see how, instead, she was constantly resisting and struggling at work (Bookman & Morgen, 1988; Collins, 1990). Berta critically assesses the power relations in the apparel industry.

Es una cadena en la que hace dinero el más poderosos. Porque ellos tienen su sueldo mas aparte su comisión. . . . No quieren que haya "damage" no quieren reparación. Quieren la mejor calidad sin pagarles! Es una cadena hay Dios mio! Ce injusticia, de hambre, de ansiedad para los trabajadores.

(It is a chain in which the one making money is the most powerful. Because at the showroom they have a salary plus commission . . . they do not want damaged garments, they do not want to repair them [coming from contractors]. They want the best quality without paying for it! It is a chain oh my God! Of injustice, hunger, anxiety for workers.)

The next three sections explore Berta's attempts to shape her work experience to fit her talents, dreams, and economic needs, within the limited opportunities offered by the garment industry. In the first section Berta discovers the constraints on workers' incomes, regardless of their skills, and searches for additional income sources. In the second section, Berta adopts several different strategies for generating income in the formal and informal economy. Eventually she finds a way to combine wage labor with labors of love. As we see in the third section, the price of her success is her complicated role as a quality-control person, someone who must translate between the sweatshops and the showrooms of the fashion industry.

From Sweatshops to Homework: Developing Skills, Remaining "Unskilled"

To find work, Berta did what other Latinas do—she walked and knocked on doors, asking for work. When she came to a shop where the owner was also a Mexican lady, Doña Carmen, Berta was hired. Berta's outgoing personality and enthusiasm got her her first job in Los Angeles.

Camine hasta que encontre un taller de costura . . . ese miso día que salí encontre trabajo . . . entonces la muchacha me dijo que necesitaban a alguien que hiciera el "blind stitch . . . " me enseño como y dió la oportunidad de aprender. . . . Yo iba desde las 6 de la mañana hasta las 7 sin sueldo. Pero queria aprender y despues de 2 meses, me pagaba 25 dolares a la semana. . . . En ese tiempo el salario minimo era de 100 dolares a la semana.

(I walked until I found a sewing shop . . . that same day I went out I found a job . . . then the girl told me they needed somebody to do blind-stitch . . . she showed me how and gave me the opportunity to learn. . . . I went from 6 in the morning to 7 at night without pay. But I wanted to learn and after two months she paid me 25 dollars a week . . . in those times the minimum wage was 100 dollars a week.)

Sure enough Berta learned to be efficient at the blind stitch, earning a very modest salary based on the piece-rate system. She made enough money to pay for a baby-sitter. She looked at it as an investment in her future work chances. She was mastering several types of sewing machines. She stayed at the shop for 2 years, earning the trust of the owner. When Doña Carmen left the shop, Berta became the person in charge of the shop. She could train new workers and oversaw production. Her salary, however, never improved.

Berta moved from shop to shop, trying to find a place that would remunerate her abilities. She soon discovered that if she worked at a regular pace, she was paid piece rate. However, whenever she excelled at an operation and became fast, the owners paid her by the hour. She was always paid whichever was lower; often she was cheated. She remembers sewing garments at a stated piece rate; the rate was lowered by the time she received her salary. The explanation given was that the contractor had losses. Some contractors also failed to pay her at the end of the week. She would come to the shop for her paycheck and they were gone. Nobody could tell her where to find her employers.

According to the master narrative, garment workers move through different shops, but they do not develop skills. Somehow after years of performing different operations at the sewing machine and learning to operate different machines, their labor remains "unskilled," thus deserving low pay. Nevertheless, when we follow the working paths of garment workers, we see that many develop valuable skills. For example, some operate various sewing machines, from the single needle to the overlock. Also very important to the industry, garment workers devise ways to finish operations in a short time. Simultaneously employers dismiss workers' skills in order to pay them the lowest possible rate. The master narrative and employers socially construct Latinas as "unskilled," therefore deserving a low wage.

Berta used to buy coffee and doughnuts at a place close to the sewing shop. One day talking to the person in charge, she found out that that employee made minimum wage selling doughnuts. Berta considered this a better deal than working at the sewing machine. Although Berta's English was not very good, the owner was willing to hire her if she knew the names of the doughnuts. Berta went home and memorized the names. In no time Berta was selling doughnuts. With this new job Berta had more time on her hands. She decided to expand her meager English vocabulary. Berta had tried the local night school and took classes in English as a Second Language. Disappointed with the slowness and low level of the classes offered, she bought a dictionary and began her self-teaching program. Berta would write one word and repeat it until she could use it comfortably in conversation. And she would ask customers for help in pronunciation. Soon she was functional in English. After a few months at the doughnut shop Berta grew bored and decided that sewing was what she really enjoyed most; she returned to work at the sewing machine.

At the beginning Berta made tremendous sacrifices with her husband. The little money the couple earned was spent on their rent, bills, and food. Berta recalls the difficult times:

> Había veces que solamente trabajabamos por la renta. E ibamos al "market" y procurabamos la comida del niño y si nos quedaba solo suficiente para comprar un paquete de tortillas y dos paquetitos de sopa. . . . Bueno me fué demasiado dificil. De pasar hambres . . . pero de no darnos por vencidos.

> (There were times that we only worked to pay for rent. And we went to the market and we procured the child's food and we were left with only enough to buy a bag of tortillas and two little packets of soup . . . well it was very tough. We starved . . . but we never gave up.)

For several years Berta worked in many shops, eventually becoming an expert sewing machine operator.[6] However, Berta's developed skills and work ethic never translated into an improved salary. This unresponsive market situation drove Berta to another practice common to garment workers—taking work home from the factory to sew overnight. Homework (Boris, 1994; Fernandez-Kelly & García, 1985; Hadjisconti, 1990) allows workers to make some extra money. Eventually, instead of taking work home on weekends or overnight, she just did homework. She could stay and sew at home and never have to work at the factory. Berta judged that staying at home and sewing clothes was a smarter choice for someone raising children. Now with three children, she could always stay home while working. Doing homework also made sense in terms of saving childcare expenses. For several years Berta continued to sew garments at home. Homeworkers, according to the master narrative, are all "unskilled." However, there are different garments produced by homeworkers, each demanding different levels of skill. The master narrative assumes that homeworkers only produce cheap garments, yet I interviewed garment workers who produced elaborate, expensive designer's gowns at home. A high level of skill is required to sew cocktail gowns with elaborate stitching and shirring, and sheer materials are difficult to manipulate and control under the sewing machine.

Using the Informal Economy to Survive

More family members came from Mexico to start a new life. Berta and José always opened their doors to their relatives in need. At some point Berta had at least four adults, plus her children, living in a small apartment. Around this time José was laid off from his job, and the family faced very difficult times. Berta decided she could clean homes during the day and sew clothes at night to make ends meet. Relatives worked doing casual labor, while Berta's earnings provided for most of the family's living expenses. When Berta remembers this harsh time, she recalls most of all her exhaustion.

Berta began cleaning several homes but soon a woman offered her a permanent cleaning job in Beverly Hills. Every day Berta returned from cleaning the mansion to her small apartment. She would be so tired that, on many occasions, she opted to take a nap instead of eating. By ten at night Berta would sit at the sewing machine and work until three or four in the morning.

Pero así pasaron bastantes años de dormirme a las 2 o 3 de la mañana y levantarme a limpiar casas. . . . Así trabaje limpiando casas y cosiendo. Llegaba sin nada de ganas a trabajar en mi costura. . . . Me estaba atrasando.

(So many years went by I would go to bed at 2 or 3 in the morning and wake up to clean homes. . . . Thus I worked cleaning homes and sewing. I used to come without any energy to work in my sewing . . . I was slacking.)

In this way, she kept the family afloat. Berta and José worked several jobs to save money. The informal economy always represented a way out for them. José worked doing handy jobs at nights and on weekends; Berta always worked at sewing, often combining homework with whatever job was available. Berta knew how to be thrifty and save money. She knew how to buy groceries in bulk, to plan meals, and inexpensive outings for the children. They eventually saved enough for a down payment for a modest home in Los Angeles. Once settled in their home, they had more to look forward to. Berta decided she could have her own contracting shop. José built a small sewing shop for Berta in their backyard. The master narrative dismisses the experiences of working-class Latinas who buy homes or start their own businesses; only workers living in dire poverty are visible. Some immigrant workers in Los Angeles through years of savings and sacrifices own homes or pay mortgages in poor sections of the city; in some instances the most dangerous areas cater to Latino/a immigrants. Many immigrant Latinos/as thrive and even establish their own businesses, which are always at risk of failure. Yet many Latino businesses have their own clientele in areas where they are needed.

Since Berta had made enough connections among contractors, she went into her own contracting business. Berta owned a couple of sewing machines and rented five more. She hired some of her friends at the sewing shop and offered to treat them well and pay them decent salaries. She planned to pay more than the minimum wage plus overtime. She went so far as to provide refreshments. Her kitchen at home remained open to her workers. There were always free sodas and a place to eat a warm lunch. She did not want to reproduce the working conditions and miserable salaries so prevalent in the industry. Idealistically Berta wanted to correct the exploitative system of clothing production.

Her contracting dream shop lasted only 6 months. The cruel realities of production and fierce competition forced Berta out of business. She had to pay for incidental expenses such as electricity and servicing of sewing machines. She also had to pay taxes. Berta remembers working double shifts without receiving a salary. After she paid everyone else there was no salary left for herself. Competition also represented a strong factor. Prices were ridiculously low. Many new contractors were willing to produce for much less, in other words to squeeze their workers. By the late 1980s when Berta opened her own contracting shop, more competition appeared and prices were being driven down.

> ¡Y por eso le digo que antes lo sentí como trabajadora, ahora lo sentí como contratista que es todavía peor! Tenemos la presión de que firmamos un contrato. Pegamos mucho dinero, "taxes" más muchas otras cosas, más aparte no hacemos nada para nosotros.

> (That is what I told you before, I felt like a worker, now I felt like a contractor, which is even worst! We have the pressure that we signed a contract. . . . We pay a lot of money, taxes, and many other things, plus on top of that we make nothing for ourselves.)

She gave up and dismissed her workers. She could not afford to pay fair salaries. If the option was to abuse workers to stay afloat, then she preferred to close down.

The sewing shop José built for Berta, now no longer a contracting shop, became her retreat. Berta converted it into her own workshop. She produces one gown at a time as a project of art and dedication. She can distinguish, and appreciates the difference between, mass production and custom-made clothing that she makes at her leisure. She really enjoys her work at home. Every day after her 8-hour shift at "Garras"[7] as a quality-control person, Berta sews at home. She arrives home to have dinner with her family. After dinner she goes to her backyard and works on her gowns. She enjoys this labor of craftsmanship. She delights in the different textures, materials, and possibilities. This is the time for Berta to be creative and to enjoy herself.

Attending classes on clothing construction at a local *academia*[8] once a week, Berta continues to perfect her craft. Now she not only makes gowns but also designs and creates the accessories such as the headdress, the bouquet, and other ornaments. Every gown she completes, represents a work of pride for Berta. She is invited to weddings and *quinceañera*[9] parties where she is publicly recognized for her work. It is at these rite-of-passage celebrations in her Latino(a) community that she is affirmed as an artist. This recognition as an expert seamstress gives Berta a strong sense of accomplishment and affirmation. When she labors at her workshop, it represents a labor of love and craftsmanship.

Estoy sorprendida conmigo misma, porque lo que empezo como una ocupación. Lo hice con una satisfacción tan grande que no sé ni como explicarlo.

(I am surprised with myself, because what started as an occupation. . . . I do it with a tremendous satisfaction that I do not know how to explain.)

Berta has made business cards and become well known to her customers. Her *quinceañera* gowns are quite popular among young Latinas. Berta can enjoy her work at night because her salary at the firm is supplemented with the constant flow of orders for her gowns. As if this were not enough to keep anyone busy, Berta fills other orders. She seasonally sews pajamas for a lady at the "swapmeet" and squares individually crafted for quilts. A company catalogue sells these quilts every Christmas.

After much hardship Berta's quality of life has improved. This is possible because she continues to work several jobs, even though she has acquired new skills and speaks English fluently. Her experiences deny the assumption that Latina garment workers are uneducated victims without options. Berta has worked hard and creatively to support herself and her family. Hardship still exists at the present time; however, the conditions of her labor are different. She has mastered English and developed her skills. Investing in her "human capital" (Mincer & Polacheck, 1974) has not translated into a great job in the garment industry. Meanwhile, her salary has not allowed her to stay at only one job; she still has to combine earnings in order to survive.

As Berta stated, her survival has been predicated on multiple jobs. Berta recognizes and states that her quality of life will decline once she is older. She asks herself, how long can she remain a young, healthy, strong woman? After 15 years of working in the garment industry she finally has access to a benefit package through her job at the firm. In the past Berta never received any form of benefits. By the time Berta retires she will have a small pension only from her last employer and maybe some social security. There was nothing set aside for her for all the years she gave to the clothing industry.

Her multiple participation in different jobs will soon be over. Thus she is not the triumphant Horatio Alger who with hard work succeeds and prevails. Her story demonstrates the way Latinas are forced to participate in a system of superexploitation just to make ends meet. Berta, despite all her hard work, did not become rich or independent.

TRAVELING FROM SHOWROOM TO SWEATSHOP

Because the firm at which Berta earns her salary contracts out most of its production, she visits sweatshops regularly as part of her job. As a quality-control person Berta travels between worlds; she makes the trek from the firm to different contracting shops. This journey takes her to two separate worlds characterized by polar opposites in terms of working conditions, salaries, and people employed. She inspects the quality of garments produced, while at the same time she observes the quality of life of those working in showrooms and sweatshops. Her angle of vision is enriched by her own experience in this industry. She has been through all the levels a Latina can occupy in the apparel industry.

The "Garras" firm and showroom where Berta works are located in an accessible neighborhood to the west of the city. Some firms prefer to keep a showroom in a central area in the same building with other firms. The California Mart, which houses many showrooms under one roof, represents a good example of this in downtown Los Angeles. Characterized by comfortable surroundings, good lighting, windows, and air conditioning the firm boasts functional spaces. Sometimes classical or elevator music fills the air, providing an environment to create and relax. The fancy spaces the designers, pattern makers, and sample makers enjoy are both geographically and socially separated from the sites of production where manual labor occurs. From Berta's standpoint, the quality of life and work ambiance at the top is filled with possibilities. Good salaries are a must. The staff orders lunch and coffee from posh restaurants. Those like Berta who cannot afford such luxuries look on. Talk in the office is about conspicuous consumption and trivialities. They imagine they are at the same level with famous designers; their salaries afford them this illusion.

At the high end of production, the lives of workers who labor at the sewing machines and contractors are erased. Distant and alien, the lives of contractors and sweatshop laborers are of no meaning to this side of production. Somehow their existence at the upper levels of fashion and design, their business and their salaries are totally disconnected from the producers of finished garments. The erasure of garment workers and contractors is possible in part because most people on top do not interact with people who work at the sewing machine. They do not see the people involved at the various levels of production. Production at the lower level is invisible to them or totally distorted. Only quality-control personnel witness both sides of production at the firm.

At the showroom, designers work with pattern makers and sample makers, who have an important part in the business because they help to come up with the next product. The creative side is tightly bound to economic considerations. Since the bulk of production is farmed out to contractors, production managers make sure to price every item and produce it at the lowest price possible. Quality and timely return of finished items must be guaranteed. Thus contractors sign a contract, which dictates penalties if garments are not delivered on time. Quality-control persons mediate negotiations between the firm and contractors. This is a job Berta accomplishes and understands well.

Moreover, the quality-control person helps solve problems in midproduction. They can explain how a particular sewing operation must be completed to get results. Since quality controllers are experienced at all aspects of clothes making, they are extremely valuable resources to both the firm and contractors. Their responsibility goes beyond just checking the quality of clothes during production.

As a quality controller, Berta earned $12 an hour in 1989, a good salary compared to the minimum wage she earned as a garment worker. Berta knew all facets of production. After her contracting shop failed, she ventured to look for something better. She discovered this position in the newspaper.

> Entonces estaba demasiado deprimida y dije, deje mi trabajo de limpieza pero mis hijos aun necesitan. . . . Tome el periodico y busque en lo que yo podía hacer. . . . Vi ese anuncio que decía "quality control," que para mi era algo que nunca había oido antes. . . . Me subscribi a un periodico relacionado solamenete con la industria del vestido. . . . Habian muchos anuncios que decian "quality control." . . . Tome tres anuncios y direcciones. Salí a las diez de la mañana y para la una ya tenía trabajo!

> (Then on a Sunday I was very depressed. I told to myself, I quit my cleaning job but my children still have needs. . . . I took the paper and I looked for something that I could work at. . . . the advertisement said "quality control," for me it was something that I had not heard before. . . . I subscribed to a paper only related to the apparel industry . . . there I saw many ads that said "quality control." . . . I took three ads and addresses. . . . I went out at ten in the morning and by one in the afternoon I found a job!)

Interestingly she learned, in comparison to other people working in the firm, her salary was quite low. She notes this by the cars the pattern makers and production manager drive—Mercedes Benz and Volvos. All of them have car phones, dress in style, and eat out for lunch. There is also talk of expensive condominiums.

In contrast to the showroom, at the sweatshops Berta visits every day the environment is unsanitary. Workers labor under poor ventilation; windows and doors remain locked. Air does not circulate properly. Layers of heavy lint float in the air constantly released from fabric under sewing machines. Space in the sweatshop is cramped; there is no room to move around. Sewing machines are lined up next to each other. Workers sit at sewing machines on uncomfortable folding chairs without back support. Because many shops are not registered with the state they remain hidden; windows and doors are locked. Sweatshops are unmarked and concealed. Owners fear labor inspectors or Immigration and Naturalization Service raids at their shops.

At the sweatshop, Berta notes that the racial makeup of the majority of workers is markedly different from the firm. The women who work in the sweatshop are young and middle-aged Latinas and Asians who labor long hours for piece rates. Workers strive to earn the minimum wage while working for piece rates. Berta also disapproves of the way workers are treated and abused by certain owners. Some owners use physical force and abusive language as part of their management techniques. Recently Berta observed how an elderly Asian woman was humiliated:

> Tienen personas trabajando entre sesenta y setenta años de edad. . . . Y estan sentaditos ahi cortando herbras, y los regañan igual y les gritan igual. . . . Me dan ganas de llorar. . . . He visto muchos ancianitos "orientales". . . ¿Venir hasta aca a esa edad para sufrir?. . . Vi a una que temblaba y casi lloraba porque cometio un error planchando. . . . ¡La planchada es muy dificil y la operación peor pagada!

> (They have persons working who are between 60 and 70 years old. . . . They sit there cutting threads, [contractors] scold them the same and they scream at them the same. . . . I feel like crying. . . . I have seen a lot of elderly Asians. . . . To come all the way here at that age to suffer? . . . I saw one that trembled and almost cried because she made a mistake ironing . . . ironing is very tough and the worst-paid operation!)

This broke Berta's heart because the industrial iron is heavy, weighing about 4 pounds. Ironing, which is a very difficult job, is terribly paid, but constitutes a key aspect of clothing production. Sometimes ironing corrects sewing mistakes such as hiding seams or changing the way the material drapes. Berta always witnesses some type of abuse during her visits to sweatshops. Supposedly owners behave in her presence. She does not want to imagine what they do when she leaves the place.

In Berta's own experience working as a sewing-machine operator, she recalls how difficult it was to confront abusive contractors. Berta survived the humiliations and low salaries working in sweatshops. She understands both the plights of contractors as well that of workers. She is fully aware of the vulnerability of both groups. She herself failed as a contractor and knows how unfair the system is.

CONCLUSION

The master narrative and the apparel industry's hierarchy tends to erase and objectify the contributions and experiences of Latinas who work in contracting shops, sweatshops, and doing homework. The global apparel industry discourse presents immigrant women as if their social class is the only important factor to take into consideration. Seeing Berta's account as translocal we can look at her shifting social locations through her lived experiences. From Berta's standpoint in the garment industry individuals are marked not only by social class but also by race, ethnicity, gender, and immigrant status among other factors. Berta's story reflects the complexity of Latinas' lived experience in Los Angeles.

Berta's oppositional voice to totalizing accounts and assumptions of the global apparel industry demonstrates the way she experiences globality in her everyday world. The master narrative of the global apparel industry claims to be superior, to account for all social locations and to stand as a universal framework. Berta's story disrupts the assumptions of the master narrative; her experiences stand within the context of the global and the local Los Angeles clothing industry (Cvetkovich & Kellner, 1997). Her translocal account purports to intervene and disrupt the taken-for-granted homogenization and objectification of Latinas in metanarratives. Her story allows us to reflect on both what passes for research on immigrant Latina workers and how these women struggle against subordination to capital, race, and gender divisions.

NOTES

1. The overlock sewing machine sews, binds, and cuts threads and fabric to prevent seams from fraying.

2. All names have been changed to protect confidentiality.

3. A quality-control person denotes the individual in charge of farming out production to contractors, checking the quality of garment production, and intervening when production problems arise. Depending on the size of the firm, there might be several quality-control persons.

4. Developing countries join the global economy assembling clothing where start-up capital is relatively low. Similarly, since clothing production does not require developed skills from workers, immigrant workers get their first jobs in the garment industry in the United States (Bonacich, et al., 1994). Immigrant workers provide the cheap labor necessary to further increase profits. Apparel production chains are global, and commodity production occurs between nations. Simultaneously economically dislocated populations migrate to "Third World Cities" where jobs await immigrant workers.

5. Dorothy Smith (1987) proposes that our understanding departs from the experiences of actors in their everyday world. "The movement of research is from a woman's account of her everyday experience to exploring from that perspective the generalizing and generalized relations in which each individual's everyday world is embedded" (p. 185).

6. Some of the skills that the master narrative and industry value and recognize are those of pattern makers, cutters, or specialized tailors, all predominantly male occupations.

7. "Garras" is the name of the firm at which Berta works.

8. The *academia* denotes a small private school where training is bilingual. In Los Angeles "Academias de Costura" have proliferated.

9. A *quinceañera* is a celebration of a girl's 15th birthday.

REFERENCES

Bonacich, E. (1994). The garment industry in the restructuring global economy. In E. Bonacich, L. Cheng, N. Chinchilla, N. Hamilton, & P. Ong. (Eds.), *Global production: The apparel industry in the Pacific Rim* (pp. 3–18). Philadelphia: Temple University Press.

Bookman, A. & Morgen, S. (Eds.) (1988). *Women and the politics of empowerment.* Philadelphia: Temple University Press.

Boris, E. (1994). *Home to work: Motherhood and the politics of industrial homework in the United States.* New York: Cambridge University Press.

Carrillo, J. V. (1994). The apparel maquiladora industry at the Mexican border. In E. Bonacich et al. (Eds.), *Global production: The apparel industry in the Pacific Rim* (pp. 217–29). Philadelphia: Temple University Press.

Collins, P. H. (1990). *Black feminist thought: Knowledge, consciousness, and the politics of empowerment.* Boston: Unwin Hyman.

Cvetkovich, A. & Kellner, D. (Eds.) (1997). *Articulating the global and the local: Globalization and cultural studies.* Boulder, CO: Westview Press.

Furio, C. M. (1979). Immigrant women and industry: A case study of the Italian immigrant women and the garment industry 1880–1950. Unpublished dissertation, New York University.

Fernandez-Kelly, M. P. (1983). *For we are sold: I and my people: Women and industry in Mexico's frontier.* Albany: State University of New York Press.

Fernandez-Kelly, M. P. & Garcia, A. M. (1985). The making of the underground economy: Hispanic women, homework, and the advanced capitalist state. Washington, D.C.: The Institute for the Study of Man.

Glenn, S. A. (1983). The working life of immigrants: Women in the American garment industry 1880–1950. Unpublished dissertation, University of California at Berkeley.

Hadjicostandi, J. (1990). Façon: Women's formal and informal work in the garment industry in Kabala Greece. In K. Ward (Ed.), *Woman workers and global restructuring* (pp. 64–81). Ithaca, NY: Cornell University Press.

Hondagneu-Sotelo, P. (1994). *Gendered transitions, Mexican experiences of immigration.* Berkeley and Los Angeles: University of California Press.

Lamphere, L. (1987). *From working mothers to working daughters.* Ithaca, NY: Cornell University Press.

Mincer, J. & Solomon, P. (1974). Family investments in human capital: Earnings of women. *Journal of Political Economy, 82* (2), 76–108.

Smith, D. (1987). *The everyday world as problematic: A feminist sociology.* Boston: Northeastern University Press.

Tiano, S. (1987). Gender work and world capitalism. In B. Hess & M. Marx Ferre (Eds.), *Analyzing gender: A handbook of social science research* (pp. 216–43). Newbury Park, CA: Sage.

Waldinger, R. (1986). *Through the eye of the needle: Immigrants and enterprise in New York's garment trades.* New York: New York University Press.

Contributors

MARIXSA ALICEA is Associate Professor in the School for New Learning at DePaul University. She has published articles in the areas of Puerto Rican migration, women and drug use, and teaching methodologies. Marixsa has recently completed a book-length manuscript on women heroin users with Jennifer Friedman, entitled *Through the "I" of the Needle.*

JOAN MECHELLE BROWNE entered the Social Psychology Program at Howard University in 1996, with an MS degree in clinical psychology from Alabama A & M University and a BA in social work from Oakwood College in Huntsville, Alabama. Inspired by her mentor, Dr. Sandra Schwartz Tangri and her mother (now deceased), Joan is committed to the advancement of the study of the psychology of women. Her immediate research interest is the study of the life path of African American midlife women; however, it is her hope that she will, in the near future, be able to extend her research to include the life path of Caribbean midlife women.

ROSARIO CEBALLO is Assistant Professor of Psychology and Women's Studies at the University of Michigan. She received her doctorate in clinical and developmental psychology and a graduate certificate in women's studies from the University of Michigan. Her primary research interests focus on the impact of poverty on family functioning and children's psychological well-being.

JENNIFER FRIEDMAN is Associate Professor and Director of Graduate Studies in the Department of Sociology at the University of South Florida. She received her Ph.D. from Northwestern University in 1988. Since then, she has conducted research in the areas of substance use, gender, and Latina issues. Jennifer has completed a manuscript on women heroin users with Marixsa Alicea, entitled *Through the "I" of the Needle.*

AÍDA HURTADO is Professor in the Department of Psychology at the University of California at Santa Cruz. Dr. Hurtado's research focuses on the effects of subordination on social identity, educational achievement, and language. Her most recent publications include *Strategic Interventions in Education: Expanding the Latino Pipeline* (co-edited with Professors Richard Figueroa and Eugene Garcia. [1996]. [Santa Cruz: University of California, Latino Eligibility Study]) and *The Color of Privilege: Three Blasphemies on Race and Feminism* ([1996.] [Ann Arbor: University of Michigan Press]. Dr. Hurtado received her BA in psychology and sociology from

Pan American University in Edinburg, Texas, and her MA and Ph.D. in social psychology from the University of Michigan.

FAYE KNOKI received her BA in education from the University of Arizona in 1975, after working for a number of years for the Bureau of Indian Affairs. She taught with the Ganado Public Schools, working with elementary, middle, and high school students. For several years, she served as a counselor with the Ganado Public Schools and enjoyed her work with children and families. She retired in 1983 but continues to be actively involved with young people through her grandchildren. Faye continues to live near Ganado where she was born and raised.

URSULA KNOKI-WILSON received her BSN from Loretto Heights College and her MSN from the University of Utah. She is currently Supervisor of Nurse-Midwifery Service at the Chinle Comprehensive Health Care Facility in Chinle, Arizona. She serves as adjunct faculty/preceptor for student nurse-midwives for the universities of New Mexico, Colorado, and California, and Community-Based Nurse-Midwifery Education Programs for the Frontier School of Midwifery and Family Nursing. In addition to her professional work as a nurse-midwife, she is a student of Navajo healing practices and serves as a consultant for a variety of organizations focusing on the health and well-being of Native American women. She has published in the areas of providing nursing care for Native American women and cultural guides for health care practitioners working with Native Americans.

LORA BEX LEMPERT is Associate Professor in the Department of Sociology and the Director of Women's Studies at the University of Michigan at Dearborn. She is also an assistant research scientist at the Institute for Research on Women and Gender at the University of Michigan at Ann Arbor. She studied grounded theory at the University of California, San Francisco, with Anselm Strauss. She has published numerous articles on issues of family, gender, and intimate violence against women and is beginning to report on findings from a study of African American grandparents who are raising their adolescent grandchildren.

LISA KANE LOW, MS (University of Illinois), RN, and CNM, has been a certified nurse-midwife since 1986 and is currently a doctoral student at the University of Michigan School of Nursing with a concentration in Women's Studies. She has taught in both midwifery and women's health courses and is in clinical practice as a nurse-midwife at the University of Michigan Health System.

JANET E. MALLEY is currently senior research associate at the Murray Research Center of Radcliffe College. She received her Ph.D. in personality psychology from Boston University and subsequently completed a postdoctoral fellowship at the University of Michigan's Institute for Survey Research. Her research interests are in the area of adult development, focusing particularly on how the process of development may be mediated by individual life experiences as well as more broadly based work and family roles.

KARIN A. MARTIN is Assistant Professor of Sociology and Women's Studies at the University of Michigan. Her research is in the areas of gender, body, and the self. She is author of *Puberty, Sexuality, and the Self: Girls and Boys at Adolescence* (Routledge, 1996).

PJ MCGANN is a visiting scholar at the Murray Research Center at Radcliffe College, and visiting research associate in Women's Studies at Brandeis University. PJ is on leave from St. Lawrence University, where she was Assistant Professor in the Department of Sociology and Director of the Gender Studies Program. Her areas of specialization include gender/sexuality; the body, deviance, and medicalization; social psychology; and qualitative methodology. Her ideas about gender culture and narrative, social control and resistance, and the discursive production of identity are explored more fully in her forthcoming book, *The Ballfields of Our Hearts: Tomboys, Femininity, and Female Development,* Temple University Press (a life-story-depth interview-based study of the gender identity development of 35 former tomboys, the adult legacies of a childhood tomboy past, and social construction of the tomboy in discourses of medicine/psychiatry, social science, and everyday life).

DONNA K. NAGATA is Associate Professor in the Department of Psychology at the University of Michigan, Ann Arbor. She has conducted research on the long-term psychosocial consequences of the Japanese American internment for more than 10 years. Included among her publications in this area are the book, *Legacy of Injustice: Exploring the Cross-Generational Impact of the Japanese American Internment* (Plenum, 1993), an article entitled "Long-term effects of internment among third-generation Japanese Americans" in the *American Journal of Orthopsychiatry,* and another article "Coping and resilience across generations: Japanese Americans and the World War II internment" in *The Psychoanalytic Review.*

ANNA NEUMANN is Associate Professor in the Department of Education at Michigan State University. She is the editor (with Penelope L. Peterson) of *Learning from Our Lives: Women, Research, and Autobiography in Education* (Teachers College Press, 1997), and is currently conducting a 3-year study of professors' learning and identity development in four major research universities. Neumann's interests center on learning and intellectual development across the life course, with particular attention to learning in scholars' lives. Her studies of scholars' development, academic leadership, and university cultures have been published in a number of books and journals including *Curriculum Inquiry, American Educational Research Journal,* the *Journal of Higher Education,* and the *Review of Higher Education.*

JOAN M. OSTROVE is currently a research associate with the MacArthur Research Network on Socioeconomic Status and Health at the University of California at San Francisco. Beginning in the fall of 1999, she will be Assistant Professor of Psychology at Macalaster College. She received her Ph.D. in psychology and a certificate in women's studies from the University of Michigan. She is particularly interested in understanding the intersection between individual psychology and social structure. Her research focuses on social class and health and on the psychological implications of social-class background, feminist identity, and political activism.

MARY ROMERO, Professor at Arizona State University, is the author of *Maid in the U.S.A.* (Routledge, 1992), co-editor of *Challenging Fronteras: Structuring Latina and Latina Lives in the U.S.* (Routledge, 1997), *Women at Work: Exploring Race, Ethnicity, and Class* (Sage, 1997), and two volumes of published National Association for Chicano Studies Conference proceedings. She is the editor of four sets of *Syllabai and Instructional Materials for Chicano and Latino Studies in Sociology* for the American Sociological Association Teaching Resource Center. Her teaching and research areas are in qualitative methods and narrative analysis; race relations in the United States; and Latina/o studies, gender, race, and ethnic issues in the labor market, and higher education.

AMY SCHULZ is a research scientist in the School of Public Health at the University of Michigan. She received her Ph.D. in sociology from the University of Michigan. Her current work focuses in two broad arenas: the intersection of identity, meaning, and action; and the relationships among ethnicity, social inequalities, and health. She teaches courses in qualitative methods, gender, and community organizing and multicultural practice.

SANDRA SCHWARTZ TANGRI is Professor in the Department of Psychology at Howard University in Washington, D.C. Her research has focused on women and work, including career development, dual-career couples, role conflict for working women, sexual harassment, and gender and race discrimination. She received her Ph.D. in social psychology from the University of Michigan at Ann Arbor. She founded the Women's Life Paths Studies at both the University of Michigan and Howard University.

MARÍA A. GUTIÉRREZ SOLDATENKO is Assistant Professor with a joint appointment in Chicano Studies and Gender Feminist Studies programs at Pitzer College in Claremont, California. Her research focuses on Chicana and Latina garment workers and the participation of Latinas in organized labor in Los Angeles. She has contributed work to *Aztlan* and *Cultural Studies Journals*. Currently she teaches courses on the areas of women of color in the United States, Chicanas and Latinas, and women in the Third World.

ABIGAIL J. STEWART is Professor of Psychology and Women's Studies at the University of Michigan and a former director of the Women's Studies Program. Since 1995, she has been director of the Institute for Research on Women and Gender. Her research combines qualitative and quantitative methods and focuses on the psychology of women's lives, personality, and adaptation to change. She has recently written or co-edited books on women's lives (*Women Creating Lives: Identities, Resilience, and Resistance,* with Carol Franz, 1994, Westview), feminist theory (*Theorizing Feminism: Parallel Trends in the Humanities and Social Sciences,* with Anne Herrmann, 1994, Westview), women's studies (*Feminisms in the Academy,* with Domna C. Stanton, 1995, University of Michigan Press), and families (*Separating Together: How Divorce Transforms Families,* 1997, Guilford).

BEVERLY DANIEL TATUM is Dean of the College and Professor in the departments of Psychology and Education at Mount Holyoke College. Her research has been focused on issues of racial/ethnic identity development and its impact in educational settings. She is the author of *"Why Are All the Black Kids Sitting Together in the Cafeteria?" and Other Conversations about Race* (Basic Books, 1997).

THAOMEE XIONG graduated cum laude from Mount Holyoke College in 1998. She has received local and national recognition for her dedication to empowering Southeast Asian refugees. Currently, she is the Project Director of SEARCH, a mentorship and education project she founded for Southeast Asian refugee girls in western Massachusetts.

Index

abortion, xiv, 12, 129, 168
abuse: physical, 130, 167; psychological, 126; sexual, 45, 47, 49, 167
abusive relationships, 172
acculturation, 143
activism, 216, 220, 222, 224, 233, 237–39; 1960s, 212–26; antiracist, 198, 203, 205; civil rights, xviii; of Hmong women, xviii, 227–42; political, xviii, 195–211, 216, 220; student, 212–26; white women's, xviii
activists, xviii; antiwar, 215–16, 220; civil rights, 210; sixties, 212–26
addiction: medical model of, 165
Adler, Margot, 213, 220
adolescence, 106, 111–14
adoption, 8, 15, 16, 17; informal, 15–16
adulthood, 106, 114; activism in, 212–26
affirmative action, 144–45, 148, 156
African American women, 37, 38, 42, 229 (see also black women); and incest disclosure, 37–52; and infertility, xvii, 3–19; multiple births among, 3–4; public images of, 4, 13; rape of, 4, 13; stereotypes of, 4
African American(s), 14, 50, 126, 217, 227 (see also blacks); children, 13; church, 13; communities, 13, 15; families, 13, 39, 42; fertility, 4; husbands, 11, 15; infant mortality rate, 17; men, 38, 39, 50; mothers, 126; sextuplets, 3; sexuality, 4; society, 125
age, xii, 106, 257; adolescence, 231–33, 237; adulthood, 106, 114; childhood, 106, 112, 118; developmental stages of, 73, 80, 82; infancy, 21; old, 268; puberty, 80, 109, 113–14
agency, 259; in women's life narratives, 207–8, 258
ambiguity and incest, 42, 44–48
America: corporate, 212–13, 215
American Indian(s), 174–91; forced removal of, 176; groups, 176 (see also Indians; Navajo; Native Americans)
American(s), 148; citizens, 78; culture, 73, 234, 238, 240; European, 176, 181; family, 142; history, xvii, 81; male-dominant values, 73; Nazis, 201; society, 53; universities, 246; values, 232
Americanization process, 147, 155, 232
Anglo(s), 177, 180, 186; culture, 180; knowledge dominance, xviii; language, 183
apparel industry, 256, 259, 266–68 (see also garment industry; global apparel industry)
Asian American(s), 144, 228, 237; community, 227–28; dropout rates for, 228; stereotypes of, 237; writers, 227
Asian Pacific Americans, 228
Asian(s), 227–28, 268; ethnic groups, 230; model minority stereotype, 227–28; students, 234; women, xviii
assembly centers, 75–76, 77
assimilation, 142–45, 147, 154–55, 176–78, 182, 232; ideology of, 148; role models of, 157

B'Hai faith, 109
baby- boom generation, 5, 53

back talk, 107, 122n. 2
Baptist churches, 198
beliefs, 155, 179; cultural, 182; traditional, 182
belonging: sense of, 142–58
benefits, 265; health, 96, 152
biculturalism, 97, 143, 155, 231–33, 236
bilingual education, 143, 144, 148
binarism: gender, 108, 112, 117, 119–21; male/female, 117
biography, 106, 109, 202
birth, xix, 23, 25, 32–35, 36; experiences, 22, 35; home, xvii, 9, 20–36; hospital, xvii, 20, 22, 25, 28, 31, 36; labor, 20, 24, 25–7, 28–31, 33; narratives, of, 21, 22, 24–35
black women, xvi, 21, 125–41, 203, 205, 229 (see also African American women); and infertility, 3–19; in U.S. slavery, xv; role of in political economy, 4; sexuality of, 4; stereotypes of, xvi, xvii
black(s), 144 (see also African Americans); children, 198; church, 205; men, 38, 128; middle class, 125–41; people, 196, 204; students, 200, 238
border: crossings, 259; patrol, 93
Brownsville, Texas, 94, 96–97

capitalism, 152
capitalist production, 257
career: academic, 243–55
caregivers, 39, 165, 168, 170–72
Central America, 54, 59
Cesarean section, 20, 23, 32
Chicanas, 144–45, 155
Chicano(s), 144, 155–56, 227; studies, x
child rearing, 231
childbearing, 13; delayed, 5
childcare, 167–68, 259; costs, 94, 262
childhood, 106, 112, 118
children, 39, 44, 53–54, 57, 60, 65, 106, 112, 166–69, 171–72, 221, 224, 230; biological, 15, 17; black, 198; disabled, 218; homeless, 126; immigrant, 155; Latino/a, 17; of color, 17; refugee, 228; sexual assaults on, 42, 47; white, 17
Chinese, 237; Americans, 76
Christianity, 109
civil rights, xix, 73, 144–45, 206, 212, 214, 217
civil rights movement, xviii, 127, 156, 214, 220; and white women, 195–211; feminism in, xviii
civilization: narrative of, 176
class, xii, xv, xix, 94, 105, 106, 125, 127, 172, 213, 216, 224–25, 256–57, 259; bias, 16, 18; conflicts, 58; issues, 149, 151; middle, 155; norms, 128, 133; social, 176; transformation, 258; working, 144, 215, 263
classism, 165
clothing: custom-made, 264; industry, 256–70
collective memory, 185
colonialism, 13
community(ies), 143, 155; of color, 157, 231; reservation, 182; work, 233
consciousness-raising, xii
conservatism, 212

contractions, 25–28, 29–30, 31–33
counternarratives, xii, xvi, xix, 143, 147, 160, 173. *See also* narratives; of academic work, 243–46; to global apparel industry, 258–69; to the immigrant experience, 145, 147–57
Crisis, The, 200
critical: legal theory, xiii; pedagogy, xiii; race theory, xiii
cross genderism, 112, 116
cross-border existence, 83–101
cultural: assumptions, 106, 120; beliefs, 182; change, 94; competence, 148; expectations, 171; forms, xvi, 106; ideal, xii; images, 44, 106; models, 50; representation, 212; stereotypes, 40; transformation, 241; values, 185, 230
culture, x, xiii, 39, 99, 112, 144–45, 147, 155–57, 180, 239; and gender, 107–109, 120; Anglo, 180; dominant, 171, 232; Puerto Rican, 172
CWRIC (Commission on Wartime Relocation and Internment of Civilians), 71

daughters: of incest. *See* incest; of Nisei women, 80
democracy, 200
democratic: issues, 237; process, 142, 157, 200
deportation, 88
depression, the, 53, 55, 56, 57
desire, 106–107, 115, 120; heterosexual, 112, 116, 120; homosexual, 134; lesbian, 109, 116
developing countries: clothing production in, 257
development: adult, xviii; female, 107; feminist models of, 107; stages of, 73, 80, 82
disabilities: developmental, 216, 218
discourse, 160, 173; globality, 257–58, 269; medical, 160; of division, 246; public, 246
discrimination, 68, 69n. 4, 160, 234; class-based, 225; in the workplace, 55; racial, 55, 232; sexual, 55
domestic service work, 259, 263; folklore in, 152; systems of gifts and obligations, 152–53
domestics, 79, 87, 142–58; and relationships with employers, 142–58; familial relationships with employers, 152–53
dominant: cultural narratives, xv, 21, 150; culture, 171, 232, 236; group, xiii; master narratives (*see* master narratives); social and cultural systems, xiv, 160, 178; society, 38, 155, 185, 230; stories, 165
domination, 188; processes of, 187; systems, 154
drug addiction: women's, 159–73
drug dealing, 167–68
dualisms, 245; male/female, 117
Du Bois, W.E.B., 199, 202

economic: access, 145; dislocation, 256
economy: informal, 262–65
education, x, 74, 93–94, 98, 127, 143, 197, 225, 228, 233; higher, 138, 243–55; intercultural, 199–200, 210; pregnancy and birth, 21; religious, 207; self-, 210; special, 216; women's, 86
el norte, 92, 99, 258
embodiment, 107, 120–21
employment benefits, 157
empowerment, xi, xii, 35
environmental issues, 223
equal opportunity, 142
equality, 154; racial, xviii

ethnic: difference, 157; groups, 73, 143, 155, 177, 227; heritage, 73; identity, 80, 148, 157, 237–38, 240; issues, 157; literature, 227; minorities, 18; neoconservatives, 144; studies, 148
ethnicity, ix, 105, 106, 176, 239, 269
exploitation, xix, 64, 68, 149, 153–54, 160, 221, 258–59, 265

faith, 13–15, 130
family, 46, 58, 60, 83, 98, 99, 143, 145, 147, 151–52, 156, 183, 252; American, 157; breakup of, 125; caretakers, 67; dysfunctional, 44; extended, 16, 170, 230; ideology of, 46, 48; images of, 45–46; life, 54, 65–67, 68; networks, 91; nuclear, 40, 219, 230; of incest, 42–3; restrictions, 99
fashion industry, 260 (*see also* apparel industry; garment industry; global apparel industry)
FBI, 74, 77
Felix, Maria, 83
female, 108, 115, 117; sexuality, 119
feminine, 110, 115, 117; incompetence, 118–19
femininity, 107–108, 111, 114–15, 118–20; traditional, xvii, 68, 106, 108, 116, 120–21
feminism, xiii; in the U.S., xii; second wave, xii
feminist(s): consciousness, 209; depictions of girls and women, 107; ideology, xviii; methods and research, xi, xixn. 5; process, ix; scholars, xiii, 4; self-help movement, 20; theorists, 44; theory, 44, 121, 123n. 8; writers, 84, 91
fertility, xix; treatments, 3
foster care, 167–68
free speech, 214, 220
friendships: between women, 91, 197, 202–203; interracial, 37, 203–205, 208–209

garment industry, xviii, 146, 256, 258, 260, 265, 269 (*see also* apparel industry; global garment industry)
gay(s), 18; community, 134
gay, lesbian and queer theory, xiii
gender, ix, xii, xv, 57, 58, 73, 82, 84, 94, 97, 106–108, 110, 114–15, 117, 120–21, 125, 142, 176, 213–14, 216, 224–25, 230, 256–57, 269; and culture, 107–109, 120; and immigration narratives, 97–100; as moral boundary, 108; as performance, 116–19; binarism, 108, 117, 119–21; constraints, 170–71; construction of, 111, 259; cross-, 108, 116; deviance, 108, 121; differences, 10–11, 73, 120; dysphoria, 109; expectations, 109, 171–72; fluidity, 118; hierarchy, 46, 258; identity, 109, 115, 117–18; inequality, 88; issues, 237; meanings of, 107, 112, 120; normal divide, 105–24; norms, xiv, 67, 108, 127–28, 136, 236, 239–40; order, 105–24; politics, 44, 208; roles, 39, 61, 64, 81, 195, 230–31; stereotyping, 61, 108, 110, 122n. 5; theory, 115; traditional expectations of, 160, 165, 195, 236; warrior, 122, 123n. 9
gendered restrictions, 111
Genné, Joe, 200, 203, 205–208
Genné, Noma Jensen, xviii, 196–202
genocide, 176
German Americans, 71, 79
girlhood, 105, 120
girls, 108–111, 120

global: apparel industry, 257, 269 (see also fashion industry; garment industry); industry, xviii; social relations, 258
globalization, 88
Good War, the (see also World War II), 53, 55–56, 58, 62, 64, 68
Graham, Shirley, 199, 203, 207–208
grape boycott, 216
green card, 88, 97

healing practices, 175
health care services, 96
health insurance: employer-sponsored, 17
helplessness, 133, 207
heroin, 159–73
heterosexuality, 107, 120–21, 165
hierarchies, 42, 257; gender/racial, 258
Hispanic(s), 157; businesses, 156; women, 21
history: American, xvii, 81; oral, 94, 100
Hmong American(s), 240; men, 229, 240; women, 228, 231
Hmong refugees, 230, 234; first generation adolescent girls, 231–33, 237
Hmong women, 232, 237–41; activism of, xviii, 227–42; refugees, 233; students, 228
Hmong, the, 229–30, 234, 236, 238, 240; adolescent girls, 231–33, 235–37; children of, 231; community, 228–29, 235–40; culture, 238–39; elders, 231; experience in the U.S., 229; families, 233; folklore of, 238; genocide among, 230; identity, 235, 240; population, 230; roles of, 230–31; society, 230; students, 234; values, 231–32
Hmong/U.S.: cultural conflict, 231–33
Ho Chi Minh Trail, 229–30
home births, xvii, 20–36; planned, 21; unplanned, 21
home-front life, 53–70 (see also World War II)
homeless, the, 125–41; children, 126; people, 125–41; shelters, 131–33; women, 125–41
homelessness, xvii, 125–41; factors contributing to, 125–26; in the U.S., 125–26; politics and policies of, 139
homemaker: role of, 59–60
homework, 262–63, 269
homeworkers, 262
homosexuality, 107
hospital practices and policy, 21
housewives, 60; experiences of World War II, 53–70; traditional, 60
Huang, L.N., 230
husbands, 98, 128–29

idealism, 212–13
identity, xiii, xiv, 106–107, 109, 117, 120, 131, 142–58, 174–91, 228–30, 240, 256, 258; and language, 180–82; bicultural, xvii, xviii, 232, 236–37; collective, 176, 180; construction of, 105, 121, 176, 178–82; cultural, 176; desire-based, 121; development, 254n. 2; ethnic, 80, 237–38, 240; gendered development of, 106; group, 177, 187; Hmong, 235, 240; hyphenated, 232; Japanese, 80; Mexican, 147; multiple, 178; naming, xviii; Navajo (see Navajo, identity); political, xix, 176; self-, 176; sexual, 106; social, 106, 176; tomboy, 106, 118, 120; tribal, 176–77

ideology, xiii, 154–55, 188
immigrant(s), 147, 155–57, 230; American, xix; children of, 155, 157; European, 144, 232; experience of, 142–58; Hmong, 227–42; Latina/o, 256, 263, 269; Mexican, 83–101, 142–58; networks, 88, 91; of color, 231; parents, 156; Southeast Asian, 227–42; status, 257, 269; women, 83–101, 146, 153, 269
immigration, xvii, 83–101; and gender, 97–100; of women, 83–101; patterns of, 92
incarceration: responses to, 71–82; wartime, 71–82
incest, xvii; ambiguity in disclosure of, 44–48; behaviors, 44; daughters of, 37–52; definitions of, 49–50; disclosure of, 37–52; families of, 42–3; paternal, 37, 40–1, 43–44, 46, 49; perpetrators, 42–3, 44; taboo, 40; victims of, 39
Indian: assimilation, xviii; boarding schools, 178–79, 182–83 (see also American Indian; Navajo; Native American)
indigenous people, xix
individualism, 156, 230–31, 236
inequality, 176–77
infertility, 11, 16; and black women, 3–19; public image of, 3
infertility treatments, 4–5, 7–8, 18; insurance coverage for, 17
injustice, 223, 256, 260
INS (Immigration and Naturalization Service), 88, 267–68
integration, 144–45, 202
internment, xix, 69n. 2, 71–82; Japanese American women's experience of, xvii, 71–82; male perspective on, 72–73; of Japanese Americans in Hawaii, 71
internment camps, xix, 71–82; redress movement of, 76, 78–81; reunions, 76, 79
isolation, 99, 234–35
Issei, the, 74, 76

Japanese, 237; children, 73; hatred for, 74; identity, 80; immigrants, 72; language and culture, 77–78, 80; territories, 78
Japanese American women: experiences of internment, xvii, 71–82; roles of, 72
Japanese American(s), 69n. 2, 71–82; children, 77; first generation (Issei), 74; men, 72–73; second class citizen status, 75–76; second generation (Nisei), 72
Japanese ancestry: people of, 71–72
Japanese Latin American(s), 79–80
Japanese Peruvian(s), 78, 79, 81; women, 81 (see also Latin Japanese)
Japanese values: male-dominated, 77; traditional, 73
jobs: loss of, 125; multiple, 259, 262–63
justice, 139, 223; equal, 210; racial, 210; social, 208, 217–18; studies, x

kinaaldá, 175
knowledge, 174–91; academic, 243–55; collective, 185–88; domains of, 249; Navajo, 180; scientific, 248, 252; self as source of, 182–87; subjective, 25, 181, 185–87; women's connection to, 248

labor: artisan, 264–65; camp, 89; casual, 262;

cheap, 257, 259; domestic, 142–58; emotional, 153; farm, 90; manual, 152–53, 266; market, 60, 84, 92; of love, 260; organizations, 259; paid, 151, 207; relational, 248–51; seasonal, 91; unpaid, 151–52; wage, 146, 151–52, 260
language, 144, 157, 174–91; and identity, 180–82
Lao, the, 229
Laos, 229, 230, 233–34; secret war in, 229
Latin Japanese, 78, 81
Latina women, xviii, 98–99, 151, 256, 259–63, 265–66, 268–69; garment workers, 256–70
Latino(s), 126, 144, 147, 156–57, 259, 263; businesses, 263; community, 258–59, 264; racial constructions of, 259
lesbianism, 109, 112, 114–15, 120
lesbians, xv, 18, 106, 107, 116, 121, 134–36; desire, 109, 116; identity, 109; mothers, 172; sexuality, 109
life-story method, 121

maids, 87, 142–58; live-in, 145–46, 148
male, 108, 115, 117; -dominated cultural norms, 99; body, 117; employers, 62; privilege, 73
mannishness, 109, 112, 120
marginalization, 64, 206
marginalized populations, 55, 154, 236
marriage, 40, 48, 202, 206, 210; interracial, xv, 128
Marshall, Thurgood, 199, 202, 204
Martin, Karen, xvii
masculine, 108, 110, 115, 117
masculinity, 107, 114–15, 120
master narratives, x–xi, xviii, 17, 48, 69, 169, 173, 188, 259; and how they construct women, xiii–xv; countering, xvi–xix; dominance of, xvi; oppression of, xvii; racist, 240; reistance and reproduction of, 166–72; sexist, 240; stories outside of the, xi
master narratives of: academic work, 243–46; American history, 71; Asian Americans, 227; assimilation, 154; birth in the U.S., 20, 23; class, xiii, xiv; coming out, 134; European immigrants, 142; garment workers, 261; gender, xiii, xiv, 43; global apparel industry, 256, 258; homeless people, 125–41; homogeneity of Asian American community, 237; immigration, 83–85, 94, 98, 100, 143, 145, 148, 154; Latinos, 144, 156; migration, 259; military necessity, 72; motherblame, 38–9; motherhood, xix, 168, 171–72; Nature/Civilization, 183; normal girls, 108; passive Asian women, 238–39; progress, assimilation, and civilization, 178; race, xiii, xiv, 38, 43; Rosie the Riveter, 56–58, 60–61, 63 (see also Rosie the Riveter); sexuality, xiii, xiv; social mobility, 156; the "good mother," 42; the "Good War," 53; the female drug addict, xviii; the immigrant maid, 142; the passive model minority, 237; tomboys, 106–109, 119; women, 39; women's substance abuse, 159, 165; young adults in the 1960s, 212
Matamoros, Mexico, 87, 92, 96–97
medical: establishment, 7, 36; interventions, xvii, 7–8; professionals, 6–8, 12, 20, 26, 31
medical model, 160; of addiction, 165
men, 58; and immigration, 83; experiences of, 72; infertile, 11; roles of, 63
mental: health services, 218; illness, 126

meritocracy, 142, 154
metanarratives, 176–78, 269; racialized, 176
methadone, 159–73; clinics, 160, 170
Mexican Americans, 98, 142–58
Mexican immigrant(s), 142–58; children of, 147; community, 147, 148; workers, 145
Mexican(s), 148; community, 155; construction of experience, 143–47; culture, 143; garment workers, 148; identity, 147; women, 146, 152
Mexico, 83–101, 146–47, 257, 258–59; maquiladora industry in, 257
midwives, 20, 22, 23, 27, 29, 34, 84, 85, 86–87, 178–79, 184
migrants, 83–101; seasonal, 89
migration, 83–101, 258; circular, 84
migratory: experiences, 87; status, 127
military wives, 59 (see also housewives)
minorities, 55, 68, 200, 227; objectification of, 187; student, 98
model-minority myth, 227–28, 235, 240
mother-blame, 42–43, 47, 48–49
motherhood, 6–7, 10, 17; construction of, 167; images of, 46; mandatory, xiv, 6; master narratives of, xix; narratives of, xvi
mothering, xvii, 165
mothers, xvii, 48, 50, 60; "good enough," 168; African American, 126; at-home, 53; good, 44, 166, 168–69, 172; lesbian, 172; of incest victims, 37–52; other, 170; role of, 165; single, 152, 216; sociocultural expectations about, 44; teenage, xvi; welfare, 4

NAACP (National Association for the Advancement of Colored Peoples), 195–96, 199–204, 206–7, 209–10
narratives, x–xi, xiv, xix, 18, 121, 202; bicultural, 240; collective, xvi; constitutive power of, 38–39, 121, 139; counter- (see counternarratives); dominant, 20, 169, 171; gender, 108; ideological, 44; ideological function of, xv; immigration, 83–101; life, ix; master (see master narratives); of civilization, 176; oral, 188n. 1; otonological, 178; personal, xix, 38, 43; process of, 38; sexist, 11; subjugated (see master narratives); women's, 178, 207–20
narratives of: academic work, 243–46; civilization, 176; gender, 44; Japanese American internment, 71–82; migration, 83–101; motherhood, 44; Nisei women, 73–82; scholarly work, 246–53; Tomboys, 105–24; women's experiences of the war, 55; women, race, and fertility, 5
National Survey of Family Growth, 15
Native Americans, 144, 174–91, 227; reservation communities, 182 (see also American Indians, Indian, Navajo)
naturalization, 93
Navajo, 174–91; culture, xviii, 183; identity, xviii, 178–81, 187; knowledge, xviii, 180; language, xviii, 181, 183, 186; Nation, 175, 178; relocation of, 182; rug weaving, 184; spiritual practices, 175, 182–87; values, 185–86; women, 174–91 (see also American Indian; Indians; Native American)
New Left, the, 213; sexism in, 214; white males in, 213

Nisei, 75–76, 81–82; men, 72, 81; women, 72, 73–82
nurse-midwives. *See* midwives
nursing, x, 84, 85, 86, 88, 91

oppression, xix, 143, 145, 152, 160, 165, 237; of teenaged girls, xiv; of the Hmong, 229
other, the, 231; construction of, 176–78

paid employment, 56, 68
parenthood, 212
parenting, 69; part-time, 15
Parenting for Peace and Justice, 221
parents, 16, 17; rights of, 168; single, 219; Southeast Asian, 228; stay-at-home, 126
Paris Peace Accords, 230
Passages Conference, 135, 138
passivity, 111, 119–20, 133, 207
paternalism, 7, 153
Pathet Lao government, 230
patriarchy, xiii, 42, 99, 240
peace, 223; issues, 221; movement, 221
Pearl Harbor attack, 55, 71–72, 74, 75, 76, 77
people of color, 196, 237
physical: abilities, xii; abuse, 130, 167
Plummer, Ken, xiv, 38
political: activism, 195–211, 217; change, 214; process, xiv, xv; values, 218
politics, 208, 216; ethnic, 147; nonethnic, 156; women's participation in, xviii
popular: culture, 143, 160, 213; media, 83
poverty, 17, 62, 86, 93, 126, 131, 140, 160, 165; culture of, 145
power structures, xiii, xiv
pregnancy, 6–7, 9, 17, 20–1, 23, 75, 87, 98; adolescent, xvi; premarital, 129
prejudice, 140, 196, 199–200, 232
prenatal: care, 21; classes, 22
privileges, 114, 145, 147, 154–55, 205
psychological abuse, 126
psychology, x, xi
puberty, 80, 109, 113–14; ceremony, 175
public: health, x; issues, 106; policy, xiv, xix, 17; sphere, 209
Puerto Rican: culture, 172; women, 161–72 (*see also* Latinas)

race, xii, xv, xix, 38, 105, 106, 125, 154, 172, 200, 205, 216, 225, 257, 269; issues of, 7, 17, 234, 237; politics of, 208; privilege, 205; relations, 156, 201–203, 206–208
racial: bias, 16; differences, 11, 203; discrimination, 55; ethnics, 156–57; identity development, 237; minorities, 18; norms, 133
racial stereotypes, 18; internalization of, 11–13
racism, 13, 69n. 4, 84, 160, 165, 196–97, 199, 201–202, 205, 208, 221, 227, 231–35, 237; institutional, 157
rape, xv (*see also* African American women)
redress movement. *See* internment camps
refugee(s), 228, 236; camps, 229–30, 233; children, 228; Hmong, 230
religion, 13–15, 84, 105, 182, 196–97, 200
relocation, 125, 182

reproduction, 13, 16, 18, 173
reproductive technology, 5
residency: legal, 88; U.S., 88
resident visas, 96
resilience, 160
resistance, xi, 121–22, 165, 173, 177, 256, 259; female, 105; to patriarchy, 99
restriction, 119–20
rights, 154; disability, 225; parental, 15; political, 176, 195; reproductive, 17; women's, 207; workers', 152
Roosevelt, Eleanor, 202, 210
Rosie the Riveter, 53, 55, 56–58, 59, 64, 68 (*see also* master narratives of Rosie the Riveter)

scholars, 243–55
scholarship, 243–55; as a relational labor, 248–51
SDS (Students for a Democratic Society), 213
segregation, 127, 144; in the workplace, 55, 69n. 4
self, 177, 184; -affirmation, 258; -construction, 252; definition, 131, 187; -esteem, 131; -reliance, 9–11, 16; -sufficiency, 65; as source of knowledge, 182–87; images of, 46; in relation to group, 180
service occupations, 154
sewing skills, 260–61, 264–65
sex, 106–108, 114–15, 117, 120; identity, 118; roles, 63
sexism, 42, 84, 127, 160, 165, 214, 221, 231, 233
sexual: abuse, 45, 47, 49, 167; assault, 13; discrimination, 55; harassment, xv, xvi; identity (*see* identity, sexual); incest (*see* incest); self-denial, xiv; victimization, 43
sexuality, ix, xii, xv, 13, 107, 115, 117, 121, 125, 134, 176; black women's, 4; construction of, 4, 111; female, 119; norms of, 133; women's, 4
sexually transmitted disease, 7
silence, 82; code of, 13; cultural, 13; social, 43
sixties, the, 212–26
social: change, 208, 212–26; class, 176, 212, 257; constructions, 47, 139, 160, 176, 187; contexts, 37; control, xv, 112, 114; discourse, 38; groups, 75; history, xviii; ideals, 218; identity (*see* identity, social); ideology, 38; ills, 140; institutions, 243; issues, 237; justice, xviii, 208, 215; mobility, xvii, 142–58, 212; networks, 64, 91–92; order, 63, 139; organization, 38; policy, xix, 219; processes, 43, 88, 121, 178, 187; relations, 187, 257–58; services agencies, 133, 218; structure, xiii, 121; systems, 140, 177; transformation, xiii, 214; values, 17, 218
society, xiv, 62, 63, 157, 173; African American, 125; American, 156, 230; dominant, 38, 155, 185–86; Hmong, 230; patriarchal, 231; U.S., 72, 231; white, 125
sociocultural: assumptions, 39; ideologies, 42
Southeast Asian(s), 228, 232; community, 228, 240; girls, 232, 240; parents, 228; refugees, 228, 240
spirituality, 183–85, 219
stereotypes, xiv, 42, 168; internalization of, 11–13; of Asians, 227; of pathology, 42
sterilizations: forced, 18
stories, xii–xiii, 188; birth, 24–35; dominant, 165; forms of, xiv; teaching, 185; women's, xii, xiv, 17, 55, 81, 202, 207–8
storytelling, 121; women's, xii–xiii

students, 245, 247–48, 252
sweatshops, xviii, 146, 256–70

teaching, 243–55
Thailand, 229, 233
tomboyness, 108–109, 112, 114–15, 122
tomboys, 105–24, 127; heterosexual adult, xvii; identity of, 106, 111–12, 118, 120; imagery of, 106–107, 122n. 5; reformed, 112
transgender experience, 115
translocal, 257, 269; analysis, 257
transsexuality, 106, 109, 117
transsexuals, 117, 120–21
transvestites, 109, 117, 120
trauma, 73–74
tribal: identity, 177; members, 176; status, 182
tribal language: destruction of, 176
Tuskegee Syphilis Experiment, 17

U.S.: -Mexico border, 258; citizenship, 79, 96–97; culture, 235; government, 229; history, 214; job market in the, 95; labor structure, 258; poverty rate, 126; residency, 88; society, 227, 231; spouses, 93
union system, 92, 259
United States, 55, 83, 88–89, 92–94, 96, 99, 155, 224, 228, 230–31, 233, 256, 259; citizens, 71; government, 71; history of, xix; internment camps (see internment camps); migration to, 83–101 (see also immigration); slavery in, xv; sweatshops in, 256–70; unemployment rate, 55
University of Michigan, 215
Upward Bound program, 98

values, 94, 97, 179, 185–86, 218
Veracruz, Mexico, 85, 87, 92
Vietnam, 229
Vietnam War, the, 40, 212, 214, 217, 228–30
violence, 125, 221; against women, 126; domestic, xv, 43, 171; racial, 200
Voting Rights Act, 144

Weber, A.D., 94
welfare, 216
white women, 5, 11, 21, 22, 37, 58, 68, 69n. 4, 128, 210, 212, 224; and infertility, xvii, 11; and the civil rights movement, 195–211; political activism in, xviii
white(s), 3, 126, 210; America, 157; and infertility, 4; communities, 75, 156, 229; culture, 155; domination, 157; male, middle-class students, 214; men, 137; multiple births among, 3–4, 17; racists, 205; students, 200, 213, 227
White, Walter, 199, 200–201, 204, 207
whiteness, 142, 176, 205
Whitman Walker Alcohol and Substance Abuse (WW) program, 134, 138
Wilkins, Roy, 199–201, 204
Wise, N. B., & Wise, C., 56

wives, 83 (see also housewives)
womanhood, 58, 185
women, x, xii–xiii; abused, 37; academics, ix, 243–55; African American (see African American women); American, 58; and political activism, 195–211; Asian (see Asian women); birthing, 25; black (see black women); drug addicts, 159–73; employed, 17; Hmong (see Hmong women); homeless, 125–41; immigrant, 83–101, 154; infertile, 11; Japanese American (see Japanese American women); Japanese Peruvian (see Japanese Peruvian women); junkies, 160; low-income, 21; Mayan, 87; Mexican immigrant women, 142–58; middle-class, 17, 18; Navajo. See Navajo, women; of color, 18 (see also women of color); poor, xix, 17, 18; pregnant, 20; professors, 243–55; representations of, 63; rural, 21; stereotypes of, xix; students, ix; traditional roles of, 56; unmarried, 18; upper-class, 18; violence against, 125; white (see white women), working, xviii, 56, 58, 60
women drug addicts: images of, 159
women of color, xiii, 12, 18, 160; and infertility, 3; stereotypes of, xix
women's: accounts, xiii; biography, 202; birth experiences, 22; bodies, 22, 25; career opportunities, 57; consciousness, 214; development, 248; drug addiction, 159–73; educational needs, 245; employment, 57, 60, 62, 68, 91; experiences, xix, 80, 94, 257; friendships, 91, 197, 202–3; groups, 214; health care choices, 21; immigration patterns, 84; liberation, 212; lives, xiii, xvii, xix, 54, 72, 73, 195, 202, 207–8, 245; medical care, 20; networks, 84, 87–92; nontraditional jobs, 57, 62, 68; opportunities, 80; perspectives, 73; public lives, xviii; relations to others, 253; roles, 217; scholarship, 243–55; sexuality, 4; social lives, 91; social roles, 58, 61, 63, 68; spirituality community, 224; stories (see stories, women's); storytelling (see storytelling, women's); studies, x; traditional roles, 59–60, 63–64, 68; work, 91
Women's International League for Peace and Freedom, 221
Women's Life Paths Study, 215
women's movement, xii, 195, 217–18, 224; second wave, 195, 209, 214
workers: domestic, 142–58; garment, 256–70; in industry, xix; seasonal, 91; undocumented, 84, 88, 93; unskilled, 84
World War I, 55
World War II, xvi, xix, 53–70, 182 (see also Good War, the); all-Nisei combat troops in, 72; employment during, 57; hardships during, 56; housewives' experiences of, xvii, xix, 53–70; internment of Japanese Americans, 71–82; production for, 56; soldier husbands during, 65–67, 68

Yamada, Mitsuye, 227

Zavella, P., 87